Studies on Entrepreneurship, Structural Change and Industrial Dynamics

Series editors

João Leitão
University of Beira Interior, Covilhã, Portugal

Tessaleno Devezas
University of Beira Interior, Covilhã, Portugal

The 'Studies on Entrepreneurship, Structural Change and Industrial Dynamics' series showcases exceptional scholarly work being developed on the still unexplored complex relationship between entrepreneurship, structural change and industrial dynamics, by addressing structural and technological determinants of the evolutionary pathway of innovative and entrepreneurial activity.

The series invites proposals based on sound research methodologies and approaches to the above topics. Volumes in the series may include research monographs and edited/ contributed works. Please send the completed proposal form downloadable from this page (see "For Authors and Editors") to the series editors.

More information about this series at http://www.springer.com/series/15330

Serena Cubico • Giuseppe Favretto • João Leitão •
Uwe Cantner

Editors

Entrepreneurship and the Industry Life Cycle

The Changing Role of Human Capital and Competences

 Springer

Editors
Serena Cubico
Department of Business Administration
University of Verona
Verona, Italy

Giuseppe Favretto
Department of Business Administration
University of Verona
Verona, Italy

João Leitão
Department of Management and
Economics
University of Beira Interior
Covilhã, Portugal

Uwe Cantner
Friedrich Schiller University Jena
Jena, Germany

ISSN 2511-2023   ISSN 2511-2031   (electronic)
Studies on Entrepreneurship, Structural Change and Industrial Dynamics
ISBN 978-3-319-89335-8   ISBN 978-3-319-89336-5   (eBook)
https://doi.org/10.1007/978-3-319-89336-5

Library of Congress Control Number: 2018944276

Printed on acid-free paper

This Springer imprint is published by the registered company Springer International Publishing AG part of Springer Nature.
The registered company address is: Gewerbestrasse 11, 6330 Cham, Switzerland

Contents

Part II   Innovative Networks and Entrepreneurial Activities

Part III   Entrepreneurship for Change

Introduction

Serena Cubico, Giuseppe Favretto, João Leitão, and Uwe Cantner

Abstract This volume emerges in an especially competitive, challenging and uncertain context, around which the current digital transformation, artificial intelligence and intelligent machines tend to take over from the human workforce. However, creativity combined with some irrationality of aptitudes and behaviour, as well as the growing importance of the network value (or utility) of future expectations and those realized, reveal the importance of directing additional research efforts towards better understanding of the importance of developing behavioural and technical competences, especially those oriented towards entrepreneurship and innovation systems, which distinguish human capital as a highly differentiating production factor which, together with knowledge, form the endogenous motors of growth and change.

1 Setting the Ground

This volume emerges in an especially competitive, challenging and uncertain context, around which the current digital transformation, artificial intelligence and intelligent machines tend to take over from the human workforce. However,

S. Cubico (✉) · G. Favretto
Dipartimento di Economia Aziendale, University of Verona, Verona, Italy
e-mail: serena.cubico@univr.it; giuseppe.favretto@univr.it

J. Leitão
Faculty of Social Sciences and Humanities, Department of Management and Economics, University of Beira Interior, Covilhã, Portugal

CEG-IST, University of Lisbon, Lisbon, Portugal

C-MAST, UBI & Instituto Multidisciplinar de Empresa, Universidad de Salamanca, Salamanca, Spain
e-mail: jleitao@ubi.pt

U. Cantner
Department of Economics, Friedrich-Schiller-University Jena, Jena, Germany
e-mail: uwe.cantner@uni-jena.de

© Springer International Publishing AG, part of Springer Nature 2018
S. Cubico et al. (eds.), *Entrepreneurship and the Industry Life Cycle*, Studies on Entrepreneurship, Structural Change and Industrial Dynamics,
https://doi.org/10.1007/978-3-319-89336-5_1

creativity combined with some irrationality of aptitudes and behaviour, as well as the growing importance of the network value (or utility) of future expectations and those realized, reveal the importance of directing additional research efforts towards better understanding of the importance of developing behavioural and technical competences, especially those oriented towards entrepreneurship and innovation systems, which distinguish human capital as a highly differentiating production factor which, together with knowledge, form the endogenous motors of growth and change.

In our framework, an innovation system is defined as a network of actors who interact in the processes of the generation, diffusion, and utilization of new, economically useful knowledge under a distinct institutional framework (Cantner and Graf 2003).

Following Cantner and Graf (2006), the dynamics of the system is directed towards an increasing focus on core competences of the local innovation system; i.e. innovators on the periphery of the network exit and new entrants position themselves closer to the core of the network. Thus, a shared knowledge base prior to cooperation is an important prerequisite for partners in research and development (R&D) activities.

Cantner and Graf (2006) revealed that personal relationships, which arise through the job mobility of scientists, are an important variable in explaining the formation of cooperation networks.

Crossing literature streams, at the level of entrepreneurial and organizational studies, there has been a growing interest on the connection between human capital and competences, which are quite complex, multifaceted and multidisciplinary. Nevertheless, there is plenty of room for adding research efforts in order to formalize and explore the concept of knowledge competences, using an evolutionary lens crossed with human capital and competences dynamics.

The European Union (2006, p. 13) underlines the values of the competences in the economic and social growth, in particular, entrepreneurship is considered one of the eight key-competences for «personal fulfilment and development, active citizenship, social inclusion and employment».

Considering a suggestion posed by Unger et al. (2011) our volume investigates the relationship between knowledge competences in innovative and entrepreneurial activities, for addressing the caveat previously identified by the same authors, which resides, until now, in the use of static views on human capital, competences, entrepreneurial success and industrial dynamics.

Cubico et al. (2017) attempted to address the competences dynamics subject, in the context of family firms, and they identified mutual competences and different components that characterize the intergenerational coexistence of entrepreneurs, which is a critical way for managing the generational transition process. It is also important to understand the differences between senior and junior entrepreneurs and whether if they can help along the different stages of their firm's life cycle. In fact, the dynamic competences influence relationships and the possibility of having a rewarding work life.

This perspective opens the door of a challenging research task, that is, to consider an industry life cycle approach, for analysing how entrepreneurs, innovation systems and industries change over time, through their own processes of evolution, as first analysed by Joseph Schumpeter.

What remains to be addressed is the role played by innovative and entrepreneurial activities, plus dynamic knowledge competences, on the evolutionary pathway of industries and regions, especially the ones that face turbulence, but demonstrate to be resilient, by revealing special dynamics moving through intrinsic upturns and downturns, which are not necessarily related to the macroeconomic fluctuations. In fact, they could be associated with intrinsic and behavioural features connected to the human capital interacting with different dimensions: environmental; organizational; or individual level; along the industry life cycle.

The set of contributions joined here is particularly relevant and innovative, inasmuch as it is a pioneering approach to a vast set of competences, skills and aptitudes it is necessary to develop throughout the life cycles of organisations and production and innovation ecosystems, affecting both incumbent, established units and new entrants.

What are the right competences, skills and aptitudes to initiate a business activity and successfully lead that entrepreneurial and innovative unit throughout its non-linear life?

The work published here has no one answer to this challenging question, but makes contributions regarding the importance of the open participation of external and internal stakeholders in design and co-creation exercises, integrating organisations' external and internal dimensions.

In terms of objectives and knowledge transfer of the current edited volume, firstly, it presents a multidisciplinary approach by providing an up-to date state of the art on knowledge competences and human capital, as well as structural and changing dynamics and their links with the entrepreneurial activities, using both evolutionary and behavioural approaches.

Secondly, it makes available a set of international benchmarking case studies (i.e. in developed and developing economies) on initiatives (at the national, regional or individual level) oriented to entrepreneurship development in different environments, systems and life cycle stages, namely: young, established, mature and transition industries and markets; and regions.

Thirdly, it is positioned as a reference guide for scholars, policy makers and practitioners interested on innovation, entrepreneurship, knowledge competences, human resources management, leadership and organizational behaviour.

Concerning knowledge transfer, it should be outlined that these international benchmarks on entrepreneurship, knowledge competences, human capital, innovation systems and industrial dynamics now presented, require further research efforts aiming to create efficient, innovative and entrepreneurial units; and to promote organizational change, in different dimensions, such as, environmental (institution, network, policy, financial, infrastructures, information, economic system, region, etc.), organizational (vision, mission, goals, strategy, form of ownership, corporate governance, family legacy, business area, management, resources, etc.) and individual (culture, entrepreneurial education, competences, skills, aptitudes, human capital, etc.), deepening knowledge on their evolutionary pathways along the industry life cycle, taking both the individual and the organisation, as units of analysis to be further explored.

Looking inside the organisation, positioning intrapreneurship as the organisational culture, and combining the values of corporate social responsibility and sustainability are critical actions requiring the mapping and development of competences, skills and aptitudes (Cubico et al. 2010) at the intersection of a variety of specialized scientific areas as yet unemphasized, such as education, philosophy, spirituality, psychology, health and well-being, sustainability, behavioural economy, circular economy, information systems and organisational design, among others.

At an individual level, gender, enthusiasm, socio-emotional wealth, social networks, values, self-esteem and self-efficiency are behavioural characteristics still revealing some difficulty in being transferred to the domain of knowledge and behavioural competences, which should certainly be worked on and perfected throughout the personal and organisational life cycle.

Also empathy, relationship management, inherited relational legacy, and above all, the analysis capacity of social networks, for better mapping of the network nodes and the groupings to reach in order to improve efficiency and productivity, are considered determinant factors in the decision to innovate and enter, and in the evolutionary process of survival, and even in strategic exit by different planned, or alternatively contingency routes.

The individual entrepreneurship capacity (Leitão and Franco 2011) is a critical concept that needs deepening, following an integrated logic, for example, following the intellectual capital approach and adopting a dominant triad of components typologies (Pedro et al. 2018), namely human capital, structural capital and relational capital. Each of these components *per se* can be an area of work to be explored not only as a simple direction of the causal nexus for economic, innovative and non-economic performance of organisations and industries, but also as crossable and symbiotic elements of complex and multi-dimensional situations for analysis, increasingly called ecosystems, whose functioning is based on networks and interconnections (Leitão et al. 2018).

In our view, the evolutionary path of those ecosystems depends on the quality and persistence of the competences, skills and aptitudes of the actors in those networks, forming the competences dynamics. Here, formal and informal education, culture, religion and social change are additives or restrainers to bear in mind, according to the context (Welter 2011).

Nevertheless, education based on and oriented towards competences, skills and aptitudes should be translated by a new construction that needs expansion and depth, in order to stimulate a genuine 'managerial culture' and a renewed culture of innovation and entrepreneurship.

In the context of this volume, competences, skills and aptitudes are therefore positioned as new knowledge assets needing mapping and continuous accompaniment, in order to last and be perfected to the point of being an integral part of individuals and organisations' entrepreneurial and innovative culture.

The transposition of this new theoretical and applied construction is a challenge that can be self-designated as a 'knowledge challenge' which, from an evolutionary perspective, would be subject to adaptations and changes, through substituting old and not so old competences, skills and aptitudes and stimulation of the new knowledge assets mentioned above.

In this line of reasoning, it is necessary to identify the gaps and promote new behaviours and aptitudes integrating competences of organisation, leadership, motivation, empathy, spirituality, design, emotional intelligence and others. Considering the gaps already mapped, it becomes necessary to reveal the role of stress, time management, gentrification, social exclusion and individual isolationism, in order to construct a new map and code of competences necessary for competitive adaptation and survival, in the context of increasingly complex and dynamic ecosystems in need of greater understanding, knowledge and human intervention.

Promoting the visibility and comparability of the theoretical and applied approaches at the international level, concerning the identification of competences, skills and aptitudes considered critical to promote the innovative and entrepreneurial culture, is also at the heart of the exercise of preparing and organising the collection of international and multi-dimensional cases, of exceptional quality and originality, which is now presented for the first time, from a behavioural point of view, with the as yet unexplored issue of dynamic knowledge competences in the background.

The organisers' boldness is also underlined, by joining in the same volume a eclectic set of dimensions and methodologies of analysis, based on the lessons of evolutionary theory and this new dynamic competences approach, both transferable to various open areas of work they point out as critical and relevant for advancing scientific knowledge, think-tanks on technological and social change, equality and inclusion, and above all innovation and entrepreneurship founded on the individual, because at the end we are all interested parties in the co-creative design of evolutionary processes of engineering and social economy, embraced recently as a priority task for the architects of social change, in particular, and for social scientists in general.

2 The Volume's Structure and Outline

The volume is divided into three parts: Part I—Entrepreneurial and knowledge competences; Part II—Innovative networks and entrepreneurial activities; and Part III—Entrepreneurship for change.

Part I opens the volume offering different visions and eclectic approaches to entrepreneurs and entrepreneurial competences. The contributors analyse the entrepreneurial field through study of the variables that appear "inside" and "outside" the entrepreneurial choice and life. Different and eclectic perspectives exploring entrepreneurial competences, teams, culture, leadership and knowledge offer the possibility to understand the development of an enterprise and the human resources involved, using a complex and evolutionary approach.

In Chapter "Entrepreneurial Competences: Comparing and Contrasting Models and Taxonomies", Giovanna Gianesini, Serena Cubico, Giuseppe Favretto, and João

Leitão reflect on three models of entrepreneurial competences pointing out the risk of confusing them with the measurement of individual traits or cognitive styles. Competences have their own wide literature that the authors analyse in detail by comparing and contrasting three well-known models. The main output is a taxonomy proposal that synthesizes and regroups a multifaceted list of entrepreneurial competences in three areas (ideas, resources and actions) defining the knowledge, skills, and personality of the entrepreneur's profile.

In Chapter "Heterogeneity and the origin of the Founding Team: How the concepts relate and affect Entrepreneurial Behavior?", Gertie M. Agraz-Boeneker and Maria del Mar Fuentes-Fuentes create a transition from "subjectivity" to "collectivity". They read entrepreneurial competences in a broader way: the founding team designs the history of an enterprise. The study helps to understand the relation between team heterogeneity and specific entrepreneurial behaviours (effectuation and causation). Founded on the theoretical and empirical approaches developed, the authors propose an original behavioural classification of founding teams.

In Chapter "Entrepreneurial aptitude and gender-related stereotypes. A study of competences, policies and practices to foster entrepreneurial culture in a less favored environment", Stefano Noventa, Serena Cubico, Maddalena Formicuzzi, Piermatteo Ardolino, Giuseppe Favretto, Francesco Ciabuschi and João Leitão open the research context. The sample of the quantitative study is young men and women from a territory characterized by unfavourable socio-economic conditions (Sardinia, Italy); the data highlight the risk that gender stereotypes and inequality affect the possibility of creating fruitful entrepreneurial network despite education, aptitude, competences and opportunities being similar between genders.

In Chapter "Co-leadership and performance in technology-based entrepreneurial firms", Daniel Pittino, Francesca Visintin and Cristiana Compagno introduce the recent construct of co-leadership. The co-leadership notion appears as an important variable in the management of entrepreneurial firms. An extensive quantitative study reveals the impact of co-leadership on the performance of technology-based companies. The different types of "leadership in plural form" have specific effects on the enterprise's performance. It is worth noticing that "distributed leadership", contrary to the shared one, has a positive effect. Another notable contribution of the study lies in deepening knowledge in the literature related to co-leadership and performance of entrepreneurial ventures.

In Chapter "Human Capital, Organizational Competences and Knowledge & Innovation Transfer: A Case Study Applied to the Mining Sector", Margarida Rodrigues and João Leitão provide a set of insights into the role played by knowledge competences in innovation transfer processes. Through a case study of a company in the mining sector during a restructuring process, the authors reveal that the organizational competences become a common benefit if shared and communicated. The authors conclude that human capital is a critical variable for success in the restructuring process, but it is not enough without specific knowledge and communication culture.

In Chapter "Specific practices of Human Resource Management in the creation and development of micro and small firms, case studies in Portuguese firms", Helder

Antunes and António Nunes present a study taking as the unit of analysis a Portuguese region characterized by a large concentration of micro and small companies. The study identifies a set of recruitment and selection practices outlining the importance (and sometimes the lack) of managerial competences in human resource management processes. Notably, the methodological choice of an idiographic perspective, emphasizing real life situations, allows the reading of different sides of the company behaviour (within each specific case).

Part II explores the intersection of innovative networks and entrepreneurial activities in distinct sectors. The authors describe "when and where" the innovative factors are present in networks, countries, entrepreneurial phases and economic activity sectors.

In Chapter "The selective nature of innovator networks: from the nascent to the early growth phase of the organizational life cycle", Uwe Cantner and Tina Wolf focus their research efforts on the phases between nascent entrepreneurship and early growth of the firm. The authors underline the role of the network and the effect of the company's position in it. They reveal that a central position in the network is not always favourable.

In Chapter "The decline of innovation in the antibiotics industry and the global threat of antibiotic resistance; when entrepreneurial efforts are not enough", Francesco Ciabuschi and Olof Lindahl provide us with a reflection on a crucial sector for our health. This is a very interesting case dealing with the declining industry in the antibiotic field, where entrepreneurial activity needs to be reinvigorated by public intervention, as entrepreneurial orientation, although important, is not enough.

In Chapter "Entrepreneurship success factors in high and low early stage entrepreneurship intensity countries", Ruth Alas, Tiit Elenurm, Elizabeth Rozell, and Wesley Scroggins synthesize the results from two extended datasets on entrepreneurial attributes and competences. The studies on early stage entrepreneurship activities reveal the importance of a positive behavioural pattern in terms of image associated with successful entrepreneurs, in particular in the countries in which people are more active in new venture creation.

In Chapter "Reasons for the almost complete absence of high-growth ambition and innovation activity of early-stage entrepreneurs in Brazil", Ronald Jean Degen and Nicholas Harkiolakis provide a set of results obtained from a qualitative study based on a theoretical framework that includes cognitive variables, environment and opportunities. In terms of main insights, culture and education are positioned as potential improvement areas to favour the creation of entrepreneurial settings in all different family status in Brazil.

In Chapter "Hindering factors to Innovation. A Panel Data Analysis", Joana Costa, Anabela Botelho and João Matias analyse the innovation processes in Portugal's companies and reveal the variables involved in this type of organizational decision-making process. A counter-intuitive result points out that entrepreneurs continue to invest in innovation despite the economic crisis, useful information to understand and design policies more appropriate for these enterprises.

Part III draws attention to the place where entrepreneurship has its origin and how this process can contribute to changing the context. The authors create a journey through different cultures and ways of managing life and enterprise in light of the relationships with the existing social and political roles.

In Chapter "Women Entrepreneurship in India: A Work-Life Balance Perspective", Ajay K Jain, Shalini Srivastava and Serena Cubico analyse a crucial factor in the daily life of the female entrepreneur. The study carried out in North India to better understand a national phenomenon, confirms the traditional female work-life balance variables and reveals the importance of the supporting network as moderator of personal and professional obstacles.

In Chapter "The Pentagonal Problem and the Offshore Energy Sector in Portugal. Why Does It Matter?", Ana Pego addresses a key-topic in the ongoing debate on the issue of sustainable economic development. The case of the offshore energy sector becomes a focus that allows understanding of the chance to apply a circular economy based on innovation and technology. The proposed (pentagonal) way of reading and studying the factors involved helps to deal with that issue in a more effective and efficient way.

In Chapter "Entrepreneurial Urban Revitalization", Carlos Balsas addresses the linkages between the growth of enterprises and the rise of cities (or part or them). Applying the model of Business Improvement Districts, the town becomes more livable for the inhabitants and more attractive for tourists or investors. This type of intervention proves to be dynamic, proactive, and able to engage all elements of the city in partnerships.

In Chapter "Unconventional Entrepreneurship and the Municipality: The Role of Passion and Competences", Francesca Simeoni and Federico Testa describe an example of an original, or rather, unconventional form of entrepreneurship. The qualitative and in-depth research reveals the importance of Municipalities' trust in business creators and the competences and passion they demonstrate in terms of problem solving.

Lastly, in Chapter "Assessing Entrepreneurial Profiles: A Study of Transversal Competence Gaps in Four European Countries", Marlene Amorim, Marta Ferreira Dias, Helena Silva, Diego Galego, Maria Sarmento and Carina Pimentel present a set of notable considerations emerging from quantitative research on entrepreneurial competences. By involving entrepreneurs and employees, it is possible to draw the "identikit" of the desired collaborator and the profile of young graduates. Unfortunately, a lack of transversal competences emerges in young professionals, which needs to be overcome with life-long skills training programmes.

References

Cantner, U., & Graf, H. (2003). *Interaction structures in local innovation systems*, Jena Economic Research Papers, #2008–40, Friedrich Schiller University and the Max Planck Institute of Economics. Germany: Jena.

Cantner, U., & Graf, H. (2006). The network of innovators in Jena: An application of social network analysis. *Research Policy, 35*(4), 463–480.

Cubico, S., Bortolani, E., Favretto, G., & Sartori, R. (2010). Describing the entrepreneurial profile: The entrepreneurial aptitude test (TAI). *International Journal of Entrepreneurship and Small Business, 11*(4), 424–435.

Cubico, S., Favretto, G., Ardolino, P., Noventa, S., Bellini, D., Gianesini, G., & Leitão, J. (2017). Family business and entrepreneurship: Competencies and organizational behavior. In T. Devezas, J. Leitão, & A. Sarygulov (Eds.), *Industry 4.0 – Entrepreneurship and structural change in the new digital landscape, Studies on entrepreneurship, structural change and industrial dynamics*. Cham: Springer.

European Union. (2006). *Recommendation of the European Parliament and of the Council of 18 December 2006 on key competences for lifelong learning*. Accessed online http://eur-lex.europa.eu/legal-content/EN/TXT/PDF/?uri=CELEX:32006H0962&rid=3

Leitão, J., & Franco, M. (2011). Individual entrepreneurship capacity and SME performance: A human and organizational capital approach. *African Journal of Business Management, 5*(15), 6350–6365.

Leitão, J., Alves, H., Krueger, N., & Park, J. (Eds.). (2018). *Entrepreneurial, innovative and sustainable ecosystems – best practices and implications for quality of life, Applying quality of life research: Best practices*. Cham: Springer. https://doi.org/10.1007/978-3-319-71014-3. Hard cover ISBN 978-3-319-71013-6.

Pedro E, Leitão J, Alves H (2018). Intellectual capital and performance: Taxonomy of components and multidimensional analysis axes. *Journal of Intellectual Capital 19*(2). https://doi.org/10.1108/JIC-11-2016-0118

Unger, J.-M., Rauch, A., Frese, M., & Rosenbusch, N. (2011). Human capital and entrepreneurial success: A meta-analytical review. *Journal of Business Venturing, 26*, 341–358.

Welter, F. (2011). Contextualizing entrepreneurship: Conceptual challenges and ways forward. *Entrepreneurship: Theory and Practice, 35*(1), 165–184.

Part I
Entrepreneurial and Knowledge Competences

Entrepreneurial Competences: Comparing and Contrasting Models and Taxonomies

Giovanna Gianesini, Serena Cubico, Giuseppe Favretto, and João Leitão

Abstract The emphasis on competences as capturing key aspects of entrepreneurship is relatively recent and quite distinct from research on entrepreneurial traits or cognitive styles in that competences represent observable and measurable knowledge, behaviour, attitudes and skills. Many competency taxonomies and models have been proposed by scholars, as frameworks organized into tiers of competences including descriptions of the activities and behaviours associated with that competency (Chouhan and Srivastava, IOSR Journal of Business and Management, 16(1): 14–22, 2014). However, no comprehensive set of entrepreneurial competences has emerged from these distinctions and no or little empirical evidence has been provided to validate these categorizations (Morris et al., Journal of Small Business Management 51(3): 352–369, 2013). This study compares and contrasts three traditional models (Morris et al., Journal of Small Business Management 51(3): 352–369, 2013; Bartram's, Journal of Applied Psychology 90(6): 1185–1203, 2005, with the EU Entrepreneurship Competence Framework; Bacigalupo et al., EntreComp: the entrepreneurship competence framework, EUR 27939 EN, Publication Office of the European Union, 2016) previously empirically validated by the authors.

Keywords Entrepreneurship · Competences · Taxonomies · European competence framework

G. Gianesini · S. Cubico (✉) · G. Favretto
Dipartimento di Economia Aziendale, University of Verona, Verona, Italy
e-mail: serena.cubico@univr.it

J. Leitão
Department of Management and Economics, School of Social and Human Sciences, Universidade da Beira Interior, Covilhã, Portugal

NECE—Research Centre in Business Sciences, Covilhã, Portugal

© Springer International Publishing AG, part of Springer Nature 2018
S. Cubico et al. (eds.), *Entrepreneurship and the Industry Life Cycle*, Studies on Entrepreneurship, Structural Change and Industrial Dynamics,
https://doi.org/10.1007/978-3-319-89336-5_2

1 Introduction

Entrepreneurship in todays' economy means the creation of new opportunities in an environment characterized by a high degree of complexity and uncertainty. It represents a key driver of the growth and sustainability of the economy, as well as a mechanism of social development (Farhangmehr et al. 2016). Therefore, the promotion of an entrepreneurial culture has become a priority area around the world for public-policy makers, educators and researchers. Entrepreneurship links two cornerstones of economic development, industrial dynamics and innovation, and they all influence each other. New firms with differentiated growth influence industrial development and create innovation, but at the same time the industrial context and innovative technologies can shapes the entrepreneurial activities. Innovation is increasingly considered the key to elevating prosperity and securing sustainable long-term economic growth.

Scholars have been examining the meaning of what constitutes entrepreneurship and the activities which define entrepreneurship for decades. The prevalent view being based on someone who starts or owns a business, suggesting that a person can be classified as being entrepreneurial based on the organizational or ownership status, which represents a static view of entrepreneurial action (Audretsch et al. 2015, 2016). On the other hand, in dynamic terms, entrepreneurship is inferred on the basis of change, and in particular, changing products or processes through innovative activity. Leyden and Link (2013) have proposed a dynamic theory of entrepreneurship to apply to decision making and behavior within the context of both the public and private sector and explained in terms of the human capital. Moreover, the dynamic nature of entrepreneurship is defined through the actions of the entrepreneur. Teece (2012) articulated the dynamic nature of entrepreneurial capabilities as falling into three clusters of activities and adjustments: opportunity identification and assessment (sensing), resource mobilization (seizing) and continued renewal (transforming).

The distinction between dynamic and static entrepreneurship is innovation. Generally knowledge has been identified as the driving force underlying innovative activity (Koskinen and Vanharanta 2002). Greater knowledge, greater experience, and greater education, all lead to a greater capacity of human capital, which can accelerate true innovation (Audretsch et al. 2016). Entrepreneurs with a greater endowment of human capital have access to the particular knowledge resources that are requisite for fueling innovation (Lazear 2004). Knowledge is gained experientially at different rates by different people depending on their subjective abilities. Human capital, the skills and capacities that reside in people and that are a more important determinant of long term economic success than virtually any other resource, is the important link between innovative activity and individual entrepreneurs (Davidsson and Honig 2003). Human capital is viewed traditionally as a function of education and experience, the latter reflecting both training and learning by doing.

2   Human Capital

The conceptualization of human capital attributes beyond its static concept implies looking at the actual outcomes of learning experiences and how they differently related to entrepreneurial success, in terms of acquisition and transfer. Acquisition refers to the transformation from experience (and not knowledge) to skills, while transfer is the application of knowledge acquire in one situation to another (Unger et al. 2011).

The task-relatedness of human capital explains the differential effects of human capital on entrepreneurial success (Unger et al. 2011). The entrepreneurial literature provides a number of arguments on how human capital should increase entrepreneurial success (Cubico et al. 2013), but limited evidences are available on the circumstances and the context of entrepreneurial growth. Entrepreneurial alertness (Westhead et al. 2005), exploitation of opportunities (Shane 2000), planning and venture strategies (Frese et al. 2007), organization, management and leadership (Shane and Venkatraman 2000) are among the competences related to entrepreneurial success. Human capital, as well as success, are multidimensional construct (Combs et al. 2005). In their meta-analysis Unger et al. (2011) evidenced indicators of human capital investments (education, start-up experiences, industry specific experiences, management experience, experience in trade, technology and small business venture, having a self-employed parent) versus human capital outcomes (entrepreneurial skills, competences and knowledge), building on Becker's (1964) differentiating between task-related and not-related-to-task human capital attributes. They found the success relationship to be higher for outcomes human capital indicators rather than investments, although the success relationship of human capital was smaller than those of personality and entrepreneurial orientation (Unger et al. 2011). Moreover, in addition to individual differences and motivation (De Tienne et al. 2008), learning behaviours and processes (for example adaptive expertise, Smith et al. 1997 and stream of experience, Reuber and Fisher 1999) are relevant human capital aspects.

3   Entrepreneurial Competences

Generally, competence is defined as the knowledge, skills, attitudes and abilities required to perform a specific job (Baum et al. 2001). Competences are changeable, learnable and attainable though experience, learning and coaching (Volery et al. 2015). As an integrated component of knowledge, skills and attitudes, the notion of competence focus on the ability to successfully meet the complex demands of a particular context (Mulder et al. 2007). Entrepreneurial capability refers to ability to identify a new opportunity and develop the resources and capital needed to pursue it (Arthurs and Busenitz 2006). Entrepreneurial competences have been identified as a particular group of competences that is significant to the practice of successful entrepreneurship (Mitchelmore and Rowley 2010) which, according to Bird (1995) includes specific knowledge, motives, traits, self-images, social roles, and skills. They refer to a variety of skills, abilities, and knowledge, not just in terms of technical, financial, organizational, and legal know-how (Kuratko 2005). The resource-based view focused on enterprise resources as the key elements of enterprise performance, resulting in the venture's birth, survival and growth (Peteraf and Barney 2003). Entrepreneurial competences are not entirely separate from the entrepreneur's personal characteristics, traits and motivations (Lee et al. 2016), are multidimensional in nature and dynamic because entrepreneurs make decisions under uncertainty and are rational, they do not create "once-and-for-all" solutions or routines but continually re-configure or revise the capabilities they have developed (Zahra et al. 2006). In a recent systematic literature review on key entrepreneurial characteristics empirically related to venture performance, Lee et al. (2016) identified five dimensions of entrepreneurial competences related to: (1) recognizing, developing and assessing opportunities through insight (Opportunity competences): (2) operating well and have administrative skills (Administrative competences): (3) hiring trainable candidates, build trust and healthy relationships with employees, communicating and leading to good corporate culture (Relationships Competences); (4) individual traits reflected in the behaviour of the entrepreneur (Personal Competences) and (5) going forward with perseverance and tenancy notwithstanding uncertain situations (Commitment competences). Entrepreneurial competences refer, as seen, to a variety of abilities and characteristics that make an entrepreneur successful in a competitive and increasingly unstable and unpredictable environment. Although researchers have devoted considerable time and effort to identifying characteristics, traits, values, affective states and cognitive styles associated with entrepreneurial success, the unique and peculiar competences that support venture creation and are vital in navigating the entrepreneurial contexts remain elusive (Morris et al. 2013). Despite the interest in entrepreneurial capacity building, there is still no consensus on what the distinctive elements of entrepreneurship as a competence are. Previous research has attempted to identify, define, and categorize these competences and a multitude of multidimensional models have been proposed in the research literature, drawing upon strategic management, organizational behaviour theories and various entrepreneurship models.

4 Entrepreneurial Competences Models

Recent studies have proposed that individual, organizational, and environmental dimensions combine to provide a more comprehensive prediction of venture development and growth than any one dimension in isolation (Baum et al. 2001). These comprehensive and multilevel model of entrepreneurial competences, have included research domains traditionally and theoretically identified as antecedents of venture performance at the individual, organizational, and environmental level. The great heterogeneity of entrepreneurs and firms can be better understood by a framework combining individual, relational and contextual characteristics and dimensions. Studies on entrepreneurial competences have attempted to organize entrepreneurial competences into various sub-constructs. For example, Man et al. (2002) identified six competency areas: opportunity, organizing, strategic, relationship, commitment, and conceptual competences. On the other hand, Priyanto and Sandjojo (2005) divided entrepreneurial competency into four scopes: management skills, industry skills, opportunity skills, and technical skills. More recently, Kyndt and Baert (2015) assessed behavioral indicators in actual and aspiring entrepreneurs as proximal outcomes of entrepreneurial competences and identified 12 competences, from Perseverance to Social and Environmental conscious conduct. Unfortunately, only two competences (Perseverance and Insight into the market) predicted entrepreneurship three to five years after their survey, Social, and Environmental conscious conduct related negatively to entrepreneurship. These results demonstrate that entrepreneurship is a complex phenomenon that requires further research efforts.

In this chapter we aim at contributing to such research efforts by comparing and contrasting a recent EU integrated theoretical framework (EntreComp; Bacigalupo et al. 2016) with two previous taxonomies, the 13 Entrepreneurial Competences Models by Morris et al. (2013) and Bartram's Great Eight (2005)

4.1 The 13 Entrepreneurial Competences Model

Building on structuration theory, and approaching competences as the results of interactions between the individual and environment, Morris et al. (2013) distinguished a core set of 13 entrepreneurial competences, employing a Delphi methodology and pre- and post-measures in a sample of students (see Table 1). Structuration theory provides a framework to understand competency development by capturing the recursive process and explaining how scripts develop into competences and the factors that can facilitate or impede this development. Scripts are defined into three broad categories: signification, legitimation, and domination (Giddens 1984). Signification scripts influence how individuals search for environmental change, legitimation scripts influence how individuals interpret and evaluate this change, and domination scripts influence how individuals respond to this change. Their findings evidenced behavioral competences, such as opportunity recognition, opportunity assessment, resource leveraging, and developing business models, as well as attitudinal competences, including resilience, self-efficacy, and tenacity. Moreover, they results highlighted the complexity of entrepreneurial action and showed that particular competences remained stable while others can be enhanced based on exposure to an entrepreneurship program and intense experiential learning. Creating successful entrepreneurs requires a shift from studying intentions and business formation alone to actually studying successful business development and growth as desired outcomes of an educational effort (Morris et al. 2013). The 13 Entrepreneurial Competences Model aimed at creating general awareness of what entrepreneurship entails, as well as guiding the development of entrepreneurship educational curricula

Table 1 The 13 Entrepreneurial competences model

1. Opportunity Recognition: the capacity to perceive changed conditions or overlooked possibilities in the environment that represent potential sources of profit or return to a venture
2. Opportunity Assessment: ability to evaluate the content structure of opportunities to accurately determine their relative attractiveness
3. Risk Management/Mitigation: the taking of actions that reduce the probability of a risk occurring or reduce the potential impact if the risk were to occur
4. Conveying a Compelling Vision: the ability to conceive an image of a future organizational state and to articulate that image in a manner that empowers followers to enact it
5. Tenacity/Perseverance: ability to sustain goal-directed action and energy when confronting difficulties and obstacles that impede goal achievement
6. Creative Problem Solving/Imaginativeness: the ability to relate previously unrelated objects or variables to produce novel and appropriate or useful outcomes
7. Resource Leveraging: skills at accessing resources one does not necessarily own or control to accomplish personal ends
8. Guerrilla Skills: the capacity to take advantage of one's surroundings, employ unconventional, low-cost tactics not recognized by others, and do more with less
9. Value Creation: capabilities of developing new products, services, and/or business models that generate revenues exceeding their costs and produce sufficient user benefits to bring about a fair return
10. Maintain Focus yet Adapt: ability to balance an emphasis on goal achievement and the strategic direction of the organization while addressing the need to identify and pursue actions to improve the fit between an organization and developments in the external environment
11. Resilience: ability to cope with stresses and disturbances such that one remains well, recovers, or even thrives in the face of adversity
12. Self-Efficacy: ability to maintain a sense of self-confidence regarding one's ability to accomplish a particular task or attain a level of performance
13. Building and Using Networks: social interaction skills that enable an individual to establish, develop, and maintain sets of relationships with others who assist them in advancing their work or career

Source: (Morris et al. 2013, p. 358)

4.2 The Great Eight Model

Bartram's (2005) criterion-centric model explores the validity of various potential predictors of workplace performance, he refers to as the Great Eight (see Table 2). These eight broad competence factors have emerged from factor analyses and multidimensional scaling analyses of self- and manager ratings of workplace performance. The author has explored the predictor-outcome relationships through a meta-analysis of 29 validity studies. The model showed a complete and consistent pattern of relationships between predictors and workplace performance. The Great Eight structure provides an articulation of the work performance domain that is consistent with a wide range of models used by practitioners in competency practice and supported empirically by the way in which competency ratings cluster when subjected to factor analysis. The model has been elaborated in terms of 112 component competences, which were linked both to competence assessment measures and

Table 2 The Great Eight model

Factor and competency domain title	Competency domain definition	Hypothesized big five, motivation, and ability relationships
1. Leading and Deciding	Takes control and exercises leadership. Initiates action, gives direction, and takes responsibility	Need for power and control, extraversion
2. Supporting and Cooperating	Supports others and shows respect and positive regard for them in social situations. Puts people first, working effectively with individuals and teams, clients, and staff. Behaves consistently with clear personal values that complement those of the organization	Agreeableness
3. Interacting and Presenting	Communicates and networks effectively. Successfully persuades and influences others. Relates to others in a confident, relaxed manner	Extraversion, general mental ability
4. Analyzing and Interpreting	Shows evidence of clear analytical thinking. Gets to the heart of complex problems and issues. Applies own expertise effectively. Quickly takes on new technology. Communicates well in writing	General mental ability, openness to new experience
5. Creating and Conceptualizing	Works well in situations requiring openness to new ideas and experiences. Seeks out learning opportunities. Handles situations and problems with innovation and creativity. Thinks broadly and strategically. Supports and drives organizational change	
6. Organizing and Executing	Plans ahead and works in a systematic and organized way. Follows directions and procedures. Focuses on customer satisfaction and delivers a quality service or product to the agreed standards	Conscientiousness, general mental ability
7. Adapting and Coping	Adapts and responds well to change. Manages pressure effectively and copes well with setbacks	Emotional stability
8. Enterprising and Performing	Focuses on results and achieving personal work objectives. Works best when work is related closely to results and the impact of personal efforts is obvious. Shows an understanding of business, commerce, and finance. Seeks opportunities for self-development and career advancement	Need for achievement, negative agreeableness

Source: (Bartram 2005, p. 1187)

to personality, motivation, and ability scales in the predictor domain. Consequently, the model provides a single framework for making predictions from measures of competence potential (ability, personality, and motivation) to ratings of actual behavior: work performance (Bartram 2005). Bartram's findings evidenced that Personality based predictors had moderate to high validities for all of the Great Eight, ability tests only added to the prediction of criteria for four of the eight competences. Ability was the most strongly predictive of competences in the areas of Analyzing & Interpreting and Creating & Conceptualizing. His results showed that personality and ability together and in isolation predict competency performance ratings in a meaningful manner. Personality provided a far broader coverage of the competence domain than ability, but ability data added to the level of prediction obtained from personality measures in those areas where ability was relevant. The Great Eight model provides a framework for integrating measures of ability, personality, and motivation performance consistently across jobs, measurement instruments, and cultural contexts. Interestingly, the personality-based Great Eight predictors differentiated competences into two principal components in terms of potential: the first reflects motivation, extraversion, and openness to new experience, whereas the second represents conscientiousness and related aspects of thinking styles.

4.3   The EntreComp Framework

Developed in 2016 through a mixed-methods approach, the EntreComp framework (Bacigalupo et al. 2016) proposes a shared definition of entrepreneurship as a competence and consists of 3 interrelated and interconnected competence areas: 'Ideas and opportunities', 'Resources' and 'Into action' (See Table 3). Each of the areas is made up of five competences, for a total of 15 competences along an 8-level progression model with a list of 442 learning outcomes. These resources can be personal (self-awareness and self-efficacy, motivation and perseverance), material (production means and financial resources) or non-material (specific knowledge, skills and attitudes). The progression in entrepreneurial learning is made up of two aspects: a) developing increasing autonomy and responsibility in acting upon ideas and opportunities to create value; b) developing the capacity to generate value from simple and predictable contexts up to complex, constantly changing environments.

The first component of entrepreneurial competence in the EntreComp model is "Ideas & Opportunity Recognition" this area consists of entrepreneurial skills to identify, seize and create opportunities, and pursue them vigorously: spotting opportunities, creativity, vision, valuing ideas, ethical and sustainability thinking. Shane and Venkataraman (2000) argued that identifying and exploiting opportunities are focal concepts in entrepreneurship that distinguishes entrepreneurship from management. Entrepreneurial ideas include creativity, innovation, risk-taking, and the capability to understand successful entrepreneurial role models and opportunity identification (Bacigalupo et al. 2016).

The second component of entrepreneurial competences in the EntreComp model is "Resources" which represents the entrepreneurial 'know-how', skills or knowledge, and includes self-awareness and efficacy, motivation and perseverance, mobilizing resources, financial and economic literacy, and mobilizing others. These resources support problem solving and decision-making, the capabilities and enhance interpersonal relationships, cooperation, and management of money.

Table 3 The EntreComp model

	Competences	Hints	Descriptors
Area: IDEAS	1.2 Creativity	Develop creative and purposeful ideas	– Develop several ideas and opportunities to create value, including better solutions to existing and new challenges – Explore and experiment with innovative approach-es – Combine knowledge and resources to achieve valuable effects
	1.3. Vision	Work towards your vision of the future	– Imagine the future – Develop a vision to turn ideas into action – Visualise future scenarios to help guide effort and action
	1.4 Valuing ideas	Make the most of ideas and oppor-tunities	– Judge what value is in social, cultural and eco-nomic terms – Recognise the potential an idea has for creating value and iden-tify suitable ways of making the most out of it
	1.5 Ethical and sustaina-ble thinking	Assess the con-sequences and impact of ideas, opportunities and actions	– Assess the consequences of ideas that bring value and the effect of entrepreneurial action on the target community, the market, society and the environ-ment – Reflect on how sustainable long-term social, cultural and economic goals are, and the course of action chosen – Act responsibly
Area: RESOURCES	2.1 Self-awareness and self-efficacy	Believe in your-self and keep developing	– Reflect on your needs, aspira-tions and wants in the short, medium and long term – Identify and assess your individual and group strengths and weaknesses – Believe in your ability to influence the course of events, despite uncertainty, setbacks and tempo-rary failures
	2.2 Motivation and perseverance	Stay focused and don't give up	– Be determined to turn ideas into action and satisfy your need to achieve – Be prepared to be patient and keep trying to achieve your long-term individual or group aims – Be resilient under pressure, adversity, and tempo-rary failure

(continued)

Table 3 (continued)

	Competences	Hints	Descriptors
	2.3 Mobilizing resources	Gather and manage the resources you need	– Get and manage the material, non-material and digital resources needed to turn ideas into action – Make the most of limited resources – Get and manage the competences needed at any stage, including technical, legal, tax and digital competences
	2.4 Financial and economic literacy	Develop financial and economic know how	– Estimate the cost of turning an idea into a value-creating activity – Plan, put in place and evaluate financial decisions over time – Manage financing to make sure my value-creating activity can last over the long term
	2.5. Mobilizing others	Inspire, enthuse and get others on board	– Inspire and enthuse relevant stakeholders – Get the support needed to achieve valuable out-comes – Demonstrate effective communication, persuasion, negotiation and leadership
Area: ACTIONS	3.1 Taking the initiative	Go for it	– Initiate processes that create value – Take up challenges – Act and work independently to achieve goals, stick to intentions and carry out planned tasks
	3.2 Planning and management	Prioritize, organ-ize and follow-up	– Set long-, medium- and short-term goals – Define priorities and action plans – Adapt to unforeseen changes
	3.3 Coping with uncertainty, ambiguity and risk	Make decisions dealing with uncertainty, ambiguity and risk	– Make decisions when the result of that decision is uncertain, when the information available is partial or ambiguous, or when there is a risk of unintend-ed outcomes – Within the value-creating process, include struc-tured ways of testing ideas and prototypes from the early stages, to reduce risks of failing – Handle fast-moving situations promptly and flexi-bly

(continued)

Table 3 (continued)

	Competences	Hints	Descriptors
	3.4 Working with others	Team up, collaborate and net-work	– Work together and co-operate with others to develop ideas and turn them into action – Network – Solve conflicts and face up to competition positively when necessary
	3.5. Learning through experience	Learn by doing	– Use any initiative for value creation as a learning opportunity – Learn with others, including peers and mentors – Reflect and learn from both success and failure (your own and other people's)

Source: (Bacigalupo et al. 2016, p. 12–13)

The third component of entrepreneurial competences in the EntreComp model is "Actions" and includes the ability to mobilize and inspire others, take initiatives, planning and managing, making decisions dealing with uncertainty, team up, collaborate and learn though experience.

5 Comparing and Contrasting Models and Taxonomies

Entrepreneurship is a way of thinking that emphasizes opportunities over treats (Krueger et al. 2000) and characterized by uncertainty, as outcomes are unknown and uncontrollable (Alvarez and Barney 2005). Its essence lies in pursuing opportunity regardless of resources controlled (Stevenson and Jarillo 1990).

The unique, heterogeneous, action-based nature of entrepreneurship suggests that development of such competences may require a multivariate approach. Little consensus exists in literature regarding the relative importance of particular competences in an entrepreneurial context (Morris et al. 2013). Research seems to suggest a broader definition of entrepreneurships to include proximal and distal variables, as well as moderators, predicting both business creation and business success in different contexts (Rauch and Frese 2007). Such variables should differentiate entrepreneurs from managers or other business roles, be related to economic outcomes and business performance, and predict entrepreneurial behaviours in favourable and unfavourable environments, independently from the seize of business.

While some authors have suggested the development of a fuller contingency theory of entrepreneurs' personality trait along the lines of Situation x Traits interactions (Rauch and Frese 2007), others have organized specific entrepreneurial traits into meaningful clusters of ideas, resources and behavior (Bacigalupo et al. 2016). In this chapter we compare and contrast three recent models and taxonomies of entrepreneurial competences (see Table 4) and critically analyse them in light of major clusters of variables predicting entrepreneurship as reviewed in recent literature and the components of competence (knowledge-K, skills-S, personality-P).

Table 4 Three Entrepreneurial Models Compared: EntreComp, The Great Eight, 13 Entrepreneurial Competences Model

	EntreComp	The Great Eight	13 Entrepreneurial Competence	Type
IDEAS	1.1 Spotting opportunities	8.2.2 Identifying Business Oportunities	1 & 2 Opportunity recognition & assessment	S
	1.2 Creativity	5.2 Innovating	5 Creative problem solving/ imaginativeness	P
	1.3 Vision	5.2.4 Visioning	4 Conveying a compelling vision	S
	1.4 Valuing ideas	5.3.1 Thinking broadly		S
	1.5 Ethical and sustainable thinking	2.2 Adhering to principles and values	9 Value creation	S
RESOURCES	2.1 Self awareness & self efficacy	1 Leading & deciding	12 Self efficacy	P
	2.2 Motivation and perseverance	8.1 Achieving Personal work goals and objectives	5 Tenacy/ perseverance	P
	2.3 Mobilizing resources	4 Analazying & Interpreting	7 Resource leveraging	S
	2.4 Financial & economic literacy	8.2.2 Entrepreneurial and commercial thinking		K
	2.5 Mobilizing others	2.1 Working with people		S
			11 Resilience	S
ACTIONS	3.1 Taking the initiative	1.1 Deciding & Intitiating Action	3 Risk management/ mitigation	S
	3.2 Planning & management	6.1 Planning & Organizing		S
	3.3 Coping with uncertanty, ambiguity and risk	7 Adapting & coping	10 Maintain focus yet adapt	P
	3.4 Working with others	3 Interacting & Presenting	13 Building and using networks	S
	3.5 Learning trough experience	5.1 Learning & Researching		S
			8 Guerrilla skills	S

Note: Numbering refers to the original for each model
Legenda: *P* personality, *K* knowledge, *S* skills

5.1 Personality Variables

Depth meta-analyses found evidence for the predictive validity of appropriate personality traits in entrepreneurial research (Zhao and Seibert 2006). Specific traits, such as achievement motive, creativity, risk taking, consciousness, openness to experience, dependability, proactivity, self-efficacy, stress tolerance, need for autonomy, internal locus of control, risk taking propensity, innovativeness, passion for work, tenacity, cognitive alertness, goal setting and practical intelligence are considered distal variables affecting entrepreneurial behavior and performance indirectly (Rauch and Frese 2007). Some of these variables yielded mixed results, while others were not studied enough to reach consistent results. Personality variables can explain entrepreneurial behavior not just as a trait component but also as mediational process, as in the case of situation-specific motivation (Baum and Locke 2004) or active planning (Frese et al. 2007). Rauch and Frese (2007) identified 11 personality traits matched to entrepreneurship self-efficacy, proactive personality, tenacity, need for achievement, stress tolerance, goal orientation, need for autonomy, innovativeness, endurance, flexibility and passion for work. In the three models considered in this chapter, three personality traits are included:

- *Tenacity* (13 Entrepreneurial Competences Model)
- *Creative problem solving/Imaginativeness* (13 Entrepreneurial Competences Model, EntreComp, Great Eight)
- *Self-efficacy* (13 Entrepreneurial Competences Model, EntreComp)
- *Adaptability* (13 Entrepreneurial Competences Model, EntreComp, Great Eight)
- *Motivation & Perseverance* (EntreComp)

Self-efficacy is related to business creation and success though perseverance and search for challenges, personal initiative, higher hope for success, long-term perspective, active search for information and thus better knowledge (Chen et al. 1998). Adaptability, like stress tolerance, is essential in entrepreneurship characterized by high insecurity, risks and pressure (Haynie et al. 2012).

Creativity helps entrepreneurs to foster innovation by generating novel and useful ideas for business ventures (Ward 2004). Tenacity is the ability to sustain goal-directed action and energy when confronting difficulties and obstacles that impede goal (Morris et al. 2013). The entrepreneurial event is denoted by initiative-taking, consolidation of resources, management, relative autonomy, and risk-taking (Shapero and Sokol 1982).

The relationship between personality traits and entrepreneurial behavior is not static. Researcher need to account for mediational variable as well as processes, like intentions, goals setting and self-regulatory processes (Rauch and Frese 2007).

5.2 Entrepreneurial Knowledge

Entrepreneurial Knowledge refers to what is understood and known about entrepreneurship and has important curricular implications for entrepreneurship education. Kourilsky and Walstad (1998) found low level of entrepreneurship knowledge in youth age 14-19, especially females to be detrimental to the interest in starting a business. Knowledge of key entrepreneurship concepts, as well as of the economy and the competitive market system, and the concepts and practices of entrepreneurship is fundamental. According to the knowledge spillover theory of entrepreneurship, knowledge creates endogenously results in knowledge spillovers, which allow entrepreneurs to identify and exploit opportunities (Acs et al. 2009). Evidence exists which suggests that both entrepreneurial knowledge and skills may have a direct impact on attitudes toward entrepreneurship (Peterman and Kennedy 2003; Watchravesringkan et al. 2013). According to the literature, the types of knowledge important for entrepreneurs are wide ranging, including content as well as domain-specific knowledge (Morris 1998). Omerzel and Antoncic (2008) found education level, work experience, knowledge about functional disciplines, and self-confidence positively related to entrepreneurship knowledge, which, in turn, was positively linked to firm performance. Moreover, Uger et al. (2009) found deliberate practice to have a strong, direct effect on entrepreneurial knowledge as well as an indirect effect on business growth via entrepreneurial knowledge. Education showed positive indirect effects on business growth and cognitive ability was positively related to deliberate practice and to entrepreneurial knowledge and had an indirect effect on business growth. Knowledge is related to the discovery of opportunities, firm growth, and overall venture success (Romanelli 1989). Entrepreneurial knowledge and skills enhance students' attitudes toward entrepreneurship. (Watchravesringkan et al. 2013). Entrepreneurship education should then focus on key entrepreneurship concepts, as well as the fundamental linkages between the dynamics and assumptions of a competitive market system and the concepts and practices of entrepreneurship. In the three models considered in this chapter, entrepreneurial knowledge was included in relation to:

• *Financial and Economic Literacy* (EntreComp)

5.3 Skills

Skills exhibited by successful entrepreneurs are diverse, spanning leadership, management, communication, organization, and opportunity recognition (Watchravesringkan et al. 2013). Social skills in particular play a role in entrepreneurs' success. Baron and Markman (2000). A high level of social capital, built on a favorable reputation, relevant previous experience, and direct personal contacts, often assists entrepreneurs in gaining access to venture capitalists, potential customers, and others. Specific social skills, such as the ability to read others accurately, make favorable first impressions, adapt to a wide range of social situations, and be persuasive, can influence the quality of these interactions. Moreover, by helping entrepreneurs expand their personal networks, social skills may also contribute to their social capital. Some researchers believe that skills predominantly result from experiences and knowledge (see Becker 1964), while other consider experience- and knowledge-based human capital indicators, such as schooling, industry experience and management experience to play some role in entrepreneurial skills. Stuetzer et al. (2013) found that traditional human capital indicators individually have little or no influence on entrepreneurial skills and that a varied set of work experiences rather than depth of any particular type of experience or education is important for the development of entrepreneurial skills. Lazear (2005) proposed a theoretical model highlighting the importance of a varied set of experiences for Entrepreneurs. This varied work experience was measured as the number of distinct functional areas in which the entrepreneur had work experience prior to start-up: marketing, sales, promotion; accounting, controlling, financing; engineering, R&D; production; and personnel. They controlled for gender, age, Ethnicity, origin, having self-employed parents and generalized self-efficacy to eliminate any biasing effect. A varied work experience leads not just to an increased tendency to engage or persist in entrepreneurial endeavours, but also to perform better at them (Lazear 2005). Similarly, Smith, Schallenkamp and Eichholz (2006) proposed set of seventeen skills entrepreneurs may possess at the different level, technical, managerial, entrepreneurial (i.e. Business Concept, business plan, presentation skills, Environmental Scanning, recognize market gap, exploit market opportunity, Advisory Board and Networking), and personal maturity skills (i.e. Self-Awareness, Accountability, Emotional Coping, Creativity). Recent research has gone beyond identifying types of knowledge and skills to assess the impact on firm performance as well as entrepreneurship success (Watchravesringkan et al. 2013). Sambasivan, Abdul and Yusop (2009) examined the influence of personal qualities, management skills, and opportunity recognition skills of entrepreneurs on venture performance in Malaysia. Their results revealed that the stronger the personal qualities and management skills, the better the opportunity recognition skills. In addition, the better the opportunity recognition skills, the greater the success of the venture in terms of sales volume and growth. In the three models considered in this chapter, the entrepreneurial skills included were:

- *Mobilizing resources* (EntreComp)
- *Interacting & Presenting* (Great Eight)
- *Organizing & Executing* (Great Eight)
- *Leading & Deciding* (Great Eight)
- *Analyzing & Interpreting* (Great Eight)
- *Entrepreneurial and commercial thinking* (Great Eight)
- *Identifying (and assessing) business opportunities* (all three models)
- *Risk management* (and coping with risk) (all three models)
- *Planning & Management* (EntreComp)
- *Convey a compelling vision* (13 Entrepreneurial Competences Model, EntreComp)

- *Mobilizing resources/networking* (13 Entrepreneurial Competences Model, EntreComp)
- *Value creation/Ethical and sustainable thinking/ Adhering to Principle and values* (all three models)
- *Resilience & Coping* (all three models)
- *Mobilizing others/networking/supporting and cooperation* (all three models)
- *Learning* (EntreComp, Great Eight)

6 Discussion

In this chapter, three competing models and taxonomies of entrepreneurial competences were compared and contrasted. Some competences were found, with similar names or concepts in all three models, while others were exclusive and peculiar to only one. We grouped all competences into three clusters: personality, knowledge and skills. Comprehensively five personality variables were agreed upon (tenacity/perseverance, creativity/ imaginativeness, Self-efficacy, Adaptability, and Motivation), however only two (Creativity/Imaginativeness and Adaptability) were present in all models. Self-efficacy/awareness is absent in the The Great Eight model and motivation is coupled with perseverance in The EntreComp model and absent in the 13 Competence model. Only one traditional personality trait often found in entrepreneurial literature, risk-taking propensity, was not accounted for by any of the three models examined. It is, however, included in The Great Eight as competency component (1.1.6 Taking calculated risks) of the competency dimension Leading and Deciding, considered as a skill and behavior, rather than a personality characteristics. Risk management and reduction are also represent in the EntreComp (3.3 Coping with uncertainty, ambiguity and risk) and the 13 Entrepreneurial competences model (3. Risk Management/Mitigation), considered action and decision-making process. Surprisingly, only the EntreComp model included a rather generic knowledge (Financial & Economic literacy), whereas The Great Eight model refers to entrepreneurial knowledge-based skills in the competency dimension Enterprising and Performing, component Entrepreneurial Thinking, which includes Monitoring Markets and Competitors, Demonstrating Financial Awareness, Controlling costs) and the Managing of Knowledge in the competency dimension Learning and Researching. All three model seem to mainly focus on entrepreneurial skills and behaviors, accounting overall for a list of 12 skills, 5 of which are present in all three models (Identifying & Assessing opportunities, Visioning, Ethical and Sustainable thinking, Mobilizing Resources, Working with people), whereas Valuing ideas or Thinking broadly and Planning and Management are absent in the 13 competence Model. Finally, resilience and guerrilla skills (the ability to do more with less) are peculiar to the 13 competence model. The three models, however, greatly vary in aims and methodology. The EntreComp model is theoretical and have been tested only recently on empirical data in a sample of college students (Cubico et al. 2017). Findings revealed that the framework identifies, directly or indirectly, key entrepreneurship competences related to students' entrepreneurship mindset. Specifically, Ideas & Opportunities were confirmed as predictive of entrepreneurship and positively related to students' entrepreneurial intention. However, the same was not true for Resources and Actions which were found indirect relevant competences for entrepreneurship determining students' Attitude toward Entrepreneurial Behavior. Moreover, when we examined the three models based on the interrelated and interconnected competence areas proposed by the EntreComp: 'Ideas and opportunities', 'Resources' and 'Into action', we found the three model quite balanced in number and type of competences for each area. The EntreComp proposed division seems to better capture the unique characteristics of entrepreneurship competences. Ideas (i.e. creativity, opportunity, and feasibility) stimulate entrepreneurship, Resources (i.e. personal, human capital, economic) represent incentives and barriers to the successful launching of new ventures, and Action (i.e. initiative, management, planning, adapting) sustains the development of a business and materialize the ideas in an entrepreneurial act.

7 Conclusion

Entrepreneurship is a way of thinking but also a planned, intentional behavior. Yet, certain specific attitudes and personality traits predict intention, and the way new opportunities are perceived and pursuit (Krueger et al. 2000). The complexity of the entrepreneur's role calls for a comprehensive and detailed taxonomy of entrepreneurial competences. No single cluster of entrepreneurial competences, either defined as Personality, Knowledge and Skills, or as Ideas, Resources and Actions alone can significantly predict entrepreneurial activity and success. Although the three models analyzed in this chapter seem to agree on the competences' domains, they showed different levels of specificity and details and no one model examined was clearly superior to another in all respects. More importantly, they offered different measures (or none) for the assessment of such competences, which at the individual level appears to offer a promising arena for future research we propose, in that respect, the development of a complex and comprehensive taxonomy shared across the three models, by combining categories and including unique dimensions to some models and a validated tool to measure them. Any competence must be describable in terms of a specific label, a clearly worded definition, and at least three unique and more specific behavioral elements and belong to one of the three domain, either ideas, resources or actions. Moreover, the taxonomy we propose should balance personality characteristics, knowledge and skills, as an excessive emphases was detected on skills in all the three models examined. Finally, the model should account for both proximal and distal variables predicting entrepreneurship, and their mediating and moderating effects.

Acknowledgments The study benefits from the financial support from the EU HoB-House of Brains Project (Grant Agreement No. 2014-1-IT02-KA203-003520) and from ESU Verona (Agency for the right to study).

References

Acs, Z. J., Braunerhjelm, P., Audretsch, D. B., & Carlsson, B. (2009). The knowledge spillover theory of entrepreneurship. *Small Business Economics, 32*(1), 15–30.

Alvarez, S. H., & Barney, J. B. (2005). How do entrepreneurs organize firms under conditions of uncertainty? *Journal of Management, 31*(5), 776–793.

Arthurs, J., & Busenitz, L. (2006). Dynamic capabilities and venture performance: The effects of venture capitalists. *Journal of Business Venturing, 21*(2), 195–215.

Audretsch, D. B., Kuratko, D. F., & Link, A. N. (2015). Making sense of the elusive paradigm of entrepreneurship. *Small Business Economics, 45*(4), 703–712.

Audretsch, D. B., Kuratko, D. F., & Link, A. N. (2016). Dynamic entrepreneurship and technology-based innovation. *Journal of Evolutionary Economics, 26*(3), 603–620.

Bacigalupo, M., Kampylis, P., Punie, Y., & Van den Brande, G. (2016). *EntreComp: the entrepreneurship competence framework, EUR 27939 EN*, Luxembourg: Publication Office of the European Union. https://ec.europa.eu/jrc/en/publication/eur-scientific-and-technical-research-reports/entrecomp-entrepreneurship-competence-framework

Baron, R. A., & Markman, G. D. (2000). Beyond social capital: How social skills can enhance entrepreneurs' success. *The Academy of Management Executive, 14*(1), 106–116.

Bartram, D. (2005). The Great Eight competencies: a criterion-centric approach to validation. *Journal of Applied Psychology, 90*(6), 1185–1203.

Baum, J. R., & Locke, E. A. (2004). The relationship of entrepreneurial traits, skill, and motivation to subsequent venture growth. *Journal of Applied Psychology, 89*(4), 587–598.

Baum, J. R., Locke, E. A., & Smith, K. G. (2001). A multidimensional model of venture growth. *Academy of Management Journal, 44*(2), 292–303.

Becker, G. S. (1964). *Human capital*. New York, NY: Columbia University Press.

Bird, B. (1995). Towards a theory of entrepreneurial competency. *Advances in Entrepreneurship Firm Emergence and Growth, 2*(1), 51–72.

Chen, C. C., Greene, P. G., & Crick, A. (1998). Does entrepreneurial self-efficacy distinguish entrepreneurs from managers? *Journal of Business Venturing, 13*(4), 295–316.

Chouhan, V. S., & Srivastava, S. (2014). Competencies and competency modeling – A literature survey. *IOSR Journal of Business and Management, 16*(1), 14–22.

Combs, J. G., Crook, T. R., & Shook, C. L. (2005). The dimensionality of organizational performance and its implications for strategic management research. In D. J. Ketchen & D. D. Bergh (Eds.), *Research methodology in strategic management*. The Netherlands: Elsevier.

Cubico, S., Formicuzzi, M., Ardolino, P., Noventa, S., Ferrari, A., Sartori, R. and Favretto, G. (2013). Entrepreneurial human capital: A model for analyzing and validating the key competences for entrepreneurship. *Conference Papers of RENT XXVII – Research in entrepreneurship and small business*, http://www.rent-research.org/default.asp?iId=GGEHHJ

Cubico, S., Gianesini, G., Favretto, G., Cesaroni, F.M., Sentuti, A. and Pajardi, D. (2017). Exploring students' entrepreneurial ideas, resources, and actions: The EntreComp framework. *Conference Papers of RENT XXVII – Research in entrepreneurship and small business*, http://www.rent-research.org/conference-final-papers-2017

Davidsson, P., & Honig, B. (2003). The role of social and human capital among nascent entrepreneurs. *Journal of Business Venturing, 18*(3), 301–331.

DeTienne, D. R., Shepherd, D. A., & De Castro, J. O. (2008). The fallacy of "only the strong survive": The effect of intrinsic motivation and the persistence decisions for under-performing firms. *Journal of Business Venturing, 23*(5), 528–546.

Farhangmehr, M., Gonçalves, P., & Sarmento, M. (2016). Predicting entrepreneurial motivation among university students: The role of entrepreneurship education. *Education + Training, 58* (7/8), 861–881.

Frese, M., Krauss, S. I., Keith, N., Escher, S., Grabarkiewicz, R., Luneng, S. T., & Friedrich, C. (2007). Business owners' action planning and its relationship to business success in three African countries. *Journal of Applied Psychology, 92*(6), 1481–1498.

Giddens, A. (1984). *The constitution of society.* Berkeley, CA: University of California Press.

Haynie, J. M., Shepherd, D. A., & Patzelt, H. (2012). Cognitive adaptability and an entrepreneurial task: The role of metacognitive ability and feedback. *Entrepreneurship Theory and Practice, 36* (2), 237–265.

Koskinen, K. U., & Vanharanta, H. (2002). The role of tacit knowledge in innovation processes of small technology companies. *International Journal of Production Economics, 80*(1), 57–64.

Kourilsky, M. L., & Walstad, W. B. (1998). Entrepreneurship and female youth: Knowledge, attitudes, gender differences, and educational practices. *Journal of Business Venturing, 13*(1), 77–88.

Krueger, N. F., Reilly, M. D., & Carsrud, A. L. (2000). Competing models of entrepreneurial intentions. *Journal of Business Venturing, 15*(5), 411–432.

Kuratko, D. F. (2005). The emergence of entrepreneurship education: development, trends, and challenges. *Entrepreneurship Theory and Practice, 29*(5), 577–598.

Kyndt, E., & Baert, H. (2015). Entrepreneurial competencies: Assessment and predictive value for entrepreneurship. *Journal of Vocational Behavior, 90*(1), 13–25.

Lazear, E. P. (2004). Balanced skills and entrepreneurship. *The American Economic Review, 94*(2), 208–211.

Lazear, E. P. (2005). Entrepreneurship. *Journal of Labor Economics, 23*(4), 649–680.

Lee, H., Lee, J., Shim, K., & Lee, H. (2016). *Entrepreneurial characteristics: A systematic literature review, PACIS 2016 Proceedings,* http://aisel.aisnet.org/pacis2016/81

Leyden, D. P., & Link, A. N. (2013). Knowledge spillovers, collective entrepreneurship, and economic growth: the role of universities. *Small Business Economics, 41*(4), 797–817.

Man, T. W. Y., Lau, T., & Chan, K. F. (2002). The competitiveness of small and medium enterprises: A conceptualization with focus on entrepreneurial competencies. *Journal of Business Venturing, 17*(2), 123–142.

Mitchelmore, S., & Rowley, J. (2010). Entrepreneurial competencies: A literature review and development agenda. *International Journal of Entrepreneurial Behavior & Research, 16*(2), 92–111.

Morris, M. H., Webb, J. W., Fu, J., & Singhal, S. (2013). A competency-based perspective on entrepreneurship education: Conceptual and empirical insights. *Journal of Small Business Management, 51*(3), 352–369.

Morris, M. H. (1998). *Entrepreneurial intensity.* Westport, CT: Quorum.

Mulder, M., Lans, T., Verstegen, J., Biemans, H., & Meijer, Y. (2007). Competence development of entrepreneurs in innovative horticulture. *Journal of Workplace Learning, 19*(1), 32–44.

Omerzel, D. G., & Antoncic, B. (2008). Critical entrepreneurial knowledge dimensions for the SME performance. *Industrial Management and Data, 108*(9), 1182–1199.

Peteraf, M. A., & Barney, J. B. (2003). Unraveling the resource-based tangle. *Managerial and Decision Economics, 24*(4), 309–323.

Peterman, N. E., & Kennedy, J. (2003). Enterprise education: Influencing students' perceptions of entrepreneurship. *Entrepreneurship Theory and Practice, 28*(2), 129–144.

Priyanto, S. H., & Sandjojo, I. (2005). Relationship between entrepreneurial learning, entrepreneurial competencies and venture success: Empirical study on SMEs. *International Journal of Entrepreneurship and Innovation Management, 5*(5/6), 458–468.

Rauch, A., & Frese, M. (2007). Let's put the person back into entrepreneurship research: A meta-analysis on the relationship between business owners' personality traits, business creation, and success. *European Journal of Work and Organizational Psychology, 16*(4), 353–385.

Reuber, A. R., & Fisher, E. (1999). Understanding the consequences of founders' experience. *Journal of Small Business Management, 37*(2), 30–45.

Romanelli, E. (1989). Environments and strategies of organizational start up: Effects on early survival. *Administrative Science Quarterly, 34*(3), 369–387.

Sambasivan, M., Abdul, M., & Yusop, Y. (2009). Impact of personal qualities and management skills of entrepreneurs on venture performance in Malaysia: Opportunity recognition skills as a mediating factor. *Technovation, 29*(11), 798–805.

Shane, S., & Venkataraman, S. (2000). The promise of entrepreneurship as a field of research. *Academy of Management Review, 25*(1), 217–226.

Shane, S., & Venkatraman, S. (2000). The promise of entrepreneurship as a field of research. *Academy of Management Journal, 25*(1), 217–226.

Shane, S. (2000). Prior knowledge and the discovery of entrepreneurial opportunities. *Organization Science, 11*(4), 448–469.

Shapero, A., & Sokol, L. (1982). The social dimensions of entrepreneurship. In C. Kent, D. Sexton, & K. H. Vesper (Eds.), *The encyclopedia of entrepreneurship*. Englewood Cliffs, NJ: Prentice-Hall.

Smith, E. M., Ford, J., & Kozlowski, S. W. J. (1997). Building adaptive expertise: Implications for training design strategies. In M. A. Quinones & A. Ehrenstein (Eds.), *Training for a rapidly changing workplace: Applications of psychological research*. American Psychological Association: Washington DC.

Smith, W. L., Schallenkamp, K., & Eichholz, D. E. (2006). Entrepreneurial skills assessment: An exploratory study. *International Journal of Management and Enterprise Development, 4*(2), 179–201.

Stevenson, H. H., & Jarillo, J. C. (1990). A paradigm of entrepreneurship: Entrepreneurial management. *Strategic Management Journal, 11*(4), 17–27.

Stuetzer, M., Obschonka, M., Davidsson, P., & Schmitt-Rodermund, E. (2013). Where do entrepreneurial skills come from? *Applied Economics Letters, 20*(12), 1183–1186.

Teece, D. J. (2012). Dynamic capabilities: Routines versus entrepreneurial action. *Journal of Management Studies, 49*(8), 1395–1401.

Uger, J. M., Keith, M., Hilling, C., Gielnik, M. M., & Frese, M. (2009). Deliberate practice among South African small business owners: Relationships with education, cognitive ability, knowledge, and success. *Journal of Occupational and Organizational Psychology, 82*(1), 21–44.

Unger, J. M., Rauch, A., Frese, M., & Rosenbusch, N. (2011). Human capital and entrepreneurial success: A meta-analytical review. *Journal of business venturing, 26*(3), 341–358.

Volery, T., Mueller, S., & von Siemens, B. (2015). Entrepreneur ambidexterity: A study of entrepreneur behaviors and competencies in growth oriented small and medium-sized enterprises. *International Small Business Journal, 33*(2), 109–129.

Ward, T. B. (2004). Cognition, creativity, and entrepreneurship. *Journal of Business Venturing, 19*(2), 173–188.

Watchravesringkan, K. T., Hodges, N. N., Yurchisin, J., Hegland, J., Karpova, E., Marcketti, S., & Yan, R. N. (2013). Modeling entrepreneurial career intentions among undergraduates: An examination of the moderating role of entrepreneurial knowledge and skills. *Family and Consumer Sciences Research Journal, 41*(3), 325–342.

Westhead, P., Ucbasaran, D., & Wright, M. (2005). Decisions, actions, and performance: do novice, serial, and portfolio entrepreneurs differ? *Journal of Small Business Management, 43*(4), 393–417.

Zahra, S. A., Sapienza, H. J., & Davidsson, P. (2006). Entrepreneurship and dynamic capabilities: A review, model and research agenda. *Journal of Management Studies, 43*(4), 917–955.

Zhao, H., & Seibert, S. E. (2006). The big five personality dimensions and entrepreneurial status: A meta-analytical review. *Journal of Applied Psychology, 91*(2), 259–271.

Heterogeneity and the Origin of the Founding Team: How the Concepts Relate and Affect Entrepreneurial Behavior

Gertie M. Agraz-Boeneker and Maria del Mar Fuentes-Fuentes

Abstract Although discovery and exploitation of entrepreneurial opportunities have often been attributed to an individual entrepreneur, scholars have increasingly recognized that entrepreneurship is a task performed by teams more than individuals and that the dynamics of entrepreneurial teams add new insights to entrepreneurship research (Klotz et al., Journal of Management 40: 1–30, 2013). It has also been suggested that the traditional way of performing the entrepreneurial process, is not the only way and other alternatives have been proposed to explain how individuals and teams perform this process. Findings of this work suggest differences among founding teams relative to their composition at the moment of creation of their ventures, and to whether they were formed before or after the entrepreneurial opportunity was discovered or created. Relationships are suggested between teams' heterogeneity and the use of Effectuation and Causation as entrepreneurial behaviors by Founding Teams. Additionally, a *Behavioral Classification of Founding Teams* is proposed, based on the analysis of the behaviors reported by entrepreneurs from nine Founding Teams.

Keywords Founding teams · Entrepreneurial teams · Entrepreneurial behavior · Effectuation · Heterogeneity · Startups

G. M. Agraz-Boeneker (✉)
Tecnologico de Monterrey, Hermosillo, México

M. del Mar Fuentes-Fuentes (✉)
Universidad de Granada, Granada, Spain
e-mail: mfuentes@ugr.es

© Springer International Publishing AG, part of Springer Nature 2018
S. Cubico et al. (eds.), *Entrepreneurship and the Industry Life Cycle*, Studies on Entrepreneurship, Structural Change and Industrial Dynamics,
https://doi.org/10.1007/978-3-319-89336-5_3

1   Introduction

Opportunities are at the top of the Entrepreneurial Process whether we conceive them as latent and waiting to be discovered (Shane and Venkataraman 2000) or as circumstances that have to be constructed through experimentation (Sarasvathy 2001).

Discovery and exploitation of entrepreneurial opportunities have often been attributed to an individual entrepreneur that has been mystified as a "lone hero" (Cooney 2005). Notwithstanding this general conception, entrepreneurship scholars have come to acknowledge that the formation of new ventures is usually accomplished by teams (Klotz et al. 2013) rather than by individuals and that ventures led by teams are more successful than those of lone entrepreneurs (Kamm et al. 1990).

On the other hand, most entrepreneurship research has focused on the discovery and exploitation of entrepreneurial opportunities as a goal-driven process, where entrepreneurs foresee a business opportunity and assemble the necessary resources to exploit it (Fisher 2012; Perry et al. 2011; Sarasvathy 2001).

Complementing this view, new thinking has presented different perspectives to explain the actions and logic that underlie entrepreneurial behavior (Fisher 2012), *effectuation* being one that "assumes not that opportunities are waiting to be discovered, but that opportunities emerge when created by an entrepreneur and her partners" (Read et al. 2009, p. 573).

Sarasvathy (2001) refers to the traditional model as *causation* and introduces *effectuation* as an alternative model of opportunity identification and exploitation.

Effectuation is built on the idea of co-creation of the entrepreneur with her partners (Dew et al. 2009; Read et al. 2009) leading one to suspect that it might be more a team effort than an individual endeavor. Nevertheless, although several works about *effectuation* have been written (Perry et al. 2011; Read et al. 2009) few have explicitly referred to the use of *effectuation* by teams (Alsos and Clausen 2016). In that case, this approach might add new information to the extant literature about both *effectuation* and *entrepreneurial teams*.

Klotz et al. (2013) recognize that to this point most entrepreneurship research about new venture team functioning and performance has followed the lead of Upper Echelons (UE) research which states that the characteristics of individuals in Top Management Teams (TMT) predict the team's organizational outcomes, i.e. their strategic choices and performance levels (Hambrick and Mason 1984). This has been a useful approach so far, however such studies have been limited to publicly available data, and have often failed to explain *how* and *when* teams' characteristics influence firm performance. To address these questions, an Input-Mediators-Outcomes (IMO) framework has been proposed, to achieve better knowledge about team dynamics and performance (Klotz et al. 2013).

Bird and Schjoedt (2009) refer to *Entrepreneurial Behavior* as the concrete enactment of individual or team tasks or activities "chosen with the intention of finding and exploiting an opportunity and forming an organization of human, financial, physical, social, and intellectual resources" (p. 328). According to this definition, teams and organizations do not behave but individuals comprising them do and their actions derive from the characteristics they own, such as their experience, knowledge, skills, abilities, cognitions, intelligence, learning, intentions, and motivations which, according to Sarasvathy (2001) become the *means* of the entrepreneur, or the team, i.e. *"who they are*, *what they know*, and *whom they know*—their own traits, tastes, and abilities; the knowledge corridors they are in; and the social networks they are a part of" (p. 250, italics added).

Each entrepreneur brings her own resources to the endeavor depending on the means that he/she can control and draw upon to establish and grow the new venture. Consequently, when a group of entrepreneurs get together, it can be expected that the variety of means available to start the new venture might be wider, allowing the team to develop more innovative ventures than an individual acting alone would (Kamm et al. 1990).

When studying Top Management Teams (TMT's) under the Upper Echelons perspective (Hambrick and Mason 1984), the idea of heterogeneity of characteristics among team members affecting firm's performance has been widely referred to (Nielsen 2010). The same is true in works addressing Founding Teams (Klotz et al. 2013) although extant studies support the idea that the latter are formed by individuals who are more alike than complementary (Ruef et al. 2003).

Even though several forms of heterogeneity in founding teams have been researched and tested by different authors, the results have been misleading because a mixture of demographic characteristics and/or knowledge backgrounds has been used by authors to illustrate heterogeneity (Klotz et al. 2013); and, on the other hand a variety of outcomes has been related, making it difficult to establish a consistent theory about entrepreneurial teams' heterogeneity and its effect on either team's or firm's performance, and/or behavior.

On the other hand, as Chowdury (2005) points out, research has been lacking studies on entrepreneurial team diversity related to personality characteristics of entrepreneurs, which might be combining with demographic characteristics and thinking style to influence entrepreneurial team dynamics and team effectiveness.

Despite differences in works relating heterogeneity to team or firm outcomes, several works test some form of *informational diversity* (Jehn et al. 1999).

Informational diversity refers to heterogeneity related to human capital, i.e knowledge of the entrepreneurs that is acquired either through years of study or experience (Davidsson and Honig 2003), such as educational background (either type of knowledge and/or years of training), previous work experience and, previous entrepreneurial experience and/or entrepreneurial education and training (Martin et al. 2013).

Human capital can be generic when acquired through formal education and professional experience, or specific when it relates directly to the industry of the venture (industry-specific), or to the capabilities needed by an individual to start a new firm (entrepreneur-specific) (Colombo and Grilli 2005). Complementary context-specific knowledge needs to be integrated to successfully exploit a business opportunity, and this integration is best achieved if experts are members in the founding team (p. 800).

From the conclusions of most works relating informational heterogeneity to team or firm outcomes, previous work experience (*functional experience*) is usually the one type of heterogeneity that positively affects firm's or team's performance (e.g. Eisenhardt and Schoonhoven 1990; Colombo and Grilli 2005; Beckman and Burton 2008; Hmieleski and Ensley 2007; Eesley et al. 2014; Zhou et al. 2015; Muñoz-Bullon et al. 2015; Ensley and Hmieleski 2005) which leads us to think that heterogeneity in context specific knowledge is more important to Founding Teams than other types of human capital (Colombo and Grilli 2005), or types of diversity among team members.

To explain the dynamics of Founding Teams following Klotz' et al. (2013) IMO framework, we propose a model where inputs (I) are represented by the "means" of the team as described by Sarasvathy (2001); both Effectuation and Causation as frameworks of entrepreneurial behavior (Fisher 2012) are considered mediators (M) linking Inputs to firm Outcomes (O) which are represented by sales growth, employee growth and innovativeness. Outcomes, however will not be specifically addressed by this work.

The present work analyzes, first the characteristics (*means*) of nine Founding Teams (i.e. Teams starting New Ventures) and secondly the activities and actions that each of the teams followed to identify and exploit a business opportunity, with the aim to answer the following questions: Who is included in the Founding Team at the moment of venture creation and what are the different (or not so different) attributes that team members bring to the team in terms of knowledge, social networks and other personal characteristics? What are the different behaviors and actions by which the Founding Team identifies an entrepreneurial opportunity, creates and develops the new venture and subsequently makes the important decisions that affect it?

We describe findings related to Founding Team composition; Founding Team behavior and the relationship between both concepts. Also, a Behavioral Classification of Founding Teams is proposed for future research and validation.

The rest of this paper proceeds as follows:

First the theory is presented related to Entrepreneurship and Teams as well as Entrepreneurial Behavior, focusing on the logics of Causation and Effectuation. Secondly the research design of the study is explained, followed by a presentation of results and conclusions based on the observations obtained from the analysis of the participating Founding Teams and their behaviors at pre-startup and startup phases.

2   Entrepreneurship and Teams

Kamm et al. (1990) established that "teams are significant for researchers and entrepreneurs in two primary ways: (1) they are a more common occurrence than the entrepreneurship literature leads one to expect; and (2) they affect their firms' performance" (p. 7).

Founding Teams form under conditions of uncertainty, in which "similar trusted alters" (Ruef et al. 2003) perceive they can jointly reach an objective that would not be achieved individually by any one of them (Harper 2008).

It is not always clear whether the team originates from one individual assembling it together once a business idea has been developed, or if the idea develops from an already committed group of people that share a specific social context and experience (Kamm and Nurick 1993; Cooney 2005; Beckman 2006).

Cooney (2005) and Beckman (2006) similarly explain a process of team formation in which both the idea and the team evolve and take form together in a dynamic and alternative fashion after which the idea will be evaluated by the team and the necessary resources will be acquired to develop and launch the new venture.

Cooney's (2005) model sustains the idea of organizations emerging in stages (Kamm and Nurick 1993) starting with the developing of the business idea by a "lead entrepreneur" as the first stage; although, in other circumstances, an "event" might trigger the venture creation process even before a business opportunity is identified, such as: the assembly of a team of friends or colleagues in pursuit of a common endeavor or by social convention; or the occurrence of an "external enabler" (Davidsson 2015) (e.g. demographic shift, technological breakthrough, regulatory change) that creates disequilibrium in the market and allows entrepreneurs to think about new economic activities that can be explored.

After a decision has been made about formalizing the relationship between partners and/or take action on the idea of developing a new venture, a new set of decisions follows related to getting resources and more information that may modify the initial idea, and how to implement it (Kamm and Nurick 1993). The process then becomes iterative and turns an informal social group into an entrepreneurial team.

Several terms have been used by scholars when referring to teams starting new ventures, such as *founding teams* (Brinckmann et al. 2009; Colombo and Grilli 2005; Beckman and Burton 2008; Brinckmann and Hoegl 2001; Ruef et al. 2003; Kamm and Nurick 1993; Fern et al. 2012; Visintin and Pittino 2014; Eesley et al. 2014); *entrepreneurial teams* (Blatt 2009; Chowdury 2005; Harper 2008; Zhou et al. 2015); *new venture teams* (Klotz et al. 2013; Lim et al. 2012); *new venture top management teams* (Ensley et al. 2002) and, *startup teams* (Klotz et al. 2013) among others.

Furthermore, there is no clear agreement about the definition of this type of teams.

For this work, building upon the different definitions that we found in the literature, we will use the term *founding team*, to refer to the first team that is formed to create the venture, described as a *group of two or more people who jointly create and manage a new venture, have an equity stake in the business and are responsible for taking the strategic decisions that affect it.* We will also use the term *entrepreneurial team* as a generic term when referring not necessarily to the first team but to one that *might include some or all the founders and is set at a point in time which is different from that of the creation of the new venture.*

2.1 Heterogeneity in Founding Teams

Following the lessons from Upper Echelons theory (Hambrick and Mason 1984), several authors assert that heterogeneity of the Founding Team is beneficial for the new venture and its subsequent success (Zhou et al. 2015; Eesley et al. 2014; Visintin and Pittino 2014; Beckman and Burton 2008; Colombo and Grilli 2005), however, there are also works claiming that Founding Teams are not necessarily diverse (Ruef et al. 2003) setting the tone for the development of new insights that might give us some clues about whether heterogeneity of the Founding Team really occurs and, if not, to understand how teams manage to solve the problems and needs of their ventures.

The composition of founding teams is important because they perform the entrepreneurial action that leads to the new venture and, even though, the initial team might evolve as time passes and new challenges are faced by the new ventures, research has recognized that the founding team has an imprinting effect on subsequent executives and firm structures (Boeker 1989; Kamm et al. 1990; Beckman 2006; Beckman and Burton 2008; Eesley et al. 2014) which are the ones that will support the venture to become an established company.

Although the composition of Entrepreneurial Teams has been studied before, most works have focused on member entry and exit (Forbes et al. 2006; Chandler et al. 2005; Ucbasaran et al. 2003) and have found difficulties to go into detail about how Founding Teams actually form (Forbes et al. 2006).

Some research has developed supporting the idea that founding teams are formed by individuals that are more alike than complementary (Ruef et al. 2003) nevertheless, several forms of heterogeneity in founding and entrepreneurial teams have been researched and tested by different authors (Klotz et al. 2013).

Jehn et al. (1999) distinguish three types of diversity in teams: *Informational diversity* related to differences in knowledge bases and perspectives that members bring to the group; *Social category diversity* that refer to explicit differences among group members such as race, gender or age; and *Value diversity* that occurs when members of a workgroup differ in terms of what they think the group's real task, goal, target or mission should be.

Most studies relating team's heterogeneity and firm's performance include some form of *informational diversity* (e.g. work experience diversity; educational diversity and/or entrepreneurial experience diversity) to find that it is positively related to either team's performance (Ucbasaran et al. 2003; Zhou et al. 2015; Muñoz-Bullon et al. 2015) or firm's performance (Visintin and Pittino 2014; Hmieleski and Ensley 2007; Colombo and Grilli 2005; Eisenhardt and Schoonhoven 1990).

Social category diversity (Jehn et al. 1999) has also been considered in some works, assessing age, gender and ethnicity differences among team members as control variables (Auh and Menguc 2005; Carson et al. 2007; Zheng 2012), or as independent variables (Ruef et al. 2003; Chowdury 2005; Chandler et al. 2005) related to team effectiveness, team turnover or team performance. Nevertheless, the effect of this type of heterogeneity, has not always been reported as significant (e.g. Chowdury 2005; Chandler et al. 2005).

It is suggested that the effect of Social category diversity might be indirect, by affecting or creating other types of heterogeneity such as diversity of information or perspective (Jehn et al. 1999); however, the debate about its effect remains open and calls for further research.

Value diversity on the other hand has not been addressed by the literature referring to Entrepreneurial Teams. According to Jehn et al. (1999) for a team to be effective it should have high *informational diversity* and low *value diversity*.

Additionally, personality traits diversity has recently been addressed as beneficial for the team to achieve the growth of their new venture. Especially when referring to relationship-oriented personality traits such as extraversion, agreeableness and emotional stability, diversity has been found to positively affect team processes and enhance team performance.

On the other hand, characteristics such as humility of founders and/or team leaders, together with proactive personality traits of team members may add up for the team to develop Shared leadership (Chiu et al. 2016).

D'Innocenzo et al. (2014) define *Shared leadership* as "an emergent and dynamic team phenomenon whereby leadership roles and influence are distributed among team members" (p. 5).

According to Hoch (2014) Shared leadership is directly associated with information sharing among team members when diversity is high, allowing for the team to enhance its performance by using the diverse information and knowledge backgrounds of all team members.

The heterogeneity construct in entrepreneurial teams' theory has been developed from a mix of different attributes without always making a separation between those referring to individual demographic or social characteristics of team members (*Social category diversity*) and those referring to their previous experience or knowledge (*Informational diversity*).

Adding up to the difficulties in establishing a consistent theory about entrepreneurial teams' heterogeneity and its effect on either team's or firm's performance (Klotz et al. 2013), a variety of outcomes has been considered by different authors, such as: innovativeness and/or product innovation (Eisenhardt and Schoonhoven 1990; Auh and Menguc 2005; Henneke and Lüthje 2007); firm growth related to increase in number of employees (Colombo and Grilli 2005; Beckman 2006) or sales growth (Visintin and Pittino 2014); time to receive venture capital or to initial public offer (IPO) (Beckman and Burton 2008; Eesley et al. 2014); team effectiveness and/or team performance (Chowdury 2005; Zhou et al. 2015; Muñoz-Bullon et al. 2015) and, type of strategy (Fern et al. 2012) among others.

In any case, the effect of different types of heterogeneity cannot yet be dismissed from studies about entrepreneurial teams although a greater consistency is required around the factors that are considered to delineate the different forms of heterogeneity as well as to understand the mechanisms through which heterogeneity influences behavior and/or performance outcomes (Klotz et al. 2013).

3 Entrepreneurial Behavior: About Effectuation and Causation

Bird and Schjoedt (2009) define *Entrepreneurial Behavior* as a research construct involving the concrete enactment of the individual or team tasks or activities required to start and grow a new organization.

Numerous theoretical perspectives have emerged to explain the actions and logic that underlie entrepreneurial behavior. The traditional model is described as one in which an individual or firm takes entrepreneurial action to discover, evaluate and exploit an entrepreneurial opportunity.

Sarasvathy (2001) refers to the traditional model as *causation* and introduces *effectuation* as an alternative model of opportunity identification and exploitation. In her work, she defines both concepts as follows: "*Causation* processes take a particular effect as given and focus on selecting between means to create that effect. *Effectuation* processes take a set of means as given and focus on selecting between possible effects that can be created with that set of means" (Sarasvathy 2001 p. 245).

While causation is consistent with planned strategy approaches, including such activities as opportunity recognition and business plan development, effectuation processes are consistent with emergent strategy and include a selection of alternatives based on loss affordability, flexibility, and experimentation (Chandler et al. 2011).

When effectual reasoning is used by entrepreneurs, subjects start with a given set of means which open up a set of possibilities: things entrepreneurs can afford to do based on who they are, whom they know and what they know, being able to create the opportunity and the market itself (Read and Sarasvathy 2005) using the means they can control. We can expect that entrepreneurs that use the effectual model are able to exploit opportunities quicker and more often than those who follow the causal model.

According to Fisher (2012) behaviors associated with causation and effectuation are not purely present in entrepreneurial action by an individual or a team; more often, the "traditional model" of causation needs to be combined with other emerging models (e.g. effectuation and bricolage) to explain how entrepreneurs behave when they launch their new ventures.

As Dew et al. (2009) explain, it is expected to see novice entrepreneurs to perform by the traditional *Causation* model because they are taught to master business plans and market research (Read and Sarasvathy 2005); while expert entrepreneurs follow an *Effectual* behavior, ignoring predictions about markets and working with things within their control to achieve goals that were not anticipated.

Entrepreneurial expertise as Read and Sarasvathy (2005) assert—i.e. a set of skills, models and processes that can be acquired with time and deliberate practice—is a significant factor that can explain entrepreneurial performance, and also "enables us to identify testable elements of entrepreneurship that are teachable" (p. 4).

Dew et al. (2008) contrast the differences between Effectuation and Causation models showing how prediction defined by given goals determine a future world desired by the entrepreneur and his partners who will do whatever is at hand to reach that future. This reasoning describes the Causation Behavior Model, as opposed to the Effectuation Behavior Model which is defined by design and co-creation along with stakeholders, where a set of means is given as the distinctive characteristics of the entrepreneur and her partners which consequently determine a combination of possible worlds that can be reached.

When the Effectual approach is followed, ventures are never finished and new possibilities arise as the entrepreneur accumulates resources, either human, financial or physical.

4   Research Design

Our study was based upon the analysis of nine cases, developed to understand the dynamics of Founding Teams, i.e: how teams form; which characteristics of team members, if any, are relevant when teams make decisions about their new ventures and, whether diversity in those characteristics is determinant of the behavior the team follows to identify and exploit a business idea.

The study follows a theory-building approach, which is well-suited to new research areas or research areas for which existing theory seems inadequate (Eisenhardt 1989). Qualitative methodologies based on case studies may shed light on "how" questions (Yin 2014). We thus adopt an inductive multiple case-study method, using a system of replication logic, with each case treated as an independent experiment (Yin 2014). This method allows comparison across cases, accumulating evidence in the process and increasing the validity of the findings (Yin 2014).

4.1   Case Selection

The cases for this study were selected from a database of Mexican firms that were part of ENLACE E+E mentoring program.

ENLACE E+E[1] is a mentoring program pertaining to Tecnologico de Monterrey (ITESM), which is the largest private university in Mexico. ENLACE E+E was initiated in Monterrey, Mexico in 2008 by a group of alumni to give support and advise to new ventures graduating from the university's incubators and accelerators as well as to high potential startups located in the community. The program is conducted by assembling a group of the most recognized business owners and CEOs of the largest companies in every region where an ITESM campus is located, who act as a board of advisors to new ventures with the potential to generate

---

[1]http://tec.mx/es/ee-connections-network

high growth in sales and employment in the 2 years following their selection to the program.

The cases were chosen from a group that answered a questionnaire about Founding Teams and voluntarily left their e-mail for further questioning.

The questionnaire was applied as a pre-test for a quantitative study to be made about the use of Effectuation and Causation by Founding Teams in Mexico. Several categories were included to measure different types of informational heterogeneity: educational background; educational level; work experience; and entrepreneurial experience.

Seven companies agreed to be contacted after the application of the questionnaire. Two more teams were selected by convenience of the authors. For the latter, information from the questionnaire was not available.

Companies' tenure ranged between 1 and 5 years, although three of them were more than a decade old. Companies were located in different parts of Mexico: three in the State of Sonora, and the rest in Mexico City, Puebla, Nuevo León, Jalisco, Querétaro and Sinaloa. In each case, the level of analysis is the team, and the unit of analysis is the entrepreneurial behavior they develop.

A brief description of each company is summarized in Tables 1, 2 and 3.

4.2 Data Collection

Semi-structured interviews were conducted to one or two members of each founding team still working for the company; in every case, one of the respondents was the appointed CEO or General Manager of the company. Three of the interviews were personally carried out in October 2014 and the rest were conducted through Skype in October 2015. The duration of the interviews was approximately 1 h and the procedure was recorded and fully transcribed to analyze the information provided by the respondents.

For those companies that participated in the questionnaire, heterogeneity was calculated from their answers using Blau's heterogeneity index as used by Chowdury (2005). This index was used just for reference, to be contrasted with the answers given by the CEO during the interview.

A self-reported index of Shared leadership was calculated for each Founding Team adapting the density measure used by Carson et al. (2007).

It is suggested that Shared leadership might benefit constructive discussion and diminish conflict when it is present in entrepreneurial teams (Hoch 2014; Bird and Schjoedt 2009). As we deal with heterogeneity of the founding team, and heterogeneity is believed to ignite conflict among team members and negatively affect performance of the team (Amason et al. 2006), we considered it of interest to understand if and how Shared leadership affects the interaction among team members as well as the behavior of the team.

Our measure of Shared leadership has its limitations because it is the view of only one member of the Founding Team, however, the obtained measurement was

Table 1 Characteristics of founding teams in the sample (1)

	PL1	HE2	GLOB3
No. of founders	2	3	3
Actual size of the team	2	4	4
Core product/ service	Communication through screens: On site, closed circuit TV	To develop already existing businesses in an innovative way: e.g. Carpentry, Barber shop, App programming, Branding agency, open workspace...	Application development for in site meteorological forecasts in agricultural fields
Origin of the team	Family: Brothers	Two friends since childhood started the team. Other two members with no previous relationship were added later	All acquaintances from University The fourth member with business background shares family ties with the lead entre-preneur and was invited later
Team/Idea first	Team	Idea	Idea
Age[a]	0	0	0
Formal educa-tion (field)[a]	0.5	0.625	0.375
Formal educa-tion (level)[a]	0	0	0
Work experience[a]	0.5	–	0.625
At least one member had started a previ-ous company	YES	YES	YES
One previous startup by the same team	YES	YES	NO
Shared leadership	4.5	2.5	3.25

[a]Heterogeneity

consistent with the distribution of leadership reported by the respondents during the interview.

We utilized Fisher's (2012) alternate templates as a reference of the behaviors displayed by entrepreneurs that follow the Causation and/or Effectuation models which have been consistently compared and presented in opposition by several authors (Blauth et al. 2014; Chandler et al. 2011; Read et al. 2009; Dew et al. 2009; Sarasvathy 2001), and understand from our sample which logic is preferred by entrepreneurs in Founding Teams and whether teams' composition influences the selection of either logic. Tables 4, 5, 6 and 7 show the results of this analysis of respondent statements.

Table 2 Characteristics of founding teams in the sample (2)

	ID4	H5	MAG6
No. of founders	3	2	5
Actual size of the team	3	2	4
Core product/ service	Consultancy and construction of food products' manufacturing facilities	Manufacture of "fat-burning" beverages. High R&D activity to develop different types of beverages	Design and implementation of entertainment devices and Services: 4D cabins, Dancing Fountains, Robot configuration, 4D Theaters, Holograms, 3D Mapping
Origin of the team	Friends from university. Two of them were friends since childhood	Friends since childhood	Family: Brothers and one sister
Team/Idea first	Team	Idea	Idea
Age[a]	0	0.5	0.72
Formal education (field)[a]	0.444	0.5	0.72
Formal education (level)[a]	0	0.5	0.56
Work experience[a]	0.444	0.5	0.72
At least one member had started a previous company	YES	YES	YES
One previous startup by the same team	YES	NO	NO
Shared leadership	5.0	3.5	2.6

[a]Heterogeneity

5   Results

5.1   Characteristics of the Founding Team

Our first research question is related to the composition of the Founding Team, i.e. who is included at moment of venture creation and what are the different attributes that each member brings to the team.

All nine Founding Teams in our sample were created by "similar alters" (Ruef et al. 2003), either family or friends from childhood or from college. With exception of one team (GLOB3), none were formed with the goal of complementarity of characteristics or of filling in certain positions for the new venture.

Table 3 Characteristics of founding teams in the sample (3)

	VIR7	SI8	RA9
No. of founders	7	2	4
Actual size of the team	5	2	5
Core product/ service	Distribution, design and Integration of vehicle location technology	Credit management Systems. Design, adaptation and installation	Industrial automation (Mostly Automotive); Innovation services (Startup Factory); Innovation consultancy
Origin of the team	Mostly friends from university. Two team members with no previous relationship but who had entrepreneurial experience also invested to launch the firm	Friends from university: MBA colleagues	Friends from university in an engineering field. One newly added team member is a woman with design background
Team/Idea first	Idea	Team	Team
Age[a]	0.64	0.5	0
Formal education (field)[a]	0.32	0.5	0.48
Formal education (level)[a]	0.625	0	0
Work experience[a]	0.64	0.5	0.375
At least one member had started a previous company	NO	YES	NO
One previous startup by the same team	NO	NO	NO
Shared leadership	2.6	4.0	3.4

[a]Heterogeneity

Stories about how the Founding Team came into being are more related to friends or family wanting to do something together:

> ... we were colleagues of the same career program: Electronic Engineering. One of the partners was my boss, where I was doing my internship... With the other partners ... I did some work with them in our Free Software Development Laboratory. . . so, we also were all in the faculty. . . that is where the human capital came from. (VIR7)

Table 4 Causation action framework (1)

No.	Item	PL1	HE2	GLOB3	ID4
1	Identified an opportunity before developing anything else (Not in Fisher (2012))	YES		YES	
2	Identified and assesed long-run opportunities in developing the firm	YES		YES	
3	Calculated the return of various opportunities				
4	Wrote a business plan	YES	NO	YES	
5	Organized and implented control processes				YES
6	Gathered and reviewed information about market size and growth	YES	NO	YES	
7	Gathered information about competitors and compared their offerings		NO		
8	Wrote up or verbally expressed a vision for Ventures	YES	YES	YES	YES
9	Developed a project plan to-develop the product and/or services	YES	NO	YES	YES
10	Wrote up a marketing plan for taking the products/services to market			YES	

Adapted from Fisher (2012)

Table 5 Causation action framework (2)

No.	Item	H5	MAG6	VIR7	SI8	RA9
1	Identified an opportunity before developing anything else (Not in Fisher (2012))	YES	YES		YES	
2	Identified and assessed long-run opportunities in developing the firm	YES		NO		NO
3	Calculated the return of various opportunities		YES			
4	Wrote a business plan	YES	YES	NO	YES	NO
5	Organized and implented control processes		YES		YES	
6	Gathered and reviewed information about market size and growth	NO		NO		NO
7	Gathered information about competitors and compared their offerings	YES	YES	YES		NO
8	Wrote up or verbally expressed a vision for Ventures	YES			YES	NO
9	Developed a project plan to-develop the product and/or services	YES	YES		YES	
10	Wrote up a marketing plan for taking the products/services to market	YES	YES	NO	YES	

Adapted from Fisher (2012)

... we met at college, we had worked together, we got along very well and went out together a lot... we also respected each other's work very much... the big strength that we saw is that we were impeccable, in our engineering... (RA9)

(My brother) lived in the United States and worked there... and for years, when we reunited we talked about doing something together... (PL1)

Table 6 Effectuation action framework (1)

		PL1	HE2	GLOB3	ID4
	Experimentation				
1	Developed multiple variations of a product or service in arriving at a commercial offering		YES		
2	Experimented with different ways to sell and/or deliver the product in arriving at a commercial offering				YES
3	Changed the product or service substantially as the venture developed		YES		
	Affordable loss				
4	Committed only limited amounts of resources to the venture at a time	NO	NO		YES
	Flexibility				
5	Responded to unplanned opportunities as they arose		YES		YES
6	Adapted what they were doing to the resources on hand				YES
	Pre-commitments				
7	Entered into agreements with customers, suppliers and other organizations	YES	NO	YES	YES

Adapted from Fisher (2012)

Table 7 Effectuation action framework (2)

		H5	MAG6	VIR7	SI8	RA9
	Experimentation					
1	Developed multiple variations of a product or service in arriving at a commercial offering					YES
2	Experimented with different ways to sell and/or deliver the product in arriving at a commercial offering			YES		
3	Changed the product or service substantially as the venture developed	NO	NO			YES
	Affordable loss					
4	Committed only limited amounts of resources to the venture at a time	YES	NO		YES	NO
	Flexibility					
5	Responded to unplanned opportunities as they arose			YES	NO	YES
6	Adapted what they were doing to the resources on hand			YES		YES
	Pre-commitments					
7	Entered into agreements with customers, suppliers and other organizations	YES	YES	YES	NO	YES

Adapted from Fisher (2012)

As Francis and Sandberg (2000) point out, friendship in teams facilitates group processes and performance of a management team by promoting accountability and honest exchange of information, while discouraging negative opportunism. In our sample, when team members that were not previously related were present in the founding team, those members eventually left the team:

> We always had our differences about how we wanted to operate the business, *they* had a very rigid structure because their previous company was a security firm. *They* were not very open to new strategies, new ideas ... and *we* were more like "Montessori kids"... ideas came from everywhere and *we* wanted to innovate, ... and *they* never had enough empathy to make changes... So, after some years, *we* had enough profits to buy *their* shares. (VIR7)

> The decision was totally forced by the group of investors... (the exit of the former CEO). ...We were going to let him go, anyway, because it was not working... he was not in our age range, he had different ideas... (GLOB3)

The size of the Founding Teams in the sample ranged from two to seven members. Members were only men, with exception of three of the teams (ID4, RA9 and MAG6) which included one woman each.

Contrary to what could be expected (Discua-Cruz et al. 2012) teams formed by family members showed higher diversity in educational areas and prior work experience (PL1, MAG6), while the less heterogeneous teams were represented by those that were formed by university colleagues (GLOB3, ID4, RA9, VIR7).

All but two teams (VIR7, RA9) had at least one member with previous entrepreneurial experience. The teams with no previous entrepreneurial experience started their ventures right-out-of-college.

In two of the teams, members were highly diverse in terms of age. One of these teams was formed by family members (brothers and one sister) and the other one was the team with the largest number of members. In these cases, *value diversity* (Jehn et al. 1999) was reported which delayed decision making at some point during start-up.

> ... Our first challenge was to come to agreement among ourselves, because we are siblings, it is a family enterprise, and it was my oldest brother's, 100%. He is the one that develops the technology. So, it took us almost 2 years, practically, to agree on how we wanted to operate... (MAG6)

> One of the partners is older than the rest of us and he had a complete business perspective. ... But the younger part, they said, well I "extend my hand", right? "I have a business. I am already selling... Why don't I have money in my pocket?". So, those differences in age were somewhat complicated. (VIR7)

Heterogeneity and complementarity of the founding team in the sample had more to do in some cases with personal characteristics of team members than with their functional backgrounds (RA9, HE2, ID4). For the following examples, although team members have similar educational backgrounds or share previous work experience, personal characteristics such as: risk aversion, discipline and organization, negotiation ability and people skills were determinants of complementarity among team members:

> ... I am the conflicting one, the quicker one and, when we debate, I always crash into the two (team members) that are more conservative... *They* are very good at solving logical and technical problems... *they* do have an entrepreneurial vision but, a very conservative one. ... And the other person that I mentioned ...he has always been a mediator...I think that we

might have ended the company already if it wasn't for him. . . mediating between us when it was needed. (RA9)

For example, the architect is very good dealing with suppliers, he is technically very skilled and convinces people. . . and the client. And, also in his specialty he knows what he is offering. . . (My other teammate) who makes the designs, he is technically very good, very analytic, I mean, he checks on everything, he asks a lot of questions. . . And I am a lot about discipline and order. . . about getting ahead and. . . pushing them to do new things. . . (ID4)

As a group, I. . . take care of everything that has to do with the numbers, finance, management and (my team mate) deals with the people. . . because he is better dealing with people than I am. (HE2)

Although personal traits of individuals have been dismissed as a cause that separates those who become entrepreneurs from those who do not (Gartner 1988; Gartner et al. 1992; Sarasvathy 2001), it might be insightful to understand how personal traits of individuals in a Founding Team are a source of complementarity even when team members have similar backgrounds related to education or work experience (Chowdhury 2005).

5.2 Entrepreneurial Behavior of Founding Teams

Our second question inquires into the different behaviors and actions by which the Founding Team identifies and exploits an entrepreneurial opportunity.

The findings in this study partially agree with Fisher's (2012) statements indicating that entrepreneurs employing behaviors associated with causation also employ behaviors associated with effectuation alongside.

Although behaviors of Causation and Effectuation action frameworks were reported to be used in combination, some teams demonstrated behaviors more inclined to the causation framework whereas others where more inclined to the effectuation framework; the latter sometimes even rejecting the use of causal behaviors such as the elaboration of business plans or the execution of competitive analysis:

We are so clear about where we are going, what we want to do and, who we are as a company that we never look at our competition. Basically, every time, when we develop something, we never think. . . well it is not that we do not think about them. . . but we do not limit ourselves. (HE2)

We were technical people, and we still are. . . and as technical people what talked for us was the prototype. . . we used all the tools that we had at hand and that was enough for us to convince (investors). (VIR7)

When Founding Teams were assisted by business incubators or groups of investors they usually reported behaviors that fit the Causation Action Framework (e.g. MAG6). This is consistent with statements by Dew et al. (2009) about business schools and incubators teaching entrepreneurs the Causation Model "by the book".

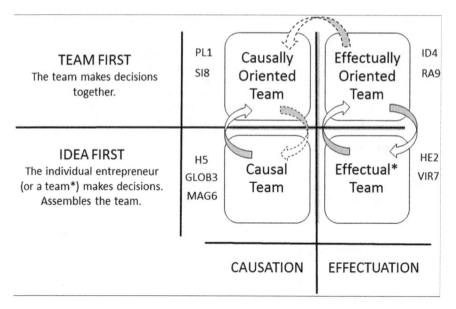

Fig. 1 Behavioral classification of founding teams. Developed by the authors

6 Behavioral Classification of Founding Teams

From the analysis of the behaviors displayed by the teams in this study, four categories of Founding teams are developed: Causally Oriented Teams; Effectually Oriented Teams; Causal Teams and Effectual Teams.

Figure 1 shows how these four different categories are related and which teams from this study represent each category.

As Cooney (2005) describes, two different events might trigger the formation of a Founding Team, one being the development of a business idea by one "lead entrepreneur" that subsequently assembles the team; another being the formation of the team by friends or colleagues who afterwards develop a business idea.

We have found that whether the first stage is the formation of the team or the development of the idea, is an important feature that might influence the behavior of the Founding Team.

6.1 Team First Categories

Team First categories refer to those cases in which the Founding Team existed before the business idea was envisioned or created. The Founding Team makes decisions with the participation of every team member, and performs either Causally or Effectually depending on the team's characteristics.

Teams in this classification are less heterogeneous related to age, type of education, level of education, and work experience, compared to the teams in the *Idea First Categories*, mostly because these Founding Teams are formed by colleagues from University. They also show higher levels of shared leadership and report less or no conflict.

6.2 Idea First Categories

Idea First Categories include Founding Teams that were assembled after an individual entrepreneur or a group of two or more developed a business idea. Teams in this classification can be *Effectual Teams* or *Causal Teams*.

Teams in the *Idea First Categories* show higher heterogeneity than the teams in the *Team First Categories*, regardless of the behaviors they perform (i.e. Effectuation or Causation).

Causal Teams were assembled by one individual entrepreneur who identified *a priori* a business opportunity and later invited others to join the team, depending on the resources that they could supply to achieve the envisioned venture.

> He (The lead entrepreneur) is a meteorology lover... He studied his career in Information Technologies but followed his curiosity. In 2009, he opened a Twitter account with information about the weather and many people started following him and most of his followers were farmers... so he realized there was a need for information of this type and that his tool could cause a great impact. .... One day, he came to the office and said: "I have this idea and I want to make an application"... that is how our relationship started. (GLOB3)

Effectual Teams in this study started with two or more entrepreneurs who began developing an "artifact" (Read and Sarasvathy 2005) (i.e. a product or service) and later added team members from their personal networks to accrue needed knowledge or financial resources. The only difference that is evidently observed between *Effectual Teams* and *Effectually Oriented Teams* (Team First category) is that *Effectual Teams* added team members at some point during the startup phase.

> ... We all were university colleagues. One of us dropped school and started to work ... he made the installation of this equipment... we were close (friends), so he tells me "if we design these equipments, it is not so complicated"... we had the tools to do it, so ... we saw the opportunity to start the company... half of the team members, we made an initial product to found the company, but we partnered with other people because they already had a company... (VIR7)

The line between *Effectual Teams* and *Effectually Oriented Teams* is not an easy one to draw as none of the Effectual Teams in this study started with only one individual entrepreneur nor even with an idea. As we can observe, it is the very nature of Effectuation as entrepreneurial behavior (Sarasvathy 2001; Read et al. 2009; Fisher 2012) what hinders this classification, leading us to suggest that Effectuation is a team endeavor and that Effectually Oriented Teams become Effectual Teams and vice versa, in a continuous manner as they add (and/or drop) team members.

6.3 Effectuation and Causation Categories

Represented by arrows in Fig. 1, are the different transitions that could be observed in teams that were part of this study: (1) from Effectual Team to Effectually Oriented Team; (2) from Effectually Oriented Team to Effectual team and, (3) from Causal Team to Causally Oriented Team.

1. From Effectual Team to Effectually Oriented Team. This transition refers to those teams that started as Idea First Teams behaving according to the Effectuation Action Framework. The transition shows a team that added or dropped members during startup but has remained the same after the venture has been established and new projects are developed with the participation of everyone involved in the team. (e.g. VIR7)
2. From Effectually Oriented Team to Effectual Team. This transition refers to those teams that started as Team First Teams, in which team members developed the idea for the startup together following the Effectuation Action Framework. After the venture was established the team added new members when new projects were created to become Effectual Teams. (e.g.ID4, RA9)
3. From Causal Team to Causally Oriented Team. As occurs with the first transition, in this case the founding team started as an Idea First Team, adding members according to the needs of the new venture being started. After the venture is established, the team remains the same for future projects that are envisioned following a Causation Action Framework. (e.g. GLOB3, H5)

No transition was observed from a Causally Oriented Team to a Causal Team, although the effect is suggested by a dotted arrow. Teams in the Causation categories were more static in terms of membership changes, even in the case of Causal Teams that added (or dropped) new members during startup, which showed no evidence of considering subsequent member additions or exits.

7 Conclusions

This study presents a different view of the dynamics of Founding Teams based on team composition at pre-startup and startup phases and, on the behavior they report from the moment they conceive their business idea to the moment when the interviews take place which is a different stage of development for each of the participating teams.

We agree with several works stating that founding teams are formed by "similar alters" (Francis and Sandberg 2000; Ruef et al. 2003; Henneke and Lüthje 2007) as all the teams included in this work are formed either by family or friends.

As has been noted, informational heterogeneity (Jehn et al. 1999) (i.e. heterogeneity related to knowledge bases and perspectives such as: work experience; educational diversity and entrepreneurial experience diversity), is the one type of heterogeneity which is mostly addressed as significant in several works relating it to firm's or team's performance (Eisenhardt and Schoonhoven 1990; Ucbasaran et al. 2003; Colombo and Grilli 2005; Hmieleski and Ensley 2007; Visintin and Pittino 2014; Zhou et al. 2015; Muñoz-Bullon et al. 2015). In our findings informational heterogeneity represented by educational background and previous work experience is also salient as a source of diversity in most of the teams, overshadowing other types of heterogeneity such as age, educational level and entrepreneurial experience.

Existing theory has concluded that individual personality characteristics are not decisive in predicting who will be an entrepreneur, nor who will succeed in their venture creation path (Gartner 1988; Gartner et al. 1992; Sarasvathy 2001). Our findings suggest that differences in individual personality traits might be a source of complementarity in founding teams (Chowdury 2005), even when other types of heterogeneity are not present.

Although the purpose of this work was to find a relationship between the heterogeneity of characteristics of the founding team and the entrepreneurial behavior it performs, we could not find a direct relationship between both concepts. Our findings, however led us to develop a new classification of Founding Teams based first, on how and/or when during the entrepreneurial process the team forms, and second, on the entrepreneurial behavior the team performs.

Kamm and Nurick (1993) state that "multi-founder" organizations emerge in stages, where the first stage is the *idea*. As Cooney (2005) points out, the *idea*, can be identified or created by an individual or by a team. Considering the latter we conclude that there is a moment in which the team forms, and this moment can occur before the idea is discovered or created. We therefore develop two categories of founding teams: (1) Team first Teams, and (2) Idea first Teams.

Ensley and Hmieleski (2005) assert that university-based firms are less heterogeneous than independent firms. Although none of these ventures are university-based firms, Team first Teams in our sample are formed mostly by university colleagues that share the same educational background and/or educational level and report to be in the same age range. Our first proposition is related to this observation:

P1 Team First founding teams are less heterogeneous than Idea First founding teams when heterogeneity refers to informational diversity, i.e. previous work experience and formal education.

As Ensley et al. (2002) explain, there are two dimensions of conflict that must be understood when dealing with entrepreneurial teams: *Cognitive conflict* is focused on the task at hand bringing together the different perspectives of the team and promoting creativity, decision quality and understanding. *Affective conflict* is personally focused, highlighting interpersonal dislikes and disaffections that both undermine the quality of decisions and reduces the satisfaction and affection among team members (Amason and Sapienza 1997). To achieve superior performance, entrepreneurial teams must be able to nurture *cognitive conflict* while avoiding *affective conflict*, although as Ensley et al. (2002) point out, both types of conflict might be fueled simultaneously and intermittently.

Cognitive conflict, however, can be developed when leadership is shared by all the participants within the founding team (Bird and Schjoedt 2009; Hoch 2014).

When conflict was reported in the interviews, it was present in Idea First Teams. Teams in this category also showed lower levels of shared leadership and higher heterogeneity, specially related to age. On the contrary, Team First Teams showed higher levels of shared leadership and reported less or no conflict. We could not conclude, however, whether shared leadership is an effect of a more homogeneous composition of the team or a feature that was developed from the interaction among team members during the startup phase of their venture. In any case, our observation leads us to the next proposition:

P2 Team First founding teams exhibit higher levels of shared leadership and less conflict than Idea First founding teams.

No relationship has been addressed between personal traits of the entrepreneur and Effectuation; on the contrary Sarasvathy's (2001) seminal work on Effectuation and Causation dismisses the influence of individual characteristics in the success of any firm or organization.

It is relevant to notice that, in the examples depicted in this work, when individual personality characteristics are referred to as means of complementarity in the founding team the actions and behaviors of the team were more related to the Effectuation Action Framework.

In this regard, a recent work by Engel et al. (2014) relating self-efficacy to the use of Effectuation in university business students might start the debate about whether personality characteristics influence the use of Effectuation or any other entrepeneurial behavior by an individual or a team. Also Welter et al. (2016) argue that there might has been a misconception about which personality-traits actually matter and are able to explain aspects of opportunity discovery. With respect to founding teams, our findings suggest that when personality traits of team members are a source of complementarity, the behavior of the team is more inclined to the Effectuation action framework, which leads us to the next proposition:

P3 When heterogeneity of personal characteristics (i.e. personality traits) is present in the founding team, the behavior of the team is more related to the Effectuation action framework.

Klotz et al. (2013) propose an Input-Mediators-Outputs framework to explain the dynamics of New Venture Teams (NVT). We refer to this framework when suggesting that entrepreneurial behavior is a mediator between team heterogeneity and firm performance. Although we are not addressing outcomes of the new ventures in this work, the following proposition remains for future research:

P4 Entrepreneurial Behavior of founding teams (i.e. Effectuation and Causation) has a mediating effect linking founding team's heterogeneity to the outcomes of their new ventures.

These propositions challenge the traditional model of entrepreneurial behavior and develop a new framework to study the dynamics of founding teams.

More detailed quantitative and qualitative studies are recommended in order to describe the dynamics of Founding Teams: how they form, and how the characteristics of team members affect the behavior of teams and the outcomes of their new ventures.

Longitudinal qualitative studies would be useful to understand if the distribution of teams according to their origin and preferred behavior remains, or is modified as time passes; such studies would also help to confirm if Shared leadership that is present at the startup phase contributes to the maintenance of the team (Kamm et al. 1990) and the venture.

The usefulness of our behavioral classification of Founding Teams (i.e. Team first Teams and Idea first Teams) also presents a case for further study:

Firstly, it will be of interest to verify quantitatively with a sufficient sample, if Team first Teams are in fact less heterogeneous than Idea first Teams, and also if the former demonstrate higher levels of shared leadership as is suggested by this qualitative study.

Secondly, as Shared leadership has been proposed to enhance cohesion in the Founding Team (Ensley et al. 2003) which increases the chances of the team to engage in cognitive conflict and fruitful decision making (Amason and Sapienza 1997) we posit that the ventures created by Team first Teams will have larger tenures and will perform better over time than Idea first Teams.

The behavioral classification that is proposed by this study presents a framework to develop new studies and conclusions about how founding teams can be nurtured and guided to create new ventures that grow and endure over time.

References

Alsos, G. A., & Clausen, T. H. (2016). Team-level effectual and causal behavior: From individual decision-making to collective behavior. *4th Effectuation Research Conference*, (pp. 1–8). Bødo, Norway.

Amason, A. C., & Sapienza, H. J. (1997). The effects of top management team size and interaction norms on cognitive and affective conflict. *Journal of Management, 23*, 495–516.

Amason, A. C., Shrader, R. C., & Thompson, G. H. (2006). Newness and novelty: Relating top management team composition to new venture performance. *Journal of Business Venturing, 21*, 125–148.

Auh, S., & Menguc, B. (2005). Top management team diversity and innovativeness: The moderating role of interfunctional coordination. *Industrial Marketing Management, 34*, 249–261.

Beckman, C. M. (2006). The influence of founding team company affiliations on firm behavior. *Academy of Management Journal, 49*, 741–758.

Beckman, C. M., & Burton, M. D. (2008). Founding the future: Path dependence in the evolution of top management teams from founding to IPO. *Organization Science, 19*, 3–24.

Bird, B., & Schjoedt, L. (2009). Entrepreneurial behavior its nature, scope, recent research and agenda for future research. In A. Carsrud & M. Brännback (Eds.), *Understanding the entreprenurial mind (International studies in entrepreneurship)* (pp. 327–358). New York: Springer.

Blatt, R. (2009). Tough love: How communal schemas and contracting practices build relational capital in entrepreneurial teams. *Academy of Management Review, 34*, 533–551.

Blauth, M., Mauer, R., & Brettel, M. (2014). Fostering creativity in new product development through entrepreneurial decision making. *Creativity and Innovation Management, 23*, 495–509.

Boeker, W. (1989). Strategic change: The effects of founding and history. *Academy of Management Journal, 32*, 489–515.

Brinckmann, J., Salomo, S., & Gemuenden, H. G. (2009). Financial management competence of founding teams and growth of new technology-based firms. *Entrepreneurship Theory and Practice, 35*, 217–243.

Carson, J. B., Tesluk, P. E., & Marrone, J. A. (2007). Shared leadership in teams: An investigation of antedecent conditions and performance. *Academy of Management Journal, 50*, 1217–1234.

Chandler, G. N., Honig, B., & Wiklund, J. (2005). Antecedents, moderators, and performance consequences of membership change in new venture teams. *Journal of Business Venturing, 20*, 705–725.

Chandler, G. N., DeTienne, D. R., McKelvie, A., & Mumford, T. V. (2011). Causation and effectuation processes: A validation study. *Journal of Business Venturing, 26*, 375–390.

Chiu, C.-Y., Owens, B. P., & Tesluk, P. E. (2016). Initiating and utilizing shared leadership in teams: The role of leader humility, team proactive personality, and team performance capability. *Journal of Applied Psychology, 101*, 1–16.

Chowdhury, S. (2005). Demographic diversity for building an effective entrepreneurial team: Is it important? *Journal of Business Venturing, 20*, 727–746.

Colombo, M. G., & Grilli, L. (2005). Founders' human capital and the growth of new technology-based firms: A competence based view. *Research Policy, 34*, 795–816.

Cooney, T. M. (2005). Editorial: What is an entrepreneurial team? *International Small Business Journal, 23*, 226–235.

Davidsson, P. (2015). Entrepreneurial opportunities and the entrepreneurship nexus: A re-conceptualization. *Journal of Business Venturing, 30*, 674–695.

Davidsson, P., & Honig, B. (2003). The role of social and human capital among nascent entrepreneurs. *Journal of Business Venturing, 18*, 301–331.

Dew, N., Read, S., Sarasvathy, S. D., & Wiltbank, R. (2008). Outlines of a behavioral theory of the entrepreneurial firm. *Journal of Economic Behavior & Organization, 66*, 37–59.

Dew, N., Read, S., Sarasvathy, S. D., & Wiltbank, R. (2009). Effectual versus predictive logics in entrepreneurial decision-making: Differences between experts and novices. *Journal of Business Venturing, 24*, 287–309.

D'Innocenzo, L., Mathieu, J., & Kukenberger, M. R. (2014). A meta-analysis of different forms of shared leadership-team performance relations. *Journal of Management, 20*, 1–28.

Discua-Cruz, A., Howorth, C., & Hamilton, E. (2012). Intrafamily entrepreneursip: The formation and membership of family entrepreneurial teams. *Entrepreneurship Theory and Practice, 37*, 17–46.

Eesley, C. E., Hsu, D. H., & Roberts, E. B. (2014). The contingent effects of top management teams on venture performance: Aligning founding team composition with innovation strategy and commercialization environment. *Strategic Management Journal, 35*, 1898–1817.

Eisenhardt, K. M. (1989). Building theories from case study research. *Academy of Management Review, 14*, 532–550.

Eisenhardt, K. M., & Schoonhoven, C. B. (1990). Organizational growth: Linking founding team, strategy, environment, and growth among U.S. semiconductor ventures, 1978–1988. *Administrative Science Quarterly, 35*, 504–529.

Engel, Y., Dimitrova, N. G., Khapova, S. N., & Elfring, T. (2014). Uncertain but able: Entrepreneurial self-efficacy and novices' use of expert decision-logic under uncertainty. *Journal of Business Venturing, 1–2*, 12–17.

Ensley, M. D., & Hmieleski, K. M. (2005). A comparative study of new venture top management team composition, dynamics and performance between university-based and independent start-ups. *Research Policy, 34*, 1091–1105.

Ensley, M. D., Pearson, A. W., & Amason, A. C. (2002). Understanding the dynamics of new venture top management teams cohesion, conflict and new venture performance. *Journal of Business Venturing, 17*, 365–386.

Ensley, M. D., Pearson, A., & Pearce, C. L. (2003). Top management team process, shared leadership and new venture performance: A theoretical model and research agenda. *Human Resource Management Review, 13*, 329–346.

Fern, M. J., Cardinal, L. B., & O'Neill, H. M. (2012). The genesis of strategy in new ventures: Escaping the constraints of founder and team knowledge. *Strategic Management Journal, 33*, 427–447.

Fisher, G. (2012). Effectuation, causation and bricolage: A behavioral comparison of emerging theories in entrepreneurship research. *Entrepreneurship Theory and Practice, 36*, 1019–1051.

Forbes, D. P., Borchert, P. S., Zellmer-Bruhn, M. E., & Sapienza, H. J. (2006). Entrepreneurial team formation: An exploration of new member addition. *Entrepreneurship Theory and Practice, 30*, 225–248.

Francis, D. H., & Sandberg, W. R. (2000). Friendship between entrepreneurial teams and its association with team and venture performance. *Entrepreneurship Theory and Practice, 25*, 5–25.

Gartner, W. B. (1988). Who is an entrepreneur? Is the wrong question. *Entrepreneurship Theory and Practice, 13*, 47–68.

Gartner, W. B., Bird, B. J., & Starr, J. A. (1992). Acting as if: Differentiating entrepreneurial from organizational behavior. *Entrepreneurial Theory & Practice, 16*, 13–31.

Hambrick, D. C., & Mason, P. A. (1984). Upper Echelons: The organization as a reflection of its top managers. *Academy of Management Review, 16*, 193–206.

Harper, D. A. (2008). Towards a theory of entrepreneurial teams. *Journal of Business Venturing, 23*, 613–626.

Henneke, D., & Lüthje, C. (2007). Interdisciplinary heterogeneity as a catalyst for product innovativeness of entrepreneurial teams. *Creativity and Innovation Management, 16*, 121–132.

Hmieleski, K. M., & Ensley, M. D. (2007). A contextual examination of new venture performance: Entrepreneur leadership behavior, top management team heterogeneity, and environmental dynamism. *Journal of Organizational Behavior, 28*, 865–889.

Hoch, J. E. (2014). Shared leadership, diversity, an information sharing in teams. *Journal of Managerial Psychology, 29*, 541–564.

Jehn, K. A., Northcraft, G. B., & Neale, M. A. (1999). Why differences make a difference: A field study of diversity, conflict, and performance in workgroups. *Administrative Science Quarterly, 44*, 741–763.

Kamm, N. B., & Nurick, A. J. (1993). The stages of team venture formation: A decision-making model. *Entrepreneurship Theory and Practice, 17*, 17–27.

Kamm, J. B., Shuman, J. C., Seeger, J. A., & Nurick, A. J. (1990). Entrepreneurial teams in new venture creation: A research agenda. *Entrepreneurship Theory and Practice, 14*, 7–17.

Klotz, A. C., Hmieleski, K. M., Bradley, B. H., & Busenitz, L. W. (2013). New venture teams: A review of the literature and roadmap for future research. *Journal of Management, 40*, 1–30.

Lim, J. Y.-K., Busenitz, L. W., & Chidambaram, L. (2012). New venture teams and the quality of business opportunities identified: Faultlines between subgroups of founders and investors. *Entrepreneurship Theory and Practice, 37*, 47–67.

Martin, B. C., McNally, J. J., & Kay, M. J. (2013). Examining the formation of human capital in entrepreneurship: A meta-analysis of entrepreneurship education outcomes. *Journal of Business Venturing, 28*, 211–224.

Muñoz-Bullon, F., Sanchez-Bueno, M. J., & Vos-Saz, A. (2015). Startup team contributions and new firm creation: The role of founding team experience. *Entrepreneurship and Regional Development, 27*, 80–105.

Nielsen, S. (2010). Top management team diversity: A review of theories and methodologies. *International Journal of Management Reviews, 12*, 301–316.

Perry, J. T., Chandler, G. N., & Gergana, M. (2011). Entrepreneurial effectuation: A review and suggestions for future research. *Entrepreneurship Theory and Practice, 36*, 1–25.

Read, S., & Sarasvathy, S. D. (2005). Knowing what you do and doing what you know: Effectuation as a form of entrepreneurial expertise. *The Journal of Private Equity, 9*, 45–62.

Read, S., Song, M., & Smit, W. (2009). A meta-analytic review of effectuation and venture performance. *Journal of Business Venturing, 24*, 573–587.

Ruef, M., Aldrich, H. E., & Carter, N. M. (2003). The structure of founding teams: Homophily, strong ties, and isolation among U.S. entrepreneurs. *American Sociological Review, 68*, 195–222.

Sarasvathy, S. D. (2001). Causation and effectuation: Toward a theoretical shift from economic inevitability to entrepreneurial contingency. *Academy of Management Review, 26*, 243–263.

Shane, S., & Venkataraman, S. (2000). The promise of entrepreneurship as a field of research. *Academy of Management Review, 25*, 217–226.

Ucbasaran, D., Lockett, A., Wright, M., & Westhead, P. (2003). Entrepreneurial founder teams: Factors associated with member entry and exit. *Entrepreneurship Theory and Practice, 28*, 107–127.

Visintin, F., & Pittino, D. (2014). Founding team composition and early performance of university-based spin-off companies. *Technovation, 34*, 31–43.

Welter, C., Mauer, R., & Wuebker, R. J. (2016). Bridging behavioral models and theoretical concepts: Effectuation and bricolage in the opportunity creation framework. *Strategic Entrepreneurship Journal, 10*, 5–20.

Yin, R. K. (2014). *Case study research. Design and methods* (5th ed.). Thousands Oaks, CA: Sage Publications.

Zheng, Y. (2012). Unlocking founding team prior shared experience: A transactive memory system perspective. *Jornal of Business Venturing, 27*, 577–591.

Zhou, W., Vredenburgh, D., & Rogoff, E. G. (2015). Informational diversity and entrepreneurial team performance: Moderating effect of shared leadership. *International Entrepreneurship Management Journal, 11*, 39–55.

Entrepreneurial Aptitude and Gender-Related Stereotypes: A Research on Competences, Policies and Practices to Foster Entrepreneurial Culture in a Less Favoured Environment

Stefano Noventa, Serena Cubico, Maddalena Formicuzzi, Piermatteo Ardolino, Giuseppe Favretto, Francesco Ciabuschi, and João Leitão

Abstract The present work explores gender stereotypes and perception of entrepreneurship in the island of Sardinia, an Italian region characterized by unfavourable socio-economic conditions. Exploring the relation between entrepreneurial aptitude, competences, and social environment is of primary importance for developing entrepreneurship and understanding the evolution of regional human capital. Results of a questionnaire administered to a sample of aspiring, actual, and attempted Sardinian entrepreneurs, suggest that gender stereotypes and perceived inequalities endanger entrepreneurial networks, in spite of pre-existing feminine norms, and gender equality of education, aptitude, competences and regional opportunities. The findings suggest that a pervasive masculine discourse on entrepreneurship can hinder entrepreneurial perception and outcomes, and supplement the extant literature on the importance of a multiple culture perspective. It is suggested that policy-makers should pay attention to gender-related stereotypes and to entrepreneurial aptitude in order to convert detrimental regional and social networks into innovation

S. Noventa (✉)
Hector Research Institute for Education Sciences and Psychology, Universität Tübingen, Tübingen, Germany

Methods Center, Universität Tübingen, Tübingen, Germany
e-mail: stefano.noventa@uni-tuebingen.de

S. Cubico · G. Favretto
Department of Business Administration, University of Verona, Verona, Italy

M. Formicuzzi · P. Ardolino
Center for Assessment, University of Verona, Verona, Italy

F. Ciabuschi
Department of Business Studies, University of Uppsala, Uppsala, Sweden

J. Leitão
Department of Management and Economics, School of Social and Human Sciences, Universidade da Beira Interior, Covilhã, Portugal

© Springer International Publishing AG, part of Springer Nature 2018
S. Cubico et al. (eds.), *Entrepreneurship and the Industry Life Cycle*, Studies on Entrepreneurship, Structural Change and Industrial Dynamics,
https://doi.org/10.1007/978-3-319-89336-5_4

59

systems. Practises for future investigations and recommendations to develop knowledge competences are also discussed.

Keywords Entrepreneurship · TAI · Entrepreneurial aptitude · Gender issues · Sardinia · Uxorial norms · Multiple cultures perspective

1 Introduction

The island of Sardinia is an economically backward region, geographically separated from Italy, and endowed with both special government autonomy and singular social norms which are more feminine-oriented than the national ones. Such a background has proven to be a challenging ground for entrepreneurship and innovation systems, meant as networks of actors that interact on the generation, diffusion and utilization of useful knowledge under a distinct institutional framework (Cantner and Graf 2004, 2008). In particular, previous attempts to top-down build industrial clusters and innovative systems in the region have failed to account for the unique structure of the island (Hospers et al. 2009). Nonetheless, the isolated characterization of the area, together with its peculiar social norms, offer an interesting ground to explore the process of innovation between people engaged in entrepreneurial networks. Sardinia might be indeed considered as a regional innovation system in which abilities and incentives of firms and individuals should be studied together with the social norms characterizing its institutions.

Fostering of entrepreneurship is indeed a key feature for regional development (Beugelsdijk 2007; Welter et al. 2008) and in this perspective, a local innovation system is fundamental to understand diffusion of knowledge, competences and practises in different areas through networks of relations developed between the regional system and actors like people and businesses. Local innovation systems are indeed grounded on the geographical space from which they arise: they concentrate and cluster proportionally to the knowledge involved; geographical and spatial proximity of their actors are fundamental, as well as the presence of regional spillovers, and of technological and knowledge transfers that are favoured by concentration of education institutions (see, e.g., Cantner and Graf 2004, 2008; Breschi and Lissoni 2001).

Nonetheless, these systems rely on two fundamental assumptions: the presence of a connected set of actors that ensure the flow of information and knowledge, and the social embedding of networks within institutional 'sets of common habits, norms, routines, established practices, rules or laws that regulate the relations and interactions between individuals, groups and organizations' (Edquist and Johnson 1997). These assumptions, however, are not independent and constitute the backbone of the entrepreneurial effort in general. They are more primitive, essential, and chronologically antecedent to any boost provided by knowledge concentration or technological transfer. For this reason, it is important to explore their interaction in regions like Sardinia that show geographical, spatial and social proximity, singular social norms, but not a fully developed concentration of knowledge and technological transfer. Most of all, it is paramount to understand how these assumptions affect the first steps of venture creation and the mentality of soon-to-be entrepreneurs. There appears indeed to exist an interrelation between sex, socialized gender-roles, and culture that influence entrepreneurial intention and self-efficacy (Gupta et al. 2009; Mueller and Dato-on 2013), by prevalently affecting the first stages of the entrepreneurial process, and showing strong cross-country variations (van der Zwan et al. 2012). Recent literature, for instance, has shown that feminine norms can strengthen gender equality, improving women's performances and intention, thus also improving the work-life balance of both genders by allowing a choice between growth-driven approaches or moderate ones, instead of forcing individuals to adhere to economic models that clash against their needs (García-Cabrera and García-Soto 2008; Nongbri 2008; Shneor et al. 2013). This is of particular interest in a region like Sardinia which is imbued with long-standing uxorial traditions (Oppo 1990; Boi et al. 1999; Bernardi and Oppo 2007) and shows geographical, structural and economic deficiencies (Hospers 2003; Hospers et al. 2009), and a risk-averse and inward-looking tendency in business (Mariotti and Piscitello 2001).

In order to explore these interrelations, this work aims to shed light on the characteristics emerging stronger in potential entrepreneurs of the Sardinian less favoured environment by investigating their competences, connections, and access to regional capital. Most of all, the analyses are carried in light of two important lenses: the fluidity of the concept of entrepreneurship, with its limits of definition and the effects of national and local stereotypes; and a multiple-culture perspective that allows to account for the presence and interaction of local norms, national stereotypes, geographical and economical background, and their effects on entrepreneurial development and behaviour. It is indeed argued that a masculine narrative of entrepreneurship can overcome local socio-cultural norms, regardless of individuals' competences and aptitude. More in detail, it is argued that, all other determinants kept equal (e.g., education, network dimension and resources, entrepreneurial aptitude and intention, access to regional capital and innovation system) the existence of a gender polarization (driven by masculine national norms and a masculine discourse about entrepreneurship) would still emerge in a feminine-oriented society in which there are strong and capable women (albeit a full equality of roles and rights is not reached). In turn, these stereotypes would affect entrepreneurial outcomes and networks, and the access to capital and information thus hindering at its own root the entrepreneurial effort and the efficacy of any local innovation system. Accounting for these determinants becomes than necessary in creating adequate policies.

For this purpose, since differences in entrepreneurship due to a gender gap appears to prevalently affect the first stages of entrepreneurial engagement (van der Zwan et al. 2012), a sample of aspiring, actual, and attempted entrepreneurs was considered from the capital city of Cagliari which, in spite of an unemployment rate that doubles the national average and a strong specialisation in oils and chemicals, accounts for the 38% of the production units of the island and has shown fertile ground for entrepreneurship with a concentrated growth in the area of financial services, ICT, and software development (Murroni 2006) which are ideal sectors of growth for innovation systems. As participants were attending an entrepreneurship preparation course, they are expected to possess high level of intention and motivation. In addition, being Sardinia imbued with uxorial social norms, the presence of strong and capable female figures is expected. Under these circumstances, participants should show no gender gap in intentions and abilities, thus being a suitable sample to explore impact of gendered stereotypes, norms, and local context on entrepreneurship and entrepreneurial network. Several variables were considered, like participants' network, education, engagement in entrepreneurship, together with access to regional capital. In particular, their entrepreneurial aptitude was measured by means of the Entrepreneurial Aptitude Test (TAI®, Cubico et al. 2010) to explore the application of a tailored instruments based on a socio-behavioural perspective to a particular social and economic context. A consistent application of TAI would indeed highlight the importance of analysing the entrepreneurial aptitude construct using important factors like need for achievement, independence, and effective leadership which are considered individual predictors of entrepreneurial success (Brockhaus 1982).

The present work contributes to the existing literature with a threefold purpose: firstly, by exploring the characteristics emerging in a less favoured environment, and the relation between gender norms and entrepreneurial performance and behaviour, it stresses that a masculine narrative about entrepreneurship can be a priori detrimental to the development of venturing; secondly, it emphasizes that a multiple cultures perspective is relevant in analysing the effects of local characteristics that constitute the institutional background of innovation networks and systems; thirdly, it supports the idea that entrepreneurial aptitude is useful to explore the potential of socially and economically singularly characterized areas. In the following sections, a brief theoretical review of the context of the study (multiple cultures perspective, gender bias, and Sardinian economy and society) is given before introducing the main research focus.

1.1 The Context of the Study

In this section, we examine three elements that characterize the context that we intend to investigate, i.e. the fluidity of the concept of entrepreneur and the importance of a multiple culture perspectives in analysing entrepreneurial phenomena, the association of this fluidity with the existence of gender differences and stereotypes, and the cultural and geographical contexts of the island of Sardinia.

1.1.1 Definition of Entrepreneur and Multiple Cultures Perspective

There is no agreement on which historical, economic, social, environmental or personal variables define an entrepreneur, and several approaches have their place in literature, from strictly economic to multi-disciplinary ones, drawing from both psychological and sociological perspectives (see, e.g., Murphy et al. 2006; Hisrich et al. 2007). Various determinants have been identified to account for macro level variations across time, regions, and countries (Grilo and Thurik 2004), yet a proper systematisation of entrepreneurship has likely been hindered by the multiple and different ways in which resources and exploitation of opportunities can manifest themselves, together with the social complexity of the phenomenon due to the interrelation of entrepreneurial behaviour, context, and social norms (Alvarez and Busenitz 2001). A particular tension between universalistic and particularistic approaches can be traced in both managerial and entrepreneurial literatures due to the difficulty of explaining entrepreneurial activity both within and across cultures. On the one hand, cross-national differences influence individuals so that countries, nations and societies are considered to represent systems of values, beliefs, attitudes and preferences (Zander and Romani 2004). On the other hand, globalisation, international mobility, and technological advancements undermine the equivalence culture/nation (Sackmann and Phillips 2004). Entrepreneurial decisions are driven both by society-specific cultural values like power distance, individualism, uncertainty avoidance and masculinity (Hofstede 2001), and common cognitive scripts that can be detected in entrepreneurs of different nations (Mitchell et al. 2000). Assumptions of cultural stability over time and of homogeneity within nations have then been argued, since intra-national differences can be more relevant than cross-national ones (Tung 2008). This highlights an interrelation between entrepreneurial culture, behaviour, socio-economic contexts, and collective norms that affects regional and urban development (Beugelsdijk 2007; Welter et al. 2008) and allows for the coexistence of effects due to both community cultures and nationwide cultures (García-Cabrera and García-Soto 2008). A multiple cultures perspective has then been advocated to understand effects of environment on entrepreneurship, as both local and national culture impact on individual beliefs which in their turn can affect entrepreneurial success or failure (García-Cabrera and García-Soto 2008; Hopp and Stephan 2012).

Conception of entrepreneurship may indeed vary depending on local realities, implying that while it is often understood in terms of venturing, starting up enterprises, and adding new value, it actually requires development of characteristics within traditions, socio-cultural norms, environmental and economic contexts, formal and informal institutions, quality of human capital, regional resources and national state conditions (Audretsch and Fritsch 2002; Fritsch and Mueller 2004; Kotey 2006; Hopp and Stephan 2012). Most of all, norms and context can affect both individual perception and characterization of entrepreneurship. An example is given by the higher levels of entrepreneurial behaviour detected in the women of Cape Verdean population or those of the Khasis in North-east India, to whom are assigned responsibilities in professional tasks in addition to family sustenance, albeit without reaching a full equality of roles (García-Cabrera and García-Soto 2008; Nongbri 2008). Notably, Cape Verdean society leans towards a feminine orientation and Khasi are an actual matrilineal society, suggesting that norms favouring females help also to strengthen individual performance and intention. Another example is given by a comparison of entrepreneurial conceptions and behaviour of Turkey and

Norway (Shneor et al. 2013); although in both nations entrepreneurship is mostly a male gendered concept, there are differences associated to cultural values: on the one hand, Turkey is a masculine oriented country, driven by strong growth ambitions, in which females entrepreneurs follow male stereotypes as consequence of gender inequality; on the other hand, Norway is a feminine oriented country, driven by moderate growth ambitions, in which females entrepreneurs can follow both male or female stereotypes as a consequence of gender equality. Interestingly, Sardinia is a region with a feminine background within Italy, which is instead a strongly masculine country (Hofstede 2001). Before introducing such a geographical and cultural context it is important however to review the main gender differences in entrepreneurship.

1.1.2   Gender Differences in Entrepreneurship

The fluid situation described in the previous section, and the difficulties in providing a common and general definition of entrepreneur, appear to be particularly evident in the case of female entrepreneurship. Indeed, women are generally associated to lower venture performances (as enterprises owned by women are much less in number than those owned by men), and are also considered to lag behind men in terms of entrepreneurial outcomes, self-efficacy, risk-taking attitude, intentions, and propensity in venturing (van der Zwan et al. 2012; Koellinger et al. 2013; Amoros and Bosma 2013). In the case of Italy, for instance, women entrepreneurs are the 6% of adult population against the 16% of men, they own small enterprises concentrated in services rather than manufacturing, earn the 55% less than men, and are more concerned than men about financing, payments for outstanding invoices, personnel, administrative and legal matters, and back up from family (OECD 2011, 2015). Yet, women participation to entrepreneurship has been increasing all around the world and their contribution is a relevant and growing quota of the global market (Kelley et al. 2014), it covers a relevant share of the employment market, hiring the 50% of individuals in sole proprietor low size enterprises (OECD 2012), and has revealed positive personal effects as women are more satisfied than their male counterpart, showing higher levels of work-life balance and subjective well-being (Amoros and Bosma 2013). Fostering of women's entrepreneurship is thus beneficial in terms of equality, empowerment, social inclusion, and creation of jobs based on different perspectives on management and organization, which add heterogeneity and variety at regional and national levels (OECD 2012).

However, women's entrepreneurship is still considered understudied (Brush and Cooper 2012) and women's contribution to employment creation poorly documented (OECD 2012). Most of all, effects of gender on self-efficacy, attitudes, entrepreneurial intentions, and social norms change across cultures so that the rationale behind any perceived gap in motivations and intentions is debated, with the extant literature divided even on the existence and definition of a 'gender gap' (Shneor et al. 2013). The supposed 'gender gap', indeed, measured by the Global Entrepreneurship Monitor as the ratio of women to men participating in entrepreneurship, is actually a collection of differentials concerning participation to the various stages of the venturing process, characteristics and motivations of women entrepreneurs, societal attitudes and impact indicators (Kelley et al. 2014). Several determinants have been suggested to account for the existence of this supposed gap, ranging from internal and individual to external and socio-economic ones (see, e.g., Klapper and Parker 2011). Examples of internal determinants are: individual differences in motivation and expectations in business growth, where men are primarily driven by financial success while women account for recognition, innovation and self-realization (Manolova et al. 2012); differences in traits and attitudes, with women showing lower levels of self-efficacy and self-confidence (Wilson et al. 2007; Klyver and Grant 2010), and a risk-adverse attitude that pushes them toward low capital businesses (Brindley 2005); women's higher concern regarding failure (Shinnar et al. 2012; Koellinger et al. 2013); or gender differences in recognizing and seizing opportunities (De Tienne and Chandler 2007). It has also been argued that the gender gap might be due to differences in experience and training in previous firms, independently on education or business motivations (Fischer et al. 1993). Examples of external and contextual effects are instead given by differences in intention toward entrepreneurship due to gender-specific relations with the organizational context (Walter et al. 2013), or differences due to a contextual uneven distribution of human, family and financial capital (Cetindamar et al. 2012; Shinnar et al. 2012), and to the differences between how genders perceive themselves and the environment (Langowitz and Minniti 2007). In particular, albeit the environment is hostile for both genders, women perceive it as more challenging and less rewarding and supportive (Zhao et al. 2005; Shinnar et al. 2012; Shneor et al. 2013). Differences in networking are also relevant, with women that adopt a more integrated perspective thus dealing with entrepreneurial relations as cooperative networks of both familiar, societal and personal relationships (Brush 1992). Network composition differs also among genders, with women's that are more homogenous with respect to kin composition (Popielarz 1999), present fewer weak ties than man's and a lower level of available resources, conditions which can be detrimental to entrepreneurial performances (Kim and Sherraden 2014). As a consequence, women are more likely to become necessity entrepreneurs rather than opportunity ones (Pines et al. 2010) as they are often involved in the informal sector, can be less educated than men, possess backgrounds in social sciences and liberal arts rather than technical or scientific disciplines, and find more barriers to finances, loans and funding due to their restricted access to formal networks and the existent gender norms about domestic work (Warneke 2013). Barriers like lack of support and competency, or fear of failure, are also enhanced in women, although there are differences due to the cultures (Shinnar et al. 2012). Normative support for women is however embedded within cultural and social structures that represent values, expectations and roles (Baughn et al. 2006). As women appear to be more influenced than men in their decisions by cultural factors like family or community, they might be pushed toward their choices from socialization processes implicitly based on patriarchal norms (Klapper and Parker 2011). This might have a double drawback: on the one hand, talented women might be hindered by masculine norms (Marlow and Swail 2014; Goktan and Gupta 2015); on the other hand, in spite of an equal distribution of talent between genders, untalented females might react to discrimination by pursuing an entrepreneurial career in spite of their lacks, thus contributing to a general underperformance (Rosti and Chelli 2005).

As social norms are however institutionalized over time, they are not perceived as discriminatory, and gender inequalities root within traditions and formal and informal institutions, which are fundamental to economic, social behaviours and attitudes, thus creating a hiatus between 'de jure rights (what the law says) and de facto rights (what actually happens in practice) for women' (Warneke 2013). It has been suggested that assumptions of homogeneity and meritocratic equal opportunity among entrepreneurs, which underlie most of the extant literature, are debatable (Alh 2006; Gupta et al. 2009; Shneor et al. 2013; Marlow and Swail 2014; Goktan and Gupta 2015), and that women are positioned in social and economic niches that cannot conciliate the evolutionary necessities of their life course and the current conception of entrepreneurship (Marlow and Swail 2014). Entrepreneurship is indeed imbued with a masculine narrative about adventure, individualism, aggressiveness and ruthlessness, which is evident in most of media representations, up to the point that women entrepreneurs are often framed within the social convention of balancing public and domestic duties (Hamilton 2013). As a consequence, women's lower propensity for venturing and higher risk avoidance should not be seen as shortcomings but as reflections over femininity itself induced by roles in labour market history, institutional constraints and norms (Marlow and Swail 2014). Indeed, gender differences decrease when one looks at own-account workers (OECD 2012) since women often own part-time and home-made firms which are more easily funded and managed at an informal level (Thompson et al. 2009).

In conclusion, notwithstanding evolutionary and individual differences, it appears that a relevant quota of entrepreneurial differences might be ascribable to how masculinity and femininity are defined within social institutions and normative contexts, and to how the concepts of entrepreneurship and entrepreneur are characterized with respect to these conventions. A gendering effect can then be detected as a deviation between these characterizations and the perception of proper gender behaviour (Shneor et al. 2013). To analyse within a multiple culture perspective how regional and national context and norms affect the definition of entrepreneurship and the entrepreneurial behaviour in the specific context of Sardinia it is finally important to introduce the actual social and economic context of the island.

1.1.3 Sardinian Economic and Social Context

Sardinia is a part of the underdeveloped Italian Mezzogiorno and, due to its distance from the mainland, is one of the less favoured regions of European Union (Hospers 2003). Its economy is mainly based on agriculture, products of pastoralism, and tertiary activities; it underwent in the fifties a sectorial and concentrated process of industrialization which drove the island on top of southern regions, but still far from European standards (King 1977). Sardinia's GDP was the 78.3% of EU27 GPD in

2010. National export contributes to 14% of the GDP and is mostly based on petroleum related products and by-products. Primary sector accounts for the 24% of enterprises, industry for 8%, accommodation and food services for 8%, construction sector for 15%, commerce for 28%, while only 15% accounts for real estate, professionals and person services (data taken from Cerina 2006; Pulina and Biagi 2006; CRENoS 2010, 2014). Services for tourism are the most relevant businesses and, in spite of the risks of seasonal incomes, over-exploitation of ecosystems, and unregulated construction, they are considered the most important export industry and the most promising development strategy for a region that is weak in terms of industry, infrastructures and services (Paci 1999; Hospers 2003; Murroni 2006). Notably, informal sector increased of the 24% during the recent crisis (Di Caro and Nicotra 2015).

Sardinia's geographical, structural, and economic backwardness and its risk-averse and inward-looking tendencies in business, have contributed to the development of a weak entrepreneurial tradition in comparisons to other Italian regions (Boi et al. 1999; Mariotti and Piscitello 2001; Murroni 2006). In addition, the clientelism rooted in rural traditions has turned patronage into a common mechanism of distribution of power, influence and resources, so that services and information are considered in the same way of favours, and a rent seeking behaviour is enhanced thus affecting social interactions (Batterbury 2002). In particular, access to state apparatus and resources is often monopolised by local cliques organized on kinship relations (Bodemann 1982). In spite of this, the Island has shown solid ground for entrepreneurship: an example is given by the capital city of Cagliari, in which entrepreneurial culture has led to the concentrated growth of few large players like TISCALI and several small ICT businesses and software developers (Murroni 2006). Besides, it supports entrepreneurship by means of initiatives like the 'Città dell'Impresa' (City of Enterprise), which is a meeting place where people can learn about emerging local markets and consult experts in the field. Notably, the presence of a concentrated but not fully developed entrepreneurial and a services-oriented market in which technological players have been successful, characterizes this region as a fruitful field for the development of the particular stream of entrepreneurship which is expected in an innovation system. In addition, the island also shows strong social norms that suggests an ideal context to analyse institutionalized gender stereotypes and their interplay with the entrepreneurial social network.

Female entrepreneurs, indeed, are emblematic: they are a growing component of Sardinian society and economy (though concentrated in the tertiary sector), and are generally more educated than their male counterpart; in particular, they are not necessity entrepreneurs, as they prefer autonomous work primarily as a means of emancipation and freedom (Boi et al. 1999). This is in contrast with the rest of Italy, where women appear to choose self-employment to avoid inactivity or unemployment rather than as a means of personal motivation or desire to improve their career (Rosti and Chelli 2005), and appears to be related with Sardinian distinct and peculiar division of roles in family which resulted in the emergence of both a relative gender equality, with strong and active female figures, and enhanced horizontal ties between female siblings, which affect and influence women attitudes towards family and work (Boi et al. 1999; Bernardi and Oppo 2007). Although it has been suggested that Sardinian population experienced a matriarchal society which lasted until the industrialization of the fifties (Pitzalis-Acciaro 1978) such a concept has been lately criticized (Oppo 1990; Da Re 1990) as the absence of a full equality implies more a woman-centred society than a matriarchal one (Eller 2011). Indeed, Sardinian society was dominated by males, with women often excluded from main productive activities and government, so that their power was more a reflection of men absence (Oppo 1990; Eller 2011), but it was also based on nuclear families, with large numbers of children and co-residential domestic groups of kin structured on an uxorial base, and in which women held for a long time a strong position by providing household continuity (Oppo 1990; Bernardi and Oppo 2007). Traditional marriage habits and family configurations were close to the western habits of neo-locality and mono-nuclearity (Angioni 2005). While men were endowed with duties associated to livestock and countryside, women were endowed with duties about home, village and cultivated fields. They were, indeed, in charge of households, responsible for both goods and properties, with inclusion of financial aspects and the autonomous creation of a family asset, often without any initial endowment (Boi et al. 1999; Oppo 1990). They also were entrusted with the transmission of ethical values, with the inclusion of self-defense, which suggest some degree of aggressiveness (Assmuth 1997). As a drawback, this focus on household care appears however to have increased their responsibilities and workload contributing to a chronic stress burden (Oppo 1990; Eller 2011) and strengthening the difficulties in reconciling personal life with self-employment, as a relevant number of Sardinian women entrepreneurs are not married and/or without children (Boi et al. 1999). It appears then that there is an ambivalence within Sardinian social norms and traditions: on the one hand, women suffer the typical drawbacks that hinder their aspiration toward entrepreneurship; while on the other hand, they are strong figures with remarkable skills (Boi et al. 1999).

1.2 Perception of Entrepreneurship and Gender Related Stereotypes

As stated earlier, the aim of this research is to investigate perception of entrepreneurship in the presence of a masculine discourse of entrepreneurship that would overcome (or at least interact with) existing local socio-cultural norms, independently on individual characteristics and entrepreneurial aptitude. Indeed, it is expected that a masculine concept of entrepreneurship and Sardinian feminine norms should impact at multiple levels: firstly, women are expected to be at least as equally talented as men, by showing comparable levels of entrepreneurial aptitude, aptitude, education, self-perception of skills and abilities and self-efficacy, motivation and intention; secondly, entrepreneurial role is expected to be perceived as more socially suited to men rather than women, in spite of females' talent and self-perception; thirdly, such a perception is expected to be reinforced and become apparent not only in terms of difficulties associated to the entrepreneurial career but also as a gendered polarization of the concept itself of entrepreneur as it would be expected in a typically masculine oriented country like Italy. Finally, these stereotypes are expected to impact on the effectiveness of their entrepreneurial efforts and of their network, thus hindering one of the fundamental assumptions underlying the access to any innovation system.

Education, presence of an entrepreneurial social network (namely, an informal network of relatives, friends or acquaintances that are entrepreneurs), entrepreneurial aptitude, access to regional capital and actual level of involvement in entrepreneurship (whether they are entrepreneurs, aspiring ones, or attempted ones as they tried to start up a business but failed) were considered. Education shows indeed a positive relation with venture performance (Robinson and Sexton 1994), as it enhances individuals' ability and chances to exploit opportunities and support (Mitchell et al. 2000), and it increases knowledge about credit procedures by also reducing the 'fear of the bank' (García-Cabrera and García-Soto 2008). Access to regional capital, personal networks, shared information and knowledge are instead fundamental to analyse the innovation system (Cantner and Graf 2004). Presence of a network was investigated as social ties which are embedded into an entrepreneurial context allow for immediate availability of information, resources and social capital (Renzulli, Aldrich, and Moody 2000; Hoang and Antoncic 2003). Albeit differences in networking practices can be detected across cultures (Klyver et al. 2008), networks are a prominent instrument in all stages of business engagement (Birley 1985; Greve 1995) and the fundamental block of innovation systems. Indeed, not only entrepreneurs tend to have self-employed parents (Hisrich et al. 2007) but relations established with other entrepreneurs, managers and entrepreneurial associations, are even more effective than having parent in business (Fuentes et al. 2010) since weak ties are essential to spread innovativeness and information without the constraining influence to which strong ties are subjected (Ruef 2002). Finally, facilitators and barriers in accessing regional capital, meant as support to entrepreneurial behaviour regarding bureaucracy, funding or access to credit, and moral support (Audretsch et al. 2008), were considered to account for the context. A particular attention was devoted to their access to technological infrastructure as a mean to gather information. Entrepreneurial aptitude was instead measured by means of the TAI, a tailored instrument based on a socio-behavioural perspective which is briefly described in the following section.

1.3   Entrepreneurial Aptitude

An important distinction has been drawn between entrepreneurship, meant as the act of venturing within new or existing markets by means of new or existing goods or services, and the collection of processes (methods, practices, heuristics, decision-making style) which allows the act of entrepreneurship (Miller 1983; Covin and

Slevin 1989; Lumpkin and Dess 1996). In the present context, the Entrepreneurial Aptitude Test (TAI®, Cubico et al. 2010) was applied, which is a 23-items Likert scale created by reducing the 75 items of the original test by using Rasch partial credit model. Its structure is based on management, innovation, effective leadership, autonomy, need for achievement and goal orientation, thus supporting the entrepreneurial aptitude construct with important and acknowledged corollaries whose usefulness is also underlined by meta-analytical evidences on the application of social and behavioural perspectives in entrepreneurship (Zhao and Siebert 2006; Rauch and Frese 2007). In the present work, changes in TAI score were associated to variations in gender, presence and heterogeneity of the social network, level of entrepreneurship, level and type of education, while controlling for age, in order to investigate if analysis of entrepreneurial aptitude in a less favourable and socially characterized context, can be carried by means of a tailored instrument. Consistency of the TAI results would indeed support some important considerations: firstly, it would stress that an achievement orientation (here given by means of need for achievement and goal orientation) is a relevant addition to the individual perspective in spite of the fact that it is generally not considered at firm level (Krauss et al. 2005); secondly, it would highlight that, since entrepreneurial aptitude is a good indicator of individual propensity in different cultural and business contexts. Thirdly, an individual measure of entrepreneurial aptitude might be directly useful for training and selection purpose as a possible predictor of individual business performance.

2   Data and Methods

A sample of 314 Sardinians was interviewed. Seventeen participants were removed as they showed unit non-response or evidences of response set bias. The final sample consist of 297 participants (Male 42%, Female 58%; Mean age 31.96, SE = 0.52, range: 1959). A questionnaire with 57 group items was administered to record their personal and demographic data, engagement in entrepreneurship, structure of their entrepreneurial social network, personal experience and expectation on employed and self-employed work, perspectives on future job situation, propensity towards entrepreneurship, entrepreneurial aptitude measured with the TAI, perceptions about male and female entrepreneurs, self-perception of abilities, competences, attitudes and skills, information about bureaucracy, investments, difficulties, environmental and familiar support in venturing. Data collection was carried while participants were attending to an entrepreneurship preparation course financed by the European Social Fund and promoted by different training and orientation centres in the city of Cagliari. The percentage of missing data is 7.6% and can be considered to not excessively bias statistical analysis.

Items were either dichotomous or on a five points scale (Not at all, A little, More or less, Much, Very much). Semantic differentials were on a seven points scale. To account for the ordered nature of items, non-parametric tests were applied: Wilcoxon Mann-Whitney U test (Wilcoxon signed-rank V for paired samples) and Kruskal

Wallis K were respectively applied to dichotomous variables and categorical variables. In both cases, the r effect size $(r = Z_U/\sqrt{N})$, that divides the standardized score of the test by the square root of the sample dimension, was associated. For the Kruskal Wallis tests, the r effect size was derived for each single pairwise comparison, and p-values were Bonferroni adjusted (p_B). In the case of both dichotomous variables, Fisher's exact test was given with odds ratio (OR) as effect size. Finally, TAI score was analysed with linear mixed-effect models to verify changes in relation to gender, age, presence and heterogeneity of the network, degree and type of education, level of entrepreneurship. For mixed models, p-values for the test statistic were derived using Kenward-Roger approximation for the denominator degrees of freedom, which is considered to be less affected by unbalanced design (Schaalje et al. 2002). Type III sum of squares was also applied to account for unbalancing. Analyses were carried with the open source software R (R Development Core team 2017). For logistic regression and log-linear analysis, the *glm* function of the native *stats* package was used. Psychometrics properties of the TAI were evaluated using the *psych* package (Revelle 2017). Linear mixed effects models were evaluated using the packages *lme4* (Bates et al. 2015), *nlme* (Pinheiro et al. 2017) and *lmerTest* (Kunetsova et al. 2014).

3 Results

3.1 Descriptive Analysis of the Sample

The 55% of participants has a secondary degree, the 40% is graduated or attending a university course. Only the 5% has a primary degree. Degrees are in humanities (30%), technical or applied sciences (25%), accounting and economics (18%), tourism related (15%), environmental sciences (10%). Women are more educated than men (46% against the 31% is graduated). ANOVA reveals an interaction ($F_{(6281)} = 4.28$, p < 0.001, partial eta squared = 0.09) of education with levels of entrepreneurship. Participants with primary education are older (M = 41.45, SE = 2.37), those with a university degree are younger (M = 30.81, SE = 0.48), while in those with a secondary degree aspiring entrepreneurs are younger (M = 29.0, SE = 1.0) than both entrepreneurs (M = 39.1, SE = 2.2; p_B < 0.001) and attempted ones (M = 34.3, SE = 1.3; p_B < 0.01). There are no differences due to gender or social network. Aspiring entrepreneurs are the 58% of the sample, actual ones the 14%, and attempted ones the 28%. There is a slightly higher number of female non-entrepreneurs ($\chi^2(2) = 5.59$, p = 0.06, V = 0.14) and a slightly higher presence of secondary degrees with respect to university degrees amongst attempted entrepreneurs ($\chi^2(2) = 4.95$, p = 0.08, V = 0.13) when primary degrees are not considered. The 56% of the sample has some network of entrepreneurial acquaintances (the 36% has one type of connection, the 15% two types, only the 5% more than two types). The most common connection is friends (31.7%), followed by

Table 1 Distribution of participants

(N = 297)		Entrepreneurs (%)	Non entrepreneurs (%)	Attempted entrepreneurs (%)
Presence of network	Males	5.7	13.8	4.0
	Females	2.7	19.5	9.8
Absence of network	Males	2.0	7.7	9.1
	Females	3.7	17.2	4.7

Distribution of participants among gender, social network and level of entrepreneurship

father (14.8%), uncles/aunts or grandparents (14.8%), siblings (10.4%), mother (8.1%) and companion (2%). There are neither gender differences in the type of connections and in presence of a network, nor differences in its dimension and composition with respect to the engagement in entrepreneurship. If one however considers the nature of ties (none, friends, relatives, relatives plus friends), there is a slightly higher percentages of men with friendly connections and of women with family connections ($\chi^2(3) = 6.85$, p = 0.076, V = 0.15).

Log-linear analysis shows that independence between levels of entrepreneurship, gender, education and social network does not hold ($\chi^2(29) = 57.27$, p < 0.01). An independent effect for education and a three way interaction between the other factors have a significant likelihood ratio respect to the independence model ($G^2(7) = 23.49$, p < 0.01) and a non-significant one respect to the saturated model ($G^2(22) = 30.51$, p = 0.11). This model has an improved AIC index while the BIC index is not significantly affected with respect to the independence model ($\Delta AIC = -9.49$, $\Delta BIC = 1.58$).

As in Table 1, percentages of men and women entrepreneurs and attempted entrepreneurs change with presence or absence of a social network. While in presence of a network there are more male entrepreneurs than female ones, the opposite holds in its absence. The situation is reversed for attempted entrepreneurs. Interestingly, both in presence and absence of network there are more attempted female entrepreneurs than entrepreneur ones. It appears that, while male entrepreneurs benefit of the presence of a network, the same might not hold for females. Noticeably, if one considers the type of ties (none, friends, relatives, relatives plus friends), the same model holds and all type of ties show more attempted women entrepreneurs than entrepreneur ones.

3.2 Future Perspectives and Self-Perception

As expected, participants are motivated towards entrepreneurship. They foresee themselves in 5 years to be employed in private firms or to be entrepreneurs (Mdn = 3), rather than in the public sector (Mdn = 2) or unemployed (Mdn = 1). In ten years they see themselves as entrepreneurs (Mdn = 4), while others conditions are unchanged. Intention toward entrepreneurship is enhanced by education, with graduated participants more confident than those with a secondary degree, and by social ties (which reduces fear of unemployment). Entrepreneurs are more confident about self-employment respect to non-entrepreneurs and attempted entrepreneurs. There are no gender differences so that women perceive to become entrepreneurs as likely as men, but gender effects appear in association to perception of employability: men are more confident to find a satisfying job after graduation ($U = 9445$, $p < 0.01$; $r = 0.19$), they also believe, more than women, that the genders must face similar difficulties in becoming entrepreneurs ($U = 13{,}790.5$, $p < 0.001$, $r = 0.27$). Finally, men are less receptive toward the idea that an entrepreneurial lifestyle requires more sacrifices to women ($U = 7463$, $p < 0.001$, $r = -0.26$). There are neither effects of network nor of level of entrepreneurship and education. These results depict a situation in which women, albeit motivated as much as men are, might perceive gender-inequality and an unfavourable environment.

As to self-perception, participants declare to have a positive attitude and to possess good abilities in evaluating, planning, organizing, communicating, and identifying their weaknesses and strengths (Mdn = 4). They consider themselves as goal-oriented, enterprising, innovative, and independent (Mdn = 4), capable of handling risks (Mdn = 3.5), and moderately proficient in analytical, leading and managing skills, in technical expertise like accounting and managing stock levels, and in the capability of foreseeing events (Mdn = 3). Attempted entrepreneurs feel less capable of both entrepreneurs and non-entrepreneurs. Participants integrated in a social network envisage themselves as more skilled in managing ($U = 6915$, $p < 0.05$, $r = 0.13$), more endowed with analytical skills ($U = 7007.5$, $p < 0.05$, $r = 0.17$), more effective in risk handling ($U = 6915.5$, $p < 0.05$, $r = 0.14$) and by aptitude as more independent ($U = 7443$, $p < 0.01$, $r = 0.17$), and more innovative ($U = 7351.5$, $p < 0.01$, $r = 0.18$). Hence social ties enhance confidence in several skills and self-perception of independence and innovative behaviour; participants with a university degree are more confident than those with a secondary degree; participants with a primary degree are the least confident. There are no effects of gender as women perceive themselves as capable as men. These results underlie that the social network has a positive impact on entrepreneurial and innovative behaviour.

3.3 Gender Differences in Entrepreneurial Profile

Participants conceive a generic entrepreneur as someone characterized by leadership, innovation, need for achievement, flexibility and independence (Mdn = 4), and that seek personal and social affirmation (Mdn = 3), independently on level of entrepreneurship, gender, network, or education. However, male and female entrepreneur profiles are different. As it can be seen in Table 2 (on the left), a male entrepreneur is differently characterised by men and women, with women expressing lower scores in almost all attributes (positive effect sizes), while a female entrepreneur receives similar rating by men and women in almost all attributes (negative effect sizes).

Table 2 Gender differences

Gender differences	Between (Men vs. Women rating)				Within (Male vs. Female profile)			
	Male profile		Female profile		Men rating		Women rating	
Attribute	U	r	U	r	V	r	V	r
Determination	12,500.5 (***)	0.22	(n.s.)	–	127 (*)	−0.23	385 (***)	−0.55
Initiative	11,662.5 (***)	0.20	8240 (*)	−0.13	(n.s.)	–	297.5 (***)	−0.57
Inner strength	12,544 (***)	0.28	(n.s.)	–	213 (*)	−0.22	193 (***)	−0.65
Preparation	12,489 (***)	0.25	(n.s.)	–	171 (***)	−0.31	318 (***)	−0.56
Management skills	11,844 (***)	0.22	(n.s.)	–	(n.s.)	–	614 (***)	−0.40
Leadership	10,898 (*)	0.15	(n.s.)	–	(n.s.)	–	1249 (.)	−0.12
Time management	11,023 (*)	0.15	(n.s.)	–	335.5 (**)	−0.27	571 (***)	−0.56
Courage	11,735.5 (***)	0.20	8555 (.)	−0.10	(n.s.)	–	384 (***)	−0.55
Enthusiasm	12,747 (***)	0.29	8216.5 (*)	−0.12	(n.s.)	–	145 (***)	−0.62
Relational skills	12,362 (***)	0.28	(n.s.)	–	(n.s.)	–	790.5 (***)	−0.33
Flexibility	10,912 (*)	0.15	(n.s.)	–	(n.s.)	–	859 (***)	−0.36
Hardness	8321.5 (.)	−0.11	(n.s.)	–	392.5 (*)	−0.26	(n.s.)	
Creativity	12,403.5 (***)	0.28	(n.s.)	–	262.5 (*)	−0.16	376 (***)	−0.49
Sacrifice or self-denial	13,588.5 (***)	0.36	(n.s.)	–	(n.s.)	–	234.5 (***)	−0.63
Independence and autonomy	(n.s.)	–	7487.5 (*)	−0.15	(n.s.)	–	505 (***)	−0.27

Mann Whitney U and Wilcoxon signed-rank V tests for differences between and within men and women in perception of gendered entrepreneur profiles

Mann Whitney U tests for differences between men and women in perception of male-gendered and female-gendered entrepreneur profiles (on the left). Wilcoxon signed-rank V tests for gender differences in perception of male and female entrepreneurs within men and women (on the right). r is the associated effect size

Significance level, non-significant (n.s.), $p < 0.10$ (.), $p < 0.05$ (*), $p < .01$ (**), $p < 0.001$ (***)

Perception of a male entrepreneur hence differs between men and women, with women rating lower scores for male entrepreneurs compared to men, while perception of a female entrepreneur does not differ between men and women (except for some attribute). It is also useful to consider differences between gendered profiles within men and women. As it can be seen in Table 2 (on the right) men perception of male versus female entrepreneurs does not differ, but the contrary holds for women that rates higher all female attributes. Both genders however agree that a female entrepreneur needs more determination, inner strength, hardness, preparation, creativity and ability to handle time.

As a final notice, it is interesting to observe that non-significant traits like leadership (or those with weak effects like relational skills and independence) can be easily related to a generic and abstract entrepreneur profile, while other traits and abilities (particularly those with the strongest effect sizes) are more subjective and influenced by social exogenous and environmental conditions.

3.4 Test of Entrepreneurial Aptitude

Results appear to confirm reliability of the TAI score as a measure of entrepreneurial aptitude when applied to a sample of aspiring, actual, and attempted entrepreneurs of a marginal geographical region. Cronbach's alpha is 0.92 with a bootstrapped 95% confidence interval between 0.90 and 0.94. McDonald's omega total coefficient is 0.93, while omega hierarchical coefficient is 0.71, with a 0.49 common variance explained by the general factor. Coefficients were obtained using the psych package (Revelle 2017) to perform a hierarchical factor analysis on six factors (χ^2 (130, N = 297) = 250.32, p < 0.001; GFI = 0.99; AGFI = 0.99; RMSEA = 0.058; RMR = 0.03; TLI = 0.91; CFI = 0.95). High values of GFI and AGFI are likely upward-biased due to the size of the sample. Similarly, chi square is affected by sample size but normed chi square (χ^2/df) is below 2 and hence acceptable. Results suggest a good reliability of the scale and a good saturation in the entrepreneurial aptitude conceived as the common general factor.

TAI scores were analysed by means of linear mixed-effects model, with gender, level of entrepreneurship, education, and network as fixed effects, while controlling for the covariate age and the random effect of the type of education. Since only 5% of participants had more than two connections in their network, heterogeneity was accounted by means of a fixed effect with three levels: absence of network, homogenous (one type of connection) and heterogeneous network (more than one type of connection). Kenward-Roger's approximation for the degrees of freedom of the test statistic was considered (Schaalje et al. 2002). As a result, TAI differs between level of education ($F_{(234.7)} = 4.83$, p < 0.05), entrepreneurship ($F_{(2279.8)} = 3.37$, p < 0.05), and social network ($F_{(2282.1)} = 6.39$, p < 0.05). There are neither effects of gender ($F_{(1280.6)} = 0.37$, p = 0.55) nor of age ($F_{(1281.8)} = 0.40$, p = 0.53). Estimated effects are summarized in Table 3 with respect to a baseline given by a male graduated entrepreneur without network. Results for the t-tests follow Satterthwaite approximation and are coherent with Kenward-Roger's. TAI score appears to discriminate between actual and aspiring entrepreneurs, with attempted ones that show a tendency to perform worse than actual entrepreneurs. In addition, presence of a heterogeneous network and higher degrees of education are associated to higher scores. In addition, if one considers the types of ties instead of the heterogeneity of the network, it can be seen that the condition of familiar plus friends

Table 3 Mixed-effects linear model

Fixed effect	Estimate	Std. err.	df	t-test
Intercept	3.71	0.16	244.90	23.61 (***)
Non-entrepreneur	−0.23	0.09	280.93	−2.61 (**)
Attempted entrepreneur	−0.18	0.10	279.97	−1.87 (.)
Female	−0.04	0.06	280.22	−0.61 (n.s.)
Homogeneous network	0.06	0.06	282.64	0.32 (n.s.)
Heterogeneous network	0.27	0.08	280.60	3.57 (***)
Secondary school	−0.18	0.07	91.98	−2.68 (**)
Primary school	−0.45	0.21	18.17	−2.19 (*)
Covariate	–	–	–	–
Age	−0.002	0.004	281.57	−0.63 (n.s.)
Random effects	*Variance*	*Std. dev.*	–	–
Type of education	0.02	0.13	–	–
Residuals	0.22	0.47	–	–

Results of mixed-effects linear model

Intercept of the model corresponds to a male graduated entrepreneur without network

Significance levels: non-sign. (n.s.), $p < 0.10$ (.), $p < 0.05$ (*), $p < 0.01$ (**), $p < 0.001$ (***)

connections is the one which most improves TAI score (all other effects have the same degree of significance). Some variability is also related to the type of education received. There are no differences associated to gender.

As a finale notice, accounting for heteroscedasticity does not improve fit and estimates. Residuals are platykurtic but symmetrically distributed around zero. Visual inspection shows that the random effect is normally distributed. Correlations between fixed effects are lower than |0.4| suggesting no problems of collinearity.

3.5 Perception of Access to Entrepreneurship and Regional Capital

Participants are generally aware of their poor knowledge about venturing (Mdn = 2). Those with a network are more confident (U = 11,959.5, $p < 0.05$; r = 0.15), as well as entrepreneurs (K(2) = 32.39, $p < 0.001$) with respect to non-entrepreneurs ($p_B < 0.001$, r = 0.39) and attempted ones ($p_B < 0.01$, r = 0.41). In particular, results suggest that individuals embedded in a social network access more easily to knowledge about opportunities of local and regional innovation. Indeed, the presence of a network appears to help people sharing ideas thus stimulating development and innovation. Interviewees possessing a social network appear for instance to be more embedded in technological networks as they gather information by also browsing online content (U = 461, $p < 0.01$, r = 0.44) and by participating in forum, chat, and on-line communities (U = 204, $p < 0.05$, r = 0.36). Graduated participants are also more confident of their knowledge (K (2) = 6.35, $p < 0.05$) than those with a primary degree ($p_B = 0.052$, $r = 0.21$). Women show the same degree of awareness as men about their lack of knowledge. Entrepreneurs think that their knowledge about entrepreneurship was sufficient to start up their business (Mdn = 3) and are more confident than attempted ones (U = 1168, $p < 0.05$, $r = 0.25$). The 20% of participants had previously attended other entrepreneurial preparation courses, the 60% never attended one, but there are no significant differences with respect to gender, level of entrepreneurship, network or education. Participants perceive that bureaucracy, opportunity of finding partners, financial means, funding and capital, and trust in banks are strong difficulties (Mdn = 4), followed by support of family and social network, individuation of the correct niche for their service/product, information gathering, opportunity of becoming popular, personal aptitude and technical skills (Mdn = 3). As these items show almost no effects of gender, network, education or level of entrepreneurship, issues in accessing regional capital are equally perceived.

3.5.1 Bureaucracy

Participants that actually started a business perceived that bureaucracy stood in their way: they found difficult to obtain authorisations and they experienced excessive delays (Mdn = 3). Actual placement and location of services were poor (Mdn = 2). There are no differences due to gender or network. Yet, attempted entrepreneurs experienced more delays than entrepreneurs (U = 770, $p < 0.05$, $r = -0.22$). Participants with a secondary degree were more annoyed by these delays than graduated participants (K(2) = 10.07, $p_B < 0.01$, $r = -0.31$). Interestingly, difficulties were experienced independently on the TAI score of individuals (no significance in multivariate linear regression).

3.5.2 Financial Means, Access to Funding and Capital

Attempted entrepreneurs were more concerned about economic aspects than actual ones (K(2) = 7.68, $p_B < 0.05$, $r = -0.24$). However, only 27% of the participants who started up a business asked for loan or financing, while the 51% declared they never asked for funding. Half of those who required a loan were funded and logistic regression shows that the presence of a social network enhanced the probability of being funded (z = 2.196, $p < 0.05$) likely favouring endorsement and guarantee or personal loans. The 22% of the sample asked for incentives, while the 54% never did. A 2.3% received state incentives against a 7% that applied. A 10.3% received regional incentives against a 27% that applied. A 4.8% received private incentives against a 13% that applied. Incentives were not of help (Med = 2), though actual entrepreneurs found them more useful than attempted ones (U = 297, $p < 0.05$, $r = 0.35$), but still with a moderate appreciation (Mdn = 3). There are no effects of gender, education or social network. Funding was also independent on the TAI score of individuals.

Response rate to declare venture capital was low, with only 24% of the eligible participants answering. The average investment was 21,233.33 € with a standard error of 5752.20 € and a broad range (from 500.00 € to 150,000.00 €). However, only two participants had a venture capital higher than 100,000.00 €. All the others invested less than 50,000.00 € with a median of 10,000.00 €. ANOVA reveals no effects of gender, network, and level of entrepreneurship or education in the amount of capital invested. There is however a difference in ranking due to education (K (2) = 8.57, $p < 0.05$). Participants with a secondary degree invested on a narrow range (5000.00 € to 30,000.00 €), while graduated participants invested either lower or higher amounts, generally either below 5000.00 € or above 40,000.00 € ($p_B < 0.05$, $r = -0.49$). Interestingly, participants think that a venture capital of at least 20,000.00 € is required to start up a business, except for actual entrepreneurs that rate the budget between 10,000.00 € and 20,000.00 €.

3.5.3 Support and Back up from Families and Social Ties, Information Gathering

Women expressed higher concern about being supported and backed up from families and social ties (U = 8030, $p < 0.05$; $r = -0.13$), yet if asked whether their relatives would support them financially (Mdn = 3), there are no effects of gender. Participants with a network feel more backed up by their relatives (U = 13,459, $p < 0.001$, $r = 0.21$). Actual entrepreneurs feel more supported (K (2) = 11.65, $p < 0.01$) than both non-entrepreneurs ($p_B = 0.054$, $r = 0.16$) and attempted entrepreneurs ($p_B < 0.01$, $r = -0.31$). Similarly, if asked whether their friends would support them financially (Mdn = 2), there are no effects of entrepreneurship or gender. Again the network is supportive (U = 12,525, $p < 0.05$, $r = 0.14$). Albeit friends are the most common connection (31.65% of the sample), participants prefer strong ties for financial aid and support.

The 52.5% of those who actually started a business declared they asked for help, advice or support, while the 25% did everything on their own. Fisher's test shows that participants possessing a network are more inclined to ask for support or advice (p = 0.049, OR = 2.5). Entrepreneurs and attempted ones that asked for support considered sources of support and advice business consultants, relatives and friends, books, manuals and on-line content (Missing responses are generally between 30% and 40% so that results must be taken carefully). Satisfaction is moderate (Mdn = 3). Other sources like professional associations, other entrepreneurs, and banks are poorly considered (Mdn = 2). Lawyers are very poorly rated (Mdn = 1). Entrepreneurs are more satisfied than attempted entrepreneurs and show more satisfaction about business consultants, relatives or friends, books, manuals and online content, communities, forum and chat, and other entrepreneurs. Fisher's test shows that entrepreneurs asked for support to professional associations more than attempted ones (p = 0.003, OR = 4.62), although they were not satisfied. Similarly, they asked for online support like forum, chat and communities more than attempted ones (p = 0.03, OR = 3.27). Presence of a social network slightly increases the satisfaction regarding relatives and friends and other entrepreneurs. There are also two tendencies for gender with woman rating higher satisfaction about advice and support asked to relatives and friends or other entrepreneurs. Most of all, more women than man declared to have actually received support from their relatives and friends (p = 0.002, OR = 0.06).

4 Discussion

In order to analyse the interrelation between two of the fundamental assumptions behind an innovation system, namely the existence of an effective network of connections, and their embedding in institutions which incorporates social and local norms, the present work has explored whether a gender polarization (driven by masculine national norms and by a masculine discourse on entrepreneurship) would still emerge in a more oriented feminine society in which there are strong and capable women, thus affecting both entrepreneurial outcome and network. In order to do so, the region of Sardinia was considered as it is imbued with uxorial traditions (Oppo 1990; Boi et al. 1999; Bernardi and Oppo 2007). A questionnaire was administered to a sample of aspiring, actual and attempted entrepreneurs to record their characteristics, experience, expectations, intention, motivations, competences and perception of entrepreneurship. Entrepreneurial aptitude was measured using the TAI (Cubico et al. 2010). Presence of a social network, education, age, and experience in entrepreneurship were assessed. Several findings are worth to be reported. Results confirm that education and networking are fundamental determinants of entrepreneurial innovative behaviour. More in detail, education enhances self-efficacy, intention toward entrepreneurship, and orientation. Participants with a university degree show higher resilience toward bureaucracy and higher interest in entrepreneurship as a means to innovation. Similarly, social network enhances desirability of an entrepreneurial choice of life and strengthen self-efficacy. It fosters an independent and innovative attitude, and it increases both perception and satisfaction regarding support for advice and financial needs. In addition, it increases the participation in technological networks like chat, forum, and online communities. Most of all, it appears that a heterogeneous network is associated to a higher TAI score (in particular, coexistence of both relatives and friends within the connections appears to impact positively).

In addition, it was also confirmed the presence of gender stereotypes that appear evident in women conception of entrepreneurship and of the entrepreneurial role. Indeed, in spite of an actual equality of talent, motivation, intention, education, competences and aptitude, of the equivalence in venture capital, and of equally experienced issues in accessing regional capital and innovation networks, women perceive that inequalities hinder their access to entrepreneurship. In particular, they are less confident to find a suitable job, are more sensitive to the fact that men and women must face different obstacles to become entrepreneurs, are more concerned about being backed up and supported by their families and friends, are more concerned about the sacrifices that an entrepreneurial choice of life requires to their sex, and are more inclined to move toward entrepreneurship to seek out for a change and as a means toward personal affirmation. Most of all, masculine and feminine entrepreneurial profiles are strongly perceived as different by the genders. Indeed, a female-gendered profile is similarly perceived by both men and women and requires higher levels of several characteristics (men themselves recognize that women needs higher determination, inner strength, hardness, preparation, creativity and ability to handle time); yet a male-gendered profile receives a completely different character-ization: women give lower scores, thus expressing a perceived facilitation of male entrepreneurs in Sardinian society. Notably, the strongest effect sizes are associated to self-denial and spirit of sacrifice. Finally, the most striking gender-related result is that there is an interaction between gender, social network, and engagement in entrepreneurship, that suggests women do not benefit by the presence of a network: while there are more men entrepreneurs than attempted ones in presence of network (vice versa in its absence), the same does not hold for women as there are more attempted entrepreneurs than actual ones in both conditions. This is particularly interesting if one considers that in Italy deaths of women enterprises are lower than men's ones (OECD 2012) thus suggesting the existence of local processes and mechanisms which turn the situation around in the present sample.

Most of all, all the previous gender-related differences manifest themselves in spite of the equality of any other condition. All participants indeed confirm an unfavourable environment but they do not show gender differences, neither in access to regional capital, nor in abilities, aptitude or intention. They confirm to be difficult to find a suitable job, and confirm that access to regional capital is hindered by information gathering, bureaucracy, suitable partnership, funding availability, trust in banks and institutions, and financial weakness of their networks. Authorisations, incentives, and loans are difficult to obtain, while business support resources and services are ineffective and poorly located. As a consequence, they rely on individ-ual capital and seek support of families as they are more confident of the financial backup of their relatives rather than that of friends, which it might be expected as they are in the first stages of venturing. Notably, the previous barriers are equally perceived, irrespectively of entrepreneurial aptitude and gender. Participants are also aware of their lack of knowledge about venturing but are strongly motivated toward self-employment which is perceived in terms of personal interest, motivation and social status (though its complexity and uncertainty are recognized). They perceive themselves as moderately proficient in several abilities and skills, and they are confident of becoming entrepreneurs. Most of all, there are no gender differences in motivation, intention self-perception, confidence, risk-taking attitude as well as in entrepreneurial aptitude and aptitude. Women are more educated than men. There are also no gender differences in presence of a social network and in the types of connections available to participants (exception given for a slight prevalence of relatives in women networks and friends in men's).

These findings appear to be coherent with the uxorial background of Sardinia, which resulted in the emergence of a relative gender equality with strong female figures and ties (Oppo 1990; Boi et al. 1999; Bernardi and Oppo 2007). In particular, these findings are similar to those in Cape Verdean society and Khasi women which show high level of entrepreneurial behaviour as effect of matrilineal or feminine social norms (García-Cabrera and García-Soto 2008; Nongbri 2008). Hence, it appears that feminine norms strengthen women self-perception, abilities, aptitude, competences, and so on, yet women keep perceiving strong gender-related stereotypes and actually fail more often in the entrepreneurial effort, ceteris paribus with all the other conditions (network, financial supports, access to regional capital, dimension of the network, and so on). It then appears that most of the determinants that have been proposed to explain the gender gap (see, e.g., Klapper and Parker 2011) cannot be applied in the present case and the most likely candidate to explain these results is the masculine narrative of entrepreneurship which excessively focuses on women deficiencies and on the importance of economic growth, rather than on gender equality, gender/power relations and gender differences (Alh 2006; Gupta et al. 2009; Shneor et al. 2013; Marlow and Swail 2014; Goktan and Gupta 2015). Indeed, these results appear to be consistent with the hypothesis that masculine norms and a pervasive masculine narrative of entrepreneurship have narrowly shifted the focus towards ostensible women deficiencies and economic growth rather than on the real issues at stake (Alh 2006; Gupta et al. 2009; Shneor et al. 2013; Marlow and Swail 2014; Goktan and Gupta 2015). Since differences persist within equality of all entrepreneurial determinants, it appears that a masculine polarization of entrepreneurship overcomes (or at least coexists with) the presence of uxorial norms that enhance women's propensity and abilities. However, such a masculine polarization might be ascribable to both the strong masculinity of Italian culture and the masculine narrative of entrepreneurship, as they both likely contribute to prevent a full equality of genders in the Sardinian context, by also interacting with traditions on household continuity. Results appear then in line with the ambivalence of uxorial social norms that, on the one hand, are supportive of strong female figures with remarkable skills, while, on the other hand, let women exposed to a male-dominated society and to several barriers that hinder their aspirations toward self-employment (Boi et al. 1999).

In particular, such an ambivalence might add on gender stereotypes, likely reinforcing them by means of the traditions on household continuity, which designate women as responsible for the domestic well-being, thus increasing their workload and duties, and eventually contributing to their stress burden. Although to dissociate the entities of these contributions, and the directions of their implications, is not feasible with the present data, still it appears that there is no gender gap in self-efficacy, motivation and intention but rather an awareness of social and individual issues which are direct consequence of masculine social norms and traditions, and of the understanding of entrepreneurship in the Sardinian context in relation to the national one. These results appear also consistent with previous findings that highlighted how the relation between gender and entrepreneurial intention can be complicated, with women that perceive to be as capable as men while at the same time considering the environment as hostile and less rewarding (Zhao et al. 2005), and with previous findings highlighting that entrepreneurial propensity of women does not depend only on contextual factors but also on evolutionary behaviours

(Langowitz and Minniti 2007). The most relevant result, however, is that such an ambivalence appears to enhance differences in entrepreneurial performances by weakening the effectiveness of women's network. An aspect that becomes crucial since the effectiveness of a network is a necessary assumption of any innovation system. In order to provide a possible interpretation to this latter result some findings deserve to be detailed: firstly, networks are not heterogeneous (participants generally possess only one type of connection) and show no differences with respect to gender or to level of entrepreneurship. Relatives are preferred in spite of friends being the most common connection (nonetheless, women have slightly more family connections while men have slightly more friendly ones). Both genders rely for information and help on relatives, friends and business consultants, rather than on financial institutions, professional associations or lawyers. Resources are the same as there are no gender differences in funding and amount of invested capital. Notably, entrepreneurs resort to more heterogeneous sources of information (although not associated with a higher satisfaction), which is consistent with their tendency to higher TAI score, as they would better exploit weak ties. Secondly, women are more concerned about support and advice from their families and social ties but, once asked if they would be financially supported by their relatives and friends, there are no gender differences (both men and women rate as moderate the satisfaction about the help received from relatives and as poor that received from friends). In addition, women entrepreneurs and attempted ones asked significantly more than men for both support and advice to relatives and friends, to which they also expressed a moderately higher satisfaction.

Summarizing the previous findings, it appears that social ties in the present sample are mostly of strong nature, and that they neither characterize the degree of engagement in entrepreneurship nor a specific gender. Most of all, in spite of the hints of gender equality, women appear to do not benefit by those social ties which paradoxically they declare to exploit more than men. These results appear consistent with the fact that participants are in early stages of venturing, so that informal networks based on family, friends and financial contacts are perceived as more helpful then formal ones (Birley 1985; Hoang and Antoncic 2003), and that networking is hampered by regional deficiencies, thus being perceived more in terms of exploitation of existing connections rather than investment in potential and future ones; indeed, the poor economic context and the presence of clientelism stress the importance of family as an impacting means of support to entrepreneurial aspirations and self-employment decisions (Boi et al. 1999). In addition, these results appear also consistent with the fact that women generally perceive as more difficult to obtain support and cooperation from family (Shinnar et al. 2012) and that they put more emphasis on social supports than men do (Klapper and Parker 2011). However, these results cannot be explained by the finding, which instead holds for the rest of Italy, that less talented females react against gender discrimination by persevering in self-employment and entrepreneurship (Rosti and Chelli 2005), because education, skills and entrepreneurial aptitude and intention of Sardinian women in the present sample are the same as men's. Similarly, it appears that these results cannot be due to a lack of resources in the network that would hamper female entrepreneurship (Kim and Sherraden 2014) as women invested in venturing as much as men did, and they show the same level of access to regional capital and information sources. It is more likely that if some resource is missing is not a material one but it is associated to the social nature of their ties and context.

As these results appear not to be explainable in terms of gender gap in talent, intention, self-efficacy, or motivation, it is suggested that uxorial norms might amplify some issues which are typical of networking, with respect to family and closed bonds, exclusiveness of networks, particularly along the dimensions of information and solidarity (Zhang 2010). It is indeed acknowledged that in Sardinian society families have a strong moral (and practical) role in enterprise creation, with the presence within the same business of partners, siblings and relatives, and with women, often from both birth and extended families, that team up (Boi et al. 1999). A society characterized by uxorial ties might then enhance homophily in female relations (while favouring heterophily in male's ones), thus fostering the natural tendency of women to more homogenous network respect to kin composition (Popielarz 1999), and intensifying the strong ties on which they already rely (women of the present sample do indeed possess slightly more entrepreneurial connections made of relatives). As homophily localizes cultural, behavioural, eco-nomic and material information (McPherson et al. 2001), it might hamper women's network by framing kinship relations within the very same social norms that identify women with the providers of household continuity, thus strengthening the influence of a masculine conception of entrepreneurship which facilitates male access and/or increase women's perception of difficulties. Indeed, those very norms which are supportive of strong females do not provide an actual equality of genders, so they might affect women's attitude towards family and work by reinforcing the perceived difficulty of balancing an entrepreneurial life with family healthcare, and by hinder-ing effectiveness of social connections but not of talent, aptitude, or available resources. As a consequence, in spite of the similarities in both structure and availability of resources of men's and women's networks, women's exploitation would be different, thus possibly explaining both the coexistence of higher levels of concern and of perceived satisfaction, and the higher percentage of exploitation of these connections. In addition, this would suggest a lower exploitation of their weak ties thus making strong ties even more detrimental to women rather than men, which is interesting since social networks based on strong ties should be detrimental to entrepreneurship independently on gender (Renzulli et al. 2000).

As a final notice, the present work also aimed to explore whether the TAI score could be used as a reliable and fine-grained measure of entrepreneurial aptitude in aspiring entrepreneurs within a local context characterized by strong regional defi-ciencies and local norms. As result, TAI changes associated to gender, presence and heterogeneity of the social network, level of entrepreneurship, age, level and type of education, appear to be consistent with previous literature on determinants of entrepreneurship. Most of all, the present results highlight that supporting the entrepreneurial aptitude construct by means of behavioural and social dimensions can be particularly useful to account for the influence of cultural and local contexts.

5   Conclusions and Implications

Innovation, by promoting local identities and traditions, is a key strategy in the operational programme for Sardinia to support enterprises, employment and human resources (European Commission 2011). However, fostering of entrepreneurship in regional contexts, in order to create innovative systems that rely on efficient networks, requires that policies should be tailored on local needs rather than on abstract determinants (see, e.g., McDonald et al. 2006). Effective examples are given by geographical clusters, science parks and industrial districts that are prone to failure if local issues are not addressed (Hospers et al. 2009), and that can fall into inward-looking and conservative patterns if external resources are not matched and sustained by internal variety of skills and knowledge (Sammarra and Belussi 2006). Indeed, previous attempts to top-down build industrial clusters and innovative systems in Sardinia have turned out into disembodied results since the unique structure of the island was never properly taken into account (Hospers et al. 2009).

The present work supplements the extant literature on the interrelation between entrepreneurship and informal institutions (see, e.g., Hopp and Stephan 2012), by supporting that studies and policies on entrepreneurship and innovative systems should be tailored on regional realities, in order to account for traditions and norms within both local and national contexts that can affect the effectiveness or the networks. In particular, gender differences appear to be influenced by pervasive masculine stereotypes that interact with local norms thus creating an ambivalent (and counterproductive) effect that fosters some determinants while reversing effectiveness of others. A multiple cultures perspective appears then to be suitable to understand less favoured environment and shape policies at a contextual level (García-Cabrera and García-Soto 2008; Hopp and Stephan 2012). In addition, the present work adds to the literature on entrepreneurial aptitude, by showing that entrepreneurial aptitude is a flexible construct that offers a reliable measure that can be usefully applied within different local contexts.

From an empirical perspective, this work suggests that Sardinia can be a very favourable ground for women entrepreneurship, since women show high levels of self-efficacy, intention and orientation, but that its development is still hindered by a lack of infrastructures and policies capable of addressing the ambivalence of uxorial social norms. On the hand, indeed, venturing in a region like Sardinia requires to support access to regional capital, which needs the development of entrepreneurial skills, local resources and networks (for an example in rural Sardinia, see for instance Meccheri and Pelloni 2006); on the other hand, suitable policies are needed to handle the persistence of social stereotypes, like those associated to a masculine narrative of entrepreneurship, which are reinforced by Sardinian social norms on household responsibilities, thus contributing to homophily and to hinder the benefits of women's social networks. Failure of a social network is indeed a crucial issue in creating reliable innovative systems.

Among the limitations of the present work it should be noticed that this is a case study of both aspiring and actual entrepreneurs in the capital city of Cagliari, any generalization has a limited scope so even the extension to Sardinian population should be taken with caution. In addition, TAI score is mainly based on a socio-behavioural approach and does not take into account important dimensions like risk taking (though they were analysed with separate items). This approach do not account for the increased interest, in recent literature, for strategic, cognitive and behavioural elements like biases, resource-based heuristics, decision making (Alvarez and Busenitz 2001; Mitchell et al. 2002) and intentions as mediators of planned behaviour (Krueger and Carsrud 1993; Kautonen et al. 2013). Finally, since the present work is explorative in its essence, further investigations are needed to confirm and deepen both the structure of the entrepreneurial social networks and relations, and of the effects of the interplay between gender stereotypes associated to entrepreneurship, both as national norms or masculine narrative, and the actual role played by the existence of uxorial social norms on entrepreneurship. Most of all, social network analyses are needed to detail the complete networks of both individuals and firms as required by a complete study of innovation systems. In the present approach, indeed, only individuals have been considered, in order to compare potential entrepreneurs and actual ones (as representative of small enterprises), but thus limiting seriously the relevance of innovative systems that encompass a much larger spectrum of businesses and economical entities.

References

Alh, H. (2006). Why research on women entrepreneurs needs new directions. *Entrepreneurship, Theory and Practice, 30*(5), 595–621.

Alvarez, S. A., & Busenitz, L. W. (2001). The entrepreneurship of resource-based theory. *Journal of Management, 27*, 755–775.

Amoros, J. E., & Bosma, N. (2013). *Global entrepreneurship monitor: 2013 Global report*. Babson Park, MA/London: Babson College/London Business School.

Angioni, G. (2005). La famiglia e la donna in Sardegna, annotazioni di studio.[The family and the woman in Sardinia, study notes]. *Lares, 71*(3), 487–498.

Assmuth, L. (1997). Women's work, women's worth: Changing life courses in Highland Sardinia. In *Transactions of the Finnish Anthropological Society* (Vol. 39). Finnish Anthropological Society.

Audretsch, D., & Fritsch, M. (2002). Growth regimes over time and space. *Regional Studies, 36*(2), 113–124.

Audretsch, D. B., Bönte, W., & Keilbach, M. (2008). Entrepreneurship capital and its impact on knowledge diffusion and economic performance. *Journal of Business Venturing, 23*, 687–698.

Bates, D., Maechler, M., Bolker, B., & Walker, S. (2015). Fitting linear mixed-effects models using lme4. *Journal of Statistical Software, 67*(1), 1–48. https://doi.org/10.18637/jss.v067.i01

Batterbury, S. C. (2002). Evaluating policy implementation: The European Union's small and medium sized enterprise policies in Galicia and Sardinia. *Regional Studies, 36*(8), 861–876.

Baughn, C. C., Chua, B.-L., & Neupert, K. E. (2006). The normative context for women's participation in entrepreneurship: A multicountry study. *Entrepreneurship, Theory and Practice, 30*(5), 687–708.

Bernardi, L., & Oppo, A. (2007). *Fertility and family configurations in Sardinia* (MPIDR working paper 033).

Beugelsdijk, S. (2007). Entrepreneurial culture, regional innovativeness and economic growth. *Journal of Evolutionary Economics, 17*(2), 187–210.

Birley, S. (1985). The role of networks in the entrepreneurial process. *Journal of Business Venturing, 1*(1), 107–117.

Bodemann, Y. M. (1982). Class rule as patronage: Kinship, local ruling cliques and the state in rural Sardinia. *The Journal of Peasant Studies, 9*(2), 147–175.

Boi, D., Giancola, P., Marinelli, B., Sinis, M., Fusco, A., & Piano, M. G. (1999). *Imprese di donne. Un'indagine sull'imprenditoria femminile in Sardegna* [Womenenterprises. An investigation on female entrepreneurship in Sardinia]. Milano: FrancoAngeli.

Breschi, S., & Lissoni, F. (2001). Knowledge spillovers and local innovation systems: A critical survey. *Industrial and Corporate Change, 10*(4), 975–1005.

Brindley, C. (2005). Barriers to women achieving their entrepreneurial potential women and risk. *International Journal of Entrepreneurial Behaviour & Research, 11*(2), 144–161.

Brockhaus, R. H. (1982). The psychology of the entrepreneur. In C. A. Kent, D. L. Sexton, & K. H. Vesper (Eds.), *Encyclopedia of entrepreneurship* (pp. 39–71). Englewood Cliffs, NJ: Prentice Hall.

Brush, C. G. (1992). Research on women business owners: Past trends, a new perspective and future directions. *Entrepreneurship, Theory and Practice, 16*(4), 5–30.

Brush, C. G., & Cooper, S. Y. (2012). Female entrepreneurship and economic development: An international perspective. *Entrepreneurship & Regional Development, 24*(1–2), 1–6.

Cantner, U., & Graf, H. (2004). The network of innovators in Jena: An application of social network analysis. *Research Policy, 35*, 463–480.

Cantner, U., & Graf, H. (2008). *Interaction structures in local innovation systems* (No. 2008, 040). Jena economic research papers.

Centro di Ricerche Economiche Nord Sud (CRENoS). (2010). *XVII Rapporto sull'Economia della Sardegna*. Cagliari: Centro di Ricerche Economiche Nord Sud.

Centro di Ricerche Economiche Nord Sud (CRENoS). (2014). *XXI Rapporto sull'Economia della Sardegna*. Cagliari: Centro di Ricerche Economiche Nord Sud.

Cerina, F. (2006). La dinamica del Pil e dei consumi: i dati regionali italiani [GDP dynamics and consumption: italian regioanl data]. In *CRENoS, Economia della Sardegna-XIII Rapporto 2006*. Cagliari: CUEC.

Cetindamar, D., Gupta, V. K., Karadeniz, E. E., & Egcrica, N. (2012). What the numbers tell: the impact of human, family and financial capital on women and men's entry into entrepreneurship in Turkey. *Entrepreneurship & Regional Development, 24*(1–2), 29–51.

Covin, J. G., & Slevin, D. P. (1989). Strategic management of small firms in hostile and benign environments. *Strategic Management Journal, 10*(1), 75–87.

Cubico, S., Bortolani, E., Favretto, G., & Sartori, R. (2010). Describing the entrepreneurial profile: The entrepreneurial aptitude test (TAI). *International Journal of Entrepreneurship and Small Business, 11*(4), 424–435.

Da Re, M. G. (1990). *La casa e I Campi. La Divisione Sessuale del Lavoro nella Sardegna Tradizionale* [The house and the fields. The sexual division of works in the traditional Sardinia]. Cagliari: CUEC.

De Tienne, D. R., & Chandler, G. N. (2007). The role of gender in opportunity identification. *Entrepreneurship, Theory and Practice, 31*(3), 365–386.

Di Caro, P., & Nicotra, G. (2015). Short, long and spatial dynamics of informal employment. *Regional Studies.* https://doi.org/10.1080/00343404.2015.1072274

Edquist, C., & Johnson, B. (1997). Institutions and organisations in systems of innovation. In C. Edquist (Ed.), *Systems of Innovation: Technologies, Institutions and Organizations* (pp. 41–63). London: Pinter.

Eller, C. (2011). *The myth of a matriarchal prehistory*. The University Press Group.

European Commission. (2011). *Programme under the Regional Competitiveness and Employment Objective, cofunded by the European Regional Development Fund* (ERDF). Accessed July 10, 2017, from http://ec.europa.eu/regional_policy/country/prordn/

Fischer, E. M., Reuber, A. R., & Dyke, L. S. (1993). A theoretical overview and extension of research on sex, gender, and entrepreneurship. *Journal of Business Venturing, 8*(2), 151–168.

Fritsch, M., & Mueller, P. (2004). Effects of new business formation on regional development over time. *Regional Studies, 38*(8), 961–975.

Fuentes, M. M. F., Arroyo, M. R., Bojica, A. M., & Perez, V. F. (2010). Prior knowledge and social networks in the exploitation of entrepreneurial opportunities. *International Entrepreneurship and Management Journal, 6*, 481–501.

García-Cabrera, A. M., & García-Soto, M. G. (2008). Cultural differences and entrepreneurial behaviour: An intra-country cross-cultural analysis in Cape Verde. *Entrepreneurship & Regional Development, 20*(5), 451–483.

Goktan, A. B., & Gupta, V. K. (2015). Sex, gender, and individual entrepreneurial orientation: Evidence from four countries. *International Entrepreneurship and Management Journal, 11*, 95–112.

Greve, A. (1995). Networks and entrepreneurship, an analysis of social relations, occupation background, and use of contacts during the establishment process. *Scandinavian Journal of Management, 11*(1), 1–24.

Grilo, I., & Thurik, R. (2004). *Determinants of entrepreneurship in Europe.* ERIM Report Series Research in Management.

Gupta, V. K., Turban, D. B., Arzu Wasti, S., & Sikdar, A. (2009). The role of gender stereotypes in perceptions of entrepreneurs and intentions to become an entrepreneur. *Entrepreneurship, Theory and Practice, 33*(2), 397–417.

Hamilton, E. (2013). The discourse of entrepreneurial masculinities (and femininities). *Entrepreneurship & Regional Development, 25*(1–2), 90–99.

Hisrich, R., Langan-Fox, J., & Grant, S. (2007). Entrepreneurship research and practice. *American Psychologist, 62*(6), 575–589.

Hoang, H., & Antoncic, B. (2003). Network-based research in entrepreneurship. A critical review. *Journal of Business Venturing, 18*, 165–187.

Hofstede, G. (2001). *Culture's consequences. comparing values, behaviors, institutions and organizations across nations* (2nd ed.). Thousand Oaks, CA: Sage Publications.

Hopp, C., & Stephan, U. (2012). The influence of socio-cultural environments on the performance of nascent entrepreneurs: Community culture, motivation, self-efficacy and start-up success. *Entrepreneurship & Regional Development, 24*(9/10), 917–945.

Hospers, G. J. (2003). Localization in Europe's periphery: Tourism development in Sardinia. *European Planning Studies, 11*(6), 629–645.

Hospers, G.-J., Desrochers, P., & Sautet, F. (2009). The next Silicon Valley? On the relationship between geographical clustering and public policy. *International Entrepreneurship and Management Journal, 5*, 285–299.

Kautonen, T., van Gelderen, M., & Fink, M. (2013). Robustness if the theory of planned behavior in predicting entrepreneurial intentions and actions. *Entrepreneurship, Theory and Practice.* https://doi.org/10.1111/etap.12056

Kelley, D., Brush, C., Greene, P., Herrington, M., Ali, A., & Kew, P. (2014). *Global entrepreneurship monitor special report on women's entrepreneurship.* Babson Park, MA/London: Babson College/London Business School.

Kim, S. M., & Sherraden, M. (2014). The impact of gender and social networks on microenterprise business performance. *Journal of Sociology & Social Welfare, 41*(3), 49–69.

King, R. (1977). Recent industrialisation in Sardinia: Rebirth or Neo-colonialism? *Erdkunde, 31*(2), 87–102.

Klapper, L. F., & Parker, S. C. (2011). Gender and the business environment for new firm creation. *The World Bank Research Observer, 26*(2), 237–257.

Klyver, K., & Grant, S. (2010). Gender differences in entrepreneurial networking and participation. *International Journal of Gender and Entrepreneurship, 2*(3), 213–227.

Klyver, K., Hindle, K., & Meyer, D. (2008). Influence of social network structure on entrepreneurship participation – A study of 20 national cultures. *International Entrepreneurship and Management Journal, 4,* 331–347.

Koellinger, P., Minniti, M., & Schade, C. (2013). Gender differences in entrepreneurial propensity. *Oxford Bulletin of Economics and Statistics.* https://doi.org/10.1111/j.1468-0084.2011.00689.x

Kotey, B. (2006). Entrepreneurship and regional development: A theoretical framework. *Small Enterprise Research, 14*(2), 20–45.

Krauss, S. I., Frese, M., Friedrich, C., & Unger, J. U. (2005). Entrepreneurial orientation: A psychological model of success among Southern African small business owners. *European Journal of and Organizational Psychology, 14,* 315–344.

Krueger, N. F., Jr., & Carsrud, A. L. (1993). Entrepreneurial intentions: Applying the theory of planned behaviour. *Entrepreneurship & Regional Development, 5,* 315–330.

Kunetsova, A., Brockhoff, P. B., & Christensen, R. H. B. (2014). Tests for random and fixed effects for linear mixed effect models (lmer objects of lme4 package) [Computer software manual]. Accessed July 10, 2017, from https://cran.r-project.org/web/packages/lmerTest/lmerTest.pdf

Langowitz, N., & Minniti, N. (2007). The entrepreneurial propensity of woman. *Entrepreneurship, Theory and Practice, 31*(3), 341–364.

Lumpkin, G. T., & Dess, G. G. (1996). Clarifying the entrepreneurial orientation construct and linking it to performance. *Academy of Management Review, 21*(1), 135–172.

Manolova, T., Brush, C. G., Edelman, L. F., & Shaver, K. G. (2012). One size does not fit all: Entrepreneurial expectancies and growth intentions of US women and men nascent entrepreneurs. *Entrepreneurship & Regional Development, 24*(1-2), 7–27.

Mariotti, S., & Piscitello, L. (2001). Localized capabilities and the internationalization of the manufacturing activities by SMEs. *Entrepreneurship & Regional Development, 13,* 65–80.

Marlow, S., & Swail, J. (2014). Gender, risk and finance pp. why can't a woman be more like a man? *Entrepreneurship & Regional Development, 26*(1–2), 80–96.

McDonald, F., Tsagdis, D., & Huang, Q. (2006). The development of industrial clusters and public policy. *Entrepreneurship & Regional Development, 18*(6), 525–542.

McPherson, M., Smith-Lovin, L., & Cook, J. M. (2001). Birds of a feather: Homophily in social network. *Annual Review of Sociology, 27,* 415–444.

Meccheri, N., & Pelloni, G. (2006). Rural entrepreneurs and institutional assistance: An empirical study from mountainous Italy. *Entrepreneurship & Regional Development, 18,* 371–392.

Miller, D. (1983). The correlates of entrepreneurship in three types of firms. *Management Science, 29*(7), 770–792.

Mitchell, R. K., Smith, B., Sewright, K. W., & Morse, E. A. (2000). Cross-cultural cognitions and the venture creation decision. *Academy of Management Journal, 43,* 974–993.

Mitchell, K. R., Busenitz, L., Lant, T., McDougall, P. P., Morse, E. A., & Smith, J. B. (2002). Entrepreneurial cognition: Rethinking the people side of entrepreneurship research. *Entrepreneurship, Theory and Practice, 27*(2), 93–206.

Mueller, S. L., & Dato-on, M. C. (2013). A cross cultural study of gender-role orientation and entrepreneurial self-efficacy. *International Entrepreneurship and Management Journal, 9,* 1–20.

Murphy, P. J., Liao, J., & Welsch, H. P. (2006). A conceptual history of entrepreneurial thought. *Journal of Management History, 12*(1), 12–35.

Murroni, C. (2006). *ICT and local development: A case study of the metropolitan area of Cagliari* (CRENoS working papers). Accessed July 10, 2017, from http://veprints.unica.it/234/1/04-19.pdf

Nongbri, T. (2008). *Gender, matriliny and entrepreneurship: The Khasis of North-East India.* New Delhi: Zubaan.

OECD. (2011). *Entrepreneurship at a Glance 2011.* Paris: OECD Publishing. Accessed July 10, 2017, from https://doi.org/10.1787/9789264097711-en

OECD. (2012). *Entrepreneurship at a Glance 2012.* Paris: OECD Publishing. Accessed July 10, 2017, from https://doi.org/10.1787/entrepreneur_aag-2012-en

OECD. (2015). *Entrepreneurship at a Glance 2015*. Paris: OECD Publishing. Accessed 10 July 2017, from https://doi.org/10.1787/entrepreneur_aag-2015-en

Oppo, A. (1990). Where there's no woman there's no home: Profile of the agro-pastoral family in nineteenth-century Sardinia. *Journal of Family History, 15*(1), 483–502.

Paci, R. (1999). L'evoluzione del Sistema economico della Sardegna negli anni novanta [The evolution of the economic system of Sardinia in the nineties]. *Contributi di Ricerca CRENoS, 00/1.* Cagliari: Università di Cagliari.

Pines, A. M., Lerner, M., & Schwartz, D. (2010). Gender differences in entrepreneurship. Equality, diversity and inclusion in times of global crisis. *Equality, Diversity and Inclusion: An International Journal, 29*(2), 186–198.

Pinheiro, J., Bates, D., DebRoy, S., Sarkar, D., & R Core Team. (2017). *nlme: Linear and nonlinear mixed effects models.* R package version 3 (pp. 1–131). Accessed July 10, 2017, from https://CRAN. R-project.org/package=nlme

Pitzalis-Acciaro, M. (1978). *In Nome della Madre. Ipotesi sul Matriarcato Barbaricino* [In the name of the mother hypothesis on the Barbaricino Matriarchy]. Milano: Feltrinelli.

Popielarz, P. A. (1999). Organizational constraints on personal network formation. In S. B. Andrews & D. Knoke (Eds.), *Research in the sociology of organizations* (Vol 16, pp. 263–281). Stamford, CT: JAI Press.

Pulina, M., & Biagi, B. (2006). Regional public policy and tourism life cycle: The case of Sardinia. *46th Congress of the European Regional Science Association* University of Thessaly (Greece), 30 August–3 September 2006. Accessed July 10, 2017, from http://www-sre.wu-wien.ac.at/ ersa/ersaconfs/ersa06/papers/65.pdf

R Development Core Team. (2017). *R: A language and environment for statistical computing.* R Foundation for Statistical Computing, Vienna, Austria. Accessed July 10, 2017, from https://www.r-project.org/

Rauch, A., & Frese, M. (2007). Born to be entrepreneur? Revisiting the personality approach to entrepreneurship. In J. R. Baum, M. Frese, & R. Baron (Eds.), *The psychology of entrepreneurship* (pp. 41–65). Mahawah: Lawrence Erlbaum Associates.

Renzulli, L., Aldrich, H., & Moody, J. (2000). Family matters: Gender, networks, and entrepreneurial outcomes. *Social Forces, 79*, 523–546.

Revelle, W. (2017). *Psych: Procedures for personality and psychological research.* Northwestern University, Evanston, IL. Accessed July 10, 2017, from http://CRAN.R-project.org/ package=psych

Robinson, P. B., & Sexton, E. A. (1994). The effect of education and experience on self-employment success. *Journal of Business Venturing, 9*(3), 141–156.

Rosti, L., & Chelli, F. (2005). Gender discrimination, entrepreneurial talent and self-employment. *Small Business Economics, 24*, 131–142.

Ruef, M. (2002). Strong ties, weak ties and islands: Structural and cultural predictors of organizational innovation. *Industrial and Corporate Change, 11*(3), 427–449.

Sackmann, S. A., & Phillips, M. E. (2004). Contextual influences on culture research: Shifting assumptions for new workplace realities. *International Journal of Cross Cultural Management, 4*(3), 370–390.

Sammarra, A., & Belussi, F. (2006). Evolution and relocation in fashion-led Italian districts: Evidence from two case-studies. *Entrepreneurship and Regional Development, 18*(6), 543–562.

Schaalje, G. B., McBride, J. B., & Fellingham, G. W. (2002). Adequacy of approximations to distributions of test statistics in complex mixed linear models. *Journal of Agricultural, Biological, and Environmental Statistics, 7*(4), 512–524.

Shinnar, R. S., Giacomin, O., & Janssen, F. (2012). Entrepreneurial perceptions and intentions: The role of gender and culture. *Entrepreneurship, Theory and Practice, 36*(3), 465–493.

Shneor, R., Camgöz, S. M., & Karapinar, P. B. (2013). The interaction between culture and sex in the formation of entrepreneurial intentions. *Entrepreneurship & Regional Development, 25* (9-10), 781–803.

Thompson, P., Jones-Evans, D., & Kwong, C. (2009). Women and home based entrepreneurship: Evidence from the UK. *International Small Business Journal, 27*(2), 227–240.

Tung, R. (2008). The cross-cultural research imperative: The need to balance cross-national and intra-national diversity. *Journal of International Business Studies, 39*, 41–46.

van der Zwan, P., Verheul, I., & Thurik, A. R. (2012). The entrepreneurial ladder, gender and regional development. *Small business Economics, 39*, 627–643.

Walter, S. G., Parboteeah, K. P., & Walter, A. (2013). University departments and self-employment intentions of business students: A cross-level analysis. *Entrepreneurship, Theory and Practice, 37*(2), 175–200.

Warneke, T. (2013). Entrepreneurship and gender: An institutional perspective. *Journal of Economic Issues, 47*(2). https://doi.org/10.2753/JEI0021-3624470219

Welter, F., Trettin, L., & Neumann, U. (2008). Fostering entrepreneurship in distressed urban neighbourhoods. *International Entrepreneurship and Management Journal, 4*, 109–128.

Wilson, F., Kickul, J., & Marlino, R. (2007). Gender, entrepreneurial self-efficacy, and entrepreneurial career intentions: Implications for entrepreneurship education. *Entrepreneurship, Theory and Practice, 31*(3), 387–406.

Zander, L., & Romani, L. (2004). When nationality matters: A study of departmental, hierarchical, professional, gender and age-based employee groupings' leadership preferences across 15 countries. *International Journal of Cross Cultural Management, 4*(3), 291–315.

Zhang, J. (2010). The problems of using social networks in entrepreneurial resource acquisition. *International Small Business Journal, 28*, 338–361.

Zhao, H., & Siebert, S. E. (2006). The big five personality dimension and entrepreneurial status: A meta-analytical review. *Journal of Applied Psychology, 91*(2), 259–271.

Zhao, H., Seibert, S. E., & Hills, G. E. (2005). The mediating role of self-efficacy in the development of entrepreneurial intentions. *Journal of Applied Psychology, 90*(6), 1265–1272.

Co-leadership and Performance in Technology-Based Entrepreneurial Firms

Daniel Pittino, Francesca Visintin, and Cristiana Compagno

Abstract The notion of co-leadership, defined as a structural arrangement where the formal responsibilities at the top of the company are attributed to multiple persons, is receiving increasing attention in recent years as one of the possible conceptualizations of the leadership "in plural form". Our research aims at exploring the performance implications of co-leadership arrangements in the top management teams (TMTs) of technology based entrepreneurial firms, and at evaluating how such impact is likely to occur. The study is carried out on a sample of technology based entrepreneurial firms operating in Italy. Our study contributes mainly to the literature on co-leadership, by identifying different structural configurations of plural leadership and by shedding some light on the paths through which co-leadership arrangements have an impact on company performance.

Keywords Entrepreneurship · Co-leadership · Decision making · Teams

1 Introduction

The notion of co-leadership is receiving increasing attention in recent years in relation to company performance and change as one of the various conceptualizations of the leadership "in plural form". Distributed leadership (Gronn 2002), shared leadership (Pearce and Sims 2002), collaborative leadership (Rosenthal 1998) are other examples of constructs that, in one way or another, involve the combined influence of multiple leaders in specific organizational situations (Denis et al. 2012).

D. Pittino
Jönköping International Business School, Jönköping University, Jönköping, Sweden

F. Visintin (✉) · C. Compagno
Department of Economics and Statistics, University of Udine, Udine, Italy
e-mail: Francesca.visintin@uniud.it

© Springer International Publishing AG, part of Springer Nature 2018
S. Cubico et al. (eds.), *Entrepreneurship and the Industry Life Cycle*, Studies on Entrepreneurship, Structural Change and Industrial Dynamics,
https://doi.org/10.1007/978-3-319-89336-5_5

Co-leadership can be defined as a structural arrangement where the formal respon-sibilities at the top of the company are attributed to multiple persons (Heenan and Bennis 1999; Hambrick and Cannella 2004). Although this idea may appear contra-dictory, since leadership is typically analysed and portrayed as an individual trait (Hackman 2002), situations were the company power at the top is jointly held are increasingly common, due to the growing complexity of organizations, competitive environments and stakeholders' demands (Pearce and Conger 2003; Alvarez and Svejenova 2005).

There are several examples of partnerships at the top in large global companies: Google Inc., General Electric, Goldman Sachs, SAP are among the organizations that have been presented as successful or promising experiences of co-leadership, involving top executives with complementary skills, roles and responsibilities. On the other hand, popular failure cases include Unilever and Kraft, or Research in Motion, the Canadian high tech company, where founders' co-leadership turned from a celebrated asset into a liability.

However, despite its empirical relevance and theoretical appeal, the phenomenon of co-leadership has so far received scant attention in the academic literature. The extensive work on corporate elites drawing from the upper echelons theory (Finkelstein et al. 2009) focused either on hierarchical top management teams or on individual leaders, whereas the corporate governance literature analyses plural leadership as a means of power balance and monitoring (e.g. Goyal and Park 2002; Miller et al. 2014).

The studies addressing the effectiveness of co-leadership as a distinct phenome-non and its impact on performance and change are few in number, generally lack a consistent theoretical framework and produce conflicting results (Denis et al. 2012). In this work, we will therefore address this gap, studying the performance conse-quences of co-leadership arrangements in small technology-based firms. We decided to focus on such firms since so far research on co-leadership has almost exclusively examined large publicly listed companies (e.g. Hambrick and Cannella 2004; Krause et al. 2014; Zhang 2006), and also because we believe that the understanding of the impact of co-leadership arrangements as well as the extension of leadership theory to plural arrangements will benefit from context-based research, which is aimed at assessing the effectiveness of organizational and managerial practices not in univer-sal terms, but with respect to relevant situational factors (Johns 2006).

In particular, technology-based firms are more frequently founded and managed by entrepreneurial co-leaders rather than single entrepreneurs, since the research leading to the business idea is often the outcome of a group effort. Moreover, co-leaders seem to handle the high levels of environmental variety and uncertainty characterizing the science and technology-based sectors better than single entrepre-neurs (e.g. Schjoedt and Kraus 2009).

Our research thus aims at exploring the performance implications of co-leadership arrangements in the top management teams (TMTs) of technology based entrepreneurial firms, and at evaluating some of the causal mechanisms through which such impact is likely to occur. The study is carried out on a sample of small technology based firms operating in Italy. Our study contributes mainly to the literature on co-leadership, by identifying different structural configurations of plural leadership and by shedding some light on the paths through which co-leadership arrangements have an impact on company performance.

2 Co-leadership in the Literature

As observed by Krause et al. (2014), the theory addressing the plural forms of leadership is still in its initial stages, and therefore it often suffers from a lack of definitional clarity. Labels such as: shared leadership, collaborative leadership, distributed leadership, pooled leadership, are used rather interchangeably in the studies, indicating also that there are no established typologies or taxonomies of forms of plural leadership. So far, empirical research addressing co-leadership is predominantly based on anecdotal evidence or case studies and has often descriptive/ illustrative purposes (e.g. Gronn 1999; Gronn and Hamilton 2004; O'Toole et al. 2002; see Denis et al. 2012 for a detailed review). There is also a growing number of sample-based analyses, carried out on large publicly listed firms, which have mainly an exploratory purpose (e.g. Arena et al. 2011; Hambrick and Cannella 2004; Krause et al. 2014; Zhang 2006; Marcel 2009).

Drawing from the organizational contingency theory (Lawrence and Lorsch 1967) these studies suggest that the adoption of a co-leadership arrangement is a response through which the organization strives to align its leadership structure to the demands of the situational context.

According to this perspective, the environmental dynamism and the organizational task demands have been identified as the main drivers for the adoption of co-leadership arrangements (Hambrick and Cannella 2004). This is for example the case of the CEO-COO duo investigated by Hambrick and Cannella (2004) and Marcel (2009). External pressures may also come in the form of diverse institutional claims: the plurality of external constituencies and the related ambiguity of the company mission can generate competing logics which are pursued by the organization through plural leadership arrangements (Alvarez and Svejenova 2005). Similar arguments apply to the organizational task demands: organizational size, diversification, acquisition activity increase the administrative complexity and the variety of competences required to effectively lead the company, and thus encourage the adoption of co-leadership forms (Arena et al. 2011; Marcel 2009; Pearce and Conger 2003). Summarizing, it seems that co-leadership improves company performance when it realises a contingent fit between the power structure at the top and the internal and external environment.

Other than the contingent factors, additional explanations have been proposed for the emergence of collegial leadership structures at the top. Co-leadership for example has been viewed as the outcome of an isomorphic behaviour (DiMaggio and Powell 1983), according to which the decision makers facing uncertain situations tend to imitate what seems to work in other settings. Another explanation, rooted in the agency theory, is that co-leadership might be seen as an expression of excess of power and opportunism by the decision makers: for example, a powerful CEO may appoint a COO or a co-CEO to have more time to spend in external relationships that increase his/her own status and prestige, or to have a scapegoat in case of performance problems, and in general, to take advantage of resource slacks and poor monitoring systems (Hambrick and Cannella 2004).

The empirical results concerning the impact of co-leadership on financial performance have been mixed: Hambrick and Cannella (2004) found a negative relationship between the presence of a CEO–COO duo and the ROA performance; Marcel finds a positive impact of the CEO–COO duo on ROA performance; Arena et al. (2011) study the relationship between co-CEOs leadership and performance and find a positive association with market to book value, but negative although not significant relationship with the ROA performance. Krause et al. (2014) take a step forward, by analysing the power gap within co-CEOs arrangements, and its relationship to performance in a sample of publicly listed firms. Their results indicate that the power gap between CEOs is positively related to company profitability.

Overall, it seems that the rather inconclusive nature of findings requires a more fine-grained definition of the co-leadership arrangements and a better understanding of the mechanisms and behaviours linking co-leadership arrangements and performance.

3 Co-leadership and Performance in Technology-Based Entrepreneurial Firms

Technology-based entrepreneurial firms are an especially interesting context for the study of the forms and effects of co-leadership, because in these companies the presence of teams at the top is rather common and the impact of the leaders on the organizational performance is not mediated or constrained by articulated structures (Daily et al. 2002; Klotz et al. 2014).

In technology intensive environments, teams have an advantage over single leaders in coping simultaneously with heterogeneous and dynamic external conditions and internal complex knowledge and technological issues. Moreover, in technology-based entrepreneurial firms, the business idea and the subsequent founding of the company are often the outcome of a group effort, which lately translates in the establishment of a team at the top (Lechler 2001; Schjoedt and Kraus 2009). For these main reasons, the study of TMTs in technology-based entrepreneurial firms has received increasing attention in recent years (see Klotz et al. 2014 for a review of the literature). However, very few contributions deal with the structure of leadership and particularly with the emergence of plural leadership in these companies (e.g. Ensley et al. 2006; Hmieleski et al. 2012).

Combining this scant literature with the existing conceptualizations of plural leadership (Denis et al. 2012), we propose that the co-leadership in the TMTs of the technology based entrepreneurial firms may assume two configurations. The first configuration, which we name *shared leadership*, as defined by Ensley et al. (2006), is characterized by the equal and undifferentiated attribution of organizational leadership across TMT members. In these arrangements, each member has the same structural power in the company management (for example, all the members hold the formal CEO title) (Carson et al. 2007; Krause et al. 2014) and at the same time, company leadership is carried out by the team as a whole, with various degrees and forms of mutual influence among the members (Ensley et al. 2006; Pearce 2004).

The second configuration, which we label as *distributed leadership* (Gronn 2002), implies a sort of "division of labour" in the exercise of the organizational leadership. In this setting, there is a role specialization among the co-leaders, such that each one is in charge for a different group of tasks consistent with his/her expertise and competences. In the case of technology-based firms, for example, we could observe a specialization between co-leaders according to scientific-technological decisions and administrative/commercial ones.

These two leadership configurations are alternative to the situation where one individual emerges or is designated as the principal leader, and exerts varying degrees of hierarchical influence on the other members of the TMT (Ensley et al. 2000).

We argue that, compared to the situation of individual leadership, entrepreneurial firms in high technology sectors are more likely to benefit from the co-leadership configurations, either shared or distributed, since these arrangements allow for a better fit with the heterogeneity of the environment (e.g. Alvarez and Svejenova 2005), promote a more effective use of the distinctive professional expertise by each member, and at the same time, enable the team to fully take advantage of multiple leaders' complementary knowledge, fostering creative decision-making and more accurate critical assessment (Cox et al. 2003; Krause et al. 2014).

Thus, we propose that:

Hypothesis 1 *Co-leadership configurations, either shared or distributed, are positively related to company performance in entrepreneurial technology-based firms.*

3.1 The Mediating Role of TMT Decision Making Process

It is reasonable to argue that the structural configurations of leadership influence company performance mainly in an indirect way, through the processes taking place at the TMT level. In particular, different leadership arrangements may lead to different ways of decision making at the top of the company. The nature of decision making in TMTs ranges from autocratic through consultative, ending in team-based/participative forms (Eisenhardt 1989; Vroom and Yetton 1973). In the autocratic form, the decision maker individually gathers and processes information, develops a course of action, and then directs the implementation of the decision throughout the organization (Arendt et al. 2005). In the consultative form, the decision maker solicits information and advice from other members of the team but then makes the final decision alone (Vroom and Yetton 1973). In the participative form, the decision maker is the team as a whole: TMT members provide information to the group, jointly propose and evaluate alternative courses of action, manage disagreements to reach consensus, and together participate in the implementation of the decision (Arendt et al. 2005).

According to the input-process-output perspective in the study of the groups (Tannenbaum et al. 1992), the decision making modes, as other team processes, are directly influenced by the social structure of the TMT, in terms of roles and hierarchical relationships among members (Cohen and Bailey 1997; Stewart and Barrick 2000). Since the configuration of leadership is crucial in determining the social structure of the team, we can argue that different configurations of the leadership encourage or hinder the adoption of different modes of decision making. For example, individual leadership might favour the emergence of autocratic decision making, whereas a shared leadership structure could promote more participative forms.

In sum:

Hypothesis 2 *The leadership configuration in terms of individual or co-leadership arrangements influences the nature of decision-making process in the TMTs of technology based entrepreneurial firms.*

The nature of the decision making process, in turn, is likely to directly influence the company performance. Regarding this effect in technology based firms, two contrasting arguments can be made. The first one emphasizes the importance of an autocratic decisional process in highly dynamic settings. A centralized system, relying on a single individual for the information processing and the evaluation and implementation of alternatives, is more appropriate in a rapidly changing environment, compared to a participative system aimed at reaching consensus over the strategic decisions (Eisenhardt 1989, 2013).

If the dynamism of the context seems to favour a top-down approach to decision making, other features of technology based entrepreneurial firms encourage cooperation and integration. These companies face high degrees of both market and scientific-technological uncertainty and cope with this situation through the differentiation in their TMT structure in terms of members' backgrounds and functional expertise (e.g. Cannella et al. 2008). In order to fully capture the advantages of differentiation, the team needs to integrate the diverse perspectives in a unified strategic vision (Ensley and Pearce 2001; Ensley et al. 2003). It has been widely demonstrated, for example, that successful innovations carried out in technology intensive industries emerge from the effective integration of knowledge from different domains and at different organizational levels (e.g. Grant 1996; Hoopes and Postrel 1999; Verona 1999). At the TMT level, the integration of knowledge in unified goals is promoted by collaborative decision-making processes (e.g. Buyl et al. 2014; Lubatkin et al. 2006).

The outlined arguments, thus suggest opposite effects of autocratic versus collaborative decision making on organizational outcomes. However, both views emphasize the tight connection between TMT decision-making processes and company performance, and allow us to formulate the following:

Hypothesis 3 *The type of decision-making process in the TMTs of technology based entrepreneurial firms is related to company performance.*

Which, together with the Hypothesis 2 leads to the final:

Hypothesis 4 *The relationship between co-leadership and performance in technology based entrepreneurial firms is mediated by the TMT decision-making process.*

4 Methodology

4.1 Sample

Data have been collected on a sample of 99 entrepreneurial firms operating in technology-intensive sectors in Italy. Companies were drawn from the population of 745 firms that in the year 2009 were officially listed in the directory NETVAL of Italian companies which have been established as a result of technology transfer from universities and research institutions. Within this population, we decided to focus on the companies that were founded before the year 2004, since our aim was to target companies that have overcome the start-up phase and have reached some degree of maturity [those that Bantel (1997), for example, defines as "adolescent" technology-based firms]. This reduced the population of interest to 428 companies. Within this group we selected the companies that are led by teams having at least three members. Information was available directly from the NETVAL database. This further reduced our sample to 308 companies. In November 2010 these firms were then contacted in a first round of invitations to assess their willingness to participate to the research. Eighty-eight enterprises agreed to participate the first round of contacts.

Data on the participants were collected both from primary and secondary sources. Information on leadership structure and decision making process was collected through an online survey. Secondary data were also collected from the Italian Registry of Companies, held by the Italian network of Chambers of Commerce, and from the Amadues—Bureau Van Dijk database. Non-respondent bias was assessed through an analysis on 27 additional firms that agreed to participate after a second round of contacts. No significant differences were found between this group and a matched sample of the firms participating in the first round. The resulting sample was therefore made up of 115 companies. Since we investigated team-level processes and constructs, we asked each TMT member of the company to answer the questionnaire. We obtained a total of 194 responses and 58 of the 115 firms have multiple respondents.

We performed t-tests to investigate differences in the distributions of responses in single respondent and multiple respondent firms. No significant differences were found. In the subsequent step we excluded from the sample the firms that provided incomplete information, ending up with 99 companies. Finally, we matched the companies with their filings in the Amadeus database and in the database of the Italian Chambers of Commerce, to obtain financial data, as well as secondary information on the TMT and the leadership structure, which was compared with the questionnaire responses to check and resolve possible inconsistencies.

4.2 Variables

4.2.1 Dependent Variable

Company performance was measured by the average return on assets (ROA) over a 4 years period (2010–2013). This measure was preferred to other metrics usually employed in the case of young firms (for example, growth rate in sales and employees) because our companies are no longer in the start-up phase and the use of ROA also increases the comparability of our results, since it is commonly used in the studies that assess the impact of strategic leadership on company performance (Finkelstein et al. 2009).

4.2.2 Independent Variables

Leadership Structure

Companies were classified according to their leadership structure. We distinguished between situations of single leadership, distributed leadership and shared leadership. Respondents were asked to indicate whether their company had either a single individual formally appointed or recognized as leader (single leadership), different leaders according to different groups of tasks and functions (distributed leadership), or all the TMT members equally in charge of the overall company leadership (shared leadership). Responses were compared with the formal positions reported in the secondary datasets to identify and resolve possible inconsistencies. We then constructed three dichotomous variables accounting for the presence/absence of each type of leadership.

Decision Making Process

The decision making process adopted in the TMTs was classified according to the Vroom and Yetton's decision making styles (Vroom and Yetton 1973; Arendt et al. 2005). We constructed three dichotomous variables accounting for the presence/ absence of each type of leadership structure.

Respondents were asked to evaluate their team's decision making process on a five point scale, where each point of the scale is described by one of the decision making styles ranked by Vroom and Yetton, according to the degree of participation in the decision process. Responses where further grouped in three categories reflecting (1) autocratic decision making process (2) consultative decision making (3) participative decision making. The company membership in each category was then used to define three dichotomous variables.

Control Variables

We used company size and TMT size as our control variables.
Descriptive statistics and correlation of our variables are reported in Table 1.

4.3 *Estimation Technique*

We performed an OLS regression to estimate the relationship between co-leadership and performance and between decision-making process and performance. The relationship between co-leadership and decision making process was estimated through three probit regressions, where the dependent variables are the dichotomous measures accounting for the presence of autocratic, consultative or participative decision making.

Finally, we tested for the mediation effect of decision making by entering in different regressions the decision making process together with the co-leadership and then by assessing, according to Baron and Kenny's (1986) procedure, if the effect of co-leadership in performance previously estimated is significantly reduced by the inclusion of the variables accounting for decision making.

5 Results

Regression analysis reported in Table 2 provides support to our Hypothesis 1 only with respect to the distributed form of co-leadership. The adoption of a distributed leadership structure is positively related to performance compared to the alternative structures, namely single and shared leadership. On the other hand, and contrarily to our expectations, a shared co-leadership is negatively related to performance, although with a borderline level of significance.

Our test of the association between leadership structure and decision making process reveals that the probability to adopt an autocratic decision making is negatively affected by the use of shared leadership. Shared leadership in turn, increases the likelihood that a participative decision making process takes place. The likelihood to observe a consultative decision making process, finally, is

Table 1 Descriptives and correlations

	Mean	s.d.	1	2	3	4	5	6	7	8	9
1 Single leadership	0.24	0.43	1.00								
2 Distributed leadership	0.51	0.50	-0.57	1.00							
3 Shared leadership	0.25	0.43	-0.32	-0.59	1.00						
4 Autocratic DM	0.19	0.39	0.27	-0.08	-0.17	1.00					
5 Consultative DM	0.49	0.50	-0.12	0.18	-0.09	-0.47	1.00				
6 Participative DM	0.32	0.47	-0.09	-0.13	0.24	-0.33	-0.68	1.00			
7 Team size	2.35	1.73	0.08	-0.07	0.00	0.08	0.28	-0.37	1.00		
8 Performance	1.44	10.19	-0.07	0.19	-0.15	-0.30	0.32	-0.09	-0.08	1.00	
9 Firm size	683.77	1433	0.06	-0.02	-0.03	0.07	0.10	-0.17	-0.10	0.30	1.00

Correlations greater than 0.15 or less than -0.15 are significant at $p < 0.05$

Table 2 OLS regression analyses of the effect of co-leadership configurations on performance

	(1)	(2)	(3)
Firm size	0.00***	0.00***	0.00***
		(0.00)	(0.00)
TMT size	−0.22	−0.08	−0.17
	(0.49)	(0.50)	(0.32)
Distributed leadership		3.98**	
		(1.67)	
Shared leadership			−3.24†
			(1.92)
Constant	−0.47	−2.75	0.32
	(1.54)	(1.84)	(1.65)
N	99	99	99
F-statistic	9.98***	7.14***	6.09***
R^2	0.13	0.17	0.15

Standard errors in parenthesis
†means not significant; ***means signficant at the 0.01 level while **at 0.05

Table 3 Probit regression analyses of the effect of co-leadership configurations on decision making process

	Autocratic	Consultative	Participative
Firm size	0.00	0.00	0.00
	(0.00)	(0.00)	(0.00)
TMT size	0.06	0.25	−0.46
	(0.06)	(0.26)	(0.50)
Distributed leadership	−0.68†	0.71***	−0.17
	(0.28)	(0.22)	(0.29)
Shared leadership	−1.13***	0.18	0.91***
	(0.38)	(0.31)	(0.31)
Constant	−0.32	−0.56*	−2.24
	(0.24)	(0.24)	(2.21)
N	99	99	99
Log likelihood	−64.38	−85.37	−80.96
LR chi-square	11.79***	25.54**	4.16***

Standard errors in parenthesis
†means not significant; ***means significant at the 0.01 level, **at 0.05 and *at 0.10

positively related to the distributed leadership structure (Table 3). Overall these results provide support to our Hypothesis 2.

Hypothesis 3 suggests that the decision making process affects company performance. Our results (Table 4) reveal that consultative decision making is positively related to performance, whereas participative decision making has a negative, although small, effect on performance, and autocratic decision making has greater negative impact on performance. Hypothesis 3 is thus supported.

The relationships suggested in Hypothesis 3 were then used to test the mediation effect between leadership structure and performance (Table 5). The test for

Table 4 OLS regression analyses of the effect of decision making process on performance

	(1)	(2)	(3)
Firm size	0.00***	0.00***	0.00***
	(0.00)	(0.00)	(0.00)
TMT size	−0.84	−0.34	−0.57
	(0.52)	(0.56)	(0.50)
Consultative DM	6.80***		10.42***
	(1.71)		(2.18)
Participative DM		−1.14	6.14***
		(1.98)	(2.33)
Constant	−2.40	0.32	−7.50***
	(1.84)	(1.65)	(2.21)
N	99	99	99
F-statistic	10.09***	5.31***	10.98***
R^2	0.20	0.10	0.24

Standard errors in parenthesis
***means significant at the 0.01 level

Table 5 Mediating effect of decision making in the relationship between co-leadership and performance

	(Block 1) Distributed leadership	(Block 2) Consultative DM	(Block 1) Shared leadership	(Block 2) Participative DM
Firm size	0.00***	0.00***	0.00***	0.00***
	(0.00)	(0.00)	(0.00)	(0.00)
TMT size	−0.08	−0.70	−0.17	−0.57
	(0.50)	(0.50)	(0.32)	(0.50)
Distributed leadership	**3.98****	**2.42**		
	(1.67)	**(1.68)**		
Shared leadership			−3.24[†]	−3.23[†]
			(1.92)	(2.04)
Consultative DM		**6.11*****		
		(2.18)		
Participative DM				−0.18
				(2.05)
Constant	−2.75	−3.28*	0.32	−0.37
	(1.84)	(1.80)	(1.65)	(2.03)
N	99	99	99	99
F-statistic	7.14***	5.37***	6.09***	4.46***
R^2	0.14	0.21	0.12	0.09

Standard errors in parenthesis
[†]means not significant; ***means significant at the 0.01 level, **at 0.05 and *at 0.10

mediation indicates that the consultative decision making process mediates the relationship between distributed leadership and performance. The second regression involving distributed leadership and including consultative decision making shows that the coefficient of the distributed leadership is smaller compared to the regression with only the distributed leadership variable. On the other hand, the coefficient of the variable consultative decision-making is significant. There is also an improvement in the R^2 of the regression. On the other hand, there is no mediation effect by the participative decision making in the (negative) relationship between shared leadership and performance. Hypothesis 4 is therefore supported regarding the relationship between distributed leadership—consultative decision making and performance.

6 Discussion, Conclusion and Limitations

Our results provide some interesting evidence about the relationship between forms of co-leadership and performance. First of all, the two different forms of co-leadership we investigated have opposite effects on the performance of technology-based entrepreneurial firms. Shared leadership has a negative impact on performance whereas distributed leadership has a positive effect. This suggests, among other things, that previous studies addressing shared leadership and reporting positive correlations between shared leadership and performance (e.g. Ensley et al. 2006) might have been inaccurate in differentiating actual shared leadership from other forms of co-leadership. The positive effect of distributed leadership on company performance occurs through the mediation of a consultative decision making process. This suggests that in technology-based entrepreneurial firms a "division of labour" among co-leaders is an appropriate choice, and each co-leader should be in charge of a sub-set of issues and/or different segments of the task environment. Moreover, in the decisions regarding each area of responsibility the co-leaders are rather autonomous and seek advice from the other members, but do not expect a full consensus on the decisions they are implementing. This is consistent with the previously documented effectiveness of consultative decision-making style among high-technology firms (Buyl et al. 2014) and with the validity of the CEO-adviser strategic decision making model (Arendt et al. 2005).

On the other hand, it seems that the negative effect of shared leadership on performance does not occur through a causal path involving decision-making, thus there are probably other factors originating from shared co-leadership structure that might be detrimental for performance.

By highlighting some paths and dismissing others, this second set of results sheds some light on the mechanisms through which co-leadership affects organizational outcomes and thus contributes to the studies linking co-leadership to performance.

Our study has certainly some limitations. The main ones arise from the sample, which is rather limited, although in line with previous studies on this topic. Moreover, it is still a matter of concern that only a fraction of our sample is made up by companies with multiple TMT members responding. This could be still a threat to the validity of our results, even if we tested for the existence of significant differences between the single respondent and multiple respondents groups.

References

Alvarez, J. L., & Svejenova, S. (2005). *Sharing executive power: Roles and relationships at the top.* Cambridge: Cambridge University Press.

Arena, M. P., Ferris, S. P., & Unlu, E. (2011). It takes two: The incidence and effectiveness of Co-CEOs. *Financial Review, 46*(3), 385–412.

Arendt, L. A., Priem, R. L., & Ndofor, H. A. (2005). A CEO-adviser model of strategic decision making. *Journal of Management, 31*(5), 680–699.

Bantel, K. A. (1997). Performance in adolescent, technology-based firms: Product strategy, implementation, and synergy. *The Journal of High Technology Management Research, 8*(2), 243–262.

Baron, R. M., & Kenny, D. A. (1986). The moderator–mediator variable distinction in social psychological research: Conceptual, strategic, and statistical considerations. *Journal of Personality and Social Psychology, 51*(6), 1173.

Buyl, T., Boone, C., & Hendriks, W. (2014). Top management team members' decision influence and cooperative behaviour: An empirical study in the information technology industry. *British Journal of Management, 25*(2), 285–304.

Cannella, A. A., Park, J. H., & Lee, H. U. (2008). Top management team functional background diversity and firm performance: Examining the roles of team member colocation and environmental uncertainty. *Academy of Management Journal, 51*(4), 768–784.

Carson, J. B., Tesluk, P. E., & Marrone, J. A. (2007). Shared leadership in teams: An investigation of antecedent conditions and performance. *Academy of Management Journal, 50*(5), 1217–1234.

Cohen, S. G., & Bailey, D. E. (1997). What makes teams work: Group effectiveness research from the shop floor to the executive suite. *Journal of Management, 23*(3), 239–290.

Cox, J. F., Pearce, C. L., & Perry, M. L. (2003). Toward a model of shared leadership and distributed influence in the innovation process: How shared leadership can enhance new product development team dynamics and effectiveness. In C. L. Pearce & J. A. Conger (Eds.), *Shared leadership: Reframing the hows and whys of leadership* (pp. 48–76). Thousand Oaks, CA: Sage.

Daily, C. M., McDougall, P. P., Covin, J. G., & Dalton, D. R. (2002). Governance and strategic leadership in entrepreneurial firms. *Journal of Management, 28*(3), 387–412.

Denis, J. L., Langley, A., & Sergi, V. (2012). Leadership in the plural. *The Academy of Management Annals, 6*(1), 211–283.

DiMaggio, P., & Powell, W. W. (1983). The iron cage revisited: Collective rationality and institutional isomorphism in organizational fields. *American Sociological Review, 48*(2), 147–160.

Eisenhardt, K. M. (1989). Making fast strategic decisions in high-velocity environments. *Academy of Management Journal, 32*(3), 543–576.

Eisenhardt, K. M. (2013). Top management teams and the performance of entrepreneurial firms. *Small Business Economics, 40*(4), 805–816.

Ensley, M. D., & Pearce, C. L. (2001). Shared cognition in top management teams: Implications for new venture performance. *Journal of Organizational Behavior, 22*(2), 145–160.

Ensley, M. D., Garland, J. W., & Carland, J. C. (2000). Investigating the existence of the lead entrepreneur. *Journal of Small Business Management, 38*(4), 59.

Ensley, M. D., Pearson, A., & Pearce, C. L. (2003). Top management team process, shared leadership, and new venture performance: A theoretical model and research agenda. *Human Resource Management Review, 13*(2), 329–346.

Ensley, M. D., Hmieleski, K. M., & Pearce, C. L. (2006). The importance of vertical and shared leadership within new venture top management teams: Implications for the performance of startups. *The Leadership Quarterly, 17*(3), 217–231.

Finkelstein, S., Hambrick, D. C., & Cannella, A. A. (2009). *Theory and research on executives, top management teams, and boards.* Oxford: Oxford University Press.

Goyal, V. K., & Park, C. W. (2002). Board leadership structure and CEO turnover. *Journal of Corporate Finance, 8*(1), 49–66.

Grant, R. M. (1996). Prospering in dynamically-competitive environments: Organizational capability as knowledge integration. *Organization Science, 7*(4), 375–387.

Gronn, P. (1999). Substituting for leadership: The neglected role of the leadership couple. *The Leadership Quarterly, 10*(1), 41–62.

Gronn, P. (2002). Distributed leadership as a unit of analysis. *Leadership Quarterly, 13*(4), 423–451.

Gronn, P., & Hamilton, A. (2004). A bit more life in the leadership: Co-principalship as distributed leadership practice. *Leadership and Policy in Schools, 3*(1), 3–35.

Hackman, J. R. (2002). *Leading teams: Setting the stage for great performances*. Boston: Harvard Business Press.

Hambrick, D. C., & Cannella, A. A., Jr. (2004). CEOs who have COOs: Contingency analysis of an unexplored structural form. *Strategic Management Journal, 25*(10), 959–979.

Heenan, D. A., & Bennis, W. G. (1999). *Co-leaders: The power of great partnerships*. New York: John Wiley.

Hmieleski, K. M., Cole, M. S., & Baron, R. A. (2012). Shared authentic leadership and new venture performance. *Journal of Management, 38*(5), 1476–1499.

Hoopes, D. G., & Postrel, S. (1999). Shared knowledge, "glitches," and product development performance. *Strategic Management Journal, 20*(9), 837–865.

Johns, G. (2006). The essential impact of context on organizational behavior. *Academy of Management Review, 31*(2), 386–408.

Klotz, A. C., Hmieleski, K. M., Bradley, B. H., & Busenitz, L. W. (2014). New venture teams a review of the literature and roadmap for future research. *Journal of Management, 40*(1), 226–255.

Krause, R., Priem, R., & Love, L. (2014). Who's in charge here? Co-CEOs, power gaps, and firm performance. *Strategic Management Journal, 36*, 2099–2110.

Lawrence, P. R., & Lorsch, J. W. (1967). Differentiation and integration in complex organizations. *Administrative Science Quarterly*, 1–47.

Lechler, T. (2001). Social interaction: A determinant of entrepreneurial team venture success. *Small Business Economics, 16*(4), 263–278.

Lubatkin, M. H., Simsek, Z., Ling, Y., & Veiga, J. F. (2006). Ambidexterity and performance in small-to medium-sized firms: The pivotal role of top management team behavioral integration. *Journal of Management, 32*(5), 646–672.

Marcel, J. J. (2009). Why top management team characteristics matter when employing a chief operating officer: A strategic contingency perspective. *Strategic Management Journal, 30*(6), 647–658.

Miller, D., Breton-Miller, L., Minichilli, A., Corbetta, G., & Pittino, D. (2014). When do non-family CEOs outperform in family firms? Agency and behavioural agency perspectives. *Journal of Management Studies, 51*(4), 547–572.

O'Toole, J., Galbraith, J., & Lawler, E. E. (2002). When two (or more) heads are better than one: The promise and pitfalls of shared leadership. *California Management Review, 44*(4), 65–83.

Pearce, C. L. (2004). The future of leadership: Combining vertical and shared leadership to transform knowledge work. *The Academy of Management Executive, 18*(1), 47–57.

Pearce, C. L., & Conger, J. A. (2003). *Shared leadership: Reframing the hows and whys of leadership*. Thousand Oaks, CA: Sage.

Pearce, C. L., & Sims, H. P., Jr. (2002). Vertical versus shared leadership as predictors of the effectiveness of change management teams: An examination of aversive, directive, transactional, transformational, and empowering leader behaviors. *Group Dynamics: Theory, Research, and Practice, 6*(2), 172.

Rosenthal, C. S. (1998). Determinants of collaborative leadership: Civic engagement, gender or organizational norms? *Political Research Quarterly, 51*(4), 847–868.

Schjoedt, L., & Kraus, S. (2009). Entrepreneurial teams: Definition and performance factors. *Management Research News, 32*(6), 513–524.

Stewart, G. L., & Barrick, M. R. (2000). Team structure and performance: Assessing the mediating role of intra-team process and the moderating role of task type. *Academy of Management Journal, 43*(2), 135–148.

Tannenbaum, S. I., Beard, R. L., & Salas, E. (1992). Team building and its influence on team effectiveness: An examination of conceptual and empirical developments. *Advances in Psychology, 82*, 117–153.

Verona, G. (1999). A resource-based view of product development. *Academy of Management Review, 24*(1), 132–142.

Vroom, V. H., & Yetton, P. W. (1973). *Leadership and decision-making.* Pittsburgh, PA: University of Pittsburgh Press.

Zhang, Y. (2006). The presence of a separate COO/president and its impact on strategic change and CEO dismissal. *Strategic Management Journal, 27*(3), 283–300.

Human Capital, Organizational Competences and Knowledge and Innovation Transfer: A Case Study Applied to the Mining Sector

Margarida Rodrigues and João Leitão

Abstract This chapter aims to reveal that in certain conditions, especially in the context of restructuring processes, the articulation between organizational competences and individual competences, in terms of knowledge and innovation transfer, is not as important as pointed out by the literature on human capital. A case study is developed, presenting a situational analysis of the human capital's organizational competences in a subsidiary owned by a multinational company operating in the mining sector in Portugal. The collection of primary data is carried out through interviews with the local directors, and complemented by secondary data from document analysis. The empirical evidence obtained indicates that although the competences and specific know-how of human capital in the subsidiary play a critical role for the success of the restructuring process, they do not increase the attractiveness of the parent-company's tendency to reinforce knowledge and innovation transfer mechanisms, which could be justified by the lack of specific knowledge and (internal and external) communication culture; as well as the absence of a knowledge-sharing culture signalled by the Japanese parent-company.

Keywords Intangible assets · Individual competences · Organizational competences · Restructuring

M. Rodrigues
University of Beira Interior, Covilhã, Portugal

J. Leitão (✉)
Department of Management and Economics, University of Beira Interior (UBI), Covilhã, Portugal

Centre for Management Studies of Instituto Superior Técnico (CEG-IST), University of Lisbon, Lisboa, Portugal

Center for Mechanical and Aerospace Science and Technologies (C-MAST), Covilhã, Portugal

Instituto Multidisciplinar de Empresa, Universidad de Salamanca, Salamanca, Spain

NECE - Research Center in Business Sciences, University of Beira Interior, Covilhã, Portugal
e-mail: jleitao@ubi.pt

© Springer International Publishing AG, part of Springer Nature 2018   107
S. Cubico et al. (eds.), *Entrepreneurship and the Industry Life Cycle*, Studies on Entrepreneurship, Structural Change and Industrial Dynamics,
https://doi.org/10.1007/978-3-319-89336-5_6

1   Introduction

The subject of human capital has been widely debated in the literature of reference, especially since the publication of the pioneering work by Becker (1975), who introduced to the agenda of researchers interested in the topic the importance of concentrating on and appreciating human capital, above all through adding to the triad consisting of education, training and experience. More recently, the attention of the research community has been redirected to exploring the importance associated with different types of competences, namely organisational ones which, in theoretical terms, when they exist, could serve to facilitate the implementation of formal mechanisms of knowledge and innovation transfer, as proposed by Lengnick-Hall and Lengnick-Hall (2006).

Therefore, this chapter aims to respond to the following central research questions: are human capital and organisational competences important in determining organisations' performance? Other secondary questions to explore are: do human capital and individual competences lose importance in the context of business restructuring?; and what strategic motivations and organisational factors can limit the processes of knowledge and innovation transfer?

Generically, the aim is to examine the effective importance of having a stock of human capital accompanied by individual and organisational competences in determining organisations' performance. Specifically, the aim is to carry out a case study to respond to both the central question and the secondary questions, in the setting of a traditional industrial sector in Portugal, of worldwide strategic interest, i.e., the mining sector.

The results indicate a new contribution to the literature on the management of human capital and competences, at two levels, firstly by revealing that the stock of human capital and organisational competences in a subsidiary firm may not be sufficient to force the opening up of the parent-company, in terms of bi-directional mechanisms of knowledge and technology transfer. Secondly, the results show that organisational culture and the culture of (internal and external) communication can be factors that block the transfer of knowledge assets originating in the parent-company to the subsidiary company.

The structure of this chapter is as follows. Firstly, a literature review is carried out on the importance of the management of human capital and individual and organisational competences able to influence the implementation of mechanisms of knowledge and innovation transfer. Secondly, a case study applied to the mining sector in Portugal is presented, illustrating the relationship between the stock of human capital and its specific organisational competences, in the context of a business restructuring process, through analysis of an international economic group's strategic option of acquiring a subsidiary company, revealing its real motivations for implementing that strategic option of acquisition. Thirdly, the summarized results of the field work are presented, based on the interviews held with the director of human resources in the subsidiary firm, followed by a critical analysis of the contents. Fourthly, the conclusions are presented, together with implications for political decision-makers and managers, limitations and suggestions for future research.

2   Literature Review

2.1   Human Capital

Faced with the phenomenon of globalization, human capital has been seen as a source of long-term, sustainable, competitive advantage, which has provoked the growing interest of researchers in the academic sphere and business managers (Dyer and Reeves 1995). In this context, Becker (1975) began by studying human capital in the area of education, but his contributions were important for future study of these concepts. The same author concluded that investment in human capital leads to countries' development and economic growth (Becker 1992). Consequently, the study of human capital begins with the premise that it is individuals who make decisions about their education, training and health, whereby they assess the costs and benefits of that decision. In the same line of thought, education and training form the fundamental investment regarding human capital (Becker 1993). It is therefore pertinent to present some definitions of human capital, which during the 1960s was associated with the concept of economic value (Schuler 1990), based on the thesis that individuals have a range of capacities, skills, values and experience that are a source of economic value for organisations (Huselid et al. 1997). Parnes (1984) and Snell and Dean (1992) also argue that individuals are important capital for organisations, and so the greater the investment in the former, the greater their value, which is expressed through their increased contribution to the organisation's productivity and performance. Briefly, this concept has been approached in two ways, one emphasizing education as a form of investment, and the other through the need to qualify human capital and assessment of the corresponding return (Teixeira 2002).

The most recent conceptualizations of human capital point towards this concerning the capacities, knowledge, skills and individual experience that each person brings to the organisation, and when considered together they form an intangible asset which allows differentiation from other organisations (Lengnick-Hall and Lengnick-Hall 2006).

Following up the previous statement, human capital forms organisations' intangible assets, and so investment in this is a crucial element in defining human resource strategy (Zula and Chermack 2007), and also influences their competitiveness given the importance of organisational learning and its transformation, i.e., of organisational processes (Teixeira 2002).

This consideration leads to a crucial point: the accumulation of exceptionally talented individuals is not enough for the organisation, as there should also be a desire on the part of individuals to invest in their skills and capacities given their status in the organisation (Stiles and Kulvisaechana 2003). For these authors, individuals should make a commitment to the organisation, for there to be real effectiveness of human capital; which is naturally always based on social capital and its structure.

For Marimuthu et al. (2009), human capital includes two fundamental parts, individuals and organisations. According to these authors, human capital must have

Table 1 Evolution of human capital management

Types of approaches	Traditional view	Intermediate view	Current view
Behavioural	Leadership Motivation Quality of life; and Stress	Organisational commitment	Knowledge management; and Organisational learning
Functional	Function and salaries Performance Training Development Recruitment and selection Careers; and Routines	Variable remuneration Participation in results; and New forms of career progression	Human capital Intellectual capital; and competences
Reflexive/ critical	Work relations Collective bargaining Power Conflicts; and Industrial relations	Psychology at work; and Company culture	Subjectivity at work

Source: Adapted from Barbosa (2005)

four fundamental attributes, namely: (i) flexibility and adaptation; (ii) appreciation of individual competences; (iii) development of organisational competences; and (iv) individual employability; in order to ensure the generation of value at both the individual and organisational level.

Therefore, for organisations, human capital management has become critical in order to create processes generating added value, since the latter are crucial intangible assets for the growth of the former (Bandeira 2010).

Table 1 presents a synthesis of the evolving concept of human capital management, distinguishing: the traditional view which reflects the common practices of human resource management; the intermediate view which represents an evolution in the conceptualizations used; and the current view designated human capital management, which considers in an integrated way human resource management practices, at the same time as relational and organisational views (Barbosa 2009).

No less important is the major and growing evidence of the positive connection between human capital development and organisational performance, i.e., organisations' emphasis on human capital reflects the view that market value depends less and less on tangible resources, and increasingly on intangible ones, particularly human resources (Stiles and Kulvisaechana 2003). However, recruiting and holding on to the best employees is only one side of the equation, as argued by these authors. The organisation has to make good use of its collaborators' skills and capacities, encouraging individual and organisational learning, in order to form a favourable environment for the creation, share and application of knowledge.

Competence management has the general aim of defining the indispensible competences within the organisation, in order to develop its human capital, identifying the key areas where an individual can be allocated, for maximum benefit of their capacities and talents, and contributing to fulfilment of the strategies defined by the organisation, as well as participating in the organisation's responses to external threats and opportunities (Morcef et al. 2006).

In addition, Barbosa and Rodrigues (2006) argued that competence management corresponds to the set of knowledge, skills and attitudes that allow a pre-defined result to be achieved.

This argument is corroborated by Thévenet (2010), for whom competence management fills the existing gap in traditional practices of human resource management, in that it allows identification of that gap and the adoption of processes and practices to solve it, by adapting existing competences to organisational objectives, especially those concerning sustainability.

However, in the line of reasoning of Fleury and Fleury (2010), for this to be possible, it is crucial to understand how individuals add value to the organisation through their capacities and knowledge, i.e., individual competences.

In the perspective of Ulrich (1997), for human resource management to create value and produce results, it should have a strategic position and be oriented towards individuals and processes, so as to ensure that the configuration of the organisational system and human resource practices are in line with the business/organisational strategy.

Consequently, individual and organisational competences, as well as knowledge and innovation, are important pillars for achieving the alignment previously suggested, considering the intangible nature of human resources as elements forming human capital.

2.2 Individual Competences

Individual competences have been studied by various authors. They consist of the ability to perform tasks (Mcclelland 1973), and may result in a combination of knowledge, skills and attitudes (Boyatzis 1982). In turn, following an approach centred on the individual, those competences can also be defined as individual characteristics that are related to effectiveness and high performance in a task or job (Spencer and Spencer 1993).

By incorporating a strategic dimension in the definition of competences, these correspond to the sum of individual knowledge, aptitudes and behaviours employed in performing a given job, which allow the strategic objectives set by a given organisation to be achieved (Treasury Board of Canada Secretary 1999).

Kwon (2009) also argued that organisations' success depends to a great extent on individuals with high individual competences and on these being measured, as they generate added value for organisations as human capital.

In the scope of competences limited to individuals' characteristics, the critical character of knowledge, capacities, values, motivation, initiative and others stands out in determining the success of work performance (Cheetham and Chivers 2005).

Ceitil (2007) grouped individual competences in three categories: (i) extra-personal elements (attributes and qualifications); (ii) intra-personal characteristics (capacities); and (iii) inter-personal phenomena (behavioural).

Individual competences are found to include varied components, and so Harvey (1991) also systematized them in four items, namely: (i) knowledge (the necessary and specific information to perform tasks related to a given function); (ii) the capacities that represent skills in using instruments etc. in performing a given function (which should be acquired in the educational or informal context); (iii) aptitude (as the result of conjugating intelligence, spatial orientation and reaction time); and iv) others (which include attitudes and personality).

In the same line of analysis, Nordhaug (1998) indicates three individual competences as critical, i.e., technical competences (directed towards performing a given task, with mastery of the methods, processes and techniques involved being indispensible), inter-personal competences (for example, empathy, communication and helping capacities and the degree of social awareness); and conceptual competences (including the capacity of analysis, creativity/innovation, problem-solving capacity and the ability to identify threats and opportunities).

No less important are the various approaches focused on studying individual competences, but only those considered of greatest importance for this study are considered.

The American approach reflects the behavioural approach (Boyatzis 1982; Spencer and Spencer 1993; Mcclelland 1998; Thaler and Sunstein 2008; Thaler 2015), and according to which competences are individuals' underlying characteristics. In turn, the English approach is supported on functional competences and the individual's skill demonstrating that work is performed according to the standard performance required (Knasel and Meed 1994).

Given the diversity of theoretical frameworks/approaches for studying this concept, Le Deist and Winterton (2005) propose a taxonomy of competences, based on identifying those that are cognitive (knowledge and understanding), functional (operational or applied capacities), social (attitudes and behaviours) and meta-competences (learning capacity).

It is of note that individual competences can be increased through their development, evaluation and management (Ceitil 2006), particularly in the organisational context of human resources. It therefore becomes necessary to create a model of key competences, evaluate and analyse existing competences, standardize the competences required for a task or function, define a programme for developing competences (in order to minimize differences) and continuously monitor performance and evaluation (Sinnott et al. 2002).

However, application of a model of competence management implies thorough knowledge of organisations, including their strategies and structures (Ceitil 2006).

2.3   Organisational Competences

Organisational competences can be discussed and analysed according to various theoretical approaches, but Scianni and Barbosa (2009) concluded that, based on the theory of the resource-based vision and on that of dynamic capacities, they can be directed towards the strategic and functional dimension.

The same authors argue that the strategic dimension emphasizes the organisation's position in its sector of activity and is related to competitive advantage and to the dynamism inherent to organisations. So organisations must have essential competences, regarding knowledge of available resources, their internal and external environments, as well as having a clear definition of their organisational objectives, in order to stimulate organisational learning and ensure their resources are difficult to copy (Scianni and Barbosa 2009).

The functional dimension focuses on developing the organisation's capacities and routines included in an organisational structure, which should unite the necessary competences to manage intangible and tangible assets, as well as create and produce goods/services appropriate to the market demand, ensuring both internal and external logistics for distribution and sales (Ruas et al. 2005).

For Ruas et al. (2005), organisational competences are those that make greater benefits possible, in the form of competitive advantages, which can generate value for the customer and that the competition feels unable to imitate, in this way becoming a guideline for the business's sustainable success.

Organisations must have competences to elaborate their strategy, defining their mission and their values, to be able to integrate their individual competences and respond to the market efficiently (Sarsur et al. 2010).

From a selected set of contributions identified in the literature on the subject of competences, Table 2 identifies some organisational competences acquired from

Table 2 Organisational competences

Author(s)	Description
Prahaland and Hamel (1997)	Set of aptitudes, technology, physical and management systems
Bitencourt (2004)	Capacity to align individual competences and individuals' needs with the organisation
Barbosa and Rodrigues (2006)	Capacity to join knowledge, aptitudes and attitudes around the result defined by the organisation
Fleury and Fleury (2010)	Capacity to add value, particularly economic, to the organisation, and to value individuals' social characteristics (i.e., social value)
Kim et al. (2011)	Organisational dynamic capacities have a life-cycle that includes their origin, development and maturity
Ruuska et al. (2013)	Capacities are spread in a network and should align the knowledge of diverse actors in that network, as well as their capacities
Spithoven and Teirlinck (2015)	Resources and capacities are instruments to sustain competitive advantage or stimulate performance

Source: Own elaboration

development and knowledge, in the organisational context, which are of a critical nature in the articulation between opportunities identified in the market and the organisation's differentiating characteristics.

2.4 Processes for Transferring Knowledge and Innovation

In articulation with the previous review of individual and organisational competences, it is important to mention that the symbiosis between these two types of competences occurs within the organisation, so that both allow organisations to achieve their functional and strategic objectives, following a vision based on competences (Scianni and Barbosa 2009).

Considering that the literature on human capital goes beyond the individual, the idea should also be advanced that knowledge can be shared between groups and institutionalized within organisational processes and routines (Wright et al. 2001).

For the same authors, knowledge has been recognized by managers and economists as a valuable resource, and is a relatively recent research topic in the literature on human capital, particularly concerning matters of generating knowledge and its leverage, as well as its transfer and integration.

In other words, considering the conditions in which individuals are willing to share and act according to their knowledge, this is an important component in human capital management (Stiles and Kulvisaechana 2003). As indicated by Wright et al. (2001), the literature on human resources has traditionally focused on the development of knowledge, in individual terms, through training and incentives to apply knowledge, but the view of the literature on human capital is more concerned with organisational sharing of knowledge, making it accessible and transferable.

In this domain, Scianni and Barbosa (2009) argued that organisations transfer their knowledge to individuals, providing them with new experiences and professional skills, and simultaneously, individuals transfer their learning to the organisation; in temporal terms, when the individual transfers knowledge to the organisation, there is permanent added value through its established processes and practices, in the sphere of its organisational structure.

That knowledge transfer is related to knowledge management, whose definition is not yet consensual in the academic world. However, Rossalto (2003) defines it as a dynamic and continuous strategic process that aims to promote the management of organisations' intangible assets and their conversion into knowledge.

Generically, knowledge can be classified as: tacit (subjective); and explicit (objective); which interact (Nonaka and Takeuchi 1997). Tacit knowledge is used implicitly by individuals in organisations to carry out their work, and is assimilated through their experience in doing this, while explicit knowledge is expressed formally by using a system of coded and divulged symbols (Choo 2003).

Tanriverdi (2005) and Bogner and Bansal (2007), quoted by Birasnav (2014), converge regarding the importance of developing a single knowledge within the company, to supply new products/services, distinguish it from competitors and thereby attain competitive advantages. Supplying customers with exclusive products/services helps to improve their satisfaction, and consequently sales volume, and so companies have observed the influence of knowledge development on performance.

Since knowledge lies in employees' brains, firms have developed various strategies to create organisational knowledge, supported on developing employees' knowledge. Human capital managers must therefore engage in activities, aiming to find an appropriate leadership style to support the implementation of knowledge management programmes, in order to improve organisational performance (Birasnav 2014).

For Birasnav (2014), knowledge is of two types: tacit knowledge (knowledge that is inimitable, valuable, underused, unarticulated and lying in employees' brains) and explicit knowledge (knowledge that can be distributed, easily handled, documented and stored), which is in line with what is proposed by Choo (2003).

Organisational knowledge is created from the transformation of those two types of knowledge in another form of knowledge, which is valuable and cannot by imitated by, or transferred to other firms. Therefore, organisational knowledge becomes a source of sustainable competitive advantage. Conceiving strategies for suitable management of knowledge is a critical success factor for many organisations, due to its importance in achieving organisational results (Birasnav 2014). For this author, knowledge management corresponds to the management function that is responsible for regulating the selection, implementation and evaluation of knowledge strategies aiming to create a climate of support for work with knowledge inside and outside the organisation, in order to improve organisational performance.

The structure of knowledge management includes its process and infrastructure, and the interaction between these two components supports organisations in creating organisational knowledge and in improving organisational innovation, and consequently in the demanding task of achieving a certain level of sustainable performance (Birasnav 2014).

Both types of knowledge referred to by Choo (2003) and Birasnav (2014) imply the use of two types of knowledge management processes. For Filius et al. (2000), those two management processes are: that of tacit knowledge (employees gather information to solve problems, calculate the value of the information gathered, learn from the value and update the existing knowledge in the system); and that of strategic knowledge (organisations formulate knowledge management strategies to assess, create and sustain intangible assets and align knowledge management strategies with the business strategy).

For Filius et al. (2000), the process of managing tacit knowledge includes activities of acquiring knowledge, documentation, transfer, creation and application. Knowledge acquisition is a type of activity related to the lack of tacit and explicit knowledge in the external environment. Documenting knowledge is related to its storage and retrieval from the organisation's system, for example, databases and documents. Knowledge transfer allows employees to share their tacit and explicit knowledge with other employees, inside or outside organisations. According to Nonaka (1994), quoted by Birasnav (2014), knowledge creation means creating knowledge in both its tacit and explicit forms through a knowledge conversion process (SECI Model—Socialization, Externalization, Combination and

Internalization). The application of knowledge allows employees to use knowledge acquired inside or outside the organisation for their own purposes (Birasnav 2014).

So as to face up to changes in the environment, organisations must also develop a number of specific capacities and regenerate their essential competences. Among those firm-specific resources and capacities, intangible assets have a critical role in obtaining competitive advantages. And in turn, of all intangible assets, learning is one of the most important resources in the knowledge society, due to its highly strategic role (Lloréns Montes et al. 2005).

García-Morales et al. (2012) argue that different types of learning and innovation are related. For example, generative learning is the most advanced form of organisational learning and occurs when an organisation is willing to question long-held assumptions about its mission, customers, capacities and strategy and generate changes in its practices, strategies and values. This learning forms the basis necessary for radical innovations in products, processes and technology.

Organisational learning is an important component of any effort to improve organisational performance and reinforce sustainable competitive advantage. The development of new knowledge derived from organisational learning reduces the probability of a company's competences becoming outdated, allowing competences to remain dynamic and therefore favouring improved performance. Organisational learning generally has positive connotations, since this form of learning is associated with improved performance. Various authors have also shown that innovation is essential to improve performance and that innovation comes into play in order to improve organisational performance (García-Morales et al. 2012).

Alharthey et al. (2013) conclude that the development of an innovation culture has become essential for an organisation, as a way to hold on to its competitive position and sustainability. So organisations must give priority to innovation, as this provides them with long-term success. However, the impact of the innovation culture on human resource management practices must be identified. The need to analyse that impact was also mentioned by Chen and Huang (2009).

Alharthey et al. (2013) claim that human resource management practices are subject to change according to the innovation culture. This is due to the requirements of an innovation culture, which is marked by the need for employees' positive acceptance to ensure its implementation is successful. For employees to accept innovation, human resource managers must make changes to existing practices and policies (Denning 2011).

Nevertheless, employees' effectiveness may be greatly influenced by the strategy of human capital management, since this is directly linked to learning, compatibility, the process and performance (Alharthey et al. 2013).

Human capital management practices are focused on the transmission of internal and external knowledge, so that employees can experience different levels of knowledge and have access to innovative thoughts and ideas (Chen and Huang 2009).

Indeed, innovation can be carried out if human resource management practices are duly positioned and recreated, as that allows a group of people or individuals to be creative with their ideas and knowledge to work effectively within the innovation culture (Alharthey et al. 2013).

Innovation is a strategic option that tends to improve the organisation and increase its competitive capacity. At the same time, innovation opens the doors to differentiation, and thereby to strengthening competitive advantages in the global market context (Lloréns Montes et al. 2005).

To develop the innovation culture, human resource management should introduce changes to practices and policies to mould and develop the necessary skills, as well as in attitudes, knowledge and behaviour, with this culture becoming a management priority (Alharthey et al. 2013).

For these authors, the organisation's culture is formed basically by people's beliefs and attitudes, and so for there to be a culture of innovation within the organisation, this implies changes in human resource management. These should include supervisory programmes, training in cultural innovation for the development of new ideas, support for the creation of ideas and programmes for innovative leaders.

3   Case Study

3.1   Diagnosis of the Mining Sector: International and National

A case study will now be presented, applied to the mining industry. This is considered to be an appropriate laboratory to illustrate the importance of human capital and organisational competences in determining the performance of a business unit, owned by a multinational, which embarked on a successful process of business restructuring, through acquisition of a foreign subsidiary, despite it not being based on valuing human capital and effective reinforcement of knowledge and innovation transfer mechanisms from the Japanese parent-company to the Portuguese subsidiary.

Worldwide, the extraction industry is a strategic activity for economic growth and, no less importantly, to sustain many families (a matter of great relevance and social impact), mainly in emerging economies, playing a vital role in the global economy, as it is a major supplier of raw material and a driver of job-creation (Govindan et al. 2014).

The extraction industry, and particularly mining, creates opportunities for regional and national growth and development, through increased income (from taxes and royalties), knowledge transfer, job creation and the creation of infrastructure and social services (Franco 2014), as well as contributing to sustainable development. Kilimnik and Motta (2003) and Govindan et al. (2014) summarily characterise the world extraction industry as presented in Table 3.

Nationally, although Portugal is small in area, the country has a very diversified and complex geology, being very rich in mineral resources. This potential, together with the EU's dependence on certain mined raw materials, represents an opportunity

Table 3 Characterisation of world extraction industry

Item	Some characteristics
No. of collaborators in extraction	• 3.7 million
Environmental and social impacts	• Unplanned expansion of activities, principally in developing countries • Considered as firms that carry out their activity by contaminating the ground and water • Their activity causes major changes in the landscape
How the extraction industry is seen	• By its behaviour with regard to the environmental and social impacts it causes • Slow to implement and develop policies of corporate social responsibility, to lessen the impacts caused
The reasons for implementing policies of corporate social responsibility	• Reputation • Legitimacy • Obliged to adhere to the legislation in the countries they operate in • Attain a strategic advantage; and • A question of ethics and behaviour • Type of organisational culture, in particular of the capital holders
Human resource management	• This area is centralized and formal, but presenting some gaps regarding management that considers the different hierarchical levels and is more concerned with promoting collaborators' quality of life, principally that of basic workers • Mining companies begin to consider people as important assets (intangible assets), requiring them to be polyvalent and flexible. Besides, they recognize that talents and competences are a competitive advantage; and • Despite understanding that human capital is an intangible asset, where individual competences must be valued and managed, this sector is still in a transition stage regarding processes and practices in this area

Source: Adapted from Kilimnik and Motta (2003) and Govindan et al. (2014)

to develop the mining industry, to help improve national indigenous resources and contribute to developing the national economy, through the services involved, distribution and sale of products, job creation and export growth (Board of Geology and Energy 2015).

According to Franco (2014), the characteristics of the extraction industry require a rigorous, and sometimes delicate, balance between economic, environmental and social concerns. Mining operations inevitably cause social and environmental impacts as well as on the landscape. Moreover, the mining sector is at the root of the great majority of industrial activities downstream, with an enormous potential to create, contribute to and support sustainable development, in both the communities

Table 4 Characterization of the Portuguese mining industry

Sector of extraction industry	No. of firms	No. of collaborators	Production (tons)	Production (million euros)
Metallic minerals	5	2891	473,926	411,694
Minerals for construction	637	4987	45,335,088	309,496
Non-metallic industrial minerals	121	739	5,067,862	46,309
Mineral and source water	69	1963	1,129,862	171,371
Total	832	10,580	52,006,738	938,870

Source: Adapted from Board of Geology and Energy (2015)

where it takes place (growth and employment possibilities) and in those where the manufacturing industries that consume its products are situated.

Table 4 presents some characteristics of the Portuguese mining industry, with data from 2014, as this information is available from the regulating entities.

The Portuguese extraction industry is also considered strategic, being generally situated in inland regions, and its activities generate wealth and local employment and contribute to economic and social regional development (Board of Geology and Energy 2015).

Concerning human capital, and according to a view expressed in the Stanton Chase HR Survey (2016), the main challenges faced are as follows:

- HR results are generally very much in line with those of CEOs, which seems to demonstrate some harmony in analysis of situations and the solutions defended;
- 53% of HR managers (49% in the case of CEOs) consider that the main business strategy for the current year is "Expansion" and 68% are optimistic (CEOs—83%) about the development of their business in the next 2 years;
- The most valued competences from the selection are orientation to clients and results (62%), techniques (48%) and fulfilment capacity (39%). Besides orientation to results and clients, CEOs mention strategic vision (35%);
- The factors that can contribute most to an HR manager's professional success are leadership capacity (76%), management capacity (55%) and reinforcement of coaching and mentoring competences. More pragmatically, CEOs give more value to aspects such as international experience, mastery of soft skills and the contact network;
- The principal difficulties in managing people are, for HR managers, the creation of a business culture (48%), aligning people with organisational objectives (48%) and attracting talent (40%). For CEOs, the difficulties lie in attracting the right talent, focusing on results and motivating people;
- The principal challenges HR professionals expect to face are new working models (63%), managing different generations (44%) and the shortage of talent (38%);
- The areas on which they will focus most are internal assessment/management of talents (47%), training (47%) and employer branding (35%);

- 69% of HR managers claim that human capital management has become "increasingly important" and 62% say that the Portuguese HR manager has a "good" level of competences (52% in the case of CEOs/executive leaders); and
- Concerning the strongest aspects of the Portuguese HR manager, the answers are the technical domain (55%), dedication (48%) and flexibility (41%), which compares with 67% dedication, 63% flexibility and 55% resilience in CEOs' opinion on national managers.

In Portugal there are only three active mines, where the qualifications required of manual collaborators vary, as minimum obligatory schooling can be demanded or sometimes even less. As for senior staff, salary packages are substantially higher than those of other collaborators. It is still usual to include some benefits, such as a house, company car, health insurance and others. This human resource policy seeks to attract and retain the senior staff firms need, in the places where those industries extract and handle the raw material and generally carry out their activity.

3.2 Presentation of the Firm

The economic group behind the subsidiary was legally formed on 1 April 2003, and is involved in a wide range of business globally, including the manufacture and sale of goods, service provision, and planning and coordination of projects in its home country (domestic companies) and abroad (foreign subsidiaries). Since its foundation the group has invested in various sectors, particularly the car sector, the industrial sector, the energy sector and the extraction sector (minerals).

Its organisational structure is divided by major areas of management and type of business activity (divisions), therefore following a divisional structure.

On 31 March 2015 the group was formed of 113 domestic companies and 297 foreign subsidiaries and employed 15,936 workers. The mission and vision of this group is to create value and prosperity for its shareholders with a spirit of global integrity, based on trust, innovation, speed, change and perseverance, but only taking on calculated risks. Firms should not be concerned with seeking profit at any cost; rather, they should be concerned with doing business according to social norms, thereby contributing to society. This group believes that rigorous adherence to these premises is essential to achieve its mission and vision. It therefore tries to implant this mentality and form consensus among its collaborators to make an effort to this end, with cooperation and teamwork being important. To fulfil its mission and vision, the group promotes daily communication between its collaborators and promotes the implementation of common policies (e.g. the standard programme, with formalized procedures), aiming for these to be meticulously followed by all. It also has a Code of Ethics and Behaviour, which provides behaviour guidelines to be followed by the whole group.

The Standardization Committee, presided over by the Chief Compliance Officer (CCO), is at the centre of activities to ensure adherence to laws, regulations and

Table 5 History of the subsidiary mining company

Year	Description
1898	Mining begins
1901	Entry of English capital
1911	Company foundation
1914	Period of expansion at the beginning of the First World War
1920	Change of name
1943	The mines employed around 6000 people
Anos 70	Company restructuring, with 20% participation by the Portuguese State
1990	Sale of 80% of shares
1994/1995	Another change in the holders of capital
2003	Another change in the holders of capital
2007	Another change in the holders of capital
2015	Another change in the holders of capital

Source: Own elaboration

business ethics, in cooperation with headquarters and all subsidiaries (domestic and foreign), with scheduled meetings and visits to all companies in the group by elements from headquarters.

This is a large group with a diversified strategy and great economic and institutional power in the country of the parent-company, Japan, the reason for acquiring a subsidiary mining company in Portugal, with the support of the home country's government (see the subsidiary's history in Table 5). The investment made by this group in 2007 was with the aim of having its own supplier of the mineral product to supply its country's companies, and in this way not depend on third parties, principally China.

As for the subsidiary subject to analysis in this case study, it is situated in inland Portugal, and its activity consists of exploiting a mine, on 31 December 2015 employing around 252 collaborators and producing around 1734 gross tons of product, which amounts to 161,000 million euros of sales (exports), in the period between 2007 and 2015, according to data published in the subsidiary's annual balance sheet. This activity has existed for at least a 100 years, it being a rare fissure mine, with mineral extraction being carried out by chambers and pillars. The mine is divided vertically in four structural levels; for each level a set of base-galleries is defined, 5 m wide; at the points of intersection (between the breaking areas and the levels) there are open chimneys to transport the mined material vertically. Exploitation begins with the construction of spiral ramps or galleries to have access to the seams identified in the surveys. Then the pillars are constructed, in order to allow the theoretical recovery of eighty-four per cent of the seam. Next, controlled explosions are carried out in the places identified, with the stone being taken to the chimneys and the central belt which transports the mined material to the washing area where the final concentrate is produced and assessed.

The mission defined for the subsidiary, according to a formal communication to the collaborators of the President of the Executive Committee in 2012 is as follows:

"We are a mining company focused on the discovery, extraction and concentration of minerals, transforming those natural resources into wealth and Sustainable Development, committed to maximizing value for our shareholders, for clients and for all parties involved, creating local opportunities that support the progress of the local economy, increasing our collaborators' safety, health, well-being and environmental and social awareness." As for the firm's vision, "Our vision is to continue to be an Industrial Firm focused on the Extraction of natural mineral resources, which is greatly respected in the country and the leader in crucial mining production in Portugal." Concerning its strategy, "Our strategy is low-cost operation of the mine, which has a great potential to increase its lifetime, using the most modern and appropriate competences, and technology available, adopting modern production and business management techniques and selling the final products to a diversified market. We are focused on increasing our reserves and our mineral resources so as to ensure our asset of a long life, to continue to create and distribute value to our shareholders and the local community, and continue to satisfy our clients' needs. Our products are raw material necessary to sustain international growth not only today, but growth that will occur over a long period of time in the future. We believe that, in the long term, growing industrialization will continue to stimulate the demand for the metals we produce."

The subsidiary's capital is held only by the economic group it belongs to, i.e., the only shareholder owns a hundred per cent of the capital.

Finally, the economic activity classification code (CAE) of the subsidiary is: 07290; referring to the extraction and preparation of other metallic minerals, according to Portuguese legislation on economic activities.

3.3 Management of Human Capital and Competences: Processes and Practices

The human resource policy of the subsidiary's parent-company has the following pillars: (1) the development of human resources that are active and creative. For the firm to grow, it is essential that all the Group's employees take the initiative in identifying problems and making everyday improvements by applying new capacities and creativity, without being harnessed to conventional ideas. It intends to continue working on initiatives that promote a mentality of gradual improvement. In addition, It will constantly and systematically take on human resources for new business areas, and encourage them to gain wide business experience and apply their skills in their specialized fields; (2) as a response to globalization, the objective pursued is to use human resources from different origins, as the development of strong human resources is vital to compete successfully in an increasingly globalized business environment. Therefore, it will continue to promote the internationalization of its collaborators. The intention is also to reinforce local staff abroad and promote more diversity, so that all employees can exercise their competences in the workplace; and (3) promotion of a corporate culture to understand the exclusive strengths and identity based on trust in the Group, making its collaborators understand and accept the Group's guiding principles, namely through training, to apply them on a daily basis.

3.4 Management of Human Capital and Competences: Processes and Practices

The subsidiary follows a human resource policy based on mutual respect for the firm's and employees' rights and obligations, and on permanently seeking improved individual performance, with action being guided by the following principles: (i) recruiting the best employees regarding their basic training, creativity and capacity to perform the respective functions; (ii) seeking to be competitive in the labour market as regards salaries paid and benefits granted; (iii) promoting the internal equity of the different posts according to the obligations and competences required of each one; (iv) delegating responsibilities when necessary, according to individual merit and competences and recognized leadership capacity; (v) seeking collaborators' involvement, at the various levels of management, in decision-making which affects them, making them responsible for subsequent implementations; promoting employees' social well-being; training and awareness actions for employees towards rigorous fulfilment and adoption of the best safety and environmental practices, and for better performance of their designated functions; promoting collaborators' continuous professional training; seeking to give equal career opportunities to all, according to their capacities and observing rigorous adherence to fulfilment of personal rights contained in the Code of Work and other legislation. These principles will allow the enhancement of individual competences, whenever possible harmonizing the needs of the company and the legitimate aspirations of collaborators.

In this context, the human resource processes and practices implemented are in relation to: (i) collaborator recruitment and selection; (ii) definition of the various working schedules; (iii) control of collaborators' attendance; (iv) surveillance system; (v) absence system; (vi) holiday schedule; (vii) disciplinary processes; (viii) travel system; (ix) award system; (x) career management; (xi) social benefit system; and (xii) professional training.

Another aspect of continuous professional training should also be underlined, i.e., on-the-job training. This training is often informal and not programmed, but is as important as that carried out in the classroom. This daily practice, established in the firm, is part of a wider objective to promote life-long learning. The objective is that collaborators acquire the necessary and specific knowledge to perform their duty (KNOWING). Through contact with Managers, Specialists and more qualified Employees, collaborators will acquire and improve capacities and competences to carry out their work, i.e. acquire the necessary methods and techniques, so that, through practice and experience, they will achieve good performance (KNOWING

HOW TO DO). In addition, the aim is for that daily contact with management, specialists and their own colleagues to allow them to acquire and improve attitudes, behaviour and mentality appropriate to the function and teamwork, and ultimately be able to respond to the firm's needs (KNOWING HOW TO BE). All these aspects are assessed annually and allow collaborators showing proof of knowledge and technical aptitudes and a positive attitude and behaviour to progress to more specialized professional categories, for example machine operators, mechanics, electricians, etc. That continuous on-the-job training is one of the trademarks of these mines, which for decades have been considered in the sector as a real training school for professionals and when, for various reasons, they move to other firms, their knowledge and professionalism stands out.

There is also a job description for management, which is shown in Table 6. However, in many firms, current Human Resource Management already works more on Competence Management rather than on a simple Description of Functions, in the opinion of the interviewee, the head of human resources.

3.5 Management of Knowledge and Innovation: Processes and Practices

The head of human resources understands that in the mining sector, technological knowledge, knowledge of the applicable legislation and knowledge of human resource processes and practices is crucial, also considering that knowledge about business competitors, knowledge about the individual and organisational competences of all stakeholders is also fundamental for human resource management. For this person, all these aspects together are seen as factors ensuring the success of the subsidiary, since intangible assets should not be considered secondary capital.

In this subsidiary, knowledge management has remained at an embryonic stage (phase of study and analysis) for around 2 years, with this being the responsibility of the firm's administration. The latter is beginning to see knowledge management as a factor of competitive advantage, corresponding to alignment of the human resource strategy with the mission, its vision and values, as stated by the same person. Therefore, the human resource department has tried to adapt the best practices and processes allocating the right people to the right places, thereby seeking to maintain and develop human capital, paying attention to the individual knowledge of each collaborator, i.e., their individual competences.

This person admits that the subsidiary's organisational culture is somewhat contrary to those practices and processes related to human capital management oriented to knowledge management and innovation which is necessary nowadays, and notes communication problems that mean working-time management is often not effective. He also pointed out great resistance to new initiatives, whose results are only visible in the long-term, and this requires great discipline and persistence. This resistance has to do with the low qualifications of manual collaborators (mine

Table 6 Description of the functional scheme of top management

Status in the subsidiary	Reports to	Description of functions
President of the ExecutiveCommittee	Shareholder	Direct current management of the company as delegated by the Administrative Council; coordinate the Executive Commission formed of an Executive Administrator and a Resident Executive Administrator; represent the firm in social business, with wide-ranging authority and carrying out all actions regarding fulfillment of the social objective; and participate in meetings with the Administrative Council and meetings with the Board of Energy and Geology (DGEG)
Resident Administrator	Executive Commission	Lead all the mine's activity, ensuring fulfilment of what is previously established by the Executive Commission; participate in meetings with the Administrative Council; participate in meetings with the trade union; represent the firm in institutional connections with local authority departments and other entities; participate in monthly meetings of the Health and Safety at Work Commission
Ex-patriot Administrator	Shareholder	Control all the subsidiary's activity, as the link with the Japanese parent-company
Administrative and Financial Director (DAF)	Resident Executive Administrator	Coordinate areas reporting to the DAF: Human Resource Department, Accounting Service, Purchasing Service, Stores, Dispatch and Transport, Management Control and the area of Information Technology and Buildings; prepare the annual budget and its reviews; relations with banking institutions, namely exchange and financing negotiations; coordinate information and monthly commitments to the Tax Office and Social Security, the Bank of Portugal, the INE and others; participate in meetings with the STIM; coordinate elaboration of the monthly management "Internal Report" and justify deviations from budget; respond to enquiries from the Japanese parent-company about internal control; manage daily cash flow; Coordinate work to report to the external auditing firm; Establish contact with lawyers regarding tax, administrative and commercial litigation; invited participant in meetings of the Administrative Council; Authorize purchases and payments, according to the internal rulings in force
Director of Washing and Planning	Resident Executive Administrator	Elaborate the annual production plan, for budgeting purposes, in collaboration with the Director of Underground Work and the Director of Geology and Prospection; elaborate the monthly production plan in collaboration with the Director of Underground Work and the Director

(continued)

Table 6 (continued)

Status in the subsidiary	Reports to	Description of functions
		of Geology and Prospection; coordinate the Laboratory Sector; coordinate the team from the area of production planning; participate in the monthly meetings of the Health and Safety at Work Commission; meet and collaborate with official entities, such as the DGEG and APA; elaborate annual activity reports and annual working plans for the DGEG; direct and coordinate the head of washing production, the head of washing maintenance and the person in charge of the electrical workshop; draw up the monthly metallurgical balance sheet; direct and coordinate operation of the ETAM; Be responsible and ensure rigorous application of the rules of mining techniques in performing work; Supervise all mining activity for which he is technically and legally responsible, to include, ensuring application of health, safety and hygiene rules at work; ensure fulfilment of the legislation in force for the mining sector especially for underground work; coordinate annual elaboration of the labour report to be sent to DGEG
Director of Geology	Resident Executive Administrator	Direct the activity of the Geology and Topography teams aiming to minimize human and material means used; collaborate in drawing up the annual production report, for budgeting purposes, with the Director of Underground Work and the Director of Washing and Planning; collaborate in drawing up the monthly production Plan together with the Director of Underground Work and the Director of Washing and Planning; coordinate calculation and assessment of Reserves and Resources; manage the carrying out of surface and underground surveys and control the respective treatment and confirmation of those surveys; manage geographical mapping underground (measuring areas to be mined); coordinate organisation and management of cartography; and elaborate technical reports
Director of Underground Work	Resident Executive Adminstrator	Direct the activity of the person responsible for Mine Production, the person in charge of Maintenance of the Mine's Mobile Equipment, and the person generally responsible for the Mine and his teams; optimize the human means and equipment available; ensure fulfilment of procedures and all the legislation concerning the handling and use of explosives; coordinate all management related to the explosive stores; participate in the monthly meetings of the Commission for Health and Safety at Work

(continued)

Table 6 (continued)

Status in the subsidiary	Reports to	Description of functions
Head of Human Resources	Administrative and Financial Director	Lead/manage the Personnel Service team that deals with all administrative Staff matters—employment contracts, processing of salaries, declarations, official enquiries, Single Report, etc.; accompany area directors on a daily basis, to advise/inform/clarify about matters connected to People Management; prepare and update the subsidiary's HR Manual; participate in meetings with the STIM; participate in monthly meetings of the Commission of Health and Safety at Work; prepare/place/manage applicants for Work Placement on the site of IEFP; coordinate integration of academic/curricular work placements coming from the region's vocational schools and faculties nationally
Head of the Environment	Resident Executive Administrator	Carry out frequent and systematic visits and auditing of workplaces, in order to ensure fulfilment of the legal and regulatory requirements concerning the Environment; support all Company Areas/Departments in order to attain global objectives; propose to the Resident Administrator the necessary specific measures and control their effectiveness; promote workers' awareness of matters related to the Environment, in order to encourage a spirit of prevention; participate in the monthly meetings of the Commission for Health and Safety at Work; carry out management and updating of the subsidiary's Health and Safety Programme (PSS); accompany and assess development of the PSS in the various areas of the firm in order to minimize the time needed for its implementation; supervise the work of waste cleaning, aiming among other aspects to ensure application of the legislation in force concerning the Environment

Source: Own elaboration

and washing), where knowledge is limited. In addition, the fact that the technology used is mostly out of date leads to a culture of little innovation.

The interviewee also mentioned the shortage of financial resources as an impediment to appropriate investment in knowledge management. Despite the existence of a human resource manual adapted to that required by the Japanese parent-company, it is far from being completely implemented. In other words, he considered that human capital and knowledge management does not prevail in the subsidiary for various reasons, such as the Japanese parent-company's unwillingness to invest in this area; the organisational structure not being the most appropriate and the lack of investment in suitable technological infrastructure, despite making great efforts to persuade the administration of the urgent need to consider the importance of human capital, namely individual competences and knowledge, which must be aligned with organisational competences.

Still on the question of knowledge, he considered this is constructed on a daily basis. That construction evidently creates unique individual competences, i.e., internal talent, the identification of which is generally a process arising from the leaders' experience in each area of the firm. It is a process that includes continuous observation of the work performed each day and the evolution noted regarding know-how, often confirmed later in the annual system of performance assessment. Some talent remains in the firm for several years. The best workers are often retained in the company, through raising salaries (often being promoted to higher positions where they receive a higher salary and some other benefits). Nevertheless, it is sometimes difficult to hold onto talent as the firm cannot promote all its good workers to supervisory posts. In this case, a career plan is foreseen for those workers. Sometimes the retention of those talents is not effective and the good worker ends up leaving, either to national companies or often to work abroad where family or friends already live, despite monthly bonuses having been introduced to stimulate production (production award) and safety (safety award). It is also noted that performance assessment is not completely implemented due to some resistance from the Japanese parent-company.

One of the administrators believes that the communication channels between the parent-company and the subsidiary are mainly effective, but are found to fail somewhat due to cultural and sometimes linguistic barriers, as well as some lack of knowledge about lode mines. This implies that there is only knowledge transfer to the Japanese parent-company through the permanent ex-patriot administrator and occasional ex-patriots. The same administrator claimed that Japanese officials visit the company frequently, "Perhaps even too frequently. They're very unproductive. The focus is above all on training and teaching these people about managing some aspects of the mining industry." and "For the parent-company, the visits are also seen as "compensation for not getting long holidays" or "as a bonus for good performance".

The contribution of communication to effective firm management must be based principally on a selection of data to be analysed and on knowledge of the topics to analyse, discuss and improve. When this does not happen, there is a great amount of data communicated without any result or any practical consequence, as argued by the same administrator; "It's unbelievable the amount of rough data (not detailed) that the company sends every day to Tokyo, including data about mining activity, mineral treatment and costs. I can't help thinking most of it is completely ignored, because drawing conclusions from all that would require a lot of specialized manpower, which doesn't exist in the parent-company, because this is a lode mine and they've admitted that they don't know anything about how it operates."

Another administrator stated that although the subsidiary belongs to a large economic group, with great knowledge in their areas of business, where innovation is always present, it is clear that "about lode mines they have no experience or knowledge, and so they do nothing without the approval of the local administrators. Their culture follows very strict rules, they're very united, but they take a long time to make a decision. They will take advice, but it has to be written down formally, they don't like changes and surprises."; in other words "knowledge transfer is only towards the parent-company".

This statement is corroborated by the production director and the washing director who underline, respectively, that *"I only see a benefit for the foreign owner, because they benefit from the knowledge transfer from the local management, whereas this isn't seen in the other direction. This happens, because the shareholder only knows about rock mass mines and not fissure mines, as is the case here."* and *"The officials occasionally come to the mines to learn and not to teach".*

The geology director was more peremptory on the question of knowledge management, saying, *"Because many of the foreign officials representing the parent-company don't have a mining background, communication of the information produced leads to wrong interpretations, which is time-consuming and creates repeated information, which harms the institutional relationship. Often, these being the information channels, mining company—foreign representative—parent company, the downstream information arrives distorted and unclear."*

The whole question of knowledge transfer, and even innovation, comes down to the fact that the parent-company, as an economic group, does not have knowledge about innovation in the mining sector, and so this does not occur. This conclusion is reflected in the opinion of the ex-patriot administrator who accepts that *"First it's necessary to understand the nature of problems, and then ask for opinions about them from all the local managers. Secondly, it's necessary to compile all the information obtained about them and report to superiors in the parent-company with their opinion, which can be accepted by them or not."* and also that *"it isn't easy to understand the geological distribution of a lode mine, which hinders communication with the local managers about it".*

3.6   Critical Analysis

Based on the literature review in Section two and the evidence obtained from managers in the local subsidiary subject to study (interviews and documentary analysis), the results obtained will now be presented and discussed.

Concerning human capital, as seen, its management is critical for organisations (Bandeira 2010), as this is understood as a strategic intangible asset for their success.

In this study, although the parent-company has a human resource management according to that argument, in practice human resource management falls well short of that basic assumption. Only confirmed was the existence of a formal human resource manual reflecting the conditions of the Japanese parent-company, and an internal document describing the functions of local managers. In this context, human resource management, at the local level, does not reflect the new vision of human capital, where its organisational structure is, to some extent, the reflection of this. Here, Marimuthu et al. (2009) conclude that human capital includes individuals and organisations, so that added value will be created for both parties, with this case not revealing empirical evidence of that alignment.

In other words, the Japanese parent-company has not implemented strategic management of human capital in this subsidiary, going against the conclusion of Wright and McMahan (1992) and McMahan et al. (1999), and has not considered the subsidiary's human capital as a factor of competitive advantage (Çalişkan 2010; Joseph 2012; Progoulaki and Theotokas 2010), bearing in mind that mining is not something the parent-company is fully versed in. Comparing this question with the development of human capital management, we can conclude that its management in this subsidiary is set more in the traditional view (Barbosa 2005).

A negative point in this subsidiary is the lack of an effective system of performance assessment, which contributes to some inefficiency in human resource management, particularly the management of competences, despite career management in the hierarchical levels of manual workers. Therefore, management of human resources as an intangible asset is ineffective in terms of practices and processes, as that system is considered academically as one of the best practices in managing that asset. Nevertheless, there is a bonus system based on production, which corroborates the conclusions of Barney (2002) when studying the competences of human capital and explaining why this is intangible.

Another crucial practice in the management of human capital, and even of knowledge and innovation, is internal and external communication. In this case, this is of negligible importance for the Japanese parent-company, as in its functional structure there is no communication department. Internal communication with collaborators is not easy, with it sometimes being necessary to turn to external entities to solve internal conflicts with collaborators. External communication, in turn, is the administration's responsibility.

Summarizing, the existing communication policy, if indeed it can be called that, focuses more on solving conflicts that arise rather than on preventive action based on constructive dialogue.

Some attention is paid to internal training of manual workers, but the subsidiary has no training department in its organisational structure. The training of these collaborators agrees with the conclusions of Silva (1997) regarding the importance of emphasizing this aspect. As for the training of local middle and top management, they have to deal with this themselves, despite not openly referring to it, as they understand this to be a delicate matter. However, they show the desire to make this personal investment in accordance with their status, as mentioned by Stiles and Kulvisaechana (2003).

Although not common, this subsidiary includes a social aspect in its human resource management. That is, due to the long history implicit in its organisational culture and collaborators' view of the social obligations the organisation should respect in relation to them and the surrounding community, the administration felt the need to include some social practices in its management.

The vision and perception held by collaborators in relation to those obligations of the subsidiary imply that the recruitment policy defined is generally little applied, i.e., the history of the rooted organisation culture means the subsidiary is obliged to employ all the people from the surrounding community. In fact, it is seen as "*a family*", as mentioned by the head of human resources.

Logically, and despite all these negative points, the head of human resources tries to emphasize and value each collaborator's individual competences, through application of career management including professional assessment. However, the whole process has to be validated by the administration and directors of the collaborator's operational area. This interviewee's position reflects to a certain extent an attempt to use competence management as a process of human capital management. This evidence agrees with the conclusion of Morcef et al. (2006), who pointed out the need to identify the areas where the individual can be placed according to their individual competences and in line with the objectives and competences essential to the organisation (Fleury and Fleury 2010), as well as its strategy (Junior and Santos 2009).

As for the question of managing flows of knowledge and innovation, its effective application is still something about which the administration shows little awareness. As the mining sector is considered strategic worldwide, knowledge and innovation are fundamental aspects that the managers/administrators of mines should not consider as something residual, but rather include them in operational management and also in the strategic management of human resources, as these too are intangible assets that can be managed and possibly even measured. Junior and Santos (2009) stated that knowledge and innovation should be managed jointly and form part of organisations' strategy.

The present case is a lode mine (rare) and not a rock mass mine (more common), where the human capital holds crucial knowledge and possesses individual competences. These are aspects that should be preserved, stimulated and transferred to future generations; i.e., this human capital is a driver of the intangibility associated with its knowledge and experience in lode mines. It should be noted that the Japanese parent-company obtained great benefit from this situation, as it knew how to take advantage of its position to obtain organisational learning and knowledge transfer, i.e., it drew benefits from the tangibility and intangibility of the investment it made through total acquisition of this subsidiary. This learning by the Japanese parent-company agrees with the knowledge-sharing indicated by various authors (Wright et al. 2001; Stiles and Kulvisaechana 2003).

Being aware of possessing the knowledge and experience of its collaborators, and that this cannot be imitated, at all hierarchical levels, in recent years the local administration began to recognize the impact of knowledge management on its business and institutional environment. This produced an alignment of the mission, vision, values and strategy with this new area of management.

Nevertheless, in this subsidiary collaborators show great resistance to crucial changes to respond to this alignment, particularly in the way of managing human resources, which should include the culture of knowledge and innovation. This should obviously be an integral part of the organisational culture. It stands out that this resistance is related to the subsidiary's history with a significant reflection on its organisational culture, being seen by collaborators as a social company, where they feel they only have to perform their tasks/functions as they have done for decades, showing a lack of understanding of the need to change their attitude in the workplace.

The lack of financial resources also prevents implementation of all the processes and practices of knowledge management and innovation. Once again, the pro-activeness of the head of human resources leads to him to seek to align individual competences with organisational competences, including knowledge and innovation, to compensate partially for the lack of investment in this area and to feel personally that the way he manages human resources comes closer to the concept of human capital.

To summarize, knowledge management is still far from being the norm in this subsidiary, but the Japanese parent-company was able to benefit from the knowledge held by the former. This opinion is unanimous among the local managers, who without reservations state that knowledge transfer takes place in only one direction, towards the parent-company, either through the permanent foreign official or occasionally. This position is also mentioned by the permanent foreign official, who admits a complete lack of knowledge and understanding of how a lode mine is operated and managed.

It becomes clear that the Japanese parent-company brought no added value to the subsidiary, in terms of knowledge and innovation. Innovation in mining is fundamental regarding effective mineral production and is necessary in this case, but the parent-company has not shown any willingness to invest in this.

4 Conclusions, Implications, Limitations and Suggestions

The empirical evidence from this case study may be considered *sui generis*, inasmuch as the study applied to a subsidiary belonging to an international economic group originating in Japan revealed that despite this group making a major investment to acquire the whole subsidiary, the objective in acquiring a foreign subsidiary was only to ensure good access to the mineral (final product), a scarce resource but crucial to different industries in Japan. There was no concern/will/aim to implement human capital management in the subsidiary, considering its intangibility and value as a factor of competitive advantage. This situation is well illustrated by the fact that all the subsidiary's production is exported to industries in the country holding the capital. In addition, the Japanese parent-company demonstrated failings in formal communication processes (internal and external), benefiting from the subsidiary's knowledge of the sector but without implementing mechanisms to share the organisational cultures or to transfer knowledge and innovation, as would be expected in the global operation of a major international economic group; bearing in mind the culture of innovation usually associated with Japanese industry. In this context, individual and organisational competences were only aligned and valued locally, so that this mine could continue successfully with the business restructuring process embarked on through the strategic option of acquiring a subsidiary firm, by ensuring direct access to a good source of raw material located in Portugal. It is also of note that the local human capital, in terms of top management, is considered to be of the highest quality anywhere in the world in the mining industry, but its intellectual development is each individual's entire responsibility, with no suitable process of human capital management to extend it and increase its value.

Two types of implications can be drawn from the results obtained. Firstly, regarding political decision-makers, who should create incentives to attract forms of foreign direct investment receptive to innovation and information transfer, in order to potentialize spillover effects from the international operation of multinationals with strategic interests in different industries of weight worldwide.

Secondly, as regards the managers of parent-companies and subsidiaries, this case reveals the need to deepen formal processes to favour the share of organisational cultures, especially concerning communication (internal and external) and research and development activities, which should assume bi-directional flows of knowledge and innovation transfer, in order to ensure an inclusive approach, of the win-win type, in business restructuring processes, namely those involving merger by acquisition or absorption of foreign subsidiaries.

This approach also underlines the need to make additional research efforts on restructuring cases, considering the implementation of different strategic options, such as diversification, internationalization, enhancement of intellectual capital, open innovation, licensing, joint-ventures, etc., in order to determine the greater or lesser importance of management of human capital and individual and organisational competences in implementing mechanisms of knowledge transfer and innovation in different economic activities.

The limitations of this study concern fundamentally the subjective nature inherent to adopting a qualitative approach based on a case study. Added to this are the natural limitations associated with interpreting the views conveyed by the interviewee, which need to be contrasted with the views of other nationals and foreigners in charge of the international economic group analysed.

Suggestions for future research could include similar approaches applied to high-growth companies versus low-growth companies, in order to find out the importance of collaborators' education and behavioural competences, to determine the absorptive and innovation capacity of business units with a different organisational culture and a diversity of cultures, genders, size and age.

References

Alharthey, B., Rasli, A., Yusoff, R., & Al-Ghazali, B. (2013). Impact of innovation culture on human resources management practices. *International Journal of Academic Research, 5*(3), 60–63.

Bandeira, A. M. A. (2010). *Activos intangíveis e actividades de I&D*. Porto: Vida Económica.

Barbosa, A. C. Q. (2005). Relações de trabalho e recursos humanos em busca de identidade. *Revista de Administração de Empresas, 45*(SPE), 121–126.

Barbosa, A. C. Q. (2009). Gestão de recursos humanos: realidade atual e perspetivas. In J. R. Silva & A. C. Q. Barbosa (Eds.), *Estado, empresas e sociedade – Um mosaico luso-brasileiro*. Lisboa: Edições Colibri.

Barbosa, A. C. Q., & Rodrigues, M. A. (2006). Alternativas metodológicas para a identificação de competências. *Boletim técnico do SENAC, 32*(2), 20–29.

Barney, J. B. (2002). *Gaining and sustaining competitive advantage*. Addison: Reading, MA.

Becker, G. S. (1975). Summary and conclusions. In *Human capital: A theoretical and empirical analysis with special reference to education* (pp. 245–256). Chicago, IL: The University Press of Chicago.

Becker, G. S. (1992). Nobel lecture: The economic way of looking at life. *Journal of Political Economy, 101*, 385–409.

Becker, G. S. (1993). *Human capital: A theoretical and empirical analysis with special reference to education* (3rd ed.). Chicago, IL: The University of Chicago Press.

Birasnav, M. (2014). Knowledge management and organizational performance in the service industry: The role of transformational leadership beyond the effects of transactional leadership. *Journal of Business Research, 67*(8), 1622–1629.

Bitencourt, C. (2004). *Gestão Contemporânea de Pessoas-: Novas Práticas, Conceitos Tradicionais*. Porto Alegre: Bookman Editora.

Boyatzis, R. E. (1982). *The competent manager: A model for effective performance*. New York: John Wiley & Sons.

Çalişkan, E. N. (2010). The impact of strategic human resource management on organizational performance. *Journal of Naval Science and Engineering, 6*(2), 100–116.

Ceitil, M. (2006). *Gestão e Desenvolvimento de Competências*. Lisboa: Edições Sílabo, Lda.

Ceitil, M. (2007). Enquadramento geral e perspetivas de base sobre o conceito de competências. In M. Ceitil (Ed.), *Gestão e desenvolvimento de competências* (pp. 23–37). Lisboa: Edições Sílabo.

Cheetham, G., & Chivers, G. E. (2005). *Professions, competence and informal learning*. Cheltenham: Edward Elgar Publishing.

Chen, C. J., & Huang, J. W. (2009). Strategic human resource practices and innovation performance—The mediating role of knowledge management capacity. *Journal of Business Research, 62*(1), 104–114.

Choo, C. W. (2003). *A organização do conhecimento: como as organizações usam a informação para criar significado, construir conhecimento e tomar decisões*. São Paulo: Senac São Paulo.

Denning, S. (2011). How do you change an organizational culture? *Forbes Magazine, 23*.

Direção Geral de Geologia e Energia. (2015). Mining industry – Portugal. *Statistical Information, 17*, 1–15.

Dyer, L., & Reeves, T. (1995). Human resource strategies and firm performance: What do we know and where do we need to go? *International Journal of Human Resource Management, 6*(3), 656–670.

Filius, R., de Jong, J. A., & Roelofs, E. C. (2000). Knowledge management in the HRD office: A comparison of three cases. *Journal of Workplace Learning, 12*(7), 286–295.

Fleury, A., & Fleury, M. T. L. (2010). *Estratégias Empresariais E Formação de Competências: Um Quebra-cabeça Caleidoscópico Da Indústria Brasileira*. São Paulo: Editora Atlas SA.

Franco, A. (2014). Desafios atuais e a nova visão para o futuro da indústria extrativa. XX Congresso dos Engenheiros. Accessed June 2015, from www.ordemengenheiros.pt

García-Morales, V. J., Jiménez-Barrionuevo, M. M., & Gutiérrez-Gutiérrez, L. (2012). Transformational leadership influence on organizational performance through organizational learning and innovation. *Journal of Business Research, 65*(7), 1040–1050.

Govindan, K., Kannan, D., & Shankar, K. M. (2014). Evaluating the drivers of corporate social responsibility in the mining industry with multi-criteria approach: A multi-stakeholder perspective. *Journal of Cleaner Production, 84*(1), 214–232.

Harvey, R. J. (1991). Job analysis. In M. D. Dunnette & L. M. Hough (Eds.), *Handbook of industrial and organizational psychology* (Vol. 2, 2nd ed., pp. 11–63). Palo Alto, CA: Consulting Psychologists Press.

Huselid, M., Jackson, S. E., & Schuler, R. (1997). Technical and strategic human resource management effectiveness as determinants of firm performance. *Academy of Management Journal, 40*(1), 171–188.

Joseph, B. (2012, July). *Innovative human resource practices and employee outcomes in software firms* (Work paper 1–20).

Junior, J. C., & Santos, S. B. S. (2009). A análise do ambiente interno: competência e capacidades. In L. G. Albuquerque & N. P. Leite (Eds.), *Gestão de pessoas: perspetivas estratégicas*. São Paulo: Atlas.

Kilimnik, Z. M., & Motta, F. M. V. (2003). *Gestão de Recursos Humanos em empresas mineiras: do tradicional ao moderno ou uma solução intermediária*. Publicado em ANAPAD.

Kim, G., Shin, B., Kim, K. K., & Lee, H. G. (2011). IT capabilities, process-oriented dynamic capabilities, and firm financial performance. *Journal of the Association for Information Systems, 12*(7), 487.

Knasel, E., & Meed, J. (1994). *Becoming competent: Effective learning for competence*. Sheffield: Employment Department.

Kwon, D. B. (2009, October). Human capital and its measurement. In *The 3rd OECD World Forum on "Statistics, Knowledge and Policy" Charting Progress, Building Visions, Improving Life* (pp. 27–30).

Le Deist, F. D., & Winterton, J. (2005). What is competence? *Human Resource Development International, 8*(1), 27–46.

Lengnick-Hall, C. A., & Lengnick-Hall, M. L. (2006). HR, ERP, and knowledge for competitive advantage. *Human Resource Management, 45*(2), 179–194.

Lloréns Montes, F. J., Ruiz Moreno, A., & García Morales, V. (2005). Influence of support leadership and teamwork cohesion on organizational learning, innovation and performance: An empirical examination. *Technovation, 25*(10), 1159–1172.

Marimuthu, M., Arokiasamy, L., & Ismail, M. (2009). Human capital development and its impact on firm performance: Evidence from developmental economics. *The Journal of International Social Research, 2*(8), 265–272.

McClelland, D. C. (1973). Testing for competences rather than for intelligence. *American Psychologist Journal, 20*, 321–333.

McClelland, D. C. (1998). Identifying competencies with behavioural-event interviews. *Psychological Science, 9*(5), 331–339.

McMahan, G. C., Virick, M., & Wright, P. (1999). Alternative theoretical perspectives for strategic human resource management revisited: Progress, problems and prospects. *Research in Personnel and Human Resources Management, 4*, 99–122.

Morcef, S. O., Boas, J. A. V., Ferreira, J. C., Said, R. A., & Seabra, T. C. (2006). Gestão de Competências–Um estudo de Caso III Simpósio de excelência em Gestão e tecnologia.

Nonaka, I., & Takeuchi, H. (1997). *Criação de conhecimento na empresa: como as empresas japonesas geram a dinâmica da inovação* (A. B. Rodrigues & P. M. Celeste, Trans.). Rio de Janeiro: Campus.

Nordhaug, O. (1998). Competence specificities in organizations: A classificatory framework. *International Studies of Management & Organization, 28*(1), 8–29.

Parnes, H. S. (1984). *Peoplepower: Elements of human resource policy*. Beverly Hills, CA: Sage.

Prahaland, C. K., & Hamel, G. (1997). Incorporando a perspetiva de competência essencial. In G. Hamel & C. K. Prahaland (Eds.), *Competindo pelo futuro: estratégias inovadoras para obter o controle do seu setor e criar mercados de amanhã*. Rio de Janeiro: Campus.

Progoulaki, M., & Theotokas, I. (2010). Human resource management and competitive advantage: An application of resource-based view in the shipping industry. *Marine Policy, 34*, 575–582.

Rossalto, M. A. (2003). *Gestão do conhecimento: a busca da humanização, transparência, socialização e valorização do intangível*. Rio de Janeiro: Interciência.

Ruas, R., Antonello, C. S., & Boff, L. H. (2005). *Aprendizagem organizacional e competências*. Porto Alegre: Bookman.

Ruuska, I., Ahola, T., Martinsuo, M., & Westerholm, T. (2013). Supplier capabilities in large shipbuilding projects. *International Journal of Project Management, 31*(4), 542–553.

Sarsur, A. M., Fischer, A. L., & Amorim, W. A. C. (2010). Gestão por competências: a (não) inserção dos sindicatos em sua implementação nas organizações. In J. S. Dutra (Ed.), *Gestão de pessoas: modelo, processos, tendências e perspetivas*. São Paulo: Atlas.

Schuler, R. (1990). Repositioning the human resource function: Transformation or demise? *Academy of Management Executive, 4*(3), 49–60.

Scianni, M. A., & Barbosa, A. C. Q. (2009). Limites e possibilidades teóricas da articulação entre competências organizacionais e individuais: em direção a um novo constructo? *Boletim Técnico do Senac, 35*(3), 76–87.

Silva, S. (1997, May). Human resources development for competitiveness: A priority for employers. In *ILO Workshop on Employers' Organizations in Asia–Pacific in the Twenty-FirstCentury*, Turin (pp. 5–13).

Sinnott, G. C., Madison, G. H., & Pataki, G. E. (2002). *Competencies: Report of the competencies workgroup, workforce and succession planning work groups*. New York State Governor's Office of Employee Relations and the Department of Civil Service.

Snell, S., & Dean, J. (1992). Integrated manufacturing and human resource management: A human capital perspective. *Academy of Management Journal, 35*(3), 476–504.

Spencer, L. M., & Spencer, P. S. M. (1993). *Competence at work models for superior performance*. New York: John Wiley & Sons.

Spithoven, A., & Teirlinck, P. (2015). Internal capabilities, network resources and appropriation mechanisms as determinants of R&D outsourcing. *Research Policy, 44*(3), 711–725.

Stiles, P., & Kulvisaechana, S. (2003). *Human capital and performance: A literature review*. DTI.

Teixeira, A. (2002). *On the link between human capital and firm performance. A theoretical and empirical survey*.

Thaler, R. H. (2015). *Misbehaving: The making of behavioral economics*. New York: W.W. Norton.

Thaler, R., & Sunstein, C. (2008). *Nudge: Improving decisions on health, wealth, and happiness*. New Haven, CT: Yale University Press.

Thévenet, M. (2010). As competências como alternativas à gestão dos recursos humanos. In J. S. Dutra, M. T. L. Fleury, & R. Ruas (Eds.), *Competências: conceitos, métodos e experiências*. São Paulo: Atlas.

Treasury Board of Canada Secretariat. (1999). Framework for competency-based management in the public service of Canada. Report of joint initiative between the Treasury Board of Canada Secretariat and the Public Service Commission.

Ulrich, D. (1997). *Human resource champions: The next agenda for adding value and delivering results*. Boston, MA: Harvard Business School Press.

Wright, P., & McMahan, G. (1992). Theoretical perspectives for strategic human resource management. *Journal of Management, 18*, 295–320.

Wright, P. M., Dunford, B. B., & Snell, S. A. (2001). Human resources and the resource-based view of the firm. *Journal of Management, 27*, 701–721.

www.dgeg.pt. Accessed May 2016.

www.stantonchase.pt/. Accessed September 2016.

Zula, K. J., & Chermack, T. J. (2007). Integrative literature review: Human capital planning: A review of literature and implications for human resource development. *Human Resource Development Review, 6*(3), 245–262.

Specific Practices of Human Resource Management in the Creation and Development of Micro and Small Firms, Case Studies in Portuguese Firms

Helder Antunes and António Nunes

Abstract Practices of human resource management (HRM) have an impact on business efforts, making the acceptance of risks and innovation more pro-active. It therefore becomes necessary to understand and identify the HRM practices present in the creation of micro and small firms, as well as in their development, and characterise the needs of professional training and new competences. From a qualitative approach, in four micro and small firms, business-people and collaborators were interviewed to identify the specific HRM practices present at the beginning of activity in this type of organisation. Data treatment was through content analysis. Analysis of the organisation's creation and development stages identified as critical HRM practices recruitment and selection and professional training. Performance assessment was identified at the time of firm development, increasing in formalization and complexity over time and as the number of collaborators grows. The formalization of rewards and bonuses is affected by increased firm size, at the two stages. At the moment of creating the firm, training actions in financial management and HRM are necessary. Organisational development requires technical competences in each area of business, and also continuity and deepening of the areas of overall management and human resource development.

Keywords Human resource management practices in micro and small firms · Creation and development of micro and small firms · Necessary competences

H. Antunes
University of Beira Interior, Covilhã, Portugal

A. Nunes (✉)
Department of Management and Economics, University of Beira Interior, Research Center in Business Sciences (NECEUBI), Covilhã, Portugal
e-mail: anunes@ubi.pt

© Springer International Publishing AG, part of Springer Nature 2018
S. Cubico et al. (eds.), *Entrepreneurship and the Industry Life Cycle*, Studies on Entrepreneurship, Structural Change and Industrial Dynamics,
https://doi.org/10.1007/978-3-319-89336-5_7

137

1 Introduction

Research on Human Resources goes back to last century with studies based on the differences in practices and implementation of activities such as recruitment, selection and assessment (Huselid 2011). Recently, human resource managers have been seen as facilitators of the implementation of organisational strategies, converting them into objectives, practices and inventories of human resource talents. According to the same author, today the choice of competitive advantages from the organisation's talents is important and determinant of organisational strategic success and in management of workforce systems.

HR activities and programmes should consider the firm's internal organisation and external environment. How human resource systems and the respective policies and practices are set up contributes to the organisation's goals and is essential for strategic management of human resources (Prahalad and Hamel 1990).

The concept of the value of work and creation of human resource activities was developed by Friedman[1] and Lev (1974) and Lau and Lau (1978), who wanted to incorporate the value of human contributions in the firm's value, resorting to the development of future strategies to measure human resource activities (Steffy and Maurer 1988).

Some studies demonstrate the importance of human resources, as a competitive advantage, in business success or failure (Lepak and Snell 1999). Practices such as careful recruitment and selection, incentives, compensation and training can develop skills and aptitudes, contributing to firm performance (Miles and Snow 1984; Huselid 1995; Huselid and Becker 2000, 2011; Wright et al. 2001). According to the same authors, human resources management (HRM) practices help to create sustainable competitive advantages, especially if those practices are in line with the firm's strategy.

The importance given to HRM, the application and formalization of HRM practices in micro and small firms, as well as their evolution over time, development of the entrepreneurial intention, and the need to develop human resources through training are the main focus of this study. For subsequent in-depth analysis, the research questions are:

- What HRM practices are present in the creation and development of micro and small firms?
- In what areas is professional training necessary, considering collaborator development?

---

[1]*Human Resources Accounting* (HRA), method of systematizing the value of work and creating value from human resource activities. Development of strategies to measure collaborators' potential future activities.

With the continuous need to develop the concept of dynamic capacities (Eisenhardt and Martin 2000), HRM operates as a capacity (Hayton 2006), where application of its practices develops the levels of corporate entrepreneurship within organisations (Schmelter et al. 2010). Firm creation and growth are related to entrepreneurial behaviour (Bayon et al. 2015). In micro and small firms, growth is seen as part of the entrepreneurial process (Davidsson et al. 2002).

The literature shows there is a positive effect of training on all organisational levels (Aguinis and Kraiger 2009; Aragon et al. 2014). Training activities provide collaborators with new competences and knowledge, raising business performance (Aguinis and Kraiger 2009).

Various studies contextualize research models in large firms. These models are frequently applied to micro and small firms, where the situation and specific contexts are different (Heneman et al. 2000).

So it is urgent and relevant to understand and identify the HRM practices present in the creation of micro and small firms, due to their specificity and the lack of studies on these business entities, in order to characterise as well as possible the needs for professional training and the potential need of new competences.

To contextualize the studies by McEvoy (1984), McEvoy and Buller (2013), they used the life-cycle theory to analyse HRM practices in medium-sized firms, orienting the study from a strategic perspective of HRM. Schmelter et al. (2010) also made a study using the theory based on firms' resources, in the context of dynamic capacities, where they analysed the choice of HRM practices and their impact on corporate entrepreneurship. However, none of these studies identifies the HRM practices present in firm creation, and so in attempting to fill this gap in the research, the first specific objective of this study will be to:

- Identify the HRM practices present in the creation of micro and small firms, their development, and the importance given to those practices or restrictions to their application.

Referring to the research by Gómez et al. (2004), Kaya (2006), and Aragon et al. (2014), the following objective emerged:

- Characterise the professional training needs of entrepreneurs and collaborators.

The intention is to identify what characterises HRM policies in a typology of organisations that are not usually subject to study in this area, which should result in indications for political decision-makers and those in charge of management in micro and small firms.

Also a relevant concern is identification of policies and strategies in the area of professional training and the competences necessary for all members of the organisation when starting up activity and in the development stage, for subsequent use by organisations that embark on identical processes.

2   Literature Review

2.1   Strategic Management of Human Resources, a View Supported by the Resources-Based View of the Firm

Firms' internal characteristics (strengths and weaknesses) and the external environment (threats and opportunities) eliminate their heterogeneous resources and can become a source of competitive advantage. In the model by Barney (1991), the resources-based view of the firm (RBV) substitutes these two characteristics in the context of competitive advantage. It establishes a path between the firm's resources and sustainable competitive advantages through value, rarity, substitution and imitation (Barney 1991; Peteraf 1993).

Strategic human resource management (SHRM) emerges from exploring the role of human resources in the firm, based on support of business strategy and its affirmation (Becker and Huselid 2006).

According to the studies by Wright et al. (2001), SHRM was not born from the resources-based view of the firm, but was an instrument for its development. With the growing idea that human resources are a source of competitive advantage in firms, it is legitimate to assume that people are strategically important for the organisation's success (Wright et al. 2001).

Lepak and Snell (1999) presented a model approaching SHRM, based on RBV, and considered two dimensions, describing different combinations between collaborators' relationships and human resource systems.

The model shows how HRM practices result in competitive advantage, not in isolation but as a set of skills, capacities and knowledge related to strategically relevant behaviours (Lepak and Snell 1999).

According to the "pool" concept of human capital, HRM practices are identified as: (i) work project; (ii) personal practices; (iii) participation; (iv) training; (v) recognition and bonuses; (vi) communication and assessment, all of them having an impact on collaborators and developing their competences, cognitions and attitudes (Wright et al. 2001).

Bacon et al. (2004) also show that the business strategy has an important impact on HRM development. The theoretical integrations of RBV and strategic human resource management (SHRM) generated concepts such as knowledge, dynamic capacity, organisational learning and leadership as sources of competitive advantage, as the interception of the challenges of human resources and strategy (Wright et al. 2001; Collins and Clark 2003; Collins and Smith 2006).

2.2   Organisational Learning and Training

Organisational learning has recently come to be considered as a strategic perspective, a heterogeneous source for organisations as a possible competitive advantage

(Grant 1996). Organisational learning is understood as an essential element of success when competing in global markets (Prahalad and Hamel 1990).

Organisational learning is therefore seen as a dynamic process based on knowledge. It corresponds to passing between various levels of action, from the individual level to the group level and to the organisational level (Huber 1991; Crossan et al. 1999; Jerez-Gomez et al. 2005).

Organisational learning is multi-level, the suggestion that innovative ideas and vision occur at the individual rather than the organisational level (Simon 1991) being complemented by other authors who claim that knowledge generated individually does not influence the organisation independently. Ideas are shared, decisions are taken and a common meaning is developed (Huber 1991; Argyris and Schon 1996; Crossan et al. 1999).

In his psychological approach and focus on organisational learning, Huber (1991) proposes four constructs and processes: (i) knowledge acquisition as a process of how knowledge is obtained; (ii) distribution of information, as a process whereby information from various sources is shared and understood, or leads to new information; (iii) interpretation of information; (iv) organisational memory, as a process whereby information is kept for future use (Huber 1991).

Individual knowledge processes and organisational and social knowledge processes interact, causing group dynamics that inhibit or facilitate organisational learning (Crossan et al. 1999).

Garvin (1993) highlights that an organisation able to change behaviours by generating new knowledge is one that is skilled in the transfer, creation and acquisition of knowledge. An organisation's learning capacity is influenced by a number of characteristics that facilitate that learning. Individual thinking processes affect the organisation as a whole when shared and adopted by the organisation (Crossan et al. 1999).

Some studies suggest that training is a key factor in improving organisational learning (Garvin 1993; Gómez et al. 2004), with training being one of the HRM practices (Cabrera and Cabrera 2005) through which firms can influence collaborators' behaviours, attitudes and skills (Chen and Huang 2009).

The literature shows that training has a positive effect on all organisational levels, individual, group and organisation or social (Aguinis and Kraiger 2009; Aragon et al. 2014). Training activities provide collaborators with new competences and knowledge, thereby increasing firm performance (Aguinis and Kraiger 2009). Training oriented to learning in the firm, with long-term planning, serves as a stimulus to organisational learning (Gómez et al. 2004; Cabrera and Cabrera 2005; Chen and Huang 2009; Aragon et al. 2014).

2.3 Activities and Practices of Human Resource Management in the Organisational Context

Various studies contextualize research models in large firms. In the case of small and medium-sized enterprises (SME), large firm models are often applied, despite the specific situations and contexts being different. Variables such as structure and size should be taken into account in research focused on SMEs (Heneman et al. 2000; Pearson et al. 2006a).

According to Bacon et al. (1996), the most important question in SMEs is not what HRM practices are adopted, but how they are put into practice. Considered important are the degree of formalization of human resource practices and how they are systematized, documented and institutionalized.

In the study by Heneman et al. (2000), small business entrepreneurs gave great importance to HRM valued at the organisational and personal level. The study of these topics was appreciated and well-received by the participating entrepreneurs, but they did not reveal great concern about traditional human resource management practices, their focus being more on the person's characteristics and how they combine with the firm. They perceived HRM as a flow of related activities, attracting the right collaborators to the firm and retaining them with rewards and motivation. In this study, entrepreneurs' main concerns about HRM activities were recruitment and selection, retention of collaborators and payment of salaries and rewards (Heneman et al. 2000).

Miles and Snow (1984) introduce a comparison between HRM practices and the firm's strategic management. In its development, human resource departments should spread information about products, services and markets in order to retain and develop managers and collaborators. They should familiarize themselves with the strategy, its planning in the firm and participate in strategic management processes. The HRM department and its practices should be in line with the firm's strategy (Miles and Snow 1984; Huselid et al. 2005).

Developing the strategic dimensions of HRM practices in small and medium-sized firms, Cassell et al. (2002) proposed a study model showing some factors firms face: (i) reduced productivity and performance results; (ii) absence of competences (iii) HRM practices being influenced by factors and priorities felt in firms, such as the absence of a head of HR, with the person in charge generally accumulating other functions within the firm.

Intervention in HRM practices to solve problems is affected by decision-makers having, or not having, experience and training in HRM, with the decision being based on previous learning. The training provided by the firm regarding policies of recommendation and promotion contribute to increasing workers' commitment to the company (Chang 1999).

The type of practices to adopt and their degree of formalization are indicated as strategic factors for the firm. Managers with knowledge of HRM techniques apply them in the firm and give more value to collaborator training (Vinten 2000).

The study by Cassell et al. (2002) indicates the need to assess existing resources for the implementation of new HRM practices. The strategies to use depend on the abundance or shortage of those resources. The application of a given HRM practice depends on recognising the need to use HRM practices in response to problems, the availability of existing resources and the organisation's current priorities. Besides focusing on the strategic level, HRM should emerge from firms' current priorities in the case of SMEs. Their organisational situation is heterogeneous regarding the availability of resources, which makes uniform adaptation difficult (Cassell et al. 2002). For good configuration and prominence of HRM practices, great knowledge and experience is necessary (Kaya 2006).

2.4 Activities and Practices of Human Resource Management

2.4.1 Recruitment and Selection

Recruitment and selection is the most commonly used HRM practice in SMEs (Cassell et al. 2002). The activities of recruiting and retaining human resources determine the success of these firms (Pearson et al. 2006b). Analysis and description of functions are essential for the recruitment practice but are not always used by SMEs (Heneman et al. 2000; Kotey and Slade 2005). Documented and systematized analysis of functions varies according to company size (McEvoy 1984; Hornsby and Kuratko 1990). Pina e Cunha et al. (2012) indicate and define the stages of the recruitment and selection process with the analysis of functions; profile of competences and aptitudes; recruitment and selection decisions, attribution and study of performance and assessment.

According to Deshpande and Golhar (1994), SMEs should concentrate more on external recruitment even at a low cost. When they look outside, they prefer government employment agencies and references from other collaborators (Kotey and Slade 2005), or the word-of-mouth referred to by Cassell et al. (2002). Attracting and retaining collaborators is a challenge for SMEs (Hornsby and Kuratko 1990; McEvoy and Buller 2013).

2.4.2 Rewards, Recognition and Bonuses

According to Pfeffer (1998), rewards are important for performance in most labour systems. Rewards and benefit packages, according to Hornsby and Kuratko (1990), are influenced by companies' size, which also affects the sophistication of reward and bonus systems. So rewards are a practice that is greatly affected by firm size (Hornsby and Kuratko 1990; Cassell et al. 2002).

Salary policies also vary according to company size. The larger the organisation, the greater the capacity to provide salary policies, benefits and incentive systems. SMEs should determine incentive packages that can compete with large firms, within their available resources (Golhar and Deshpande 1997).

McEvoy (1984) considers that commission and bonuses are more effective and more used in SMEs, arguing that satisfaction with rewards and incentives contributes greatly to the level of collaborator performance. Williams et al. (2007) made a study of the causes and consequences of satisfaction with rewards, presenting as the main conclusions: (i) Satisfaction with benefits is negatively related to leaving the organisation; (ii) Satisfaction with rewards and benefits is positively related to organisational performance and effort; (iii) Satisfaction with benefits is closely related to satisfaction in the firm; (iv) Collaborators' satisfaction increases when they perceive a relationship between rewards and performance.

Cassell et al. (2002) consider that in spite of all the incentive programmes and salary policies, SMEs do not consider application of this practice as a priority, alleging in some cases that its application would become unequal between groups of collaborators.

2.4.3 Performance Assessment

This practice is also affected by company size. The larger the firm, the greater the complexity of assessment and performance systems, with diverse ways of interpreting and operationalizing this process (Cassell et al. 2002). The process of performance management should include standardised results, defined according to the organisation's values, strategies and objectives, which should be continuously improved and controlled (Pina e Cunha et al. 2012). With greater proximity between collaborators in small companies, observation of performance is the most commonly used method, as this facilitates alteration when necessary. In large firms, self-assessment and assessment of colleagues is proportional to company size and is used more the larger the organisation (Kotey and Slade 2005). McEvoy (1984) adds that the determination of individual objectives facilitates analysis of performance, improving information about the function's requirements.

Some SMEs that carry out periodic performance assessment tend to analyse collaborators' transversal competences, with less emphasis on the requirements and specificity of each function (Khan et al. 2013).

2.4.4 Career Development

The accumulation of professional experiences throughout life, normally with progression in the organisational hierarchy in one or various firms, can be defined as a professional career. Career management should not be forgotten in the organisation, as the need to retain, develop and motivate human resources as a whole is a growing requirement (Pina e Cunha et al. 2012).

Nowadays, identity and creativity in performing functions are alternative perspectives of the traditional career. New career models include a variety of options. In career management, organisations should seek new models, as organisational commitment and loyalty may no longer be as valid as they were in the past. Investment in people rather than control gives a better result in terms of commitment (Baruch 2004).

Collaborators' involvement and commitment to the organisation are increasingly part of the vocabulary in applying HRM. This is a continuous process that requires collaborators' commitment based on a focus on performance, as if they were "business partners", contributing to motivation and performance at work (Arrowsmith and Parker 2013).

2.4.5   Professional Training

Matlay (2002) says that the literature contains few studies on SMEs' needs, especially in relation to the development and training of human resources. Training was initially considered as complementary to education, serving to resolve deficits in competences which schooling did not meet. It is assumed to be a component of developing organisational competences. The author argues that training is of a more reactive than pro-active nature in micro and small firms (Matlay 2002).

According to Pina e Cunha et al. (2012), training is a process where human resources alter knowledge, capacities, attitudes and behaviours necessary to perform their functions, from the organisational point of view (Kaya et al. 2010).

SMEs use training, but without a long-term training plan, acting to solve immediate business needs rather than to develop their collaborators' competences (Cassell et al. 2002; Matlay 2002; Pina e Cunha et al. 2012). A plan with a training programme should allow attainment of the necessary competences according to objectives (Vinten 2000). The same author concludes that the smaller the organisation, the more practical training will be. Other authors, such as Kotey and Slade (2005) conclude that in SMEs training is understood as the correction of some functions and as observation of activities. Training on the job is the most frequent type in SMEs, and in micro-firms, according to Kotey and Slade (2005), intensive training actions may not be necessary since collaborators are few in number and/or family or friends.

Given the cost of training, SMEs with fewer economic resources are reluctant to introduce training activities (Marta Fernandez et al. 1999; Alasadi and Al Sabbagh 2015), and sometimes take on collaborators with more experience to avoid training costs (Khan et al. 2013). Taking the example of the United States of America, large firms use a greater variety of training types, with the most common form being training in the work context, seminars and coaching (Hornsby and Kuratko 1990; Kotey and Slade 2005). Shih and Chiang (2011) point out that externally contracted training should contain activities and be in line with the firm's strategy, so that collaborators can integrate skills in the context of their functions.

2.5   Organisational Size and Human Resource Management Practices

According to the definition of SMEs from the Agency for Competitiveness and Innovation I.P. (IAPMEI) (2015a, b) and the European Commission (2003), an SME is an organisation with fewer than 250 employees and a turnover or total balance sheet no greater than 50 million euros and 43 million euros, respectively. A micro-firm is an organisation with fewer than 10 employees and a turnover or total balance sheet under 2 million euros. A small firm has under 50 employees and a turnover or total balance sheet under 10 million euros. Medium-sized firms are SMEs that are neither micro nor small.

There are great differences in the use of HRM practices between large firms and SMEs. Hornsby and Kuratko (1990) add that training practice is more used by medium-sized firms, while in small firms the value of collaborator training is less recognised. They also say that the HRM practices used by SMEs are more sophisticated than they appear to be, with the level of sophistication increasing as firms grow. In the same way, firms' perception of future HRM trends also increases. However, small business-people, while recognising factors to consider to have a quality workforce, should increase their knowledge and understanding of HRM practices in order to improve collaborators' skills in such firms (Hornsby and Kuratko 1990). These authors' study indicates greater knowledge of HRM in SMEs, with the recruitment methods most commonly used being government employment agencies, newspaper advertisements and references, these being the least costly options.

Larger firms tend to use methods such as application forms, following up references and interviews. Indicated as selection methods were tests to assess personality and attitudes, which are less used by small companies (Hornsby and Kuratko 1990).

Deshpande and Golhar (1994) compared the application and use of HRM practices in large and small firms, finding that the former give more importance of organisational success and the latter to the capacity to control work. Both types of organisations attributed the same importance to training of new collaborators, communication, competitive salaries in relation to performance, and collaborators' participation and safety. The main conclusion of this study is that managers' perception of HRM is not accompanied by policies favouring its development, where management strategies do not stimulate HRM development (Deshpande and Golhar 1994).

As firms increase in size in terms of leaders' functions, methods of assessing performance are more varied than in relation to other employees. In small companies, performance is more easily observed, with greater proximity facilitating adjustment. Self-assessment and turning to work colleagues for assessment are proportional to firms' increased size (Kotey and Slade 2005).

Transversal competences and their development are strategies sought in today's organisations. In their study of small Irish firms, MacMahon and Murphy (1999) find that business-people identify the need for their managers to develop transversal competences through training, in various areas, rather than developing specific competences, to continuously improve flexibility in carrying out work.

From the above, in the attempt to understand and identify the topics addressed in the relevant literature, we go on to describe the empirical approach in the following chapter.

3   Research Methodology

Throughout this section, we will characterise the methodologies used. The study is a qualitative investigation. The research plan is structured according to the multiple case methodology (Yin 2009), using semi-structured interviews for data collection, which are then subject to content analysis. This is an exploratory study, with a research model in which the researcher does not manipulate the variables present, but seeks to identify certain HRM characteristics and activities present in the creation and development of sample firms, as well as the need for professional training and new competences. The case study is used in various situations in different areas, contributing to knowledge about individual, group, organisational, social and political phenomena (Yin 2009). It allows the researcher to register characteristics from real life. According to the same author, when the study covers analysis of more than one case, it provides greater sustainability and robustness (the multiple case study) than analysis of a single case.

This study follows the characteristics of case studies: an idiographic perspective, in that it analyses a particular life situation with all its specificities, analysing a set of individual cases perceiving their specificity; Dealing with contextual data, and factors, where they occurred and were influenced; Data triangulation considering information from various sources and concern about theory, where case studies facilitate and originate the formulation of hypotheses or theory formation. They may or may not be generalized to other existing cases (Willig 2001).

3.1 Selection of Participants for the Study

Regional business associations were approached to select representative cases of entrepreneurship in the creation of micro and small firms in the Beira Interior region, in various sectors of activity.

The firms selected were divided in two groups: Group I, firms operating for less than 24 months, and Group II, firms operating for more than 24 months. The criteria for selecting both groups were as follows:

- Accepting to participate in the study and the business-person showing characteristics of entrepreneurship, such as motivations, attributes and carrying out the entrepreneurial intention.
- Having more staff than when beginning activity, recruiting at least one collaborator.
- Having provided collaborators with professional training, with more than one training action for collaborators as part of a training plan with defined objectives and data proving this has taken place.
- Having developed products/services for the market, with data on the evolution of turnover and product/service development.
- Being based in, or with representation in Beira Interior.

3.2   Characterisation of Participants in the Study

Group I (operating for less than 24 months)
Firm A

The firm emerged through the entrepreneur creating employment for herself, in the estate-agency sector. The entrepreneur has a degree in law and a master in entrepreneurship and firm creation, with experience of repossession functions, in activities in land and building registry, characterisation, assessment and negotiating contracts. She holds a franchise for a brand, and the firm's main activity is estate agency mediation in selling, purchasing and renting. This includes compiling a portfolio of property, management of properties and rented accommodation, coming under activity code 68311 (estate agent activities). The main investment consisted of acquiring computer equipment. Beginning activity in 2014, the firm was created by establishing a sole proprietor limited company. The main objective was to ensure optimal results in the sale of property, providing clients with a complete portfolio of estate agent services. The selling process includes analysis of client qualification and management, product selection and after-sales service. The whole activity is supported by the experience, motivation and pro-activeness of the entrepreneur, based on effective publicity and marketing.

The potential market includes construction companies, property developers and private individuals who want to sell, buy or rent buildings. The geographical area of operation is Beira Interior and Alto Alentejo. With a strategy of quality services, initial publicity and customer loyalty, firm A finds its place in the market due to its professionalism, motivation, and constant renewal of the approach to the customer and the product. It has 3 internal collaborators and 15 external collaborators without a work contract with the firm.

Firm B

Having experience in the hotel and restaurant sector, by forming the firm the entrepreneur created her own employment, renovating a cafeteria and snack-bar in the historical part of Covilhã. With bar and restaurant services, Firm B offers a wide range of menus according to customers' choices. The good location, personal service and organisation of small events form the differentiation strategy adopted. The entrepreneur sees increasing clients and their loyalty as the main challenges, saying the project of creating the firm was due to being highly motivated, the need for personal development and the challenge to create new jobs.

Firm B has three internal collaborators, and comes under activity code 56101 (traditional-type restaurants). Formed in March 2015, as an establishment in the name of a single person, the businesswoman intends to become a limited company with the entry of a new partner. Managing purchases, organising stock, increased negotiating power with suppliers and organising a constant promotion plan, are the most urgent challenges. The market is segmented in university customers, other young customers due to the proximity of a vocational training centre and undifferentiated customers including tourists. Turnover is divided as follows; cakes and bread products represent around 20%, cafeteria/bar (sale of coffee, soft drinks, aperitifs and other drinks) represents around 25%, and the restaurant service around 55%.

Group II (operating for more than 24 months)

Firm C

Firm C, an industrial laundry, was formed in 1996 as the culmination of an investment project submitted to the Young Entrepreneur Support System (SAJE) and began operations in March 1996. Coming under economic activity code 74700 (industrial cleaning activities), the main business consists of washing and handling great quantities of textile goods for various institutions, recognized as being of high quality, guaranteeing a high level of hygiene and finishing with ironing. The firm also provides collection and delivery services. This business opportunity arose as no firm was carrying out this activity in the district, and led to various potential users opting for this service rather than have their own washing facilities. The main guidelines are based on continuing to satisfy their customers' needs and expectations. The principal areas of operation in the market are: hotel and catering (hotels, rural tourist accommodation and restaurants), health (hospitals and clinics), services (hairdressers) and private individuals.

Formed in 1996, the central objective of Firm C is complete customer satisfaction, ensuring a high quality service, both in terms of efficiency in the washing process and in relation to associated activities, such as ironing, folding, delivery and collection of clothing. Aware of its responsibility towards its collaborators and the community, the firm defined the following principles as guidelines associated with management of the environmental and health and safety at work component: Meeting all legal requirements associated with environmental aspects and the dangers and risks inherent to the activity carried out; Commitment to continuous improvement of existing processes as long as economically viable; Providing a climate of trust and internal communication with a view to constant improvement of working conditions and associated processes; Promoting an environment of partnership with customers and suppliers to stimulate a relationship of mutual help and cooperation, to seek the best solutions for both parties. At present, the firm has 14 collaborators.

Firm D

Firm D carries out its activity in the area of the sale and assembly of gas equipment, coming under activity code 47783 (retail sale of fuel), in specialized establishments. When beginning activity in 1995, Firm D only consisted of a bottle store and a distribution shop whose activity covered the sale of gas equipment, assistance and distribution in Fundão local authority. In 2000, it acquired a shop in Belmonte and began activity in this local authority. In 2001, it expanded to Covilhã local authority. In 2002, it acquired a store in Fundão industrial estate where it established the works and assistance department. In 2004, its quality management system was certified. The certification awarded confirms the company's good performance in the distribution and sale of gas, and in the sale of electrical equipment. In 2006, it decided to construct a new building and expanded its activity to the industrial gas, food and soft drink sector. In partnership with the French manufacturer Air Liquide SA., it aims to be a reference through its new and modern point of sale and filling, providing customers with a perfect balance between material technology, diversity of gas, proximity and speed of delivery. From 2009, in partnership with the BP group, it entered the business of the sale and assembly of solar panels. In 2015, it opened the point of supply of Liquefied Petroleum Gases-GPL[2] on its premises, which formed one more service in its portfolio. It increased its structures for the regional market of Viseu with the entry of new collaborators. Considered an SME of excellence in 2012 and a leading SME 2015 by IAPMEI, it now has 24 internal collaborators.

3.3   Process and Instruments for Data Collection and Analysis

The technique used in this study was the semi-structured interview, with an interview script containing all the dimensions and categories being elaborated. Field notes made when in contact with the parties involved were also used, as well as consultation of documents and procedures for internal use. Interviews are considered important sources of information in case studies, as interaction between people which in this case was semi-structured or semi-directed (Yin 2009).

Initially, the participants were contacted by telephone, asking them to take part in the research. Then a first meeting was arranged to provide all the necessary information, with the interviews being held later, in August 2015.

The questions in the interview script were organised in three dimensions, and categories and sub-categories related to the research objectives and questions were also identified.

The data were subject to content analysis, representing a set of analysis techniques that systematizes the contents of messages and communications collected (Bardin 1977). Finally, the results obtained were treated in relation to the initial goals and questions (Bardin 1977).

4   Presentation and Discussion of the Results

4.1   Individual Analysis of the Case Studies by Dimension and Categories

This section presents the case studies of all the firms involved in the research, Firms A, B, C and D. The results are presented in a descriptive form, including the transcription of some dialogues, with anonymity protecting confidentiality of all the data gathered. The interpretations presented consider participants' perceptions, analysis of the interviews and the field notes made by the researcher.

---

[2]"AutoLPG or Autogas" are the terms normally used to describe generically LPG (Liquefied Petroleum Gases) used as fuel in cars (apetro 2013).

4.1.1 Firm A

Dimension 1 and categories: Firm characterisation, attributes, entrepreneurial intention, motivations for firm creation.

This firm has been operating for about 1 year, and the businesswoman highlighted the team spirit in her human resources and the motivation of all in this phase of organisational life. The procedures and processes of the brand she represents facilitated the setting up and operationalization. The personal values and psychological characteristics of each collaborator were taken into account in the recruitment and selection process.

In the words of the interviewee: *"at the beginning it wasn't easy, but due to the efforts of everyone we achieved good results and continue on our mission. The values of the firm and our agents have produced results".*

The specific nature of the activity, by placing all the emphasis on the customer, requires great motivation on the part of the team of collaborators, aware of the need to deal with the customer in the best way possible, with continuous improvement of the creative process and good internal practices.

In the words of the interviewee *"Opening the firm arose from the opportunity to create jobs and expansion of the activity, managing people is difficult, but motivating. Competences such as financial management of the business and HRM were, and are, the challenges we continue to face and always need to improve."*

With the growth of the sector Firm A belongs to, seen in the growing levels of sales, the opportunity arose to represent a prestigious "brand" in the market, requiring the net creation of jobs. The businesswoman's motivations were to continue to develop her personal experience and the dream of having her own business, which was very well planned in an expanding sector nationally and internationally.

The businesswoman drew up her business plan with a view to the company's structure and expansion in the medium term. She participates in a programme supporting entrepreneurship (PAECPE[3]), which is formed of two methodologies: professional training with diagnosis and a development plan, and training consultancy, meaning long hours of accompaniment in the operational areas of the business.

The interviewee pointed out that the difficulties felt at the beginning were in areas of management such as: administrative organisation, billing procedures, al financial organisation and planning, tax planning and the legal deadlines to adhere to. HRM as a whole was also difficult, despite support from the franchising company where there were already procedures to apply specific HRM practices, for example: function description, allocating of responsibilities, competence scheme and operating manual (Table 1).

---

[3]Programme to Support Entrepreneurship and Self-Employment Creation—PAECPE, created by Decree n° 985/2009 of 4 September, with alterations introduced by Decree n° 58/2011, of 28 January, Decree n° 95/2012, of 4 April and Decree n° 157/2015, of 28 May, IEFP. (2015). "Summary of PAECPE". https://www.iefp.pt/en/empreendedorismo consulted in June 2015.

Table 1 Analysis of dimension 1 and categories, Firm A

Firm A	
Economic Activity Code (EAC)	68311—Estate agency activities
Date of formation	May 2014 (Group 1—less than 24 months)
Legal status	Sole proprietorship limited company
Number of collaborators	3 internal collaborators and 15 external collaborators (external consultants)
Qualifications	Average qualifications from 12th year of secondary school, six collaborators with a degree and one with a master (Businesswoman)
Product/Services	Estate agency work in purchasing, selling and renting: building up a property portfolio, property management and management of rented property
Typology of clients/geographical market	Construction companies, property developers and private individuals intending to sell, buy or rent property. Beira Interior and Alto Alentejo
Strategies	Representing the brand as a franchise quality service, initial publicity and customer loyalty, professionalism, motivation, constant renewal in dealing with the client and the product
Investment project/business plan	Yes. Creation of the job and support from the Institute of Employment and Professional Training IP (IEPT). Accompanying support for 24 months, (Programme to Support Entrepreneurship and Self-Employment Creation—PAECPE)
Personal attributes, family reasons, area of training, motivations through opportunity or need in the entrepreneurial intention	Opportunity to create her own business, apply knowledge from professional experience. Planned intention
Difficulties, obstacles, need for competences in creating the firm	Need of competences in financial management and HRM

Dimension 2 and categories: Activities and practices of Human Resource Management present in the firm's creation and development.

One of Firm A's objectives in this phase is to increase its human resource team. Over this year it has recruited consultants on various occasions. The recruitment and selection procedure is carefully planned, with curricular analysis and at least two interviews with each applicant. The reward system is assessed and accompanied at weekly meetings and presented in 3-monthly meetings, according to the objectives and development of agents and consultants (Table 2).

The entrepreneur recognised the need to improve a performance assessment system in the short term. *"Although objectives are fixed on individual results, performance assessment could include analysis of behaviour, team development and interpersonal relations, we're improving all that part of assessment"*. Career

Table 2 Analysis of dimension 2 and categories Firm A

Practices of Human Resource Management	When creating the firm	Development
Recruitment and selection	Recruitment procedure through the government employment agency, trade fairs and newspapers Selection by curricular analysis and interviews	Continued application of the established procedure, always aiming to enlarge the team of consultants
Rewards, recognition and bonuses	Three-monthly system of rewards, recognition and bonuses according to objectives	As the team grows, a bonus system is applied every 3 months
Performance assessment	System of assessment through observation by the leadership	The firm recognizes the need to develop an improved assessment and performance system in the short term
Career development, planning	Human resource planning according to the brand's criteria and those of the entrepreneur. Career development according to functions	Human resource planning according to the brand's criteria and those of the entrepreneur. Career development according to functions
Professional training	Recourse to initial training actions and internal introduction	Use of continuous development training actions in areas such as: creative thought, team management and negotiating techniques, both internally and externally

development is taken care of by the brand. It is carefully planned and allows development, recognition and good results, in financial terms, for the worker.

Firm A carries out internal training, to welcome new collaborators, and turns to external entities to develop a medium-term training plan concentrating on areas such as: creative thought, team management and negotiation techniques.

Dimension 3 and categories: Characterisation of practices of professional training and development of competences in the company's creation and development.

Development of Firm A's human resource competences is continuous, and is an internal strategy. Initially, the entrepreneur had training in areas supporting the business such as management, entrepreneurship and leadership, and the collaborators in areas related to carrying out their duties. In the words of the interviewee *"financial management is still a challenge, concentrating on the development of our human resources, retaining them and identification with the firm via competences are issues for the present and the future"*.

The process of formalizing training involved diagnosis, and holding and assessing training, but with few records, since improvement of the recording process is foreseen in the near future. The training received has been seen as positive by all and has continuously developed competences in collaborators and the leadership. It is indicated as an essential tool for everyone's daily performance.

Firm A resorts to the brand's training and also to financed training, the survey of needs being systematic and regular. According to the interviewee "*adaptation to new technology was easier for some collaborators than for others, and this is always an important area for business development.*"

The types of training most used were classroom training and coaching. Collaborators are accompanied directly by the training coordinator and by their superiors.

4.1.2   Firm B

Dimension 1 and categories: Characterisation of the firm, attributes, entrepreneurial intention and motivations for creating the firm.

Firm B is a micro-firm with three collaborators and has existed for several months. The businesswoman and collaborators are accompanied regarding training consultancy and training, as part of the programme to support entrepreneurship it is subject to.

Experience in the restaurant sector, a liking for the activity and wishing to create her own job were the reasons indicated for beginning operations. The greatest difficulties at the outset were accompanying financial management, stock management (purchases and suppliers) and HRM. Even with some initial training in these areas, these were competences needing to be improved. In the businesswoman's own words: "*dealing with suppliers, recording the planning of purchases, and carrying out the daily activities has been most difficult*" (Table 3).

The main reasons for forming the firm were the desire to work for herself, create her own job and her personal linking for this sector's activity. The businesswoman drew up the business plan considering activity in the medium term.

Dimension 2 and categories: Activities and practices of Human Resource Management present in the firm's creation and development.

Firm B began its activity recruiting and selecting collaborators based on references from friends, while recognizing the need to improve this practice due to the growth of the business and the need to structure the process.

As for performance assessment and in the businesswoman's own words: "*performance assessment is foreseen, but it is a process to improve, as well as complete description of collaborators' functions and internal regulations*".

Training activities in the initial period are recognised as important, but the logistics of working and the time available for this HRM practice did not always help in following the training timetable. However, these activities were well received, with everyone showing great interest and presenting good results in competence development. The subjects included in the firm's training plan are: event management, bookkeeping and planning marketing actions (Table 4).

Table 3 Analysis of dimension 1 and categories Firm B

Firm B	
Economic activity code (EAC)	56101—Traditional type restaurants
Date of formation	March 2015 (Group 1—less than 24 months)
Legal status	Businessperson in their own name, category B, with organised accounting
Number of collaborators	Three internal collaborators
Qualifications	12th year of schooling
Products/services	Restaurant, delivery, take-away, cafeteria and bar
Typology of customers/geographical market	Covilhã and surroundings. Business and university customers, serving groups and individuals
Strategies	Strategy of differentiation, personal service, location, organisation of small events and quality service
Investment project/business plan	Yes. Job creation and support from the Institute of Employment and Professional Training IP (IEPT) Supported accompaniment for 24 months (Programme to Support Entrepreneurship and Creation of Self-Employment—PAECPE)
Personal attributes, family reasons, area of training, motivations of opportunity or need in the entrepreneurial intention	Experience of restaurant work, the dream to have her own business and create her own job were the businesswoman's motivations
Difficulties, obstacles, the need for competences in creating the firm	Difficulty in planning marketing activities, in the planned customer increase at the beginning. Need to develop competences of financial management of stock and purchases, and HRM

Dimension 3 and categories: Characterisation of practices of professional training and competence development in creating and developing the firm.

Training actions were held on the firm's premises, face to face and involving all collaborators. The training process involves all stages including a survey of needs, planning, carrying out and assessment of training activities, but the methods and tools used in the training are aspects that should be improved in the future.

Firm B presents a training plan that is renewed annually, recognizing training as a way to develop skills such as: improved personalized service to the customer, improved marketing procedures, bookkeeping for better decision-making and increased HRM competences such as the planning and development of human resources.

The new technology introduced in the firm was well received without any resistance. The firm uses an external, certified training company within the accompaniment programme mentioned above.

Table 4 Analysis of dimension 2 and categories Firm B

Practices of Human Resource Management	When creating the firm	Development
Recruitment and Selection	The businesswoman used references from her circle of friends	Consulting government employment agency, use of interviews and curricular analysis of applicants
Rewards, recognition and bonuses	Verbal recognition from observation	Verbal recognition from observation
Performance assessment	No systematized procedure	Recognizes the importance of implementing performance assessment in the medium term
Career development, planning	There is a human resource plan that does not contemplate career progression	There is a human resource plan that does not contemplate career progression
Professional training	Training actions carried out and forecast, supported by PAECPE	Training actions forecast within the support from PACPE, in the areas of event management, bookkeeping and planning marketing actions

4.1.3   Firm C

Dimension 1 and categories: Characterisation of the firm, attributes, entrepreneurial intention, motivations in creating the firm.

Firm C highlighted that adaptation to the business was gradual and presented some initial difficulties, due to the businessman's previous experience in a different branch of activity.

In his own words *"many of the employees are the same as at the beginning, from 3 the firm came to have 17 and today we are 14. The major historical milestone was quality certification, then participation in the inPME[4] programme, through the development of consultancy measures, the production layout was analysed and new machines were acquired in 2005"*. *"One of the reasons for opening the firm was because there was nothing similar in the region, and so at the time it was innovative. When I imagined the business, it had to be something that was good for firms and for workers in the region."*

Also according to the businessman *"looking for the first customers and adaptation to the market was an obstacle, it was a service that was carried out in the firms themselves, they weren't ready to sub-contract. Adaptation to the equipment and*

---

[4]inPME, an intervention programme for consultancy and training in SMEs. An intermediate body of the Portuguese Industrial Association in the scope of the Operational Programme for Employment, Training and Social Development, Measure 2.2.—Training and Organisational Development. The inPME Project comes under the Ministry of Work and Solidarity and is supported by the European Social Fund.

fine-tuning it took some time. Nor was business management easy at the beginning, I knew about management but access to finance, deadlines, tax matters and the financial side required very specific knowledge. It was necessary to improve. Employees' initial training and adaptation to work methods was very worthwhile".

The firm drew up a business plan in 1995, and the current premises were built. According to the businessman, turnover exceeded what was forecast at the time, but in recent years the market has shrunk significantly (Table 5).

Dimension 2 and categories: Activities and practices of Human Resource Management present in creating and developing the firm.

The head of human resources in Firm C accumulates this function with others and throughout his academic studies he had training in areas of human resources.

Recruitment is sporadic, at the outset only considering: experience, qualifications from obligatory schooling and references from acquaintances. This process evolved until today when use is made of employment websites, the government employment agency, curricular analysis, analysis of experience and interviews for selection.

As for performance assessment, according to the businessman *"we have no performance assessment, at the end of the year we have a survey of collaborators' satisfaction where everyone participates".*

Table 5 Analysis of dimension 1 and categories Firm C

Firm C	
Economic activity code (EAC)	74700—Industrial cleaning activities
Date of formation	March 1996 (Group II)
Legal status	Limited company
Number of collaborators	14 internal collaborators
Qualifications	Average qualifications from the 9th year of education, 1 collaborator with a master
Products/services	Industrial laundry services, washing, treatment, ironing, folding and delivery. Rent of linen to hotel and catering units and health services
Typology of clients/geographical market	Health service units, hotel and catering establishments, restaurants and private individuals, market in North and Central Beira
Strategies	Quality of the final product, hygiene and adherence to safety and environmental norms
Investment project/business plan	Yes. Development of the activity with results above expectations
Personal attributes, family reasons, area of training, motivations of opportunity or need in the entrepreneurial intention	Innovative activity in the region at the time, the will to create his own business and create jobs. Choice of a different activity from the businessman's experience
Difficulties, obstacles, need for competences when creating the firm	Technical difficulties with machines and equipment at the beginning of operations Conquering the market. Development of competences in the area of management

Internal satisfaction is assessed annually, which is obligatory since the firm obtained quality certification.

According to the businessman "*specific training in the areas of the jobs has better results in developing competences, for example, specific treatment of textiles in the laundry*".

Firm C has an annual training plan with constantly updated records of both internal and external training. Concerning internal training, records are only kept for training actions longer than 8 h (Table 6).

Dimension 3 and categories: Characterisation of practices of professional training and development of competences in creating and developing the firm.

Since beginning operations, the most important areas of training in the firms are technical aspects with an impact on the job, developing competences related to the tasks and duties performed. At the stage of creating the firm, the businessman had training in entrepreneurship and management, declaring that training was decisive when setting up the business. He added that the areas of personal relations, and team motivation and development were important in developing human resources.

Table 6 Analysis of dimension 2 and categories Firm C

Practices of Human Resource Management	When creating the firm	Development
Recruitment and Selection	Use of references and word-of-mouth in forming the initial team, with some experience of laundry work	Use of employment websites and the government employment agency, curricular analysis, experience, selection interviews, without resorting to elaborated tests
Rewards, recognition and bonuses	Monthly bonus system in the absence of customer complaints	Monthly bonus system in the absence of customer complaints
Performance assessment	No formal performance assessment system. However, there is assessment of collaborators' satisfaction, in which collaborator teams have participated since 2005	No formal performance assessment system. However, there is assessment of collaborators' satisfaction, in which collaborator teams have participated since 2005
Career development, planning	Human resource planning without career development, being considered a "static" activity	Human resource planning without career development, being considered a "static" activity
Professional training	Annual training plans resorting to certified external entities, since 2005. Internal training on reception and Health and Safety at Work with records	Annual training plans resorting to certified external entities, since 2005. Internal training on reception and Health and Safety at Work with records. No long-term training plans

According to the businessman *"Using new technology was not a problem, there was quick adaptation without resistance"*.

Most training is financed, in an effort to reduce costs, but the contents of training in the areas approved in the projects are not always as useful as they could be, due to the specific technical nature. Together with the training entity and the trainers, Firm C adapts the content of each action when found to be necessary. All the records of the training process: needs diagnosis, pedagogical technical dossier, content files, summaries and attendance records, training assessment and training certificates are drawn up by the training entity and handed in to the firm. They develop annual training plans amounting to over 35 h[5] annually per collaborator, when considered necessary.

4.1.4   Firm D

Dimension 1 and categories: Characterisation of the firm, attributes, entrepreneurial intention, motivations for creating the firm.

The evolutionary path of Firm D was fairly linear, with little turnaround of human resources, and most collaborators have remained from the beginning until today.

In the words of the interviewee *"the entry of new collaborators was due to expanding business and the departure of some who retired"*. Firm D increased its human resources recently through opening a new unit in Viseu. The person in charge of human resources accumulates this with other functions.

The businessman's personal ambition and business expansion were the main reasons for creating the firm, as well as the business opportunity that appeared at the time. The founder's experience and technical knowledge led to exploring new products and services connected with his activity in the course of his life. Today, some members of his family are part of the firm, according to their areas of training.

Despite the initial training in management and entrepreneurship provided by the brands represented, he felt the need for knowledge of financial management, deadlines and planning, and stock organisation. Difficulties also arose in adapting to the computer system, as when the firm was created this was in constant development, largely due to the specific technical nature of the business and the use of certain specific programmes for the activity (Table 7).

Dimension 2 and categories: Activities and practices of Human Resource Management present when creating and developing the firm.

The year of 2004 is highlighted, when the firm obtained certification of its quality management system and added new processes and procedures even in its HRM.

Considering the words of the businessman *"nowadays for recruitment we use the Job Centre a lot, as it's a quicker process and also because of the financial support,*

---

[5]According to article 135, n° 2 of the Code of Work. "Each year, the worker has the right to a minimum of thirty-five hours of continuous training (. . .)".

Table 7 Analysis of dimension 1 and categories Firm D

Firm D	
Economic activity code (EAC)	47783—Retail sales of fuel in specialized establishments
Date of formation	1996 (Group II)
Legal status	Limited company
Number of collaborators	24
Qualifications	On average, the 12th of schooling, with 3 having degrees
Products/services	Distribution of gas, installation and exploitation of gas networks, distribution of *air liquide*, solar panel assembly, point of supply of LPG for cars
Typology of clients/geographical market	Private individuals and firms. Market of Beira interior and Viseu
Strategies	Extended product and service, quality service and customer satisfaction
Investment project/business plan	Yes, initial project and a development plan every year
Personal attributes, family reasons, area of training, motivations of opportunity or need in the entrepreneurial intention	Experience in the businessman's technical area, the desire to have his own business to develop a market opportunity, to include the family and personal ambition
Difficulties, obstacles, need for competences when creating the firm	Difficulties in financial management at the beginning. And developing technical, management and computing competences

and that has gone well. The firm doesn't have an introduction manual yet, but it's being developed".

The awarding of performance bonuses only concerns the technical and production side, but performance has clearly improved, justifying improvement of the reward system in the short term as it may increase employee motivation.

The performance assessment system has been applied since beginning operations, is carried out annually, involves all employees and even self-assessment is foreseen.

Career planning and development has been implemented since beginning activities, due to the requirements of the brands represented, specifically through training actions rigorously planned and carried out by certified external entities, as can be seen by consulting Table 8.

Dimension 3 and categories: Characterisation of practices of professional training, and development of competences when creating and developing the firm.

Firm D applies annual training plans in various areas, carrying out internal training with a certified trainer and also resorting to certified external training entities. The businessman felt the need for training and competence development in business management and for collaborators in technical areas in the firm's initial stages.

Table 8 Analysis of dimension 2 and categories Firm D

Practices of Human Resource Management	When creating the firm	Development
Recruitment and Selection	Recruitment of a team of collaborators with some experience and the 9th year of schooling. Selection through references from acquaintances and word-of-mouth	Recruitment and selection through interview and recourse to employment agencies. Description of functions and organogram since 2004
Rewards, recognition and bonuses	There are productivity bonuses but only on the technical side	There are productivity bonuses, but only on the technical and production side. Recognition of the need for improved attribution of bonuses in the short term. "They have served to motivate performance"
Performance assessment	Applied since 2004	There is an annual performance assessment system in which collaborators participate, various items are assessed, with self-assessment
Career development, planning	Career development through technical training from the brands represented, since 2004	Career development through technical training from the brands represented, since 2004. Collaborators are consulted to diagnose training needs
Professional training	Annual training plans resorting to certified external entities, from 2004. Internal introductory training and Health and Safety at Work, technical training with records, and e-learning	Annual training plans resorting to certified external entities, from 2004. Internal training with records. Medium-term training plans

The whole training process is based on diagnosis of employees' individual needs, and is elaborated by certified elements (internal or external), being subject to continuous assessment and planned for the medium-term. This great professionalism is related to quality certification which places high demands.

Firm D follows a strategy of training in contents and in the workplace context, considering the functions and competences to develop in relation to the objectives formed. It diagnoses training needs annually, with collaborator participation, and has a pedagogical technical dossier for each training action with notes on summaries, attendance and assessment of the action. Even when using external training, they keep their own records including assessment of the effectiveness and quality of training. Competence development is stressed in specific technical areas.

In the words of the businessman: "*areas of training in new technology, technical training at the workplace and in personal development and relations, are important areas in the firm's current situation. At the beginning, areas of business management and human resources were more important. New technology was introduced to the firm gradually and was accompanied by collaborators, because this will always be necessary*".

4.2 Comparative Analysis by Dimension and Category

This section will make a comparative analysis of all the case studies, by dimension and by categories.

The interview script was adapted considering the contextual situation of each firm. Table 9 indicates some comparative data in relation to the meetings and visits where field notes were taken, documents consulted and interviews held, with their duration and the participants.

Dimension 1: Characterisation of the firm, attributes, entrepreneurial intention, motivations for creating the firm.

The various cases were characterised taking into account the contexts, sector of activity, main markets, products, services, history, number of employees, qualifications, operational strategies and evolutionary path.

As motivations and attributes of the entrepreneurial intention, Firms A, B and D indicated reasons such as the opportunity to create their own business and apply knowledge from professional experience. Firm D adds the reasons of including the family in the firm. Firm C adds that the business was an innovative activity in the region, being a challenge and a different experience from the leader's professional activities until then. Personal ambition emerged in all cases, with this being strongest in Firm D.

The difficulties and obstacles felt by all companies were of a technical nature and specific to the business's operational activities, with special relevance for the need to develop management competences, including HRM competences, at the time of starting up the business. Difficulties in financial management were felt and indicated by all companies at one time or another in the course of their development.

Table 9 Indicators from the interviews

Characterisation of interviews and participants	Case A	Case B	Case C	Case D
Number of visits and meetings	3	3	4	4
Number of interviews	1	1	2	2
Average length of interviews in minutes	45	60	45	30
Participants	Businesswoman	Businesswoman	Businessman and head of human resources	Businessman and head of human resources
Sector of activity	Estate agency	Restaurant	Industrial laundry	Sale of fuel
Number of collaborators	18	3	14	24

Dimension 2: Activities and practices of Human Resource Management present when creating and developing the firm.

The results were analysed according to HRM practices, comparatively in all the cases studied, at the time of creating the firm and during its development. The HRM practice of recruitment and selection was identified in all the case studies, Firms A, B, C and D, at the time of creating the firm and in its development, with the degree of formalization increasing as the company developed (Table 10).

The practice of rewards, recognition and bonuses was identified in cases A, C and D, and was in effect at the moment of creating the firm and during its development. Firm B does not apply this HRM practice. Performance assessment was not present in any of the cases studied, at the time of the firm's creation. Firms C and D developed systems showing this practice over time, with Firm C only assessing collaborators' satisfaction.

Career development and human resource planning was identified in Firms A and D, which were concerned with using this practice in the organisation's beginning and development. Firm C considered the collaborators' career as "static" due to the functions implied, but human resource planning is recognised as necessary and is worked on.

The practice of professional training was identified in all the case studies, both at the firm's creation and in developing the activity, with the constant presence of training actions.

Dimension 3: Characterisation of practices of professional training, and development of competences when creating and developing the firm.

Professional training practices were identified in all companies participating in the study. It is highlighted that Group 1 firms, Firms A and B (less than 24 months

Table 10 Comparative analysis of dimension 2 and categories

Human Resource practices when creating the firm	Case A	Case B	Case C	Case D
Recruitment and Selection	Identified	Identified	Identified	Identified
Rewards, recognition and bonuses	Identified		Identified	Identified
Performance assessment	Identified			Identified
Career development, planning	Identified		Planning identified	Identified
Professional training	Identified	Identified	Identified	Identified
Development				
Recruitment and Selection	Identified	Identified	Identified	Identified
Rewards, recognition and bonuses.	Identified		Identified	Identified
Performance assessment			Analysis of collaborator satisfaction	Identified
Career development, planning	Identified		Planning identified	Identified
Professional training	Identified	Identified	Identified	Identified

since beginning activity) recognise the importance of professional training in the firm as a whole and actions are implemented according to a training cycle,[6] satisfying all stages, but there is deficient recording of evidence regarding the pedagogical technical dossier, something to be improved by the firms in the short term.

According to quality management work, as certified companies, Firms C and D registered the collaborator training process with records covering all the stages, from a survey of training needs to assessment of the training. They present annual training plans with objectives according to the competences to develop, with all agents participating in the training process. Both firms use various forms of both internal and external training, with medium-term plans, resorting to certified training entities.[7] No case showed a long-term training plan, but Firm D identified training and assessment strategies, even when using external entities, with the whole process being subject to internal treatment and assessment.

All the firms in this study considered competence development at the stage of creating the firm, in areas of management, the most prominent being: financial management (planning of bookkeeping and access to capital) and HRM (essentially planning and integration).

The new competences necessary to develop business throughout its life-cycle were in the areas of:

- Continuing to build competences in management, specifically in the financial aspect and market approach. The case of Firms A and B belonging to Group I.
- Updating and development of competences in technical matters specific to each sector of activity, in relation to collaborators' functions and according to the organisational strategy. Cases A, B, C and D.
- New HRM competences, focusing on areas of development and personal relations, teams and motivation, integrated in strategies to develop human resources. Considering participants' perception in Firms A, B, C and D.

4.3   Discussion of the Case Studies

The HRM practice of recruitment and selection was identified in all the cases studied, at the time of creating the firm and in its development, which agrees with the results of Cassell et al. (2002), with the degree of formalization increasing as the firm grows. Documented and systematized analysis of functions varies according

---

[6]The training cycle includes the survey and diagnosis of training needs, programming and planning, carrying out and assessing training, according to Pina e Cunha et al. (2012).

[7]According to the Board of Employment and Work Relations (DGERT), to carry out training activity using public funds, private training entities must be certified. These cases considered all organisation of the training cycle with records and a system of training assessment, for both individual participants and in the firm context (DGERT 2015).

to firm size, agreeing with the results of McEvoy (1984) and Hornsby and Kuratko (1990).

The practice of rewards, recognition and bonuses was identified in cases A, C and D. This was true at the time of creation and in firms' development. The practice of rewards is greatly affected by company size, and was not observed in case A. These results are also supported by Hornsby and Kuratko (1990) and Cassell et al. (2002).

Performance assessment is especially present in case D, because in case A it is a more personal and subjective assessment by leadership, in both phases studied, creation and company development. As in Cassell et al. (2002), it is found that the larger the firm the greater the complexity of assessment and performance systems. However, there is great diversity of interpretation and operationalization of this process (Cassell et al. 2002), which may go from simple assessment by leadership (case A) to more complex processes involving self-assessment by the employee (case D).

Career development and human resource planning were identified in Firms A and B, which were concerned about using this practice at the outset and in the organisation's development. Investing in people and their autonomy rather than control, as also stated by Baruch (2004), results in greater organisational commitment.

The practice of professional training was identified in all the cases studied, both when creating the firm and in developing its activity. The great importance of professional training is recognised in the cases studied as a whole, with actions being implemented throughout the training cycle, at all stages. In the case of the younger firms, records and evidence show deficiencies, in terms of the pedagogical technical dossier, which was pointed out by firms as something to improve in the short term. Formal registering of training activity seems to increase as firms become older, rather than due to an increased workforce. This conclusion does not agree with the suggestion of Kotey and Slade (2005), whereby in micro-firms it would not be necessary to apply intensive training actions. Here, we note that in Firm B, due to its sector of activity, the businesswoman recommended intensive training actions in the area of food preparation and freezing techniques.

Firms with quality management procedures, i.e., certified firms, established a training process for collaborators with records throughout all stages, from the survey of training needs to assessment of training. They present annual training plans with objectives according to the competences to develop and with the participation of all agents in the training process. They use various types of training with medium-term plans for internal and external training None had a long-term training plan. Long-term planning of learning-oriented training can contribute to developing learning competences and collaborators' development in the organisation (Aguinis and Kraiger 2009; Chen and Huang 2009; Aragon et al. 2014). MacMahon and Murphy (1999) indicate the need for managers to develop transversal competences, through training in various areas, to continuously improve the flexibility of work. Although all are SMEs, none indicates formalization of long-term training plans, which to some extent can limit the capacity of their response to demands for greater flexibility in the workforce.

All the firms in this study consider the development of initial competences in firm creation, in aspects of management, with financial management and HRM being most prominent. New competences indicated as necessary for business development were aspects of management, updating the specific technical aspects of each sector of activity and new HRM competences, focusing on development and personal relations, teams and motivation, integrated in strategies to develop human resources.

The results agree with those of Alasadi and Al Sabbagh (2015), who consider that the entrepreneur's management competences on beginning business determine business development. When this grows, it is important to invest in areas of management for better accompaniment of organisational transformation in small businesses. Their research confirmed that business-people with training clearly rose above those without training, in terms of results.

5 Conclusions

The HRM practices present in the creation and development of SMEs are multiple, and when opting to apply models for large firms to micro and small firms, where the situation and specific contexts are different (Heneman et al. 2000), it is more important the way in which human resource management practices are carried out rather than those said to be adopted. A set of recruitment and selection practices were identified, which are those observed in the literature, at the stages of creating and developing the activity, such as government agencies, references, personal knowledge, experience and interviews, based on the need for firm owners to trust in their workforce.

Even micro-firms develop these "basic techniques" of recruitment and selection, but in addition to training and curricular activities, business-people applying to financing programmes should be able to include training in techniques and methods of remote recruitment and selection, such as via the internet, which lower costs and allow wider access to the labour market. As the entry of new employees occurs above all when beginning activity, this training should be part of the requirements to gain access to financial support to create new firms.

Analysis of job descriptions, forming the profile of competences for each post, will be the basic instrument supporting recruitment and selection, but also career planning, performance assessment and reward and incentive systems, and should therefore be part of the training of all parties in the process of beginning organisations' activity, also for the reasons indicated above.

Regarding rewards and incentives and performance assessment systems, on beginning activity, no great difference was observed from what is reported in the literature on SMEs, with somewhat rudimentary systems limited to assessment of technical performance of tasks, rewards foreseen in the legislation and verbal recognition. At the development stage, there is identification of the need to use elaborated systems of performance assessment and to attribute rewards and incentives according to the organisation's strategic objectives. This need is especially evident in Firms A, C and D, but for different reasons, In Firms C and D, because they represent certified companies, regarding the quality of their processes, and are in fact "obliged" to check collaborators' level of satisfaction. In Firm A, because it is a franchise and therefore obliged to satisfy the demands of the brand, also in implementing human resource policies and practices.

Career development and human resource planning are also present at the time of creating the firm and in its development. The business-people recognise these as important, and formalization seems to increase as the number of collaborators grows. Rewards, recognition and bonuses are present in creating the firm and in its development, but the degree of formalization is affected by company size. The use of bonuses and rewards contributes greatly to collaborators' performance results, with implications for their satisfaction.

Indicated as motivations and attributes of the entrepreneurial intention were: the opportunity to create one's own business; apply knowledge from professional experience; including family in the firm; an innovative activity in the region; and personal ambition. The entrepreneurial intention mediates between systems of HRM information and business performance.

The new competences necessary for business development were in areas of management, updating of technical aspects and new HRM competences, focusing on areas of development and personal relations, team building and motivation. The management competences held by entrepreneurs and managers are determinants of business growth. When these are developed, the organisation is transformed, and investment in training improves the accompaniment transforming the firm. Entrepreneurial actions in the form of corporate entrepreneurship reveal the effectiveness of the HRM practices used in the firm, these being a vehicle for innovation, creativity and initiative. Specific and transversal competences are improved by applying training plans oriented to long-term learning.

There is clear differentiation in the use of HRM practices in SMEs that follow quality certification processes, because these are imposed at the outset and also subsequently to retain certification, a situation that is especially visible in the training processes adopted by Firms C and D. These plans are suitably supported by diagnosis of training needs and assessment of the training received. In addition, all the agents of that training (internal and external) have to follow the requirements of certification in the respective areas of training.

For those implementing policies in support of training in micro and small firms, it will be appropriate to maintain these requirements which represent organisational and individual development, and indeed medium and even long-term training plans should be imposed to gain access to, and subsequently hold on to the financial benefits received when creating a firm.

HRM practices in small firms may be more sophisticated than they appear, as claimed by some authors, but size will always be an obstacle to accessing mechanisms to implement and develop more complex activities, such as performance assessment systems and rewards and incentive systems. Those forming policies to support the creation of SMEs should encourage cooperation or even the integration of various firms/entities in "shared HRM services" which could even be created in partnership with academic institutions and subsequently provided at a low cost.

Compared to what is stated in the literature, it is observed, firstly, that the general characteristics of "basic human resource practices" are found especially when beginning activity, and secondly, that practices such as professional training are of a planned nature and are also directed to employee development, above all in firms that are obliged to adhere to quality certification processes.

Like any other, this study has limitations, with the first one being the low number of cases studied. Studying more cases would give a broader perspective. Combining qualitative methodology with quantitative methodology would facilitate the introduction of hypotheses and variables, for example, firms' turnover or business growth rates, which would enhance the study.

The fact that employees did not participate is also a limitation, and a suggestion for future research would be to include the employee perspective and extend the investigation to other sectors of activity, since only the service sector was studied here.

Other lines of research could be to measure the effects of corporate entrepreneurship through implementation of new HRM practices and the development of the entrepreneurial process throughout the organisational life-cycle.

Aknowledgments The authors are pleased to acknowledge financial support from Fundação para a Ciência e a Tecnologia (grant UID/GES/04630/2013).

References

Aguinis, H., & Kraiger, K. (2009). Benefits of training and development for individuals and teams, organizations, and society. *Annual Review of Psychology, 60,* 451–474.

Alasadi, R., & Al Sabbagh, H. (2015). The role of training in small business performance. *International Journal of Information, Business and Management, 7*(1), 293–311.

Apetro. (2013). *Associação Portuguesa de Empresas Petroliferas.* http://www.apetro.pt/index.php?option=com_content&task=view&id=71&Itemid=126, consulted on 26/08/2015.

Aragon, M. I. B., Jimenez, D. J., & Valle, R. S. (2014). Training and performance: The mediating role of organizational learning. *Brq-Business Research Quarterly, 17*(3), 161–173.

Argyris, C., & Schon, D. A. (1996). *Organizational Learning II. Theory, method, and pratice.* Reading, MA: Addison-Wesley Publishing Company.

Arrowsmith, J., & Parker, J. (2013). The meaning of 'employee engagement' for the values and roles of the HRM function. *International Journal of Human Resource Management, 24*(14), 2692–2712.

Bacon, N., Ackers, P., Storey, J., & Coates, D. (1996). It's a small world: Managing human resources in small businesses. *International Journal of Human Resource Management, 7*(1), 82–100.

Bacon, N., Wright, M., & Demina, N. (2004). Management buyouts and human resource management. *British Journal of Industrial Relations, 42*(2), 325–347.

Bardin, L. (1977). *Analise de Conteudo – Aspetos Tecnicos* (Vol. 70). Lisboa: Edições.

Barney, J. (1991). Firm resources and sustained competitive advantage. *Journal of Management, 17*(1), 99.

Baruch, Y. (2004). Transforming careers: From linear to multidirectional career paths: Organizational and individual perspectives. *Career Development International, 9*(1), 58–73.

Bayon, M. C., Vaillant, Y., & Lafuente, E. (2015). Initiating nascent entrepreneurial activities. *International Journal of Entrepreneurial Behaviour & Research, 21*(1), 27.

Becker, B. E., & Huselid, M. A. (2006). Strategic human resources management: Where do we go from here? *Journal of Management, 32*(6), 898–925.

Cabrera, E. F., & Cabrera, A. (2005). Fostering knowledge sharing through people management practices. *International Journal of Human Resource Management, 16*(5), 720–735.

Cassell, C., Nadin, S., Gray, M., & Clegg, C. (2002). Exploring human resource management practices in small and medium sized enterprises. *Personnel Review, 31*(5–6), 671–692.

Chang, E. (1999). Career commitment as a complex moderator of organizational commitment and turnover intention. *Human Relations, 52*(10), 1257–1278.

Chen, C.-J., & Huang, J.-W. (2009). Strategic human resource practices and innovation performance—The mediating role of knowledge management capacity. *Journal of Business Research, 62*(1), 104–114.

Collins, C. J., & Clark, K. D. (2003). Strategic human resource practices, top management team social networks, and firm performance: The role of human resource practices in creating organizational competitive advantage. *Academy of Management Journal, 46*(6), 740–751.

Collins, C. J., & Smith, K. G. (2006). Knowledge exchange and combination: The role of human resource practices in the performance of high-technology firms. *Academy of Management Journal, 49*(3), 544–560.

Crossan, M. M., Lane, H. W., & White, R. E. (1999). An organizational learning framework: From intuition to institution. *Academy of Management Review, 24*(3), 522–537.

Davidsson, P., Kirchhoff, B., Hatemi-J, A., & Gustavsson, H. (2002). Empirical analysis of business growth factors using Swedish data. *Journal of Small Business Management, 40*(4), 332–349.

Deshpande, S. P., & Golhar, D. Y. (1994). HRM practices in large and small manufacturing firms: A comparative study. *Journal of Small Business Management, 32*(2), 49.

DGERT. (2015). *Direção Geral do Emprego e das Relações de Trabalho.* http://certifica.dgert. msess.pt/pedir-a-certificacao/preparar-a-entidade-para-a-certificacao.aspx, consulted on 4/09/2015.

Eisenhardt, K. M., & Martin, J. A. (2000). Dynamic capabilities: What are they? *Strategic Management Journal, 21*(10-11), 1105–1121.

Europeia, C. (2003). *Recomendação da Comissão Europeia de 6 Maio de 2003 relativa à definiçao de micro, pequenas e médias empresas* (Vol. L 124, pp. 36–41). Jornal Oficial da União Europeia: Comissão Europeia.

Friedman, A., & Lev, B. (1974). Surrogate measure for firms investment in Human Resouces. *Journal of Accounting Research, 12*(2), 235–250.

Garvin, D. A. (1993). Building a learning organization. *Harvard Business Review, 71*(4), 78–91.

Golhar, D. Y., & Deshpande, S. P. (1997). HRM practices of large and small Canadian manufacturing firms. *Journal of Small Business Management, 35*(3), 30–38.

Gómez, P. J., Lorente, J. J. C., & Cabrera, R. V. (2004). Training practices and organisational learning capability: Relationship and implications. *Journal of European Industrial Training, 28* (2/3/4), 234–256.

Grant, R. M. (1996). Toward a knowledge-based theory of the firm. *Strategic Management Journal, 17*, 109–122.

Hayton, J. C. (2006). *Human capital management practices and performance in small and medium sized enterprises – A conceptual framework.*

Heneman, R. L., Tansky, J. W., & Camp, S. M. (2000). Human resource management practices in small and medium-sized enterprises: Unanswered questions and future research perspectives. *Entrepreneurship: Theory & Practice, 25*(1), 11.

Hornsby, J. S., & Kuratko, D. F. (1990). Human resource management in small business: Critical issues for the 1990's. *Journal of Small Business Management, 28*(3), 9.

Huber, G. P. (1991). Organizational learning: The contributing processes and the literatures. *Organization Science, 2*(1), 88–115.

Huselid, M. A. (1995). The impact of human-resource management-practices on turnover, productivity, and corporate financial performance. *Academy of Management Journal, 38*(3), 635–672.

Huselid, M. A. (2011). Celebrating 50 years: Looking back and looking foward: 50 years of Human Resouce management. *Human Resource Management, 50*(3), 309–312.

Huselid, M. A., & Becker, B. E. (2000). Comment on "Measurement error in research on human resources and firm performance: How much error is there and how does it influence effect size estimates?" by Gerhart, Wright, McMahan, and Snell. *Personnel Psychology, 53*(4), 835–854.

Huselid, M. A., & Becker, B. E. (2011). Bridging micro and macro domains: Workforce differentiation and strategic human resource management. *Journal of Management, 37*(2), 421–428.

Huselid, M. A., Beatty, R. W., & Becker, B. E. (2005). "A players" or "A positions"? The strategic logic of workforce management. *Harvard Business Review, 83*(12), 110.

IAPMEI. (2015a). Definição de PME. Instituto de Apoio às Pequenas e Médias Empresas e à Inovação (IAPMEI) – Agência para a Competitividade e Inovação. http://www.iapmei.pt/iapmei-art-03.php?id=1790, consulted on 5/06/2015.

IAPMEI. (2015b). Instituto de Apoio às Pequenas e Médias Empresas e à Inovação (IAPMEI) – Agência para a Competitividade e Inovação. Programa InPME – 5ª Edição. http://www.iapmei.pt/iapmei-art-03.php?id=1127, consulted on 2/08/2015.

IEFP. (2015). *Ficha Síntese do PAECPE.* https://www.iefp.pt/en/empreendedorismo, consulted on 01/06/2015.

Jerez-Gomez, P., Cespedes-Lorente, J., & Valle-Cabrera, R. (2005). Organizational learning capability: A proposal of measurement. *Journal of Business Research, 58*(6), 715–725.

Kaya, N. (2006). The impact of human resource management practices and corporate entrepreneurship on firm performance: Evidence from Turkish firms. *International Journal of Human Resource Management, 17*(12), 2074–2090.

Kaya, N., Koc, E., & Topcu, D. (2010). An exploratory analysis of the influence of human resource management activities and organizational climate on job satisfaction in Turkish banks. *International Journal of Human Resource Management, 21*(11), 2031–2051.

Khan, S. H., Cheema, F.-E. A., Syed, N. A., & Asim, M. (2013). Human resource management practices in SMEs: An exploratory study. *Global Management Journal for Academic & Corporate Studies, 3*(1), 78–93.

Kotey, B., & Slade, P. (2005). Formal human resource management practices in small growing firms. *Journal of Small Business Management, 43*(1), 16–40.

Lau, A. H. L., & Lau, H. S. (1978). Some proposed approaches for writing off capitalized human resource assets. *Journal of Accounting Research, 16*(1), 80–102.

Lepak, D. P., & Snell, S. A. (1999). The human resource architecture: Toward a theory of human capital allocation and development. *Academy of Management Review, 24*(1), 31–48.

MacMahon, J., & Murphy, E. (1999). Managerial effectiveness in small enterprises: Implications for HRD. *Journal of European Industrial Training, 23*(1), 25–35.

Marta Fernandez, B., Sanzo Perez, M. J., & Trespalacios Gutierrez, J. A. (1999). Training in small business retailing: Testing human capital theory. *Journal of European Industrial Training, 23*(7), 335–352.

Matlay, H. (2002). Training and HRD strategies in family and non-family owned small businesses: A comparative approach. *Education + Training, 44*(8/9), 357–369.

McEvoy, G. M. (1984). Small business personnel practices. *Journal of Small Business Management, 22*(000004), 1 (pre-1986).

McEvoy, G. M., & Buller, P. F. (2013). Human Resource management practices in mid-sized enterprises. *American Journal of Business, 28*(1), 86–105.

Miles, R. E., & Snow, C. C. (1984). Desogning strategic Human Resouces systems. *Organizational Dynamics, 13*(1), 36–52.

Pearson, T. R., Stringer, D. Y., Mills, L. H., & Summers, D. F. (2006a). Urban vs. rural: Human resource management in SMEs. *Academy of Entrepreneurship Journal, 12*(2), 29–46.

Pearson, T. R., Stringer, D. Y., Mills, L. V. H., & Summers, D. F. (2006b). Micro vs small enterprises: A profile of human resource personnel, practices and support systems. *Journal of Management Research, 6*(2), 102–112.

Peteraf, M. A. (1993). The cornerstones of competitive advantage – A resouce based view. *Strategic Management Journal, 14*(3), 179–191.

Pfeffer, J. (1998). Seven practices of successful organizations. *California Management Review, 40*(2), 96.

Pina e Cunha, M., Rego, A., Campos e Cunha, R., Cabral-Cardoso, C., Marques, A., & Gomes, J. F. S. (2012). *Manual de gestão de pessoas e do Capital Humano*. Lisboa: Edições Silabo.

Prahalad, C. K., & Hamel, G. (1990). The core competence of the corporation. *Harvard Business Review, 68*(3), 79–91.

Schmelter, R., Mauer, R., Boersch, C., & Brettel, M. (2010). Boosting corporate entrepreneurship through HRM practices: evidence from German SMEs. *Human Resource Management, 49*(4), 715–741.

Shih, H.-A., & Chiang, Y.-H. (2011). Exploring the effectiveness of outsourcing recruiting and training activities, and the prospector strategy's moderating effect. *International Journal of Human Resource Management, 22*(1), 163–180.

Simon, H. A. (1991). Bouded rationality and organizational learning. *Organization Science, 2*(1), 125–134.

Steffy, B. D., & Maurer, S. D. (1988). Conceptualizing and measuring the economic effectiveness or Human Resouce activities. *Academy of Management Review, 13*(2), 271–286.

Vinten, G. (2000). Training in small- and medium-sized enterprises. *Industrial and Commercial Training, 32*(1), 9–14.

Williams, M. L., McDaniel, M. A., & Ford, L. R. (2007). Understanding multiple dimensions of compensation satisfaction. *Journal of Business and Psychology, 21*(3), 429.

Willig, C. (2001). *Introducing qualitative research in psychology: Adventures in theory and method*. Buckingham: Open University Press.

Wright, P. M., Dunford, B. B., & Snell, S. A. (2001). Human Resources and the resource based view of the firm. *Journal of Management, 27*(6), 701–721.

Yin, R. K. (2009). *Case study research: Design and methods* (4th ed.). Los Angeles, CA: Sage.

Part II
Innovative Networks and Entrepreneurial Activities

The Selective Nature of Innovator Networks: From the Nascent to the Early Growth Phase of the Organizational Life Cycle

Uwe Cantner and Tina Wolf

Abstract Earlier studies have shown that entrepreneurs play a key role in shaping regional development. Innovator networks where these entrepreneurs are members of, have been identified as one among many critical factors for their firms' success. This paper intents to go one step further and analyses in how far differing characteristics of these networks lead to different firm performances along the early stages of the organizational life cycle (nascent stage, emergent stage, early growth stage). A sample of 149 innovative firms in Thuringia is analysed, using data from the commercial register and the German patent office. The results show that there is an inverted u-shaped relationship between the chances of a firm to survive and the connectivity of the network the firms are connected to but only in the later stage of the early organizational life cycle; while the structure of the ego-network never plays a role. A quite central position in the network shows-up to be unfavourable.

Keywords Innovation · Entrepreneurship · Networks · Inventor · Patents · Survival

1 Introduction

Over the 1990s, scholars have come to the consensus that networks play an important role for the emergence and survival of new ventures (Aldrich and Reese 1993; Larson and Starr 1993; Stuart et al. 1999). However, with regards to the evolutionary

U. Cantner
School of Economics and Business Administration, DFG Graduate School "Economics of Innovative Change" (DFG-GRK 1411), Friedrich Schiller University Jena, Jena, Germany

Department of Marketing and Management, I2M Group, University of Southern Denmark, Odense, Denmark

T. Wolf (✉)
School of Economics and Business Administration, DFG Graduate School "Economics of Innovative Change" (DFG-GRK 1411), Friedrich Schiller University Jena, Jena, Germany
e-mail: tina.wolf@uni-jena.de

© Springer International Publishing AG, part of Springer Nature 2018   175
S. Cubico et al. (eds.), *Entrepreneurship and the Industry Life Cycle*, Studies on Entrepreneurship, Structural Change and Industrial Dynamics,
https://doi.org/10.1007/978-3-319-89336-5_8

process behind firm growth and survival at different stages of the organizational life cycle (Hite and Hesterly 2001), recent interest has been devoted to the variable 'location' as a critical factor, shaping firm performance.

We elaborate the approach of regional innovator networks (RIN) which can be defined as networks that are built up by actors who cooperatively engage in the creation of new ideas and then economize the results (Cantner and Graf 2007), where the economization can be realized within an existing firm or by the formation of a new venture. In a previous study (Cantner and Wolf 2016) we found that for a new venture being simply connected to the innovator network increases the survival probability. The further step in this paper is to look at the "quality" of the network and of how a new venture is connected to the network (position in the network, relation to other actors, bridging functions). Examining the relationship between network position of the founder and survival of firms can provide both, an estimation of the role of different elements of network structure in firms' success and an empirical indicator for the effectiveness of knowledge flows through networks.

According to the propositions by Hite and Hesterly (2001), an analysis of the relationship between the selectivity of the innovator network and start-ups' survival cannot be conducted independently of the organizational life cycle status of the individual firm. Therefore, we consider three early stages in the life cycle, namely, the nascent stage, the founding stage and the post founding stage, and ask the following research question: *What role does the structure of the innovator network, the position of the founder(s) in the network and the structure of the founder's ego-network play for the survival of firms in the early stages of the organizational life cycle?*

To address this overarching research question, we have constructed a biographical firm dataset, based upon data on incorporations of enterprises in Thuringia as well as on patent data comprising all German patents applied for at the German Patent Office.

The reminder of the research paper goes as follows: Sect. 2 introduces the early stages of the organizational life cycle. Section 3 explains how knowledge diffuses in regional innovator networks. Section 4 combines the arguments of Sects. 2 and 3 and explains how the stages of the organizational life cycle and the regional innovator network do coevolve. Section 5 describes the database, Sect. 6 the variables and methodology used. In Sect. 7, we present the empirical results while we conclude in Sect. 8.

2 Organizational Life Cycle

In strategy and entrepreneurship research, organizational life cycles are used to explain how firms evolve through the following (mostly five) progressive stages: emergence, early growth, later growth, maturity and death (Churchill and Levis 1983; Gartner et al. 1992). These studies expect that the emergence stage of the firm, and with this it's life, begins when the organization is legally created (Gartner et al. 1992).

However, as Reynolds (2000) argues, there is also an important phase before the legal founding which is the conception or nascent stage of the firm life.

In this paper, we will concentrate on the phases between nascent entrepreneurship and early growth of the firm. Throughout all the phases of a firm's life, the strategic goals, natural resource needs and acquisition challenges are changing several times (Hite and Hesterly 2001).

A nascent entrepreneur can be defined as 'someone who initiates serious activities that are intended to culminate in a viable business startup' (Aldrich 1999, p. 77). This means that in this phase, the nascent entrepreneur is experimenting with different business ideas, starts to take care of the first stages in the founding process (like writing a business plan) and starts to collect resources along with applying for financial funds. Depending on the industry/technology the start-up will be active in, the founder(s) might also start to produce first prototypes. In this phase there seems to be no real strategic orientation but the four factors entrepreneurial personality, environment, resources, and founding process comprehensively influence founding success (Kessler and Frank 2009; Cantner and Stuetzer 2013).

After the legal founding of the firm, the emergence stage begins (Gartner et al. 1992). In the emergence stage, the firm starts to act on the real market such that one could say that after the legal founding the start-up enters in to the selective process of competition. In this phase the only strategic goal of the firm is not to die, thus to survive the selection process (Hite and Hesterly 2001). With respect to resources, these newborn firms usually lack internal resources and capabilities to reach this goal (Baum 1996). Additionally the operations of emerging firms are characterized by a high degree of uncertainty and equivocality (Gartner et al. 1992) as well as by a lower degree of legitimacy and reputation (Hite and Hesterly 2001).

If the firm enters the early growth stage, it has survived already the toughest part of the competition process, usually due to a competitive advantage. Now the firm is settled in the market and might be for the first time able to set its own conditions. Thus, when the firm enters the early growth stage it starts to make real strategic decisions and therefore requires a broader scope of resources but, however, could already gain legitimacy and reputation which reduces uncertainty (Hite and Hesterly 2001).

Organizational life cycle theory does not describe the exact time span or duration for the single phases of the life cycle. This is not surprising since the development of a firm is an individual process which differs from firm to firm. The nascent stage is usually considered to take around three years (Kessler and Frank 2009). After the legal firm founding, it is well known that survival rates are very low in the beginning due to the liabilities of newness and smallness (Parker 2009). After an initial honeymoon phase (which is the emergence stage according to the organizational life cycle theory), many small and young firms suffer from these liabilities and exit while others enter the early growth stage. Studies on the distribution of survival rates see the length of the emergence stage somewhere between five and seven years (Phillips and Kirchhoff 1989; Bartelsman et al. 2005).

Of cause along with the changes in needs for the young firms, the influence of the social (scientific) network around the founders changes. Before elaborating this, we start by describing the role of innovative networks per se.

3 Knowledge Diffusion in RINs

We define the RIN as a network that is built up by actors, living in a certain region, which cooperatively engage in the creation of new ideas and then economize on the results in the market—either within an existing firm or by the formation of a new venture (Cantner and Graf 2007; Balconi et al. 2004). Innovative actors building the RIN are employees of firms, of research institutes or of universities, students or self-employed persons who actively engage in research (Cantner and Wolf 2016).

After we have defined the innovator network, the following question arises: How can the connection of single actors to the RIN contribute to firms' innovation? As mentioned in the definition, the RIN inherits connections among actors that are engaged in research, no matter if it is basic or applied (Cantner and Graf 2007; Balconi et al. 2004). These actors usually are experienced experts and they have current knowledge in their field. Since knowledge can be codified or tacit, acquiring new knowledge pieces may require personal contacts to other actors which possess this new knowledge (Howells 2002). Breschi and Lissoni (2006) argue that pure knowledge spillovers can only take place by trade-unrelated personal communication or through reverse engineering. However, when tacitness of knowledge plays a role, knowledge spillovers are not possible anymore without active participation of the inventor. Thus, actors that are connected to the social network of innovators will receive more new knowledge pieces than an isolated actor and they will therefore have a higher probability to find new combinations.

As pointed out: Knowledge, which is possessed by actors and transferred via the RIN, is an important prerequisite for the generation of innovations within a firm. By definition, actors connected to the RIN intend to economize their research's results (Cantner and Graf 2007). This can happen within an existing firm or by founding a new one. Thus, a firm whose employees or founders are connected to the innovator network will be more likely to be innovative than firms whose employees or founders are isolated from this network (Cantner and Wolf 2016). With respect to the creation of a new firm, the interpretation of the contribution of an entrepreneur's network to the firms' scientific knowledge base is similar to the notion by Murray (2004) but we adapt it to entrepreneurship theory. Murray (2004) investigates in how far academic scientists contribute to the firm's own scientific network by providing their scientific social capital. Our notion of the regional innovator network points to the importance of the whole research community within a region. Furthermore, we expect an entrepreneur who is connected to this regional research community (from now on, we call him networked-founder), not an academic inventor as Murray (2004) does, to bring his scientific social capital to the firm and to also intent to translate it to the firms' scientific network. This so called scientific social capital of the firm is even increased if there is more than one networked-founder (team founding). Thus, the scientific human capital of the founder(s) leads a firm to become embedded within the scientific community of the region. Scholars have argued that linkages and the resulting networks are key vehicles through which firms obtain access to external knowledge (Powell et al. 1996). The connection to such a network delivers information and it is a vehicle for the rapid communication of news about opportunities and obstacles. Therefore, the generation of innovation and the recognition of new market opportunities are eased, which both are drivers of growth and survival (Audretsch 1995).

4 Early Stages in the Organizational Life Cycle and the Evolution of Firm Networks

As argued above, the needs of a firm change along its life cycle and consequently the exigence to the innovator network changes over time. At the same time, the network itself evolves and changes. This is due to the process of dynamic network evolution where firms strategically adapt and align their networks to serve their needs (Golden and Dollinger 1993; Ostgaard and Birley 1994; Balland et al. 2015). This means that the individual firm changes its ego-network but, if all firms do this, naturally the whole network changes. Therefore, in contrast to Hite and Hesterly (2001) who specifically focus on the egocentric network of the firm, we will additionally consider the structure of the whole regional innovator network as influential factor on firm success.

4.1 Structural Issues on the Diffusion of Knowledge in RINs

It has been pointed out in Chap. 3 that the connection to a regional innovator network can influence firm's innovative success and in line with this, firms' growth and survival. If we consider start-ups, connected to the RIN, specific effects of network structures on the organizational performance may play a role. These specific effects also depend on the stage in the organizational life cycle and the related strategic needs of the firms.

Considering the nascent stage of the firm's live, Cantner and Stuetzer (2013) show that factors like start-up capital, the functional background and entrepreneurial experience of the founders seem to overweight the importance of social capital for the success of the new venture. The founders are too busy in writing the business plan, getting funds and find a niche to put their business idea in that the scientific social capital plays a less relevant role in this stage of the organizational life cycle. Therefore, we expect that the structural form of the innovator network does not influence the firm in this very early stage:

*Hypothesis 1a: The connectivity of the innovator network in the **nascent stage** of the organizational life cycle does not influence the firms' chances to survive.*

In the emergent stage, the firm already entered into the market and started to compete with other actors in this market. In this phase, the founders need to know everything that is going on in the technological field. In highly connected networks where one finds connections between many of the actors, knowledge can flow quite fluently from one actor to the other. Gilsing et al. (2008) additionally argue that highly connected networks help to understand new knowledge adequately since partners may complement actors' absorptive capacities and they help building up trust by reputation. For example Fershtman and Gandal (2011) find for open source software projects that the success of the projects depends positively on the closeness centrality of the project network. Also Meagher and Rogers (2004) prove formally that there exists a feedback between spillovers and innovation and that those industries with a greater network density have a higher proportion of innovators. Cohesive networks are characterized by high density, high mutuality among ties and a relative high frequency of ties among group members, while in sparsely connected networks, where fragmentation is quite high, only a small number of knowledge spillovers may occur (Wasserman and Faust 1994). During the emergence stage, young firms profit from better access to resources and a mutual understanding which is driven by a high degree of trust and expected future reciprocity (Hite and Hesterly 2001). Therefore, we hypothesize that:

*Hypothesis 1b: Firms have higher chances to survive if the connectivity of the net their founder is connected to is high in the **emergent stage**.*

When the firm develops and enters into the early growth stage, the advantages of a very cohesive network may turn into disadvantages. First, the costs associated with maintaining contacts to many actors are quite high (Burt 1992). Second, if there are many direct and indirect ties in the net, every actor knows what the other actors know and therefore it is less likely to gain new knowledge inflows from the net (Gilsing et al. 2008). Third, there is the risk of undesired knowledge spillovers in a way that the partners of actor A's partners may receive parts of A's knowledge although A doesn't want it (Gilsing and Nooteboom 2005). Therefore, in the early growth stage, the fragmented network becomes more appropriate (Hite and Hesterly 2001). Thus, we hypothesize the following:

*Hypothesis 1c: Firms have higher chances to survive if the connectivity of the net their founder is connected to is low in the **early growth stage** of the organizational life cycle.*

4.2 Entrepreneurs Position in the RIN and Knowledge Flows to the Firm

After we have defined in Chap. 4.1 how the net as a whole should look like to positively contribute to the survival of the nascent and young firm, we now have a look at the founder's position in the net. Which position of a single node (networked-founder) is favourable to profit as much as possible from knowledge flows in the net? And how does this depend on the stage in the organizational life cycle?

If we look at the entrepreneurs' position in the network, we basically look at how important he is. In graph theory, centrality is a measure of how well connected or active an actor is in the overall network. Thus centrality helps measuring how prominent or important single actors are in the net (Wasserman and Faust 1994). The actor with the highest centrality, is the one "where the action is" as he is the most visible actor in the network (Gilsing et al. 2008).

As argued above, in the nascent stage, factors like start-up capital, the functional background and entrepreneurial experience of the founders are the main factors, influencing firm survival (Cantner and Stuetzer 2013). Therefore, we again expect that the entrepreneurs' position in the network does not influence the chances of his chances to survive. Therefore, hypothesis 2a goes as follows:

*Hypothesis 2a: A central position of the networked-founder' in the RIN in the **nascent stage** of the organizational life cycle does not influence firm survival.*

After the firm entered the market, it needs to know everything that is going on in the technological field. A networked-founder, with a high degree centrality is in direct contact or adjacent to many other actors (networked-founders or inventors) such that this founder should be recognized by others as a major channel of information. This makes it more likely for him to receive knowledge spillovers, thus information about opportunities or obstacles. Consequently, we hypothesize:

*Hypothesis 2b: The more central the position of the networked-founder' in the RIN in the **emergent stage** of the organizational life cycle the higher are the firms' chances to survive.*

We argued above that the firms' need for a cohesive network decreases over the life cycle, due to a better control of resource and knowledge flows between the other actors (Hite and Hesterly 2001). If we now consider the position of the founder in the network, we might expect that central actors may be comparably able to control knowledge flows and even use this position for his own purposes (Burt 1992). This makes it more likely for the networked founder to receive and control knowledge spillovers. Therefore, we hypothesize for the early growth stage that:

*Hypothesis 2c: The more central the position of the networked-founder' in the RIN in the **early growth stage** of the organizational life cycle the higher are the firms' chances to survive.*

4.3   Entrepreneurs' Ego-network and Knowledge Flows to the Firm

In social networks theory, a debate has arisen over the form of egocentric network structures that can appropriately be regarded as beneficial for connected firms (Walker et al. 1997). Coleman (1988) sees the optimal social structure of an ego network in dense and interconnected networks, while Burt (1992) sees a network consisting of disconnected alters as optimal. Also the number of direct and indirect ties may play a role for the advantageousness of a network structure (Ahuja 2000). As Hite and Hesterly (2001), we consider the optimal structure of the ego-network to change over the firm's life.

Again, the nascent stage is characterized by factors like start-up capital, the functional background and entrepreneurial experience rather than the social networks (Cantner and Stuetzer 2013). Therefore, we expect no connection between the shapes of the ego-networks within the innovator network and the success of the new ventures:

*Hypothesis 3a: The shape of the egocentric networks within the innovator network does not influence survival of the firm in the **nascent stage**.*

In the emergent stage, the firm needs to be informed about everything that is going on in the technology and the related market. Therefore, an ego-network that is allowing for the highest possible amount of knowledge inflow is favourable (Hite and Hesterly 2001). According to Coleman, densely embedded networks (closed networks) with many connections and thus no or less structural holes is associated with a higher innovative output. Ahuja (2000), among other factors, investigates the relationship between the number of structural holes in the ego network of a firm and innovative outputs and finds that having many structural holes is associated with reduced innovation. Since this kind of ego-network structure is exactly what a start-up in the emergent stage needs, we hypothesize:

*Hypothesis 3b: The more closed the ego-network of a networked-founder is, the higher is the survival probability of this founder's firm in the **emergence stage**.*

However, if the firm moves to the early growth stage, it rather needs an ego-network that allows a strategical use of the own position (Hite and Hesterly 2001). One characteristic of the ego-network is brokerage/structural holes (Burt 1992). Networks usually consist of one or more components. Burt defines a 'hole' /non connection between those components as structural hole. As we see nodes as actors, one could say that "people on either side of a structural hole circulate in different flows of information. Structural holes are thus an opportunity to broker the flow of information between people, and control the projects that bring together people from opposite sides of the hole" (Burt 1992). One could also say that structural holes guarantee that partners on both sides of the hole have access to different information flows (Hargadon and Sutton 1997) and the information coming from this connection is non-redundant (Gilsing et al. 2008). However, not every firm or actor has the same chance to be in a bridging position. Central firms tend to become better informed about the things happening in the network what increases their ability to form new and valuable ties (Gnyawali and Madhavan 2001; Gilsing et al. 2008). Thus, we hypothesize that:

*Hypothesis 3c: The more structural holes the ego-network of the founder has, the higher are the chances to survive when the firm moves to the **early growth stage**.*

5   Compounding the Database

To address the hypotheses introduced above, we have constructed a biographical firm dataset, based upon two data bases. First, we use data on incorporations of enterprises in Thuringia which is based on the commercial register. Second, we rely on patent data comprising all German patents applied for at the German Patent Office in the time period between 1993 and 2004.

5.1   Incorporations

Information on new ventures was collected by the Thuringian Founder Study.[1] The data base was drawn from the commercial register for commercial and private companies in Thuringia and contains information on the founders (date of birth, name, surname, academic title, address, gender) and on their respective firms (date of founding, date of closing, trade name, location, legal form, spin-off or not, industry). The survey population consists of 12,505 founders whose 7016 companies were founded between 1990 and 2006 and are either active or have failed meanwhile. After we have cleaned the data (exclusion of firms founded before 1993 since the German reunification came with a phase of many management buyouts of former state combines; exclusion of firms where the founding date was missing; extraction of only those firms that are active in innovative industries following the classification of Grupp and Legler (2000) which is classifying innovative industries by means of R&D-intensity) a population of 4566 companies was left.

5.2   Innovator Network

As mentioned in the introduction, we use patent data in order to measure the innovator network. Per definition, this network comprises persons who

---

[1]Note that this data base was just the starting point for the Thuringian Founder Study Questionnaire. It is therefore not identical to the questionnaire data collected by the Thuringian Founder Study.

cooperatively engage in the creation of new ideas and then economize the results (Cantner and Graf 2007). How these two aspects of creating and economizing new ideas can be combined into the innovator network and what this means for new ventures has been elaborated in more detail by the authors' earlier paper Cantner and Wolf (2016) and shall not be repeated here. To summarize the arguments of the paper mentioned one can say that patent data, which basically just contains information on inventions, is a sufficient measure of innovator networks since the aim of commercialization can be expected behind the legal protection of the invention.

We used data from the German Patent Office where we have in Thuringia 6969 inventors (name, surname, address) and 5381 patent applications (IPC-Code, name and address of the applicant, application date and year), resulting after checking raw data for misspelling of personal names.

It has been found that regions differ with respect to firms' success due to different infrastructural conditions (Heckmann and Schnabel 2005; Storey 1994). Additionally, the conditions for bringing competences into innovator networks may differ between functional regions since an innovator may find the competences he needs easier in large and dense networks compared to smaller ones (Ejermo and Karlsson 2006). This holds especially true for large regions with a university and several research institutes. Not just that universities and research institutes are responsible for knowledge spillovers which have a positive influence on innovations (Audretsch and Lehmann 2005), it can also be expected that actors in these networks are better connected and thus better informed than those in regions without research facilities and with less dense networks (Ejermo and Karlsson 2006). On the basis of these considerations, we have created 12 one-mode-affiliation networks of innovators (RINs) according to the Thuringian travel-to-work areas[2] (ttwa) as defined by Granato and Farhauer (2007) who applied factor analysis for commuter streams.

5.3 Combination of Both

The combination of the information from the regional innovator network with our firm database was done by matching names of firm founders with names of inventors in our innovator network. It must be pointed out that this approach does not come without bias. However, we tried to check for addresses and birth dates in order to make the matches more accurate. If one or more founders of a firm are listed as inventor on a patent, then in a first step, we counted this firm to be innovative. Sure, we here assume what we cannot observe, namely that the founder intends to economically exploit his invention within his own firm rather than selling licences

---

[2]Figure 1 in the appendix shows a card of Thuringia and its ttwas. Sonneberg, Saale-Orla-Kreis, Altenburger Land and Eichsfeld are connected to regions outside Thuringia by means of commuter streams. For the creation of the regional innovator networks, we also included patents and inventors from these regions.

or leaving the exploitation to the applicant. However, since a patent application protects the knowledge from usage by other actors, it signals an intention to further use it for example to generate an innovation, which per definition is the economization of new ideas. Furthermore, every granted patent inherits a test with respect to the commercial usability of the invention. By combining both databases, we were able to identify networked-founders in the RINs and relate their network positions, properties to their firms. They are connected to the regional innovator network of the ttwa their firm is located at. As patenting is a quite rare event, we come up with a database of 149 innovative firms out of the sample population we have from the commercial register, which was 4566 founded firms in Thuringia.

6 Variables and Methodology

The next section is dedicated to present the variables used and the methodology applied. Table 1 gives a detailed overview on all variables used in the estimations; Table 2 presents the correlations between these variables.

6.1 Estimation Framework

Since success is measured in terms of survival, we apply Cox's proportional hazards model (1972) which gives a valid estimate of the survival rate for data sets including right-censored and left truncated cases. In survival analysis typically the relationship of the survival distribution to several covariates is examined. In our model, the firms' hazard to die in the next period is dependent on covariates as the networks' structure, the founder's position in the network and the structure of his ego-network.

Since a (scientific) social network is not a static but a dynamic construct which is developing gradually (Gay and Dousset 2005), we have to take time dependent effects into account. The connectedness of the innovator network and also the founders' position in the net are changing over the organizational life cycle and it is also path dependent (Hite and Hesterly 2001). This would mean that the structure of the network and the position of the founder in this network is dependent on the past structure and position respectively. To cover the early three stages in the organizational life cycle, we decided to measure our dependent variables at three points in time: first three years before they found the firm ($t = -3$) is representing the nascent stage, exactly in the year of firm founding ($t = 0$) is representing the beginning of the emergent stage and five years afterwards ($t = +5$) is representing the beginning of the early growth stage. This allows us to control for gradual effects with respect to the development of the networks' structure and to observe the coevolution of the network structure and the organizational life.

Table 1 Description of variables used in order to investigate the selective nature of innovator networks

	Variable	Description	Obs	Mean	Std. Dev.	Min	Max
Structure of the network (H1a–c)	Net_{-3}	Density of the network 3 years before the firm founding	149	0.007	1.000	−1.063	3.308
	$Net_{-3}SQ$	Net_{-3} Squared	149	0.992	2.035	0.000	10.942
	Net_0	Density of the network in the year of founding	149	0.001	1.003	−0.821	2.915
	Net_0SQ	Net_0 Squared	149	1.000	2.334	0.001	8.495
	Net_{+5}	Density of the network 5 years after firm founding	149	0.000	1.003	−1.043	1.622
	$Net_{+5}SQ$	Net_{+5} Squared	149	1.000	0.931	0.000	2.631
Position of the founder (H2a–c)	EV_{-3}	Founders' eigenvector centrality 3 years before the firm founding	37	−0.777	17.315	−86.497	57.735
	EV_0	Founders' eigenvector centrality in the year of founding	149	0.000	0.001	0.000	0.009
	EV_{+5}	Founders' eigenvector centrality 5 years after firm founding	149	0.019	3.276	−29.564	26.400
	MC_{-3}	Binary variable, indicating whether the firm has been connected to the main component 3 years before the firm founding	149	0.007	0.082	0.000	1.000

(continued)

Table 1 (continued)

	Variable	Description	Obs	Mean	Std. Dev.	Min	Max
	MC_0	Binary variable, indicating whether the firm has been connected to the main component in the year of its founding	149	0.040	0.197	0.000	1.000
	MC_{+5}	Binary variable, indicating whether the firm has been connected to the main component 5 years after its founding	149	0.188	0.392	0.000	1.000
Ego-Net (H3a–c)	$Constr_{-3}$	Constraint of the ego-network 3 years before the firm founding	149	0.223	0.396	0.000	1.125
	$Constr_0$	Constraint of the ego-network in the year of its founding	149	0.445	0.454	0.000	1.125
	$Constr_{+5}$	Constraint of the ego-network 5 years after firm founding	149	0.677	0.381	0.000	1.125
Controls	$PatExperience$	Number of patents the firm founders applied for before the firm has been founded	149	1.309	2.205	0.000	11.000
	$\#Patents$	Number of patents the firm applied for from the year of founding on	149	2.268	4.132	0.000	28.000

(continued)

Table 1 (continued)

Variable	Description	Obs	Mean	Std. Dev.	Min	Max
#Founders	Number of founders in the team	149	1.638	0.816	1.000	6.000
Spinoff	Binary variable, indicating whether the firm is an academic spin-off or not	149	0.195	0.397	0.000	1.000
CapComp	Binary variable, indicating whether the firm has the legal form of a capital company (1) or a private company (0)	149	0.960	0.197	0.000	1.000
Acad	Variable counting the number of founders in the team having an academic title	149	0.383	0.643	0.000	4.000
OutsideConn	Binary variable, indicating whether the respective company has also connections to other networks than the one it is located in	149	0.295	0.458	0.000	1.000
Meanturb	Mean of industry turbulence in the time span of 3 years before the firm has been founded and the 3 years afterwards	149	3.235	6.466	−0.394	23.241

(continued)

Table 1 (continued)

	Variable	Description	Obs	Mean	Std. Dev.	Min	Max
Net_{-3}	$Innovators_{-3}$	Size of the innovator network the founders are connected to 3 years before the firm has been founded	149	301.691	258.600	11.000	868.000
	$Aggregation_{-3}$	Level of aggregation of the network the founders are connected to 3 years before the firm founding	149	0.054	0.055	0.013	0.273
	LC_{-3}	Size of the largest component of the network the founders are connected to 3 years before the firm founding	149	0.117	0.076	0.045	0.364
Net_0	$Innovators_0$	Size of the innovator network the firm is connected to in the year of founding	149	780.134	560.084	32.000	1836.000
	$Aggregation_0$	Level of aggregation of the network the firm is connected in the year firm founding	149	0.055	0.066	0.011	0.246

(continued)

Table 1 (continued)

	Variable	Description	Obs	Mean	Std. Dev.	Min	Max
	LC_0	Size of the largest component of the network the firm is connected to in the year of firm founding	149	0.142	0.129	0.043	0.493
Net_{+5}	$Innovators_{+5}$	Size of the innovator network the firm is connected to 5 years after the firm has been founded	149	1531.617	991.999	75.000	2875.000
	$Aggregation_{+5}$	Level of aggregation of the network the firm is connected to 5 years after the firm founding	149	0.149	0.170	0.012	0.428
	LC_{+5}	Size of the largest component of the network the firm is connected to 5 years after the firm founding	149	0.286	0.243	0.032	0.654

6.2 Variables

6.2.1 Measuring the Structure of the Regional Innovator Network

In order to measure the structure of the RIN, we use several graph-theoretic concepts. Regarding size, the straightforward way to measure is to count the number of nodes, which is the total number of inventors in the travel-to-work area (Lobo and Strumsky 2008). The variable $Innovators_t$ thus measures the total number of inventors based in a respective ttwa in the certain stage of the organizational life cycle.

We use two variables to capture the structural features of a regional innovator network. The first one is a concept we adopt from Lobo and Strumsky (2008) which

Table 2 Correlations of the variables used in order to assess the influence of the selective nature of the innovator network

	1	2	3	4	5	6	7	8	9	10	11
1 Net_{-3}	1										
2 $Net_{-3}SQ$	0.6745*	1									
3 Net_0	-0.3059*	0.0296	1								
4 Net_0SQ	-0.3157*	0.0016	0.8817*	1							
5 Net_{+5}	-0.4452*	-0.1395	0.7009*	0.4648*	1						
6 $Net_{+5}SQ$	-0.2098*	0.0133	0.5609*	0.5455*	0.7212*	1					
7 EV_{-3}	-0.3759*	-0.5851*	0.0283	0.0161	0.0537	-0.0208	1				
8 EV_0	-0.0854	0.0033	0.2395*	0.2649*	0.1329	0.1431	0.0076	1			
9 EV_{+5}	0.0475	0.0065	0.0586	-0.0095	0.0422	-0.0516	0.0111	0.0259	1		
10 MC_{-3}	0.2724*	0.4032*	-0.0509	-0.0218	-0.0858	0.0079	-0.8365*	-0.0068	-0.0005	1	
11 MC_0	0.0955	0.3298*	0.2229*	0.1793*	0.1522	0.2403*	-0.4250*	0.4013*	0.0098	0.4013*	1
12 MC_{+5}	-0.2021*	-0.0479	0.2680*	0.0815	0.4747*	0.2932*	0.0296	0.1709*	0.1678*	-0.0395	0.2510*
13 $Constr_{-3}$	-0.0084	0.0512	0.0536	0.0099	-0.0471	-0.0346	0.0751	0.0885	0.0057	0.0808	0.1661*
14 $Constr_0$	-0.0875	0.0227	0.1167	0.1329	0.0499	0.121	0.1641	-0.0381	-0.0021	-0.0173	0.0862
15 $Constr_{+5}$	0.0629	0.0023	-0.1083	-0.0477	-0.007	0.1129	0.1516	-0.1171	-0.0557	-0.0789	-0.0678
16 #Patents	-0.1708*	0.0554	0.0835	0.0061	0.078	-0.0457	-0.1137	0.2502*	0.0046	0.1007	0.1266
17 PatExperience	-0.1258	0.0225	-0.0487	-0.1093	0.0437	-0.1257	-0.0827	-0.0054	0.1034	0.0545	0.0281
18 #Founders	-0.1939*	-0.0675	0.0017	0.009	0.0191	-0.0797	-0.1158	0.1378	-0.0541	0.0367	0.0073
19 Spinoff	-0.3358*	-0.0649	0.3469*	0.3149*	0.3528*	0.2482*	0.022	0.1672*	0.0029	-0.0404	0.0718
20 CapComp	-0.0672	-0.1276	-0.1712*	-0.1779*	-0.0255	-0.0353	-0.0076	0.0168	0.0012	0.0168	0.042
21 Acad	-0.2506*	-0.0517	0.1121	0.0949	0.1685*	0.0292	0.0244	0.0792	0.0846	-0.0491	-0.069
22 OutsideConn	-0.0997	0.0155	-0.0789	-0.0506	-0.0083	-0.0661	-0.2532	0.127	0.12	0.127	0.1668*
23 Meanturb	-0.0588	-0.1453	-0.1335	-0.1072	-0.1148	-0.1339	0.2242	-0.0369	-0.0019	-0.0248	-0.089

(continued)

Table 2 (continued)

		12	13	14	15	16	17	18	19	20	21	22	23
12	MC_{+5}	1											
13	$Constr_{-3}$	0.1089	1										
14	$Constr_0$	0.0038	0.4045*	1									
15	$Constr_{+5}$	−0.0981	−0.001	0.3861*	1								
16	#Patents	0.2764*	0.3987*	0.2121*	−0.2157*	1							
17	PatExperience	0.1605	0.1245	0.0419	−0.2320*	0.4394*	1						
18	#Founders	0.0243	0.1345	0.0286	−0.1307	0.2655*	0.2095*	1					
19	Spinoff	0.1541	0.003	0.2514*	0.0695	0.0852	0.1079	0.1149	1				
20	CapComp	0.0985	0.0293	0.0413	0.0912	0.0754	0.0714	0.0767	0.0145	1			
21	Acad	0.0345	0.0589	0.0971	−0.0981	0.2544*	0.5281*	0.3177*	0.1827*	−0.0375	1		
22	OutsideConn	0.2159*	0.051	0.0274	−0.1107	0.2906*	0.4151*	0.1800*	0.2020*	0.1326	0.3712*	1	
23	Meanturb	−0.1551	0.0528	0.0174	0.1965*	−0.1285	−0.139	−0.03	−0.0603	0.0766	−0.1476	−0.1154	1

$*p <= 0.05$

is basically a Herfindahl index based on the distribution of component sizes. This variable *Aggregation$_t$* measures the proportion of inventors in a RIN who are grouped into larger components[3] and ranges between zero and one, whereupon a value close to one indicates that most inventors in the ttwa are grouped into few components. In order to measure the extent to which inventors in a ttwa are intensely linked to one another we use as second variable the *size of the largest component (LC$_t$)*, which captures the share of inventors within the ttwa that had a collaborative relationship within the largest component.

Having a look at the correlation table for variables describing the regional network structure (Table 3), it is conspicuous that the three variables describing the structure of the network (*Innovators$_t$, Aggregation$_t$* and *LC$_t$*) are highly and significantly correlated. Hence, we decided to apply factor analysis and to concentrate those variables to one factor "*Net$_t$*". Table 4 shows the results of this analysis for the three points in time nascent stage, emergence stage and early growth stage. The higher the value of this variable the larger, more cohesive and more connected is the network of the respective ttwa.

In order to test hypotheses 1a–c and to find out more on the relationship between the structure of the regional innovator network and the success (survival probability) of the firm, we regress the variable *Net$_t$* together with different firm-specific control variables on the hazard ratio of the firm (this is the basic principle of the Cox regression model).

When we assess the relationship between the founders position in the net and the structure of the ego-net on the survival probability of the firm (Hypotheses 2a–c and 3a–c), we use *Net$_t$* as regional control variable. We have argued above that the characteristics and structure of innovator networks differs regionally. The networks, we have constructed for the analysis performed here, have been created for 12 ttwas in Thuringia such that the variable *Net$_t$* basically reflects the regional endowment with respect to the innovator network.

The variable *Net$_t$* measures the overall structure of the network the firm is connected to, irrespectively of the number of founders and the question of how many founders are connected to the network. In the next two steps of analysis, we distinguish between the position of the founder in the whole network and the structure of the ego-network. This is of cause estimated for single nodes. There is a small number of cases, where more than one founder is connected to the network. In these cases, we assumed a multiplicative effect and summed up the values for the nodes.

6.2.2 Measuring Entrepreneur's Position in the Network

When analysing the founders' position in the network, we basically want to know how central he is in the network as such. In order to assess this, we use two concepts.

---

[3]For details see Lobo and Strumsky (2008, p. 876).

Table 3 Correlation table for variables describing the network structure

	Variable	1	2	3	4	5	6	7	8	9
1	$Innovators_{-3}$	1								
2	$Aggregation_{-3}$	−0.5482*	1							
3	LC_{-3}	−0.4579*	0.9178*	1						
4	$Innovators_0$	0.9518*	−0.5870*	−0.4813*	1					
5	$Aggregation_0$	0.5725*	0.0463	0.1928*	0.4457*	1				
6	LC_0	0.5993*	−0.0202	0.1792*	0.4873*	0.9734*	1			
7	$Innovators_{+5}$	0.8106*	−0.5923*	−0.4853*	0.9477*	0.2551*	0.3049*	1		
8	$Aggregation_{+5}$	0.6004*	−0.2265*	−0.0093	0.7018*	0.5638*	0.6370*	0.6901*	1	
9	LC_{+5}	0.6208*	−0.2393*	0.0033	0.7103*	0.5554*	0.6568*	0.6873*	0.9805*	1

* $p <= 0.05$

Table 4 Factor analysis network structure

Variable	Net_t	Uniqueness
$Innovators_{-3}$	-0.7271	0.4713
$Aggregation_{-3}$	0.9573	0.0836
LC_{-3}	0.9278	0.1393
$Innovators_0$	0.6847	0.5312
$Aggregation_0$	0.9523	0.093
LC_0	0.9648	0.0691
$Innovators_{+5}$	0.8427	0.2898
$Aggregation_{+5}$	0.9675	0.0639
LC_{+5}	0.9666	0.0657

First, centrality is measured here by means of eigenvector-centrality and reveals how well connected an actor is in the overall network (EV_t).[4] The eigenvector approach identifies the most central actors in terms of the "global" or "overall" structure of the network (Hanneman and Riddle 2005). Thus, by taking into account direct as well as indirect ties of single actors it assumes that a node is central to the extent that the node is connected to others who are central (Bonacich 1972). Higher scores indicate that actors are "more central" to the main pattern of distances among all of the actors, lower values indicate that actors are more peripheral. For the case that more than one founder is connected to the network, we summed up their individual values for EV_t.

The second concept we use is the membership in the main component. The main component of the network is the maximal connected sub graph. This measure thus captures the degree of fragmentation in a RIN's structure. If the network has more than one component, different information flows pass each component. Since the main component connects the largest number of nodes, being connected to this component may induce most knowledge flows (Powell et al. 1996). With respect to the RIN, this means that a networked-founder which is a member of the main component is more central to the network and thus his firm profits comparably more from network's knowledge flows. MC_t takes a value of one if (one of) the entrepreneur(s) of the firm is connected to the main component and is zero otherwise.

---

[4] We measured centrality by means of Eigenvector centrality (Bonacich 1972). There exist different measures for centrality like betweeness centrality (Anthonisse 1971; Freeman 1977), closeness centrality (Beauchamp 1965) or hub centrality (Kleinberg 1999). We decided for the Eigenvector centrality since it is a feedback centrality which is showing whether the actor is connected to the top connected other actors in the net which might be especially useful for young and small companies who are in need of good contacts.

6.2.3 Measuring the Ego-network of the Entrepreneur

In order to assess the influence of the closeness of the networked-founder's ego-network, we use the variable $Constr_t$ which is a structural hole measure introduced by Burt (1992). This is a summary measure that taps the extent to which ego's connections are to others who are connected to one another (Hanneman and Riddle 2005). A high value of this variable indicates that the entrepreneur occupies a position in the net which is less constrained and where he can broker more extensively. In other words, the higher this measure, the less structural holes the ego-network has and the more closed it is. For the case that more than one founder is connected to the network, we summed up their individual values for $Constr_t$.

6.2.4 Control Variables

In order to compare and contrast the effects of network structure as well as founders' position in the net and firms' characteristics on survival we, additionally to the dependent variables introduced in the above chapter, used a set of control variables which may influence firms' survival.

#Patents. This variable counts the number of patents the founders of the firm applied for after the firm has been founded. Founders with more patents might be more connected to the network such that in order to make statements on the main variables of interest in this paper, we need to control for the quantity of patent applications.

PatExperience. This is a variable counting the number of patents the founders of the respective firms have applied for before the firm has been founded. Cantner and Wolf (2016) found that experience in patenting is a main driver of patenting in the future such that this influences the founders future network which we want to analyze.

#Founders. This variable indicates the number of persons that has founded the respective firm. It has been argued earlier in this text that more founders may bring a broader range of scientific capital to the firm and thus also influence firms' success.

Spinoff. This dummy variable measures whether the firm is an academic spin-off or not. Academic spin-offs are usually founded on the basis of innovative products and additionally have the 'mothers' support, which makes them more successful (Utterback 1974).

CapComp. This variable indicates weather a firm has the legal form of a capital company ($Capcomp = 1$) or of a private company ($Capcomp = 0$). It has been found that private companies may have higher chances to be successful, thus to survive, since the founders adhere with their private capital (Harhoff et al. 1998).

Acad. This variable counts the number of founders with an academic title. It has been found that academics usually have a larger network of scientific contacts (Breschi and Catalani 2010) and may therefore add more to the scientific network of the firm.

OutsideConn. Being connected to more than on RIN may enlarge the scientific network of the firm. Thus, with this variable, we measure whether the firm has connections to more than the RIN where it is located at.

Meanturb. The firms in the sample are active in different industrial sectors and of cause the sector plays an important role to for the survivability of a firm. Since this paper is analyzing young firms, it is not only controlled for sectors but to also for the economic environment/stage of the sector they are active in. For this purpose, data from the IAB (Institut für Arbeitsmarkt- und Berufsforschung) has been used, which contains the number of firm founding and closing for each industry (Nace 2-digit level) for the years 1976–2010. Based on this data, the variable named *Meanturb* has been constructed, which is measuring the turbulence in the sector the firm is active in for a time span of six years, three years before the firm has been founded and three years afterwards. The turbulence is measured as number of firm founding in a certain sector in the specific years minus the number of firm close downs in the same sector in the same years. From this value, the mean over the six years around the firm founding is estimated and used for analysis.

7   Empirical Results

Hypothesis 1a states that there is no connection between the structure of the network and the chances for a firm to survive in the nascent stage of the organizational life cycle, while hypothesis 1b and 1c suggest a decreasing importance of the connectedness of the network and firm survival. In order to measure how dense the whole network is, we applied factor analysis and created the variable Net_t which is the combination of three variables describing the network as such (size of the network, aggregation level of the network and size of the largest component). The larger the variable Net_t the more connected the network in the sense that there are more actors which are highly aggregated and which's largest component is relatively big. Table 5, model 1 provides the results for all three stages in the early organizational life cycle. We do not find a significant relationship between the survival of the firm and the network structure in the nascent stage and year of firm founding/beginning of the emergent stage and thus have to accept hypothesis 1a and to reject hypothesis 1b. However, we find a significant relationship between the hazard ratio and the network structure five years after firm founding (Net_{+5}), when the early growth stage develops. The coefficient of Net_{+5} is larger than one, which means that the risk to die in the next period is increased when the connectedness of the network is increased. This supports hypothesis 1c. The squared term of Net_{+5} ($Net_{+5}SQ$) however is smaller than one which indicates that from a certain network size on, the hazard starts to become smaller again. This inverted u-shape relationship between network size and the survival of the firm indicates that there are two favorable situations for the firms. Either they are connected to a network which is quite fragmented or to a network which is extremely connected. This finding might be due to the fact that Hite and Hesterly (2001) are right in their assumption that the cohesiveness of the network decreases while the bridging of structural holes increases over time. Since we could not observe the exact date of movement between the two stages in the organizational life cycle but only narrowed this date by assuming that this might happen after roughly five years (Phillips and Kirchhoff 1989) it might just be that after five years some firms are still in the emergence firms (cohesiveness is important) and others already went to the early growth stage (structural holes are important).

Hypotheses 2a–c relate to the overall centrality of the position of the founder in the network. While hypothesis 1a suggests no relationship between the survival in the nascent stage and a central position of the founder, hypothesis 2b and 2c suggest a positive influence of a central position on the chances to survive, but for different reasons. In order to measure this relationship, we use Eigenvector centrality, as well as the membership in the main component.

Model 2 in Table 5 analyzes the variables EV_{-3}, EV_0 and EV_{+5} as representatives of the actors Eigenvector centrality. We find that only the coefficient for EV_{-3} becomes significant, a result that interestingly stands against our hypothesis 2a stating no connection between survival and centrality in the nascent stage. Rather a central position seems to hinder survival. Looking at the membership in the main component, we find a significant result for the early growth stage. However, in contrast to hypothesis 2c, we find a negative relation. If we reinterpret this result in the light of Hite and Hesterly (2001) proposition that in the later stages, firms do not need a very dense network anymore, we might say that also the connection to the main component becomes unfavourable at a certain point in the life cycle. Therefore, the power argument of being in a position to control knowledge might not be that strong for our database.

Finally, although we find significant relationships, we have to reject hypotheses 2a–c.

Hypothesis 3a states that closed ego networks of a networked-founder in the nascent stage have no influence on its survival. In model 4 of Table 5, we use the variable $Constr_{-3}$ to measure this relationship and find no significant relationship such that we cannot accept hypothesis 3a. Hypothesis 3b and 3c, taken together, state that from the emergent to the early growth stage in the organizational life cycle, the favourable network moves from a closed one to a quite fragmented one. In Table 5 we find no significant effects.

Over all models in Table 5, the variable measuring the connectivity of the whole network shows up to be significant at the beginning of the early growth stage. But this relation takes an inverted u-relationship.

8 Conclusion

Over all analyses, we find that there is no influence of the networks' structure in the nascent stage of the organizational life cycle. This supports the findings by Cantner and Stuetzer (2013) who show that factors like start-up capital, the functional

Table 5 Influence of the network structure and the ego-network on the hazard ratio

Method	Cox regression – Breslow method for ties			
	Survival			
Dep. Var.	Model 1 H1a–c	Model 2 H2a–c	Model 3 H2a–c	Model 4 H3a–c
EV_{-3}		1.034*		
		(1.721)		
EV_0		0.000		
		(−0.000)		
EV_{+5}		1.010		
		(0.168)		
MC_{-3}			6.010	
			(0.000)	
MC_0			0.000	
			(−0.000)	
MC_{+5}			4.567***	
			(2.811)	
$Constr_{-3}$				0.791
				(−0.428)
$Constr_0$				1.332
				(0.573)
$Constr_{+5}$				2.124
				(1.376)
Net_{-3}	1.214	1.192	0.938	1.172
	(0.640)	(0.579)	(−0.211)	(0.523)
$Net_{-3}SQ$	0.928	0.947	0.990	0.921
	(−0.521)	(−0.379)	(−0.068)	(−0.550)
Net_0	0.715	0.701	0.731	0.810
	(−0.577)	(−0.599)	(−0.551)	(−0.348)
$Net_0\ SQ$	1.134	1.142	1.158	1.091
	(0.523)	(0.542)	(0.607)	(0.350)
$Netplus_{+5}$	2.355**	2.512**	1.539	2.426**
	(1.982)	(2.086)	(0.974)	(2.011)
$Netplus_{+5}\ SQ$	0.509*	0.484*	0.575	0.444**
	(−1.842)	(−1.940)	(−1.535)	(−2.140)
Patthvor2	0.918	0.915	0.879	0.918
	(−0.794)	(−0.819)	(−1.165)	(−0.714)
Patth2	0.950	0.950	0.968	0.963
	(−0.941)	(−0.934)	(−0.561)	(−0.660)
Grnder	1.442**	1.473**	1.408*	1.532**
	(1.985)	(2.100)	(1.917)	(2.223)
Spinoff	0.170**	0.172**	0.169**	0.122**
	(−2.291)	(−2.283)	(−2.234)	(−2.565)
Capcomp	0.435	0.421	0.386	0.339
	(−1.234)	(−1.281)	(−1.390)	(−1.538)

(continued)

Table 5 (continued)

Method	Cox regression – Breslow method for ties			
	Survival			
Dep. Var.	Model 1 H1a–c	Model 2 H2a–c	Model 3 H2a–c	Model 4 H3a–c
Acad	1.501	1.464	1.612	1.391
	(1.249)	(1.168)	(1.375)	(0.994)
Outsideconnection	0.558	0.569	0.360*	0.605
	(−1.158)	(−1.098)	(−1.825)	(−0.995)
Meanturb	1.022	1.016	1.025	1.012
	(0.916)	(0.644)	(1.031)	(0.455)
Observations	149	149	149	149
No. Of Failures	38	38	38	38
Prob > Chi2	0.0185	0.0318	0.0042	0.0230

z-statistics in parentheses *** $p < 0.01$, ** $p < 0.05$, * $p < 0.10$

background and entrepreneurial experience of the founders seem to overweight the importance of social (scientific) capital for the success of the new venture. However, for Eigenvector centrality, we find a small negative effect indicating that a central position in the innovator network is not too favourable in the nascent stage of the firm' life. A reason might be the high inflow and redundancy of information, reaching a node in a central position. A person which has to concentrate on getting start-up capital and writing a business plan might easily be overstrained by this. For sure, this point leaves open space for further research.

Having a look at the structure of the 'home' network of the firm, we find an inverted u-shaped relationship between the survival of firms and the connectivity of the network. Thus, very loose networks and very dense networks seem to be favorable for the survival of firms but nothing in between. Additionally, we find that it becomes unfavorable to be connected to the main component when the firm enters the early growth stage. In the theoretical part of this paper, we argued that Burt (1992) and Coleman (1988) have two opposite views on the interdependency between the structure of the ego-network and the related benefits for the actor (Gilsing et al. 2008; Gilsing and Nooteboom 2005). While Burt says that a loose network is favorable since it brings possibilities to broker and control knowledge flows, Coleman says that dense networks are favorable since they allow for more knowledge spillovers. Hite and Hesterly (2001) translate these considerations to the organizational life cycle and argue that firms need a "Coleman-network" in the emergent stage but a "Burt-network" when they enter the early growth stage. The inverted u-shape we find might be due to the individuality of each firm's history. Some firms might change to the early growth stage already after two years, while others need six. What the results show is that Burt and Coleman both have their eligibility. Additionally, Hite and Hesterly seem to be on the right track with their idea of changing requirements on the network over the organizational life cycle. In a future research, it would be recommendable to have survey data and identify the moment when a firm leaves one stage and enters the other individually.

With respect to the influence of the founder's position in the network on firms' success, we looked at his centrality and on his membership to the main component. We find that being a member of the network's main component has a negative influence on the survivability of firms in the early growth stage. Thus, we disproved our theoretical argumentation, stating that the main component inherits most knowledge spillovers and thus increases the number of opportunities for innovation. However, also here, the arguments raised above may hold. In the largest component, the actors may all work in the same technology such that there is less variety of technologies which may be unfavorable for new combinations and thus firms' performance, especially in the later stage of the early firm development.

With respect to control variables we find that firms have better chances to survive if they are a spin-off and if they have connections also to other networks than only to the one in the region where they have their headquarters. This positive effect of a mother institution for highly innovative firms has already been described and empirically analyzed by Cantner and Goethner (2011). However, the influence of various connections to different networks seems to be an interesting issue. Is it important to which ones of the regional networks the firms are connected to? Is it possible for firms to be overconnected? Is there an optimal rate of outside connection? These and other questions are still open for future research.

Having a look at the mere number of founders, we find a negative effect on survival. Thus too many founders reduce a firm's chances to survive. In the theoretical part of this paper, we argued that the number of founders may have a positive influence since they may all add to the scientific network of the firm. However, Cantner et al. (2010) found that the composition of the team plays an important role for the success of a firm. Their findings may explain our results since they showed that it is not quantity but quality of the founding team that counts and our results also go into this direction.

Additionally, Lobo and Strumsky (2008) argued that the variable network aggregation also indicates whether actors in the region have worked in the same technology. Interpreting our results from that angle our results point to the interpretation that variety of technologies in a network is favorable for firms' success. Since this interpretation is very vague it leaves space for future research.

Appendix

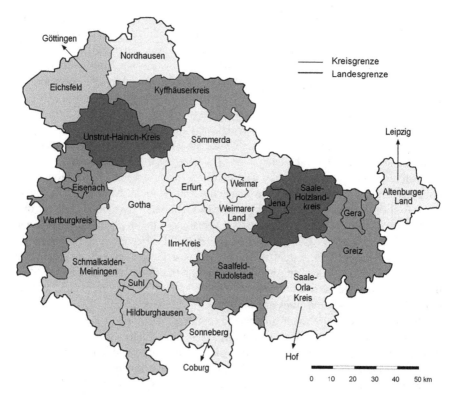

Fig. 1 Thuringia and its travel-to-work areas. Thuringian travel to work areas according to the estimations of Granato and Farhauer (2007)

References

Ahuja, G. (2000). Collaboration networks, structural holes and innovation: A longitudinal study. *Administrative Science Quarterly, 45*, 425–455.

Aldrich, H. E. (1999). *Organizations evolving*. London: Sage.

Aldrich, H. E., & Reese, P. R. (1993). Does networking pay off? A panel study of entrepreneurs in the research triangle. In N. Churchill et al. (Eds.), *Frontiers of entrepreneurship research* (pp. 325–399). Babson, MA: Babson College.

Anthonisse, J. M. (1971). *The rush in a graph*. Amsterdam: Mathematisch Centrum.

Audretsch, D. B. (1995). *Innovation and industry evolution*. Massachusetts: MIT Press.

Audretsch, D. B., & Lehmann, E. E. (2005). Does the knowledge spillover theory of entrepreneurship hold for regions? *Research Policy, 34*, 1191–1202.

Balconi, M., Breschi, S., & Lissoni, F. (2004). Networks of inventors and the role of academia: An exploration of Italian patent data. *Research Policy, 33*, 127–145.

Balland, P. A., Boschma, R., & Frenken, K. (2015). Proximity and innovation: From statics to dynamics. *Regional Studies, 49*, 907–920.

Bartelsman, E., Scarpetta, S., & Schivardi, F. (2005). Comparative analysis of firm demographics and survival: Evidence from micro-level sources in OECD countries. *Industrial & Corporate Change, 14*, 365–391.

Baum, J. C. A. (1996). Organizational ecology. In S. Clegg, C. Hardy, & W. Nord (Eds.), *Handbook of organization studies* (pp. 77–114). London: Sage.

Beauchamp, M. A. (1965). An improved index of centrality. *Systems Research and Behavioral Science, 10*, 161–163.

Bonacich, P. (1972). Factoring and weighting approaches to clique identification. *Journal of Mathematical Sociology, 2*, 113–120.

Breschi, S., & Catalani, C. (2010). Tracing the links between science and technology: An exploratory analysis of scientists' and inventors' networks. *Research Policy, 39*, 14–26.

Breschi, S., & Lissoni, F. (2006). Cross-firm inventors and social networks: Localized knowledge spillovers revisited. *Annules d'Economie et de Statistique, 79–8*, 189–209.

Burt, R. S. (1992). *Structural holes: The social structure of competition*. Cambridge: Harvard University Press.

Cantner, U., & Goethner, M. (2011). *Performance differences between academic spin-offs and non-academic start-ups: An empirical investigation*. Presented at the DIME Final Conference 2011, Maastricht.

Cantner, U., Goethner, M., & Stuetzer, M. (2010). *Disentangling the effects of new venture team functional heterogeneity on new venture performance*. Jena Economic Research Papers, 2010–29.

Cantner, U., & Graf, H. (2007). *Growth, development and structural change of innovator networks – The case of Jena*. Jena Economic Research Papers, #2007-090.

Cantner, U., & Stuetzer, M. (2013). Knowledge and innovative entrepreneurship – Social capital and individual capacities. In P. Morone (Ed.), *Knowledge, innovation and internationalization. Essays in Honour of Cesare Imbriani* (pp. 59–90). New York: Routledge.

Cantner, U., & Wolf, T. (2016). *On regional innovator networks as hubs for innovative ventures*. Jena Economic Research Papers, 2016-006.

Churchill, N. C., & Levis, V. L. (1983). The five stages of small business growth. *Harvard Business Review, 61*, 30–50.

Coleman, J. S. (1988). Social capital in the creation of human capital. *American Journal of Sociology, 94*, 95–120.

Cox, D. R. (1972). Regression models and life-tables. *Journal of the Royal Statistical Society, 34*, 187–220.

Ejermo, O., & Karlsson, C. (2006). Interregional inventor networks as studied by patent coinventorships. *Research Policy, 35*, 412–430.

Fershtman, C., & Gandal, N. (2011). Direct and indirect knowledge spillovers: The 'social network' of open source projects. *RAND Journal of Economics, 42*, 70–91.

Freeman, L. C. (1977). A set of measures of centrality based on betweenness. *Sociometry, 40*, 35–41.

Gartner, W. B., Birs, B. J., & Starr, J. A. (1992). Acting as if: Differentiating entrepreneurial from organizational behaviour. *Entrepreneurship: Theory and Practice, 16*, 13–31.

Gay, B., & Dousset, B. (2005). Innovation and network structural dynamics: Study of the alliance network of a major sector of the biotechnology industry. *Research Policy, 34*, 1457–1475.

Gilsing, V. A., & Nooteboom, B. (2005). Density and strength of ties in innovation networks, an analysis of multimedia and biotechnology. *European Management Review, 2*, 179–197.

Gilsing, V. A., Nooteboom, B., Vanhaverbeke, W., Duysters, G., & van den Oord, A. (2008). Network embeddedness and the exploration of novel technologies: Technological distance, betweenness centrality and density. *Research Policy, 37*, 1717–1731.

Gnyawali, D. R., & Madhavan, R. (2001). Cooperative networks and competitive dynamics: A structural embeddedness perspective. *Academy of Management Review, 26*, 431–445.

Golden, P. A., & Dollinger, M. (1993). Cooperative alliances and competitive strategies in small manufacturing firms. *Entrepreneurship: Theory and Practice, 17*, 43–56.

Granato, N., & Farhauer, O. (2007). *Die Abgrenzung von Arbeitsmarktregionen: Gütekriterien und Maßzahlen*. Wirtschaftswissenschaftliche Dokumentation der TU Berlin. 2007/2.

Grupp, H., & Legler, H. (2000). *Hochtechnologie 2000 – Neudefinition der Hochtechnologie für die Berichterstattung zur technologischen Leistungsfähigkeit Deutschlands*. Karlsruhe/Hannover.

Hanneman, R. A., & Riddle, M. (2005). *Introduction to social network methods*. Riverside, CA: University of California.

Hargadon, A., & Sutton, R. I. (1997). Technology brokering and innovation in a product development firm. *Administrative Science Quarterly, 42*, 716–749.

Harhoff, D., Stahl, K., & Woywode, M. (1998). Legal form, growth and exit of west German firms – Empirical results for manufacturing, construction, trade and service industries. *The Journal of Industrial Economics, 46*, 453–488.

Heckmann, M., & Schnabel, C. (2005). *Überleben und Beschäftigungsentwicklung neu gegründeter Betriebe*. Discussion Paper No. 39. Friedrich-Alexander-Universität Erlangen-Nürnberg.

Hite, J. M., & Hesterly, W. S. (2001). The evolution of firm networks: from emergence to early growth of the firm. *Strategic Management Journal, 22*, 275–286. https://doi.org/10.1002/smj.156

Howells, J. R. L. (2002). Tacit knowledge, innovation and economic geography. *Urban Studies, 39*, 871–884.

Kessler, A., & Frank, H. (2009). Nascent entrepreneurship in a longitudinal perspective: The impact of person, environment, resources and the founding process on the decision to start business activities. *International Small Business Journal, 27*, 720–742.

Kleinberg, J. M. (1999). Authoritative sources in a hyperlinked environment. *Journal of the ACM, 46*, 604–632.

Larson, A. L., & Starr, J. A. (1993). A network model of organization formation. *Entrepreneurship: Theory and Practice, 17*, 5–15.

Lobo, J., & Strumsky, D. (2008). Metropolitan patenting, inventor agglomeration and social networks: A tale of two effects. *Journal of Urban Economics, 63*, 871–884.

Meagher, K., & Rogers, M. (2004). Network density and R&D spillovers. *Journal of Economic Behavior & Organization, 53*, 237–260.

Murray, F. (2004). The role of academic inventors in entrepreneurial firms: Sharing the laboratory life. *Research Policy, 33*, 643–659.

Ostgaard, T. A., & Birley, S. (1994). Personal Networks and firm competitive strategy: A strategic or coincidental match? *Journal of Business Venturing, 9*, 281–305.

Parker, S. C. (2009). *The economics of entrepreneurship*. New York: Cambridge University Press.

Phillips, B. D., & Kirchhoff, B. A. (1989). Formation, growth and survival. *Small Business Economics, 1*, 65–74.

Powell, W. W., Koput, K. W., & Smith-Doerr, L. (1996). Interorganizational collaboration and the locus of innovation: Networks of learning in biotechnology. *Administrative Science Quarterly, 41*, 116–145.

Reynolds, P. D. (2000). National panel study of U.S. business start-ups: Background and methodology. In J. A. Katz (Ed.), *Databases for the study of entrepreneurship* (pp. 153–227). Amsterdam: JAI Press.

Storey, D. J. (1994). *Understanding the small business sector*. London: Thomson Learning.

Stuart, T. E., Hoang, H., & Hybels, R. (1999). Inter-organizational endorsements and the performance of entrepreneurial ventures. *Administrative Science Quarterly, 44*, 315–350.

Utterback, J. M. (1974). Innovation in industry and the diffusion of technology. *Science, 183*, 620–626.

Walker, G., Kogut, B., & Shan, W. (1997). Social capital, structural holes and the formation of an industry network. *Organization Science, 8*, 109–125.

Wasserman, S., & Faust, K. (1994). *Social network analysis – Methods and applications*. New York: Cambridge University Press.

The Decline of Innovation in the Antibiotics Industry and the Global Threat of Antibiotic Resistance: When Entrepreneurial Efforts are Not Enough

Francesco Ciabuschi and Olof Lindahl

Abstract In this chapter we intend to analyze the worrisome case of the antibiotics industry, as the number of active firms, innovation output and profitability has constantly declined in the last years. With a focus on factors influencing the Entrepreneurial Orientation of firms in this industry, we analyze a number of challenges and environmental contingencies unique to antibiotic innovation and entrepreneurial activity, and discuss currently debated public policy interventions intended to reinvigorate the industry. In doing so we discuss the possibility of enhancing entrepreneurial orientation by acting on the performance side through targeted public interventions such as research grants and market entry rewards. This chapter contributes to innovation and entrepreneurship literature by presenting a unique case of a declining industry, the antibiotics field, which requires public intervention to revive and meet global societal needs to face the threat of antibiotic resistance. This industry-based case analysis presents a number of interesting implications for theory on Entrepreneurial Orientation that also allows the outlining of several avenues for future research.

Keywords Innovation · Entrepreneurial orientation · Public intervention · Antibiotics industry

1 Introduction

The antibiotic industry is in decline at the same time as society worldwide desperately needs new antibiotics to face the global threat of antibiotic resistance. In the past 20 years, an increasing number of companies have exited the antibiotics market and the number of new entrants is very limited. These circumstances have today resulted in a lack of innovation with only few big pharmas still active in the field, and

F. Ciabuschi (✉) · O. Lindahl
Department of Business Studies, Uppsala University, Uppsala, Sweden
e-mail: francesco.ciabuschi@fek.uu.se; olof.lindahl@fek.uu.se

© Springer International Publishing AG, part of Springer Nature 2018
S. Cubico et al. (eds.), *Entrepreneurship and the Industry Life Cycle*, Studies on Entrepreneurship, Structural Change and Industrial Dynamics,
https://doi.org/10.1007/978-3-319-89336-5_9

a global antibiotics pipeline with extremely limited numbers of promising new molecules.

Although there still are small, entrepreneurial companies trying to develop novel antibiotics, without big pharmas to purchase their molecules there is little hope for continued innovation and improved industry dynamics. How to stimulate innovation and entrepreneurial activity in an industry in decline? In this chapter we intend to analyze the current status of the antibiotics sector with a focus on factors influencing the Entrepreneurial Orientation of firms in this industry. More specifically, we start by presenting the current status of the antibiotics industry and also by analyzing a number of challenges unique to innovation and entrepreneurial activity in this industry. We present such entrepreneurial and innovation-related challenges according to their scientific, financial, or market-specific nature. Consequently, we will also discuss potential public policy interventions to stimulate new entrepreneurial activities and related antibiotic innovation in this industry. In particular, the most important public interventions are discussed in terms of their potential effects (both benefits and risks) on future innovation and entrepreneurial activities given the previously identified challenges of the antibiotic field. Analyzing the effect of intervention mechanisms on the Entrepreneurial Orientation of firms in this industry will be given particular attention. The decline of an entire industry has been found to manifest itself through the lack of entrepreneurial orientation and firm performance (Lumpkin and Dess 2001). In this study, we attempt to explain the lack of firm performance, and by implication also long-term entrepreneurial orientation, by analyzing a number of environmental contingencies which may be suffocating the antibiotics industry.

This chapter contributes to innovation and entrepreneurship literature by presenting a unique case of a declining industry, the antibiotics field, which requires public intervention to revive and meet global societal needs to face the threat of antibiotic resistance. Analyzing this specific industry case also has a number of interesting implications for theory on Entrepreneurial Orientation that allows the outlining of several avenues for future research.

The remainder of this chapter is structured as follows: after introducing the current status of the antibiotic industry we move on to depict the current main (scientific, financial and market-related) challenges that firms face in this industry. In the part that follows we make use of the Entrepreneurial Orientation framework to analyze these challenges as well as currently discussed public interventions to stimulate investments and entrepreneurial activities in the antibiotic industry. This analysis paves the way for our concluding discussion that puts in relation targeted public interventions, environmental contingencies and firms' performance with the level of Entrepreneurial Orientation in the industry. At last we will present some suggestions for future research.

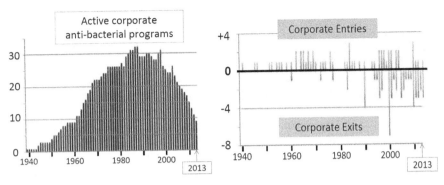

Fig. 1 The withdrawal of firms from the antibiotics industry. Source: Adapted from Kinch et al., *Drug Discovery Today* (2014)

2 The Current Status of the Antibiotics Industry

The antibiotic industry suffers from a lack of innovation and investment from the main actors in the industry, as well as a dearth of new entrants (Fig. 1). As a consequence, the industry is in a long and steep decline as pharmaceutical companies are increasingly closing down their antibiotic research and development (R&D) labs (Rex and Outterson 2016). For comparison, there were 25 large pharmaceutical firms with ongoing antibacterial drug discovery programs in 1980; in 2014 only four remained (Boucher et al. 2009) two of which had an antibacterial in phase two of development. Sadly, out of these four active programs, an additional two have been closed since 2014 (AstraZeneca and Cubist).

This decline in active antibacterial drug discovery programs has taken place in the face of rising threats from multi-drug resistant bacteria. Antibiotic resistance, i.e., when bacteria become resistant to existing antibiotics, is a growing global threat to public health and makes the decline of the antibiotics industry uniquely problematic. While considerable advances have been made in the areas of vaccines, sanitation, and infection control, antibiotics remains a pillar of infectious disease therapy. Often referred to as the backbone of modern medicine, antibiotics are used to save lives by killing dangerous bacteria in everything from pneumonia and urinary tract infections to treatments like surgery and chemotherapy.

While hard to calculate with precision, the consequences of antibiotic resistance are huge in both human health and economic cost. Since penicillin first became widely used in the 1940s, the fear has been that bacteria in time would mutate and find ways to defend themselves against the miracle drug of antibiotics. Indeed, the increasing prevalence of antibiotic resistance is eroding the efficacy of existing antibiotics (Laxminarayan et al. 2014). These antibiotic-resistant bacteria have become increasingly common and today are confirmed to kill 100,000 people per year in the US, the EU and Thailand—the only countries from which data is currently available. However, the global numbers believed to die from antibiotic-resistant bacteria are thought to be in the several hundreds of thousands (O'Neill Commission 2015).

Taken together, these developments have presented a pressing need to reverse the decline of the antibiotics industry and to restore the industry's innovation pipeline to good health. However, reversing this decline requires first identifying the main challenges to innovation in antibiotics, which, as we will discuss in the next section, are numerous.

In order to outline the situation facing the antibiotics industry, we will first present the main challenges to antibiotic innovation from a business perspective followed by examples of the main responses to the crisis of the antibiotics industry that lately have been discussed on supra-national levels, such as at the G20 and the UN. Finally, we will present a framework through which we believe that the challenges facing the antibiotics industry may be understood as a whole and the feasibility of the solutions to these problems may be evaluated—the framework of Entrepreneurial Orientation. Having analyzed the antibiotic industry through this lens, we provide important implications for firms, policy makers, and theory on entrepreneurship and innovation.

3   Challenges Facing the Antibiotics Industry

There are a number of factors conspiring to cause lack of entrepreneurial activities in the antibiotic industry.[1] The most pressing challenges are related to innovation and profitability.

From a scientific standpoint, what can be referred to as the "low-hanging fruit" has been picked and novel discoveries are increasingly both costly and scarce. Moreover, there are a number of factors related to pharmaceutical innovation regulations and so-called stewardship—the responsible (restrictive) use of new antibiotics—that increase the scientific and business challenges to antibiotics R&D.

Developers who come up with new antibiotics create considerable benefit for society but are not guaranteed to benefit financially (O'Neill Commission 2015). Industry consolidation has resulted in a major decrease in the hunt for novel

---

[1]*Methodological note:* The analysis of the antibiotics industry in this chapter is based on data collected within a larger research project in which multiple data collection methods were applied. A separate literature review of challenges facing innovation in the antibiotic industry was conducted. A focus group of experts from both academia, public health, and the pharmaceutical industry reviewed the final list of challenges. When initially analyzing the collected data we focused on facts and specific statements rather than on opinions (Eisenhardt 1989; Eisenhardt and Graebner 2007) and in our initial analysis of these challenges we did no additional interpretation of beyond that already present in the data. Our data collection efforts resulted in an exhaustive document outlining the known challenges to innovation in antibiotics. However, for the purpose of the analysis performed in this book chapter, only a subset of such challenges was used. These challenges were those most closely pertaining to the business of antibiotics, i.e., to sales market growth, competition, and innovation. These challenges are presented in the coming section in their original format to facilitate the later analysis using the entrepreneurial orientation framework.

antibiotic agents (Projan and Shlaes 2004). This, in turn, is thought to be caused by a lack of commercial attractiveness to off-set the costs and risks involved in the development of antibiotics. Most antibiotics generate annual revenues of US$ 200–300 million, while the costs of bringing any drug to market have been estimated to be as high as US$ 400–800 million (DiMasi et al. 2003). Moreover, the financial risk associated with involvement in antibiotics R&D acts as a disincentive (Pray 2008). High costs and high risk together have the effect that important investment metrics such as Net Present Values (NPVs) and Return On Investments (ROIs) for antibiotics are either negative (Spellberg et al. 2015) or lower than for other pharmaceutical treatments, making antibiotics an unattractive therapeutic investment (Payne et al. 2015; Power 2006; Projan 2003; Wright 2015). As a consequence, antibiotics get lower priority than other drugs (Projan and Shlaes 2004), as current R&D trends emphasize chronic diseases (Spellberg et al. 2004). However, these financial challenges to antibiotic innovation and entrepreneurship can be seen to have deeper root causes, which is the topic to which we turn next. Below, we present more in detail a set of challenges pertaining to the financial, market and scientific areas of the global antibiotic industry.

3.1 Pricing

Antibiotics are typically priced much lower than other drugs (Spellberg et al. 2015) and limitations on the pricing of new antibiotics persist (Harbarth et al. 2015). Moreover, reimbursement systems encourage the use of the cheapest drug (Morel and Mossialos 2010; Renwick et al. 2014) and healthcare payers are neither accustomed nor prepared to reimburse antibiotics at higher prices, which would provide incentives to start or maintain antibacterial drug development programs (Laxminarayan and Powers 2011). Additionally, tightening restrictions for placement on hospital formularies negatively affects antibiotics R&D (Harbarth et al. 2015) and increased regulatory measures negatively impact potential revenues by increasing development costs, limiting the number of indications or diseases for which a drug can be recommended as standard treatment (Power 2006). Lastly, flaunting of intellectual property laws has resulted in the proliferation of low priced generics, which created a distortion of the market for anti-infective drugs (Projan 2003). All the above listed factors point to the fact that improving revenue streams and profit margins in this industry is very difficult to accomplish.

3.2 Revenues and Market Sizes

There is tremendous uncertainty associated with the peculiar dynamics of the antibiotics marketplace (O'Neill Commission 2015). For example, it has been highlighted how hard it is for pharmaceutical firms to predict how big the health need will be in the future as they try to make decisions about very long-term investments in R&D (O'Neill Commission 2015; Zorzet 2014). This, in turn, is made particularly difficult in the antibiotics industry due to the uncertainties surrounding resistance development and as the rate of infections can change quickly (O'Neill Commission 2015).

The revenues attained from a novel antibiotic have been found to be negatively affected by the generally short courses of treatment (Renwick et al. 2014). Specifically, this affects NPV (Morel and Mossialos 2010; Spellberg et al. 2015) or ROI (Katz et al. 2006; NIAID 2014) by reducing the potential "peak" revenue attainted even if a novel antibiotic gains a large market share (Payne et al. 2015). Lastly, the potential of accruing revenues from novel antibiotics are also depressed as resistance may itself limit an antibiotic's lifespan (So et al. 2011).

Adding to the challenges of difficult-to-predict future markets and low peak-year sales, there is moreover a high level of competition for newly developed antibiotics (Payne et al. 2007; So et al. 2011; Spellberg et al. 2004). In addition, new drugs will probably only become prioritized treatments many years after introduction (O'Neill Commission 2015), pushing the prospects of much needed revenues further into the future. As a consequence of these challenges, recently launched antibiotics developed to target resistance have not captured as much of the market share as anticipated (Payne et al. 2015; Projan 2003), essentially dis-incentivizing the development of new antibiotics (Outterson et al. 2007).

Part of the reason why new antibiotics become the treatment-of-choice only after many years is that the medical community discourages the use of newly developed antibiotics to preserve their efficacy in case of rapid future increases in antibiotic resistance (Spellberg et al. 2004).

Research has estimated that the worldwide sales revenue (in 2000 US$) over the product life cycle for a new antibiotic approved in the US during 1990–1994 to be on average US$2379 million. This compares to an average of US$4177 million for central nervous system drugs and US$3668 million for cardiovascular drugs (DiMasi et al. 2004). But not only did antibiotics bring in less revenues than other drugs, they also showed an average annual growth of 4% over the past 5 years, compared with a growth of 16.7% and of 16.4% for antiviral drugs and vaccines, respectively (Hamad 2010).

Taken together, the challenges presented above point to the fact that attaining revenues and market share is particularly tough in the antibiotics industry.

3.3   Portfolio and Competition

One 'industry effect' that poses a challenge to antibiotics R&D is, in the case of larger pharmaceutical companies, that various competing projects must be prioritized relative to each other (Projan 2003). Low NPV or ROI for antibiotics incentivizes companies to shift their investments towards chronic illnesses in for example the oncology or cardiovascular therapeutic areas (Finch and Hunter 2006; Katz et al. 2006; Morel and

Mossialos 2010; Power 2006; Projan 2003; Spellberg et al. 2015), since better returns can be made in other areas than antibiotics (Payne et al. 2007).

The antibiotics industry is increasingly faced with a large number of inexpensive off-patent antibiotics (Harbarth et al. 2015; Renwick et al. 2014) and pharmaceutical companies have difficulty competing against such generic manufacturers (Projan 2003), since the latter do not bear the costs and risks of drug development (Power 2006). This competition from generic producers has in turn had a negative effect on the willingness of research-focused pharmaceutical firms to invest in antibiotics R&D (Projan and Shlaes 2004).

Funding is the lifeblood of early-stage activities in the antibiotics field. In general, small pharmaceutical firms rely on large companies to provide the funding for the expensive phase III clinical trial studies (Projan and Shlaes 2004). Yet since antibiotics traditionally fail early and often, the appetite of the venture capital market to fund small companies during discovery and early development phases of research has been much reduced (Friedman and Alper 2014). Unfortunately, this lack of funding causes many potentially valuable projects to fail to get off the ground (O'Neill Commission 2015).

All the above listed challenges suggest that antibiotics suffer from competition not only against cheap generic manufacturers and off-patent antibiotics, but also internally in large pharmaceutical firms for funding against other therapeutic areas, and in the case of small pharmaceutical firms for fundraising from VCs in competition with other pharmaceutics/biotech businesses.

3.4   Costs of Resistance and Stewardship

Antibiotics R&D is negatively affected by the fact that antibiotics are becoming progressively ineffective due to antibiotic resistance (Renwick et al. 2014), thus shortening the clinical lifespan of antibiotics (Katz et al. 2006; Morel and Mossialos 2010; Payne et al. 2015; Power 2006) and as a consequence also negatively influences the ability of sales to recoup the costs of innovation (Power 2006). Moreover, national conservation programs and other kinds of antibiotic stewardship negatively affects sales (Renwick et al. 2014; Spellberg et al. 2015) and so does public health measures that aim to limit antibiotics use (Power 2006; Rubin 2004; Spellberg 2008). Lastly, active efforts to conserve antibiotics through rational use guidelines curb the opportunity to expand markets (So et al. 2011).

As we can see, both attempts to fight antibiotic resistance (stewardship) and resistance itself are undermining the development of novel antibiotics by reducing as well as creating uncertainty around the prospects of future sales.

3.5 R&D Challenges

In recent years there has been little success in developing novel antibiotics (Payne et al. 2015). As examples of this lack of progress, only 7% (at GlaxoSmithKline) or 6.5% (at Pfizer) of search efforts directed at finding new antibiotics have been successful, while other therapeutic areas have seen approximately ten times greater success (Projan 2003).

Attempts to use new, automated, techniques to find potential new antibiotics have resulted in closures of corporate labs that used to pursue traditional, exploratory research into antibiotics. As a consequence, pharmaceutical companies now have a dwindling capacity with regards to effective antibiotics development (Laxminarayan et al. 2014). Moreover, the pharmaceutical industry has down-sized interdisciplinary innovation environments in which risk-accepting, long-term experimentation was favored, and has therefore been argued to a considerable extent have lost its capacity to discover new antibiotics (ReAct 2011). As many pharmaceutical companies have reallocated scientific talent and capacity to more profitable opportunities, they have also diminished the economies of scale they originally possessed (Renwick et al. 2014).

As the new ways of searching for potentially novel antibiotics did not produce results, firms were lead to develop drugs that were variations of old ones, rather than novel therapies (Poupard 2006). Complex regulatory requirements relating to pre-clinical data and a tendency towards misinterpretation of toxicity data (whether an antibiotic is toxic not only to the target bacteria, but also to the patient) has been identified to pose obstacles to antibiotics R&D (Bridging the Gap 2012; Friedman and Alper 2014).

Some of the scientific difficulties are due to the fact that bacteria have multiple means of defending itself from drugs, above and beyond resistance (Payne et al. 2007). These multiple means of defending against drugs seem to be at work simultaneously and have been argued not to have been given enough attention in clinical research (Stewart and Costerton 2001; ReAct 2011). Additionally, the issue of resistance potential has not been given enough attention and has likely not been assessed correctly in drug development of antibiotics (ReAct 2011).

The challenges presented above contribute to that antibiotic R&D has a higher failure rate than other therapeutics (Payne et al. 2015), that is faces increasing costs for clinical trials (Bridging the Gap 2012; Katz et al. 2006; Payne et al. 2015; Zorzet 2014) as well as increasing development time (Katz et al. 2006; Payne et al. 2015; Spellberg et al. 2004). This suggests that there are important intrinsic R&D-related challenges critically influencing the antibiotics field.

4 Public Awareness and Policy Interventions

Taken together, the many challenges facing innovation in antibiotics has had the effect of essentially suffocating this critically important industry. Although it has been long in the making, the more recent and rapid rise in antibiotic resistance has put the problems of the antibiotics industry on the agenda of policy makers, academics, and health professionals alike. There is now a common understanding that this industry must be revived if we are to avoid a post-antibiotic era where medical progress in important areas takes a 70-year step backwards.

On the policy-making level, politicians in the most advanced countries are currently discussing the emergency of the antibiotic resistance problem. For the fourth time in its history the UN has brought a health-related problem to the official agenda: the threat of antibiotic resistance.

On the industry-side, the G20 meeting in July 2017 dealt with decisions on how to best tackle this global threat as a top priority on their agenda. Media are repeatedly and increasingly taking up the antibiotic resistance issue to raise public awareness. Billions in funding from many different countries is going to be spent on tackling the problem. How to best invest these resources is crucial. The role of firms is an important, yet missing, piece of this puzzle. A *"Declaration on Combating Antimicrobial Resistance"* was drafted and signed by 85 companies and 9 industry associations across 18 countries at the 2016 World Economic Forum in Davos, Switzerland, showing their intent to take part in confronting antibiotic resistance before we find ourselves in a catastrophic post-antibiotic era.

However, on a more practical note and as a consequence of the growing insight into the need for public intervention in order to revive the antibiotics industry, a number of different kinds of such interventions are currently being planned. Two much discussed interventions discussed by policy makers in both the EU and the US are the push intervention "Targeted Grants", and the pull intervention "Market Entry Rewards". These are two quite simple and straight-forward ideas which will be presented in their essence below. However, the effects that these two different interventions may have on the antibiotic industry are much less obvious, as will be discussed at length later in the analysis.

4.1 Targeted Grants (Push)

Targeted Grants is a public intervention that serves the purpose of directly reducing firms' R&D costs for developing new antibiotics which are deemed necessary and urgent for society. This is done by providing funds to firms that are currently developing critically needed antibiotics as they are in the process of developing them. The purpose of a targeted grant is thereby to provide free funding that may "tip the scales" of a firm's investment calculation and thereby allow the development of a particular, targeted antibiotic to move forward.

4.2 Market Entry Reward (Pull)

The type of public intervention called a Market Entry Reward (MER) is a large sum of money given to any firm that brings an antibiotic with a certain ex-ante specified profile to market. Such profile is supposed to reflect the most urgent unmet clinical need, i.e., the antibiotic should target multi-drug resistant bacteria that at present is hard to kill or perhaps only can be killed with one kind of antibiotic (which might seize working in the future). The MER, then, is essentially a sum of money that is large enough to compensate the developer of the new and needed antibiotic for the risks and costs incurred.

A MER is intended to have the effect of increasing the revenue from an antibiotic at the time it is brought to market. Paying a MER provides a firm with a large revenue that offsets costs of R&D more powerfully than sales in the market would, as sales would occur over many years and thus be worth less due to the "time-value of money" where revenues in the future are worth less than the same amounts would be today.

One of the main benefits of a MER is that is can be so-called "fully delinked". This means that the MER will be awarded as a substitute, not a complement, to market sales, thereby not allowing for the antibiotic in question to be freely sold on the market. This is an attractive feature since it prevents over-consumption that may lead to resistance.

5 Entrepreneurial Orientation

To help understand the problems facing the antibiotics industry and the attempts to alleviate these problems and revive the industry through public interventions, we will make use of an analytical framework based in the literature on entrepreneurial orientation.

Research in entrepreneurship has repeatedly found that firms vary in their degree of entrepreneurial orientation and that this variation is related to differences in firm performance (Covin and Miller 2014; Lumpkin and Dess 1996; Rauch et al. 2009; Saeed et al. 2014). The particular framework of entrepreneurial orientation that we will base our analysis on, originally presented by Lumpkin and Dess (1996), was designed to explain the entrepreneurial behavior of firms in an industry and the relation between this behavior and firm performance. Lumpkin and Dess (1996) specifically contributed by summarizing literature on the topic and emphasizing what they refer to as "contingencies" on the main relationship between entrepreneurial orientation and firm performance as will be explained below. In this chapter, we will use this framework as an analytical lens through which we will attempt to explain not the link between entrepreneurial orientation and firm performance of the single firm, but rather the general decline of all firms of the antibiotics industry. A prominent reason why research on entrepreneurial orientation is suitable for analyzing the challenges facing the antibiotics industry is that an entrepreneurial orientation has been found to help firms that are facing risk and uncertainty in their industry to act entrepreneurially in seizing and exploiting business opportunities in that industry (Covin and Slevin 1991; Lumpkin and Dess 1996; Rosenbusch et al. 2013; Wiklund and Shepherd 2003). Although the entrepreneurial orientation framework has traditionally been applied to single firms, we argue that this framework can be of great value also when analyzing the overall entrepreneurial orientation of firms in an industry as a whole. This approach is particularly relevant in the antibiotics industry since it is characterized by the aggregate of a few important actors that all face similar challenges. What this essentially means is that in an industry facing strong environmental contingencies, the relationship between entrepreneurial orientation and performance becomes very similar across firms since the most powerful factors are these environmental contingencies. Thus, the analysis becomes one of the "collective" entrepreneurial orientation of all firms and the performance of the industry at large, as moderated by environmental contingencies. This is also what makes understanding the lack of entrepreneurial orientation a particularly relevant focus when considering the possibilities of reviving the antibiotics industry.

The entrepreneurial orientation of an industry as a whole is manifested through the actions of the main players in this industry with regards to developing their activities through innovation, expansion of activities or as new entrants into the industry. Another way of thinking of entrepreneurial orientation is as a proxy for the health of an industry; i.e., whether firms are investing, innovating, expanding and entering or, contrastingly, if they are drawing down activities and investments and are exiting. The central elements to the entrepreneurial orientation of firms in a particular industry are their predisposition to take action autonomously to innovate, to take risks, and to act proactively to business opportunities (Covin and Slevin 1988, 1989; Lumpkin and Dess 1996). Each one of these elements may characterize a firm's attempts to engage in an established market with innovative or existing products or services, and thus manifest its entrepreneurial orientation.

By capturing the tendency of the main players to innovate, take risks, and act proactively to seize business opportunities, entrepreneurial orientation can be seen as reflecting the health of an industry as judged by the behavior of its main players in terms of introducing new, innovative or existing, product or services. This because in doing so, these main players reinvigorate the market.

The basic relationship in this literature is thus that entrepreneurial orientation leads to firm performance (e.g. Brouthers et al. 2015; Lee et al. 2001; Teng 2007). Firm performance in turn, can be measured in terms of for example growth in sales, market share, or profitability. The main relationship between entrepreneurial orientation and firm performance is thereby that firms which are innovative, risk taking, and proactive reap the rewards of higher performance, which is what then allows for a healthy, and thereby attractive, industry as the key players are making profits or at least growing their sales.

However, this relationship is moderated by contingencies that may emanate from either the firm itself or from the business environment (Bowen and De Clercq 2008; Covin and Slevin 1989; Lumpkin and Dess 1996; Wales et al. 2013). More specifically, there are a few particularly influential environmental factors that act as external contingencies on the relationship between entrepreneurial orientation and firm performance—and thereby are seen as requirements for a healthy industry. Research emphasizes the influence of the factors referred to as dynamism (Lumpkin and Dess 2001), munificence (Lumpkin and Dess 1996), and environmental hostility (Covin and Slevin 1989). These contingencies, which are of critical importance to the relationship between entrepreneurial orientation and firm performance, will be further elaborated on below.

First, the dynamism of an industry has been found to influence the relationship between entrepreneurial orientation and firm performance in that industry (Lumpkin and Dess 2001). In essence, the dynamism of an industry reflects the uncertainty experienced by firms, i.e., the extent of unpredictable or uncertain change that occurs in particular business environments (Child 1972). Uncertainty, in turn, undermines the ability of managers to adequately predict and plan for future events although they may be critically important for the firm (Alvarez and Busenitz 2001).

Environmental munificence can be understood as the overall profitability and growth in an industry. Entrepreneurial orientation in a munificent industry is claimed to have a stronger effect on firms' performance (Lumpkin and Dess 1996) as the munificence essentially suggests that there is space to grow and money to be made in the first place. Firms active in a munificent industry can thereby reap greater profits which in turn create a degree of slack that can be used to innovate, starting a benevolent spiral for the industry (Bourgeois 1981).

Finally, Covin and Slevin (1989) found how hostile environments, i.e., industry contexts characterized by intense competition, an unforgiving business climate, and a relative lack of exploitable business opportunities moderated the relationship between entrepreneurial orientation and firm performance. A hostile environment has this moderating effect because a starved industry resource base could inhibit innovation and experimentation (Bourgeois 1981) as well as create a focus on the conservation of scarce resources, such as the shrinking of R&D departments, and a focus on existing, rather than innovative, goods and services (Chakravarthy 1982; Covin and Slevin 1988; Teng 2007). Given these hostile industry environments, entrepreneurship and innovation would dwindle and the few new entries undertaken would risk suffering from a lack of sufficient resources to be successful (Lumpkin and Dess 1996). Taken together, the scarce resources characterizing a hostile industry environment would negatively moderate the link between entrepreneurial orientation and firm's performance. Hostility can thereby be understood as reflecting a scarcity of resources as well as a high intensity of competition for these (Covin and Slevin 1989; Zahra and Covin 1995) (Fig. 2).

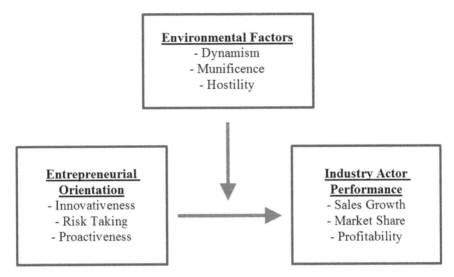

Fig. 2 Conceptual framework of entrepreneurial orientation. Source: Adapted from Lumpkin and Dess (1996)

6   Analysis

Applying the entrepreneurial orientation framework to understand the difficulties facing the antibiotics industry as a whole, the challenges presented earlier can be analyzed through such a lens as follows.

6.1   Entrepreneurial Orientation

As previously mentioned, the entrepreneurial orientation of an industry is expressed in the decisions of the main actors of that industry in terms of developing their activities by innovating, expanding their activities or in the decisions of new actors to enter the industry. The entrepreneurial orientation of firms in a healthy, vigorous industry drives them to take action to innovate, to take business risks, and to act proactively on opportunities. Looking at the case of the antibiotics industry, the entrepreneurial orientation of the actors is decidedly low. Rather than investing, innovating, expanding, or entering, firms are drawing down their activities and investments, closing labs, and are exiting the antibiotics industry.

6.2 Industry Actors Performance

The performance problems in the antibiotics industry are clear and numerous. We can see how the revenues from sales of existing antibiotics are down. We can also see how forecasting the sales of potentially new antibiotics are problematic since a new drug might be subject to minimal use to preserve its effectiveness for future resistance development. Furthermore, the market shares of many drugs are compromised by competition from generic drugs while the market is itself partly shrinking due to stewardship by hospitals and governments. Profitability in the antibiotics industry is overall very low, there have been a few "blockbusters" in the last couple of decades, but these are generally seen as unlikely to ever be repeated. Overall, the performance of the actors of the antibiotic industry is alarmingly low and very few players are still left in the industry as a consequence.

6.3 Environmental Factors

The environmental contingencies that most powerfully affects the antibiotics industry are, as we have learned from the received research discussed and illustrated above, the dynamism, munificence, and hostility of an industry.

First, the dynamism of the antibiotics market, i.e., the uncertainty and unpredictable future characterizing it, can be seen to be strongly affecting firms in the antibiotics industry. This dynamism is manifested through the uncertainty associated with antibiotics R&D, on the one hand, and with the unpredictability of the future markets for antibiotics that are being developed, on the other. There are high financial risks associated with antibiotics R&D. This as antibiotics R&D faces high and, importantly, increasing costs for clinical trials as well as long and increasing development time. For example, the difficulties in attaining enough patients in clinical trials create additional uncertainty in antibiotics R&D. It is today still particularly difficult to evaluate the resistance potential in bacteria and drug, and as a consequence this causes uncertainty in the development of antibiotics. There are substantial biological uncertainties in antibiotic R&D that make such efforts increasingly unpredictable and which require further attention from microbiology research, e.g. the ability of an antibiotic to successfully enter a bacterium, that it is not readily pushed back out, and that it is only toxic to the bacteria. There is moreover particularly high uncertainty surrounding the market for new antibiotics. It is difficult for a developer to estimate the future market due to the fact that resistance as well as the rate of infections can change quickly. As a consequence, validating the commercial potential of a promising molecule is challenging as it makes it hard to predict how big the health need will be at an early stage of development where major investment decisions need to be made. Additionally, there is considerable violation of intellectual property rights with regards to antibiotics which creates heavy price competition from both legal and illegal generic drugs. Taken together, the dynamism of the antibiotics industry seems to pose challenges to firms through the uncertainty surrounding both antibiotic R&D and the forecasting of future markets for new antibiotics.

Second, the munificence of an industry is another of the main environmental factors influencing the relationship between entrepreneurial orientation and firm performance. This is expressed through the overall profitability or growth of an industry. Looking at the antibiotics industry, we can unfortunately see little of either. Rather, this industry is characterized by a lack of commercial attractiveness and low profitability among firms active in the field. We moreover see that there are low prices on antibiotics. Although difficult to generalize, research suggests that most antibiotics generate annual revenues that fall short of adequately covering their cost of development. Adding to this is the fact that the average annual growth of the market for antibiotics was 4% over the years 2005 to 2010—which is less than a quarter of the rate by which other major therapeutic areas grew. Large and effective antibiotic education campaigns have resulted in a reduction in antibiotic use and are thereby also thought to decrease the sizes of future markets for new antibiotics. But not only antibiotic stewardship is limiting future markets, also the development of antibiotic resistance is shortening the clinical lifespan of new antibiotics with resulting smaller overall markets for new antibiotic drugs. In sum, the munificence of the antibiotics industry is close to non-existent, featuring low prices, little profitability, and shrinking markets for new drugs.

Third, and lastly, the hostility of the industry environment is the third environmental factor found to influence the relationship between entrepreneurial orientation and firm performance. This hostility is manifested in a combination of intense competition and a lack of exploitable business opportunities. What we can see in the example of the antibiotics industry is that there is significant competition in a relatively saturated market. But this is not so much a consequence of healthy competition between efficient firms, or because there is little need for antibiotics, rather this is the effect of limitations on the pricing of antibiotics by governments reimbursement rules for such drugs. It is also because it is difficult to get onto the formularies from which doctors prescribe—i.e., becoming the prioritized treatment—because use is being discouraged, and because of competition from generic (off-patent or pirated) antibiotic drugs remains strong. Furthermore, many reimbursement systems encourage the use of the cheapest drug available. Taken together, most healthcare payers are today not prepared to reimburse antibiotics at the kind of prices which would act as incentives for antibiotic drug development. Concerning the lack of exploitable business opportunities, it has already been emphasized that it is hard to find new antibiotics. It has been said that "the low-hanging fruit" has already been picked in the antibiotics industry and the remaining opportunities will not be as scientifically easy to successfully pursue. However, and arguably equally as important, it is not easy to pursue those opportunities from a financial, or business, standpoint either, as a there is considerable hesitation from investors to fund antibiotics research, and, as a consequence, many valuable projects are believed to never have gotten off the ground. All in all, a hostile business environment is clearly

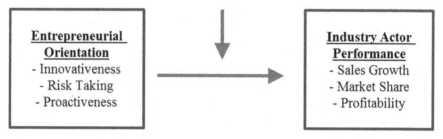

Fig. 3 Environmental factors within the framework of entrepreneurial orientation. Source: Own elaboration of Lumpkin and Dess (1996)

a salient feature of the antibiotics industry, with intense, but artificial, competition as well as few opportunities that makes "business sense" to pursue (Fig. 3).

6.4 Public Interventions

Applying the entrepreneurial orientation framework, we can see that the main environmental factors that constitute challenges facing the antibiotics industry are: the dynamism (the uncertainty and unpredictability of antibiotic R&D and future markets), the munificence (the growth and profitability of antibiotics as a field), and the hostility (the intensity of competition and lack of business opportunities in antibiotics). So, having established what several of the main problems facing this industry are, the focus now turns to what public policy interventions such as targeted grants and market entry rewards might do about these. Using the entrepreneurial orientation framework to evaluate how the suggested public interventions address, or fail to address, the environmental contingencies discussed above lead us to two key considerations.

The first consideration we want to make is if public interventions can act as antecedents of entrepreneurial orientation. In other words, is it possible for public intervention to boost firms' innovativeness, risk taking behavior and proactiveness? If this is possible, can we then argue for the inverse relationship between "performance" and "entrepreneurial orientation"? With the latter question we want to explicitly address the potential effects of a sudden increased performance (due to public intervention) on the degree of entrepreneurial orientation of the industry.

The second consideration we find worth highlighting is how different public interventions (in our case grants and MER) can not only target environmental factors, but also have different impact on the entrepreneurial orientation—performance relationship. Although, we don't know what in practice will happen in the antibiotic industry once these interventions are in place, we can still conceptually consider the differences between the two interventions and what the impact may be if they are introduced. This is represented in the figure below illustrating how public intervention (grants and MER) may affect Environmental Factors (Dynamism, Munificence and Hostility), Industry Actors Performance and indirectly Entrepreneurial Orientation.

Now, let's turn to the differences between targeted grants and MER as means of public intervention to better understand their potentially different impact on the environmental contingencies weighing on the actors of the antibiotic industry and, if successful, the overall long-term entrepreneurial orientation of an industry.

6.5 Targeted Grants

Targeted grants have the benefit of reducing the early costs of developing a new antibiotic. This is important since the considerable challenges of antibiotic R&D otherwise may make these early investments prohibitively risky. From the perspective of the entrepreneurial orientation framework, this can be seen to have three potential effects.

First, by lowering the risk of investing in R&D, it helps to mitigate some of the financial uncertainty of this kind of investment. This suggests that we can understand targeted grants as essentially de-risking the investment for the firms as the grants picks up a piece of the cost in their cost/benefit analysis. This in turn would then mitigate (albeit only marginally) the challenges caused by the Dynamism and more specifically by the uncertainty characterizing antibiotics R&D.

Second, it can moreover be seen as affecting the Munificence contingency factor of low profitability. It does so in the sense of not improving revenues, but in lowering costs and thereby improving the cost/benefit analysis of firms considering whether it is profitable to invest in antibiotic R&D.

Third, by infusing potentially cash-strapped firms with capital enough to proceed through the next step of development, a targeted grant may also incentivize development in small- and medium-sized firms where antibiotics do not need to compete with other therapy areas for funding. In doing so, the targeted grants essentially address the Hostility contingency factor of intense competition. That said, the targeted grant does little for the intense competition from generic producers and slow uptake of new drugs in the antibiotics market.

All in all, targeted grants can be thought to have a number of very possible effect on the contingencies weighing on antibiotic developers in that it targets the costs and financial risk of engaging in this activity as well as the scarcity of funds in firms already committed to further engagement. However, a public intervention relying on targeted grants does not seem to be able to mitigate the negative influences of the contingency factors of market uncertainty (Dynamism), low growth (Munificence), or lack of business opportunities (Hostility).

6.6 Market Entry Rewards (MERs)

A MER has the benefit of providing assured revenues for firms bringing new antibiotics of certain kinds to the market. This, in turn, can be thought to affect the environmental contingencies impeding antibiotic R&D in a number of ways.

First, a MER can be seen to create business opportunities in an industry which is desperately lacking these. In essence, that is what a MER is supposed to be—a business opportunity that is attractive enough to spur pharmaceutical firms into action of developing new drugs. In doing so, the MER can be seen to mitigate the Hostility contingency of lack of business opportunities.

Second, the MER can also be seen to provide certainty by essentially constituting a strong "customer" in a market that has been desperately lacking customers willing to pay enough for new antibiotics. In this sense, the MER can be understood to address the Dynamism contingency of uncertain markets. This is because it helps to correct some of the man-made market distortion that are creating such uncertainty about future markets for novel antibiotics. Being delinked in itself allows the MER to have an important effect in mitigating the environmental factors of dynamism, specifically the uncertainty brought on by the challenge of forecasting future markets for new antibiotics. Thereby a MER can be understood as potentially canceling out an important contingency that is weighing on the antibiotics industry by removing the generally considerable uncertainty surrounding future markets which in turn negatively influences investment decisions.

Third, a MER can be understood to influence the contingencies affecting antibiotic R&D by strongly increasing the profitability of antibiotics, or at least the ones targeted by the MER. By doing so, the MER can be expected to mitigate also the Munificence contingency of lack of profitability.

Fourth, by introducing a large payment in return for bringing new, much needed, antibiotics to market, the MER also addresses two aspects of the Hostility contingency of intense competition. One the one hand, it makes antibiotic projects that target the bacteria asked for by the MER more competitive internally, as the revenues from a MER could be even more than that expected from a drug in other therapy areas. On the other hand, the MER also allows a firm to essentially side-step the competition from generic producers and slow product uptake in hospitals by having a single "customer"; the public entity offering the MER, make one huge purchase of the rights for this antibiotic upon market entry, thus making competitors and hospital prescriptions irrelevant for the firms' revenues from this drug. This said, the introduction of a MER may create a different form of competition as different firms may attempt to develop in parallel what could be seen as the same drug. How this might affect entrepreneurial orientation in the antibiotics industry is difficult to gage.

Although a MER can be expected to have a number of important effects, it does however not seem not to address the environmental contingencies of uncertain R&D (Dynamism) and low growth (Munificence).

6.7 Combining Targeted Grants and Market Entry Rewards

Having discusses the individual effects of the intervention mechanisms of targeted grants and MER, we now turn to the questions of whether these two interventions can, and should, be combined in addressing the challenges facing the antibiotics industry.

There are, obviously, crowding-out effects in deciding on public intervention as spending more public funds on MER may require spending less on targeted grants (or vice-versa).

However, targeted grants and MER may also complement each other. The value of combining both targeted grants and MER is that the targeted grants can be seen as having an effect earlier in the development of an antibiotic as compared to the MER, which shows effects much later in this process. Thus, if targeted grants are given to firms developing early-stage antibiotics, there may be more antibiotics having survived late enough in development to be targeted by the MER. In essence, this suggests that certain levels of grants are needed for a MER to work efficiently as it is based on the assumption that there are enough promising late-development antibiotics to target.

In addition, there could potentially be synergies between targeted grants and MER that could allow combing them to have an effect that is more than the sum of their parts. Synergies might be possible to achieve in the sense that one of the main problems facing the antibiotics market seem to be that related to Dynamism—i.e., that there is crippling uncertainty and unpredictability in regards to both the R&D and the future markets for antibiotics. Although these two kinds of challenges are related, solving one does not solve the overall problem of uncertainty. This, in turn suggests that targeting both of these uncertainties at the same time would have a considerably more powerful effect on incentivizing antibiotics R&D than would targeting only one of them. Additionally, we need to account for the fact that grants are provided early in the R&D effort, while MERs come into play effectively only after several years of innovation (i.e., when the new antibiotic enters the market, which typically can be after 6–10 years of development time). Thus, we highlight also the importance of looking at potential effects of combined public interventions in time.

Figure 4 illustrates of how public interventions may influence the entrepreneurial orientation of the antibiotic industry as well as address environmental contingencies holding it back. The factors that are potentially influenced by the Targeted Grants are *italicized*, and the ones influenced by the MER are grey and **bold**. The gray dashed

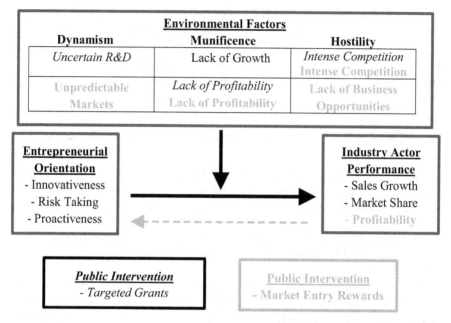

Fig. 4 Influence of public intervention on entrepreneurial orientation. Source: Own elaboration of Lumpkin and Dess (1996)

arrow illustrates the potential indirect impact of the MER on the entrepreneurial orientation—performance relationship.

7 Concluding Discussion

This chapter provides is a unique case of an important industry in health—the antibiotics industry—that is in rapid decline. This is an unusual setting as there is high demand for new antibiotics but low interest from companies to pursue the development of new ones. Combining the critical need for new antibiotics with the lack of innovation in the antibiotics industry suggests a clear proposition for public intervention to try to fix this industry. In this chapter, we outline not only the challenges facing the antibiotics industry but also two main public interventions that are currently being discussed to address the industry's decline.

Analyzing both the challenges and the suggested public interventions through the lens of the Entrepreneurial Orientation framework allows us to evaluate not only what the problems are, but importantly also how the public interventions may, or may not, address these problems and revive the antibiotics industry. In this sense, we found both promising effects and overlooked problems, and that there are important potential synergies between the public interventions discussed, which suggests they may need to be implemented in combination.

Above and beyond managerial and policy making implications, our discussions have also given rise to a number of interesting questions for theory and research on entrepreneurial orientation. For example: can public interventions influence the entrepreneurial orientation of an industry and, if so, how? Our analysis suggests that there could be reverse causalities in the relationship between entrepreneurial orientation of firms in an industry and the performance of the same. This suggests that if you can help make firms in an industry characterized by low collective entrepreneurial orientation more profitable, this could, by the extension of the entrepreneurial orientation framework, lead to increased innovation and entrepreneurial activities.

This study has a number of limitations. It is a study of a single industry yet which seeks to generalize conceptually to theory. Moreover, the study is based on a literature review of challenges to the antibiotics industry and this has no primary data that can verify if and to what extent these challenges are indeed correct. Additionally, and along the same lines, we are not able to say which challenges are more or less important for firms and why—a question that is of paramount importance for managerial practice and policy making alike.

Moreover, we left two types of environmental contingencies rather unaddressed (low growth and uncertainty of R&D), which will require further research. Although one line of thinking about such attempts at future research is that both these contingencies are not possible to address using public intervention; for example, how could we frame the relationship between uncertainty of R&D and money spent on R&D? Or, could we expect to reverse the lack of growth of the antibiotics market when stewardship is both on the rise and important? These are difficult questions; but one way to address these two contingencies could be to think of them not as direct moderating effects, but indirect ones. By this we mean that the uncertainties surrounding antibiotics R&D might not be possible to pay off, but perhaps the consequences of this uncertainty, in terms of higher failure rates, costlier projects, pickier investors, etc. could be addressed by using public interventions. Likewise, although growth may never return to the antibiotic industry in the traditional sense, due to stewardship and resistance, the market could still be expanded using public funds as long as there is a critical and concrete clinical need.

A final avenue for future research coming straight out of the results of this study is the consequences of somehow substituting traditional internal and external competition with a competition for MERs. How such a change would affect the industry and the firms' business models is to our knowledge unexplored and potentially problematic as this kind of solution might cause new challenges.

While there can be no certainty that the suggested public interventions for the antibiotic industry will work as intended, they can, from an Entrepreneurial Orientation perspective, be understood as attempts to essentially reverse the "entrepreneurial orientation—performance" relationship by creating profitability that is hoped to entice companies to start acting entrepreneurially again. This is an important theoretical contribution in the sense that it suggests that the entrepreneurial orientation framework is not so much one-way, as described in received research, but a dynamic framework where external factors may act not only on the main relationship, as moderating factors, but also (in the case of public intervention) directly on the dependent variable of Industry Actor Performance. This, in turn, may suggest that the main relationship of the framework could be reversible and that decline in important industries is far from inevitable. However, if, and under what conditions, this is correct needs to be established by further research and possibly across different industries and countries.

Specifically, we see the possibility to act on entrepreneurial orientation by acting on the market side (e.g., a MER) as long-term results if the number of successful innovations is high enough to create a healthy antibiotics R&D pipeline. At such point in time, when more firms will be attracted (again) to the industry, it could be possible to consider taking away public interventions. Such instance would be also a very interesting object of study for future research. Specifically, from a longitudinal perspective would be interesting to study the criteria and effects of introduction and subsequent elimination of public interventions from an industry. Future research should also devote some efforts to conduct cross industry analysis of public interventions effects on collective entrepreneurial innovation in the attempt to find more generalizable factors in terms of effects of public interventions.

Acknowledgments The authors have received support for part of the research developed and presented in this chapter from the Innovative Medicines Initiative Joint Undertaking under grant agreement n°115618 [Driving re-investment in R&D and responsible antibiotic use—DRIVE-AB—www.drive-ab.eu]. This grant is composed of financial contribution from the European Union's Seventh Framework Programme (FP7/2007–2013) and EFPIA companies' in kind contribution.

References

Alvarez, S. A., & Busenitz, L. W. (2001). The entrepreneurship of resource-based theory. *Journal of Management, 27*(6), 755–775.

Boucher, H. W., Talbot, G. H., Bradley, J. S., et al. (2009). Bad bugs, no drugs: No ESKAPE! An update from the Infectious Diseases Society of America. *Clinical Infectious Diseases: An official publication of the Infectious Diseases Society of America, 48*, 1–12.

Bourgeois, L. J. (1981). On the measurement of organizational slack. *Academy of Management Review, 6*, 29–39.

Bowen, H. P., & De Clercq, D. (2008). Institutional context and the allocation of entrepreneurial effort. *Journal of International Business Studies, 39*(4), 747–767.

Bridging the Gap. (2012). *Overcoming bottlenecks in the development of therapeutics for infectious diseases – Workshop summary report*. National Institute of Allergy and Infectious Diseases, National Institutes of Health.

Brouthers, K. D., Nakos, G., & Dimitratos, P. (2015). SME entrepreneurial orientation, international performance, and the moderating role of strategic alliances. *Entrepreneurship Theory and Practice, 39*(5), 1161–1187.

Chakravarthy, B. (1982). Adaptation: A promising metaphor for strategic management. *Academy of Management Review, 7*, 35–44.

Child, J. (1972). Organization structure, environment, and performance: The role of strategic choice. *Sociology, 6*, 1–22.

Covin, J. G., & Miller, D. (2014). International entrepreneurial orientation: Conceptual consider-ations, research themes, measurement issues, and future research directions. *Entrepreneurship Theory & Practice, 38*(1), 11–44.

Covin, J. G., & Slevin, D. P. (1988). The influence of organization structure on the utility of an entrepreneurial top management style. *Journal of Management Studies, 25*(3), 217–234.

Covin, J. G., & Slevin, D. P. (1989). Strategic management of small firms in hostile and benign environments. *Strategic Management Journal, 10,* 75–87.

Covin, J. G., & Slevin, D. P. (1991). A conceptual model of entrepreneurship as firm behavior. *Entrepreneurship Theory and Practice, 16*(1), 7–25.

DiMasi, J., et al. (2003). The price of innovation: New estimates of drug development costs. *Journal of Health Economics, 22,* 151–185.

DiMasi, J., et al. (2004). *Assessing claims about the cost of new drug development: A critique of the public citizen and TB Alliance reports.* Boston, MA: Tufts Center for the Study of Drug Development, Tufts University. http://csdd.tufts.edu/files/uploads/assessing_claims.pdf

Eisenhardt, K. (1989). Building theories from case study research. *Academy of Management Review, 14*(4), 532–550.

Eisenhardt, K., & Graebner, M. (2007). Theory building from cases: Opportunities and challenges. *Academy of Management Journal, 50*(1), 25–32.

Finch, R., & Hunter, P. (2006). Antibiotic resistance – Action to promote new technologies: Report of an EU Intergovernmental Conference held in Birmingham, UK, 12–13 December 2005. *Journal of Antimicrobial Chemotherapy, 58,* 3–22.

Friedman, D., Alper, J., Chemical Sciences Roundtable, Board on Chemical Sciences and Tech-nology, Division on Earth and Life Studies, & National Research Council. (2014). *Technolog-ical challenges in antibiotic discovery and development: A workshop summary.* Washington, D.C.: National Academies Press.

Hamad, B. (2010). The antibiotics market. *Nature Reviews Drug Discovery, 9,* 675–676.

Harbarth, S., Theuretzbacher, U., & Hackett, J. (2015). Antibiotic research and development: Business as usual? *Journal of Antimicrobial Chemotherapy Advance Access, 70*(6), 1604–1607.

Katz, M. L., Mueller, L. V., Polyakov, M., & Weinstock, S. F. (2006). Where have all the antibiotic patents gone? *Nature Biotechnology, 24,* 1529–1531.

Kinch, M. S., et al. (2014). An analysis of FDA-approved drugs for infectious disease: Antibacterial agents. *Drug Discovery Today, 19*(9), 1283–1287.

Laxminarayan, R., Duse, A., Wattal, C., Zaidi, A. K., Wertheim, H. F., Sumpradit, N., Vlieghe, E., Hara, G. L., Gould, I. M., Goossens, H., Greko, C., So, A. D., Bigdeli, M., Tomson, G., Woodhouse, W., Ombaka, E., Peralta, A. Q., Qamar, F. N., Mir, F., Kariuki, S., Bhutta, Z. A., Coates, A., Bergstrom, R., Wright, G. D., Brown, E. D., & Cars, O. (2014). Antibiotic resistance – The need for global solutions. *Lancet Infectious Diseases, 13*(12), 1057–1098.

Laxminarayan, R., & Powers, J. H. (2011). Antibacterial R&D incentives. *Nature Reviews: Drug Discovery, 10*(10), 727–728.

Lee, C., Lee, K., & Pennings, J. M. (2001). Internal capabilities, external networks, and perfor-mance: A study of technology bases ventures. *Strategic Management Journal, 22*(6-7), 615–640.

Lumpkin, G. T., & Dess, G. G. (1996). Clarifying the entrepreneurial orientation construct and linking it to performance. *Academy of management Review, 21*(1), 135–172.

Lumpkin, G. T., & Dess, G. G. (2001). Linking two dimensions of entrepreneurial orientation to firm performance: The moderating role of environment and industry life cycle. *Journal of Business Venturing, 16*(5), 429–451.

Morel, C., & Mossialos, E. (2010). Stoking the antibiotic pipeline. *BMJ, 340,* c2115.

NIAID. (2014). *NIAID's antibacterial resistance program: Current status and future directions.* Report.

O'Neill Commission. (2015). *Securing new drugs for future generations: The pipeline of antibi-otics.* The Review on Antimicrobial Resistance.

Outterson, K., Samora, J. B., & Keller-Cuda, K. (2007). Will longer antimicrobial patents improve global public health? *Lancet Infectious Diseases, 7*(8), 559–566.

Payne, D. J., Federici Miller, L., Findlay, D., Anderson, J., & Marks, L. (2015). Time for a change: Addressing R&D and commercialization challenges for antibacterials. *Philosophical transactions of the Royal Society of London. Series B, 370*, 20140086.

Payne, D. J., Gwynn, M. N., Holmes, D. J., & Pompliano, D. L. (2007). Drugs for bad bugs: Confronting the challenges of antibacterial discovery. *Nature Reviews, Drug Discovery, 6*, 29–40.

Poupard, J. (2006). Is the pharmaceutical industry responding to the challenge of increasing bacterial resistance? *Clinical Microbiology Newsletter, 28*, 13–15.

Power, E. (2006). Impact of antibiotic restrictions: The pharmaceutical perspective. *Clinical Microbiology and Infection, 12*, 25–34.

Pray, L. (2008). *Antibiotic R&D: Resolving the paradox between unmet medical need and commercial incentive.* Needham, MA: Cambridge Healthtech Institute (Insight Pharma Reports).

Projan, S. (2003). Why is big pharma getting out of antibacterial drug discovery? *Current Opinion in Microbiology, 6*, 427–430.

Projan, S., & Shlaes, D. M. (2004). Antibacterial drug discovery: Is it all downhill from here? *Clinical Microbiological Infections, 10*, 18–22.

Rauch, A., Wiklund, J., Lumpkin, G. T., & Frese, M. (2009). Entrepreneurial orientation and business performance: An assessment of past research and suggestions for the future. *Entrepreneurship Theory and Practice, 33*(3), 761–787.

ReAct. (2011). *Collaboration for innovation: The urgent need for new antibiotics. ReAct policy seminar, Brussels, 23 May 2011.*

Renwick M., Brogan D., & Mossialos E. (2014). *A critical assessment of incentive strategies for development of novel antibiotics.* Report, LSE.

Rex, J. H., & Outterson, K. (2016). Antibiotic reimbursement in a model delinked from sales: A benchmark-based worldwide approach. *The Lancet Infectious Diseases, 16*(4), 500–505.

Rosenbusch, N., Rauch, A., & Bausch, A. (2013). The mediating role of entrepreneurial orientation in the task environment–performance relationship a meta-analysis. *Journal of Management, 39* (3), 633–659.

Rubin, P. (2004). The FDA's antibiotic resistance. *Regulation, 27*, 34–37.

Saeed, S., Yousafzai, S. Y., & Engelen, A. (2014). On cultural and macroeconomic contingencies of the entrepreneurial orientation-performance relationship. *Entrepreneurship Theory & Practice, 38*(2), 255–290.

So, A. D., Gupta, N., Brahmachari, S. K., Chopra, I., Munos, B., Nathan, C., Outterson, K., Paccaud, J. P., Payne, D. J., Peeling, R. W., Spigelman, M., & Weigelt, J. (2011). Towards new business models for R&D for novel antibiotics. *Drug Resistance Update, 14*(2), 88–94.

Spellberg, B. (2008). Antibiotic resistance and antibiotic development. *Lancet Infectious Diseases, 8*, 211–212.

Spellberg, B., Bartlett, J., Wunderind, R., & Gilbert, D. N. (2015). Novel approaches are needed to develop tomorrow's antibacterial therapies. *American Journal of Respiratory and Critical Care Medicine, 191*(2), 135–140.

Spellberg, B., Powers, J. H., Brass, E. P., Miller, L. G., & Edwards, J. E., Jr. (2004). Trends in antimicrobial drug development: Implications for the future. *Clinical Infectious Disease, 38*, 1279–1286.

Stewart, P., & Costerton, J. (2001). Antibiotic resistance of bacteria in biofilms. *Lancet, 358*, 135–138.

Teng, B.-S. (2007). Corporate entrepreneurship activities through strategic alliances: A resource-based approach toward competitive advantage. *Journal of Management Studies, 44*(1), 119–142.

Wales, W. J., Gupta, V. K., & Mousa, F. T. (2013). Empirical research on entrepreneurial orientation: An assessment and suggestions for future research. *International Small Business Journal, 31*(4), 357–383.

Wiklund, J., & Shepherd, D. (2003). Knowledge-based resources, entrepreneurial orientation, and the performance of small and medium-sized businesses. *Strategic Management Journal, 24*(13), 1307–1314.

Wright, G. D. (2015). Solving the antibiotic crisis. *ACS Infectious Diseases, 1*(2), 80–84.

Zahra, S. A., & Covin, J. G. (1995). Contextual influences on the corporate entrepreneurship-performance relationship: A longitudinal analysis. *Journal of Business Venturing, 10*, 43–58.

Zorzet, A. (2014). Overcoming scientific and structural bottlenecks in antibacterial discovery and development. *Upsala Journal of Medical Sciences, 119*(2), 170–175.

Entrepreneurship Success Factors in High and Low Early Stage Entrepreneurship Intensity Countries

Ruth Alas, Tiit Elenurm, Elizabeth J. Rozell, and Wesley A. Scroggins

Abstract The paper links data from the research project "Entrepreneurship Work in Organizations Requiring Leadership Development" (E-World) and information from the Global Entrepreneurship Monitor (GEM) research about intensity of early stage entrepreneurship activities. Perceptions about features of entrepreneurs that enhance their success are influenced by evolution of economies from the resource-driven to the efficiency driven and to the innovation driven development stage. E-World results from 21 countries indicate stronger focus on opportunity seeking in these efficiency driven countries, where share of early-stage entrepreneurs in population is high. Opportunity seeking attributions of entrepreneurs in innovation-driven economies appeared to be stronger in countries, where early-stage entrepreneurship intensity is relatively low. Positive behavioural patterns of entrepreneurs are linked to the high early-stage entrepreneurship intensity both in efficiency-driven and innovation-driven economies and in all regions that were studied. That reflects expectations about entrepreneurship ethics in countries, where the early-stage entrepreneurship rate is high.

Keywords Success factors of entrepreneur · Cross-country comparison · Development cycle · Early-stage entrepreneurship · Innovation

---

Ruth Alas was deceased at the time of publication.

T. Elenurm (✉)
Estonian Business School, Tallinn, Estonia
e-mail: tiit.elenurm@ebs.ee

E. J. Rozell · W. A. Scroggins
Missouri State University, Springfield, MO, USA
e-mail: erozell@missouristate.edu; wesscroggins@missouristate.edu

© Springer International Publishing AG, part of Springer Nature 2018
S. Cubico et al. (eds.), *Entrepreneurship and the Industry Life Cycle*, Studies on Entrepreneurship, Structural Change and Industrial Dynamics,
https://doi.org/10.1007/978-3-319-89336-5_10

1 Introduction

The role of early-stage entrepreneurial activities and relevant knowledge competences depends on the development stage of an economy. The Global Entrepreneurship Monitor (GEM) research has applied the concept of the World Economic Forum
that classified economies into factor-driven, efficiency-driven and innovation-driven
in its Global Competitiveness Report (Schwab 2012). In factor-driven economies
international competitiveness of industries and enterprises is mainly based on cheap
labour and low cost of other production factors that support subcontracting services
for industrial customers from more advanced economies. In efficiency-driven economies success of new entrepreneurs depends heavily on their access to investments
and in many industries limited financial resources hinder early-stage entrepreneurship initiatives. Innovation-driven economies are by their nature knowledge-based
and entrepreneurial framework conditions in these countries enhance business
sophistication (The Global Entrepreneurship Research Association 2017). In
innovation-driven economies start-ups focused on business opportunities of emerging new industries and on innovative product development have better business
environment than in factor-driven or efficiency-driven countries, where more business opportunities can be still found in traditional industries. At the same time
entrepreneurs in new industries face the challenges of matching technological
changes and customer needs. They need to validate their entrepreneurship ideas by
using lean start-up tools (Ries 2011). That leads to two research questions:

1. How perceptions about entrepreneurial success attributes change when countries
   move towards the innovation-driven development stage?
2. How entrepreneurial success attributes related to intensive early-stage entrepreneurship at innovation-driven development stage differ from success attributes at
   earlier development stages?

2 Changing Role of Entrepreneurial Success Attributes
on Evolutionary Pathways of Economies

Constructs, understandings of the entrepreneurial phenomenon are complex and
represent a synthesis of the entrepreneurial self and circumstances (Welter and
Smallbone 2011). Characteristics and competences of entrepreneurs are shaped by
their personal background, entrepreneurship practices and by more or less systematic
self-reflection and self-development efforts. Kyrö (2015) refers to the consensus that
competences of entrepreneurs are related to the process of using opportunities, new
venture creation, growth, risk and acquisition and allocation of resources in order to
make things happen.

Aaltio (2013) has stressed the need to focus on entrepreneur's identity construction as a departure point for successful entrepreneurship development. Entrepreneur's identity can change during the entrepreneurial journey of an individual but

also in the changing business environment, when industry life cycles will close some 'windows of entrepreneurial opportunities' based on cheap production factors and open new opportunities that reflect innovation and higher development level of the ecosystem that can be used for entrepreneurial initiatives. McMullen et al. (2007) has explained that an entrepreneurial opportunity can be either an objective construct visible to an entrepreneur or a new construct created by a knowledgeable entrepreneur. Aidis et al. (2012) studied entrepreneurial initiatives in different countries and reported a positive and significant impact of low corruption on entrepreneurial entry and an individual's decision to become an entrepreneur. It is, however, also important to understand which features of successful entrepreneurs are perceived to be important in such countries, where bureaucratic procedures complicate the process of starting a new business.

The Global Entrepreneurship Monitor (GEM) started in 1999 as a partnership between the London Business School and Babson College. GEM has during two decades become the most comprehensive internationally comparative research tool focused on intensity of early-stage entrepreneurship initiatives. Global Entrepreneurship Monitor as international research project has used economic approach and institutional theory that can be compared to demographic and cognitive approaches (Ramos-Rodríguez et al. 2015).

GEM concept takes into consideration important societal beliefs related to early-stage entrepreneurship such as whether starting a business is considered a good career choice and if entrepreneurship activities lead to high status and positive media attention (Xavier et al. 2013). There is however a need to study in addition to general societal beliefs also specific features attributed to successful entrepreneurs as these influence the nature of entrepreneurial initiatives and priorities of potential entrepreneurs, when launching their initiatives and acquiring knowledge that they consider relevant for success.

GEM 2012–2014 Estonian surveys have demonstrated the role of team-based co-creative entrepreneurship in developing ambitious internationally oriented entrepreneurial initiatives and networking needs of early-stage entrepreneurs. Entrepreneurs that have international growth ambitions and innovation focus, often rely on knowledge sharing with people arriving from other countries while entrepreneurs that are domestically focused trust more their close friends and spouses as business knowledge sources (Venesaar et al. 2014). Barazandeh et al. (2015) in their study, based on GEM 2010 data of 59 countries, conclude that for good performance companies should not necessarily involve in export activities. Characteristics and behaviour patterns of successful entrepreneurs are however influenced by the role of international business in new venture creation. Innovative start-ups created in small economies have limited opportunities for commercializing their innovation without gaining access to international markets.

GEM surveys over many years indicate that the relationship between economic development and intensity of early-stage entrepreneurship is not linear. Wennekers et al. (2005) demonstrated U-shape relation between a country's level of entrepreneurial activity and its level of economic development. In countries that have cheap labour but undeveloped industries, people often start their own entrepreneurial initiative because they cannot find jobs in established industrial companies. Bosma et al. (2008) had pointed out that high involvement of population in attempts to set up own business in such economies reflects dominance of the necessity-driven entrepreneurship resulting from lack of employment opportunities. There is GEM evidence, that opportunity-driven entrepreneurship is more spread in advanced innovation-based market economies than in factor-driven or efficiency-driven economies (Xavier et al. 2013). In more advanced innovation-driven economies the share of new entrepreneurs in the population is in many cases lower than in less advanced economies but entrepreneurs in innovation-driven societies are more often driven by new business opportunities that they have discovered or created. Davidsson (2004) has pointed out the role of social and human capital in new venture creation processes. Recent research on social entrepreneurship has indicated influence of different values on early-stage entrepreneurship and on efficiency of entrepreneurship policies. Latin American model is characterized by a strong presence of egalitarianism and the North American model is characterized by the prevalence of mastery and autonomy values (Jaén et al. 2017). Social values shape role models of entrepreneurs. GEM surveys have demonstrated that role models of successful entrepreneurs are an important driver of new entrepreneurial initiatives (Bosma et al. 2012). Role models are influenced by features attributed to successful entrepreneurs.

In this paper we study how perceptions of characteristics that enhance entrepreneurial success can be linked to GEM data about high and low intensity of early-stage entrepreneurial activity. We assume that perception about features of entrepreneurs that enhance their success may be influenced by evolution of economies from resource-driven to the efficiency driven and further to the innovation driven development stage.

In resource-driven economies processing natural resources or sub-contracting based on cheap labour advantage set the main framework for entrepreneurial initiatives. Although innovative entrepreneurs can launch new products and services also in resource-driven developing countries, their pathway to long-term technology and product development for establishing a global brand is rockier compared to launching innovative entrepreneurial initiatives in such innovative-driven economies, where supporting infrastructure for innovation is in place. Entrepreneurship in efficiency-driven economies assumes investment and knowledge for increasing productivity in such business environment, where access to cheap resources does not give any more the same advantage as in resource-driven economies.

Competition in advanced market economies is intensive and new knowledge leading to innovating is essential for creating a new business opportunity, when entrepreneurs cannot any more rely on low labour cost advantage or on efficiency of established production processes.

Comparing E-World research data with the Heritage Foundation Economic Freedom Index has demonstrated that individuals in countries with lower economic freedom emphasised behavioural patterns more than individuals in countries with higher economic freedom. The opposite was found with opportunity seeking. The importance of administrative skills was higher in countries with lower economic freedom and effective negotiation skills were more important in countries with higher economic freedom (Alas et al. 2015). Linking E-World data to GEM results helps to interpret these findings in the context of innovation and new ventures creation.

3 Linking Global Entrepreneurship Monitor and E-World Research

3.1 Global Entrepreneurship Monitor

The GEM 2015/16 Global Report that is compared with the E-world research data is the 17th annual global survey of entrepreneurial activity. GEM sampling rules enable representative and comparable samples of adult population (18–64 years) in all involved countries. In addition GEM also collected data through national expert surveys. The main focus of GEM surveys is on measuring participation levels of individuals at different stages of the entrepreneurship process to enable comparisons within and across individual economies and economic development levels. GEM methodology uses as the primary measure of entrepreneurship the Total Early-stage Entrepreneurial Activity (TEA) index in the adult population. It includes the share of start-up nascent entrepreneurs currently setting up their business and new entrepreneurs that have been running their business more than 3 months but less than 3.5 years.

Adult population data of 60 economies were involved in the 2015/2016 GEM survey (Kelley et al. 2016) but both GEM data and E-World data were available for two factor-driven, ten efficiency-driven and nine innovation-driven economies (Appendix 1). After the name of each country the TEA index, reflecting the per cent of adult population involved in early-stage entrepreneurship in this country, is presented in Appendix 1.

During the first data analysis step GEM results were used for comparing high early-stage and low early-stage entrepreneurship intensity (TEA) countries inside regions. In Asia and Oceania region Lebanon and Turkey, Australia and China represent relatively high TEA, Philippines, Malaysia, Israel, India and Taiwan lower TEA. In Latin America Chile and Ecuador represent high TEA, Uruguay lower TEA. Europe and North America were treated as one global region. Inside this region USA, Sweden, Ireland, Romania and Estonia represent high TEA, United Kingdom, Italy, Germany and Bulgaria lower TEA for our comparison. GEM and E-World surveys involved only one country in the Northern America—USA, where TEA index was 11.9% That did not allow to present separate comparison of high and low TEA countries inside this region.

The Second step of analysis differentiated high and low TEA countries in comparison to other countries at the same economic development level stage. In India 13.6% of adult population had some involvement in early-stage entrepreneurial activity and in Philippines TEA was 14.9%. As only these two factor-driven countries were involved both in GEM and E-World studies and their TEA levels are quite similar, only efficiency-driven and innovation-driven countries were included in the second level analysis.

Among efficiency-driven countries Lebanon, Ecuador, Chile and Uruguay were treated as high TEA countries, China, Estonia, Romania, Malaysia and Bulgaria as lower TEA countries. Among innovation-driven countries Australia, Israel, United States, Taiwan and Ireland had high TEA compared to Sweden, United Kingdom, Italy and Germany. Applying both regional and development level frameworks allowed to take into consideration the economic development stages and regional differences that have influenced E-World results.

3.2　E-World Survey

The international research programme "Entrepreneurship Work in Organizations Requiring Leadership Development" (E-World) has been based on implicit/attribution entrepreneurship theory. The implicit leadership theory (Lord and Maher 1991) maintains that individuals have implicit beliefs, convictions, and assumptions concerning attributes and behaviours that differentiate leaders from subordinates, and effective from non-effective leaders. We have extended this concept to entrepreneurship by expanding the list of attributes in order to reflect business opportunity identification and other crucial entrepreneurial activities. Implicit beliefs about successful entrepreneurs can be different depending on the development stage of the economy and the cultural background of the country. Perceptions of entrepreneurship success factors may be biased interpretations of reality but these reflections still influence the actions and effectiveness of entrepreneurs and attitudes of the people who can either support or inhibit their entrepreneurial initiatives. Images of successful entrepreneurs are especially relevant for young potential entrepreneurs, when they consider entrepreneurship among other career options and assess their own opportunities of early-stage entrepreneurship.

The E-World survey tool included 115 characteristics and behaviours of successful entrepreneurs that were based on prototypes of successful entrepreneurs. The list of characteristics and behaviours reflected focus group results of the first stage in the E-World research programme. Investigators examined individual country taxonomies and listed those factors that appeared most important for comprising the entrepreneurial prototype. All investigators had to agree that the item was important enough to be included in the list, based on frequency of appearance in focus group discussions and importance in the taxonomy. Characteristics and behaviours were assessed in the E-World survey on 7-point scales, indicating the degree to which respondents felt the characteristic, trait, or behaviour either impeded or facilitated successful entrepreneurship in their country. The scale ranged from one (this behaviour or characteristic greatly inhibits a person from being a successful entrepreneur) to seven (this behaviour or characteristic contributes greatly to a person being a successful entrepreneur). For countries in which language differences were an issue, the questionnaire was translated into the host country language by host country E-World collaborators and back-translated into English by associates of the principal investigators who were fluent in the particular language. Survey instructions defined "successful entrepreneurs" as people who have started a new business and have been running it successfully. Specific criterion of success, such as profitability or value growth of the new venture, was not described in the survey instruction. Consequently, respondents were free to use their own assessment on which social and economic results are treated as success. Survey instructions however defined in one sentence what each characteristic or behaviour meant (Elenurm et al. 2014). Our present paper is based on E-World results of 4979 respondents from 21 countries, where also the Global Entrepreneurship Monitor results were available. Respondents involved entrepreneurs and persons potentially interested in entrepreneurial activities.

3.3   Combined Survey Results

A principal component analysis and factor analyses with varimax rotation was completed for the 115 items of the E-World survey for all countries. Items were selected with a factor load in this particular factor above [0.30] and the same load in other factors below [0.30]. The number of factors received was 3. (Appendix 2). Factors comprise together 38.9% of initial variability.

The first factor (Component 1 in Appendix 2) could be called 'innovative opportunity seeker'. It indicates innovative people looking carefully for changes in economic environment and markets in order to find opportunities to initiate new business and to satisfy unmet needs of customers. Being open minded, effective negotiator, resourceful, dynamic, creative, constantly learning and motivator are among characteristics represented in this factor. The second factor includes characteristics inhibiting a person from being a successful entrepreneur and could be called 'negative behavioural patterns'. This includes arrogance, dishonesty, non-delegator, ruthless, domineering, cynical and stubborn behaviour but also masculine characteristics (Component 2 in Appendix 2). The third factor includes 'positive behavioural patterns' like being compassionate, loyal, self-sacrificial, indifferent to personal gains but also procedural, tactful and cautious behaviour (Component 3 in Appendix 2). At first these three factors were calculated by countries grouped according to high and low early-stage entrepreneurship (TEA) levels inside regions of the Global entrepreneurship Monitor survey (Table 1). According to ANOVA test average values of all three E-World indexes in high and low early-stage entrepreneurship countries were statistically significantly different on 0.000 level in all three regions.

Opportunity seeking indexes in high TEA countries of Asia, Australia, Middle East and in South America are substantially higher than in the low TEA countries of these regions. In the region that includes Europe and USA, the difference between the opportunity seeking index value in high and low intensity early-stage entrepreneurship countries is marginal.

Negative behaviour patterns are treated as more serious success impeding issues in high TEA countries of Asia, Australia, and Middle East compared to low TEA

Table 1 E-World indexes in high and low early-stage entrepreneurship (TEA) countries by regions

Region	High or low intensity early stage entrepreneurship countries	Opportunity seeking	Negative behaviour	Positive behaviour
Asia, Australia and Middle East	High TEA	5.94	3.34	4.98
	Low TEA	5.79	3.58	4.81
South America	High TEA	6.02	3.22	4.74
	Low TEA	5.83	2.69	4.42
Europe and USA	High TEA	5.93	3.34	4.48
	Low TEA	5.92	3.14	4.07

Table 2 E-World indexes in high and low early-stage entrepreneurship (TEA) efficiency driven and innovation driven economies

Type of economy	High or low intensity early stage entrepreneurship countries	Opportunity seeking	Negative behaviour	Positive behaviour
Efficiency-driven	High TEA	6.06	3.25	5.07
	Low TEA	5.87	3.31	4.50
Innovation-driven	High TEA	5.86	3.42	4.65
	Low TEA	5.94	3.06	4.02

countries in this region. In Europe and USA but especially in South America negative behavioural patterns are interpreted as less impeding issue in high TEA countries than in low TEA countries. Positive behavioural patterns are assessed as more contributing to successful entrepreneurship in high TEA countries of all three regions compared to lower TEA countries of these regions.

Comparison of the same three factors was completed between high and low early-stage entrepreneurship (TEA) countries in efficiency driven and innovation driven countries (Table 2). According to ANOVA average values of all three E-World indexes in efficiency driven and innovation driven countries were statistically significantly different on 0.000 level. Table 2 reveals that the value of the opportunity seeking index is the highest in these efficiency-driven countries, where the share of early-stage entrepreneurs is larger than in other efficiency-driven countries or in innovation driven countries. Opportunity seeking index in low TEA innovation driven countries is even higher than the same index of innovation-driven countries, where early-stage entrepreneurship activities are more intensive. Negative behaviour patterns are considered to be the most serious problem in low TEA innovation driven countries and the least serious success impeding issue in high TEA innovation driven economies. Positive behaviour index is higher in more intensive TEA countries both in efficiency-driven and innovation-driven economies compared to low TEA intensity countries of the same economy development level.

In order to make more detailed comparison of specific characteristics that are considered to be most important for high and low early-stage entrepreneurship intensity countries, top ten characteristics were identified based on the mean values of survey results in efficiency-driven and in innovation-driven economies.

Table 3 Characteristics and behaviours considered having greatest contribution to entrepreneurial success in efficiency-driven economies

High early-stage entrepreneurship intensity countries		Low early-stage entrepreneurship intensity countries	
Top ten characteristics	Mean on 7-point scale	Top ten characteristics	Mean on 7-point scale
Perseverance	6.435	Administratively skilled	6.306
Constantly learning	6.435	Effective negotiator	6.287
Creative	6.431	Team builder	6.274
Administratively skilled	6.423	Good judgment	6.237
Intelligent	6.411	Open minded	6.216
Innovative	6.407	Opportunity awareness	6.206
Opportunity awareness	6.405	Adapt to new evironment quickly	6.172
Trustworthy	6.354	Understand their business	6.163
Positive	6.340	Can judge and make decisions from the perspective of an opponent	6.113
Informed	6.327	Resistance to stress	6.091

Characteristics that were considered by respondents most contributing to entrepreneurial success in efficiency-driven and innovation-driven economies have several common features. Business opportunity awareness belongs to top ten characteristics at both development levels and in countries that represent high and low early-stage entrepreneurship intensity (Tables 3 and 4).

At the efficiency-driven development stage in high early-stage entrepreneurship intensity countries perseverance, constant learning and creativity features are stressed. Respondents in lower early-stage entrepreneurship intensity countries consider most important for success administrative and negotiation skills but also team building (Table 3).

In innovation-driven economies successful entrepreneurship is associated with the entrepreneurial drive both in high and low early-stage entrepreneurship intensity countries (Table 4).

In high early-stage entrepreneurship intensity countries being positive and enthusiastic is perceived as crucial success factors more often than in countries, where early-stage entrepreneurship intensity is lower. Respondents in low early-stage entrepreneurship countries at the same time point out contribution of negotiating skills and anticipation. Resistance to stress also belongs to top ten characteristics in countries, where early-stage entrepreneurship intensity is relatively low.

Table 4 Characteristics and behaviours considered having greatest contribution to entrepreneurial success in innovation-driven economies

High early-stage entrepreneurship intensity countries		Low early-stage entrepreneurship intensity countries	
Top ten characteristics	Mean on 7-point scale	Top ten characteristics	Mean on 7-point scale
Positive	6.288	Driven	6.498
Driven	6.273	Effective negotiator	6.419
Enthusiastic	6.273	Anticipatory	6.353
Problem solving	6.244	Open minded	6.349
Constantly learning	6.244	Dynamic	6.342
Opportunity awareness	6.214	Good judgement	6.339
Open minded	6.185	Perseverance	6.323
Creative	6.157	Resistance to stress	6.301
Perseverance	6.149	Opportunity awareness	6.293
Effective negotiator	6.134	Creative	6.288

4 Discussion and Conclusions

Future development trends of entrepreneurship are influenced by features that are attributed to present successful entrepreneurs by young people that are considering entrepreneurial career. Research indicates that in high early-stage entrepreneurship intensity countries focus of successful entrepreneurs on opportunity seeking is generally stronger than in low early-stage entrepreneurship intensity countries. This perception is however not clearly evident in established European market economies. Despite high share of opportunity-driven early-stage entrepreneurs in innovation-driven economies, entrepreneur's features that support business opportunity seeking were stressed by respondents in efficiency-driven economies even more than in innovation-driven economies. In order to understand these phenomena deeper, collecting additional data that reflects difference between using an existing business opportunity versus creating a new business opportunity and a new market assumes further research in the framework of the Schumpeterian (1928) innovative entrepreneur's creative destruction logic versus the opportunistic trader logic explained by Kirzner (1978).

Positive behavioural patterns such as being compassionate, loyal, self-sacrificial, indifferent to personal gains are assessed as more contributing to successful entrepreneurship in high TEA countries of all three regions compared to lower TEA countries of these regions. That demonstrates the ethical dimension of the successful entrepreneur's image in countries, where people are more active in new venture creation. Stressing the impeding role of the negative behavioural factor that includes such features as arrogance, dishonesty, non-delegator, ruthless, domineering, cynical and stubborn behaviour, at the same time differentiated high TEA countries from lower TEA countries only in one region—Asia and Oceania. Negative behaviour patterns tend to be treated as more serious problems in low TEA innovation driven countries than in high TEA innovation driven economies. That indicates importance of entrepreneurial competences related to human relations and leadership capabilities combined with business opportunity seeking for increasing early-stage entrepreneurship activity in these countries.

In countries, where early-stage entrepreneurship is less intensive than in other sample countries representing the same economic development stage, administrative and negotiation skills are considered more crucial than in high early-stage entrepreneurship intensity countries. That may reflect perception of entrepreneurship challenges related to overcoming bureaucratic and corruptive obstacles in the business environment, making the right deals with business partners and enforcing entrepreneur's rights in interactions with stakeholders as more complicated than in high intensity early-stage entrepreneurship countries. Further longitudinal research is needed in order to understand, how in the process of moving towards innovation-driven economies changes of economic freedom and attempts of governments to strengthen innovation support policies influence early-stage entrepreneurship intensity and survival of new ventures.

Walter and Block (2016) have concluded after comparative study of 32 countries that entrepreneurship education has increased readiness of students to start their own business mainly in countries, where institutional environment to entrepreneurship is hostile. In order to develop more focused entrepreneurship education, it is crucial to overcome the 'one size fits all' approach. Potential entrepreneurs need assistance in order to understand the interplay between specific entrepreneurship opportunities emerging in their economy and evolutionary pathway of their society and industry, their own strengths and weaknesses and also role models of entrepreneurs preferred by investors and others stakeholders in order to start and continue such entrepreneurial journey that could lead to success.

Appendix 1

Countries for GEM and E-World comparison

	Factor-driven	Efficiency-driven	Innovation-driven
Asia & Oceania	India (13.6) Philippines (14.9)	China (15.3) Lebanon (35.7) Malaysia (2.9) Turkey (16.1)	Australia (15.5) Israel (14.4) Taiwan (9.7)
Latin America		Chile (29.7) Ecuador (34.3) Uruguay (20.1)	
Europe		Bulgaria (3.5) Estonia (13.1) Romania (10.8)	Germany (4.7) Ireland (9.3) Italy (4.9) Sweden (7.2) United Kingdom (6.9)
North America			United States (11.9)

In parenthesis per cent of adult population involved in early-stage entrepreneurship activities

Appendix 2

Rotated component matrix describing opportunity seeking, negative behaviour and positive behaviour factors

	Component		
	1	2	3
Opportunity awareness	0.772	−0.053	0.034
Innovative	0.761	−0.051	0.030
Adapt to new environments quickly	0.756	−0.013	0.108
Open minded	0.756	−0.083	0.076
Good judgement	0.739	−0.123	0.119
Effective negotiator	0.736	−0.098	0.019
Resourceful	0.730	−0.020	0.092
Driven	0.723	0.068	0.069
Dynamic	0.723	−0.010	0.068
Creative	0.721	−0.078	0.080
Constantly learning	0.711	−0.097	0.190
Understand their business	0.709	−0.060	0.126
Motivator	0.697	−0.057	0.098
Can judge and make decisions from the perspective of an opponent	0.685	0.022	0.136
Improvement oriented	0.680	−0.116	0.174
Problem solving	0.679	−0.057	0.139
Personal strength	0.676	0.077	0.105
Investigation skills	0.675	−0.028	0.197
Strong initiative	0.671	0.037	0.011
Intelligent	0.671	−0.087	0.122
Team builder	0.668	−0.174	0.181
Resistance to stress	0.667	−0.011	0.008
Perseverance	0.664	0.051	0.157
Flexible	0.648	−0.074	0.113
Intuitive	0.646	0.043	0.060
Brave in the face of difficulties	0.640	0.063	0.168
Prepared	0.639	−0.061	0.173
Self-confident	0.639	0.139	0.116
Coordinator	0.630	−0.029	0.208
Networking	0.628	−0.031	0.188
Ability to start with few resources	0.623	0.025	0.043
Diplomatic	0.606	−0.162	0.201
Enthusiastic	0.591	−0.062	0.139
Convincing	0.590	0.111	0.056
Positive	0.582	−0.083	0.121
Business experience	0.580	0.063	0.167
Anticipatory	0.580	−0.063	−0.012
Competitive	0.573	0.275	0.022

(continued)

	Component		
	1	2	3
Decisive	0.568	0.069	−0.024
Entrepreneurial links	0.565	0.162	0.161
Desire to change things	0.563	0.168	0.080
Ambitious	0.559	0.147	−0.052
Defines clear, concrete, and measurable goals	0.558	−0.047	0.200
Informed	0.534	−0.036	0.136
Having a different view of the market	0.529	0.129	0.173
Dependable	0.508	−0.188	0.233
Well connected	0.495	0.210	0.096
Never yielding in the face of failure	0.487	0.108	0.115
Courageous	0.486	0.146	0.228
Political links	0.425	0.267	0.070
Tolerance for ambiguity	0.403	0.122	0.100
Lucky	0.364	0.268	0.089
Independent	0.361	0.195	0.036
Willful	0.354	0.274	0.020
Unique	0.349	0.193	0.220
Arrogant	−0.159	0.606	−0.017
Dishonest	−0.269	0.601	−0.055
Domineering	0.064	0.596	0.019
Ruthless	−0.046	0.575	−0.126
Cynical	−0.228	0.561	0.118
Stubborn	0.138	0.529	0.006
Loner	−0.164	0.495	0.201
Autocratic	0.042	0.483	0.035
Nondelegator	−0.206	0.480	0.232
Wary of people who will copy their idea	0.173	0.470	0.195
Dissatisfied with former employment	0.098	0.399	−0.019
Masculine characteristics	0.287	0.348	0.049
Compassionate	0.153	−0.074	0.622
Procedural	0.177	0.015	0.582
Indifferent to personal gains	0.074	0.046	0.573
Cautious	−0.045	0.150	0.573
Loyal	0.292	−0.119	0.550
Likes security/stability	0.047	0.211	0.549
Sincere	0.294	−0.146	0.540
Not profit oriented	0.029	0.002	0.539
Class conscious	0.124	0.266	0.514
Self-sacrificial	0.255	0.144	0.401
Tactful	0.275	0.053	0.324

5

244

2R. Alas et al.

References

Aaltio, I. (2013). Management education as an identity construction: The case of Estonia and its transition background. *International Journal of Entrepreneurship and Small Business, 5*(1), 83–99.

Aidis, R., Estrin, S., & Mickiewicz, T. M. (2012). Size matters: Entrepreneurial entry and government. *Small Business Economics, 39*(1), 119–139.

Alas, R., Elenurm, T., Rozell, E. J., & Scroggins, W. A. (2015). Perceptions of entrepreneurial success factors: A cross-cultural comparison of 27 countries. *Journal of Business and Economics, 6*(9), 1570–1584.

Barazandeh, M., Parvizian, K., Alizadeh, M., & Khosravi, S. (2015). Investigating the effect of entrepreneurial competencies on business performance among early stage entrepreneurs Global Entrepreneurship Monitor (GEM 2010 survey data). *Journal of Global Entrepreneurship Research, 5*(1), 18. https://doi.org/10.1186/s40497-015-0037-4.

Bosma, N., Hessels, J., Schutjens, V., Praag, M., & Verheul, I. (2012). Entrepreneurship and role models. *Journal of Economic Psychology, 33*(2), 410–424.

Bosma, N., Jones, K., Autio, E., & Levie, J. (2008). *Global entrepreneurship monitor 2007 executive report'*. Babson Park, MA and London, UK: Babson College and London Business School.

Davidsson, P. (2004). *Researching entrepreneurship*. New York: Springer.

Elenurm, T., Alas, R., Rozell, E. J., Scroggins, W. A., & Alsua, C. J. (2014). Cultural prototypes of the successful entrepreneur: Comparison of Estonia and the United States. *Journal of Baltic Studies, 45*(4), 499–515.

Jaén, I., Fernández-Serrano, J., Santos, F. J., & Liñán, F. (2017). Cultural values and social entrepreneurship: A cross-country efficiency analysis. In M. Peris-Ortiz, F. Teulon, & D. Bonet-Fernandez (Eds.), *Social entrepreneurship in non-profit and profit sectors* (pp. 31–51). Cham: Springer International Publishing.

Kelley, D., Singer, S., & Herrington, M. (2016). *2015/16 global report. GEM global entrepreneurship monitor*. Babson Park, MA, Santiago, London: Babson College, Universidad del Desarrollo, Universiti Tun Abdul Razak, Tecnológico de Monterrey, London Business School.

Kirzner, I. (1978). *Competition and entrepreneurship*. Chicago: University of Chicago Press.

Kyrö, P. (2015). The conceptual contribution of education to research on entrepreneurship education. *Entrepreneurship & Regional Development, 27*(9-10), 599–618.

Lord, R., & Maher, K. J. (1991). *Leadership and informational processing: Linking perceptions and performance*. Boston: Unwin-Everyman.

McMullen, J. S., Plummer, L. A., & Asc, Z. J. (2007). What is entrepreneurial opportunity? *Small Business Economics, 28*(4), 363–379.

Ramos-Rodríguez, A. R., Martínez-Fierro, S., Medina-Garrido, J. A., & Ruiz-Navarro, J. (2015). Global entrepreneurship monitor versus panel study of entrepreneurial dynamics: Comparing their intellectual structures. *International Entrepreneurship and Management Journal, 11*(3), 571–597.

Ries, E. (2011). *The lean startup: How today's entrepreneurs use continuous innovation to create radically successful businesses*. New York: Crown Business.

Schumpeter, J. (1928). The instability of capitalism. *Economic Journal, 38*(151), 361–386.

Schwab, K. (Ed.). (2012). *The global entrepreneurship report 2011–2012*. Geneva: World Economic Forum.

The Global Entrepreneurship Research Association. (2017). *Global entrepreneurship monitor. Global report 2016/17*. http://gemconsortium.org/report/49812. (Accessed June 5, 2017).

Venesaar, U., Mets, T., Paes, K., Elenurm, T., Masso, J., Küttim, M., & Konsa, P. (2014). *'Globaalne ettevõtlusmonitooring 2013. Eesti Raport'* (*'Global entrepreneurship monitor 2013. Estonian report'*). Tallinn: Estonian Development Fund.

Walter, S. G., & Block, J. H. (2016). Outcomes of entrepreneurship education: An institutional perspective. *Journal of Business Venturing, 31*(2), 216–233.

Welter, F., & Smallbone, D. (2011). Institutional perspectives on entrepreneurial behavior in challenging environments. *Journal of Small Business Management, 49*(1), 107–125.

Wennekers, S., Van Wennekers, A., Thurik, R., & Reynolds, P. (2005). Nascent entrepreneurship and the level of economic development. *Small Business Economics, 24*(3), 293–309.

Xavier, S. R., Kelley, D., Kew, J., Herrington, M., & Vorderwülbecke, A. (2013). *Global entrepreneurship monitor global report* (Global Entrepreneurship Research Association). http://www.gemconsortium.org/docs/2645/gem-2012-global-report. (Accessed June 10, 2017).

Reasons for the Almost Complete Absence of High-Growth Ambition and Innovation Activity of Early-Stage Entrepreneurs in Brazil

Ronald Jean Degen and Nicholas Harkiolakis

Abstract This multiple case study contributes to identifying the reasons behind the almost complete absence of high-growth ambition and innovation activity of early-stage entrepreneurs in Brazil by investigating why they did not develop similar cognitive frameworks as the countries high-growth entrepreneurs. The understanding of the reasons can assist in the planning of programs and policies directed toward the creation of the necessary conditions to increase the number of early-stage entrepreneurs with high-growth ambition and hence promote the country's economic growth. The reasons identified by the study were that high self-efficacy in the cognition/personality traits, knowledge (human capital) acquired from family and education complemented by task-related professional knowledge, and social capital that provided support from the professional network based on professional reputation and from family are the key factors in the cognitive framework of high-growth that explains their high-growth ambition and innovation activity are rare in Brazil. These factors are rare in Brazil, particularly the high self-efficacy and knowledge (human capital) acquired from family and education, because only those who belong to the country's very small well-educated and empowered elite like the high-growth entrepreneurs possess them, whereas most early-stage entrepreneurs in Brazil that don't belong to this elite did not acquire these key factors in their cognitive frameworks and so don't have high-growth ambition and develop innovation activities.

Keyword Ambition of entrepreneurs · Innovation activity of entrepreneurs · Cognitive-framework of entrepreneurs · High-growth entrepreneurs · Self-efficacy of entrepreneurs

R. J. Degen (✉)
International School of Management (ISM), Paris, France

N. Harkiolakis
University of Liverpool, Liverpool, UK

© Springer International Publishing AG, part of Springer Nature 2018
S. Cubico et al. (eds.), *Entrepreneurship and the Industry Life Cycle*, Studies on Entrepreneurship, Structural Change and Industrial Dynamics,
https://doi.org/10.1007/978-3-319-89336-5_11

247

1 Introduction

The purpose of this study was to identify the reasons for the absence in general of high-growth ambition and innovation activity of early-stage entrepreneurs in Brazil (Macedo et al. 2013; Singer et al. 2014; WEF and GEM 2015). Since early-stage entrepreneurs with high-growth ambition is a significant predictor of the economic growth of a country (Autio 2011; Stam et al. 2011; Levie and Autio 2013) the absence indicates that entrepreneurship in Brazil is not contributing significantly to the economic growth of the country. This is contrary to the fact that neighboring countries like Chile and Colombia have successfully managed to capitalize on their high-growth early stage entrepreneurs (Singer et al. 2014: Drexler and Amorós 2015).

Brazil appears to be in what Drexler and Amorós (2015) call the entrepreneurial trap. The trap, as described by the authors, unfolds either when less competitive countries have a relatively high-rate of early stage entrepreneurial activity undertaken by entrepreneurs that are rarely innovative or create many jobs, or when more competitive countries have a very low rate of early-stage entrepreneurial activity undertaken by entrepreneurs that are more frequently innovative and ambitious in job creation. The authors explain that in each case the countries lack the conditions necessary to achieve full entrepreneurial potential.

Drexler and Amorós (2015) explain that for countries to break out of the entrepreneurial trap and become entrepreneurial all-rounder economies like Chile and Colombia, their governments must pay attention to the balance of three ingredients: the number of early-stage entrepreneurs, their innovativeness, and their high-growth ambitions. The authors point out that the pathways to a thriving entrepreneurial economy are manifold and countries that try to mimic the Chilean, Colombian or the well-known Silicon Valley models may well be disappointed.

The World Economic Forum and Global Entrepreneurship Monitor study (WEF and GEM 2015) highlights that it is difficult for countries to develop an entrepreneurship policy because entrepreneurial ecosystems are dynamic structures that do not respond in a linear manner to policy interventions. Nevertheless, the study highlights, as in the cases of Chile and Colombia, that government policies can have a positive impact on the evolution of entrepreneurship in an economy, and given the stakes involved, governments would do well to craft policies that are tailored to the needs of their entrepreneurs. The study proposes that by using knowledge about the strengths and weaknesses of an economy's entrepreneurial make-up, policymakers can clearly define objectives for interventions. In order to identify the reasons for the absence in general of high-growth ambition and innovation activity of early-stage entrepreneurs in Brazil this study examined the development patterns or formation over time of the cognitive frameworks of the high-growth entrepreneurs, the high-growth entrepreneurial opportunities they exploited, and the influences of the Brazilian environmental conditions. The results of the study could help educational institutions adopt or improve their entrepreneurship programs as well as government policy makers in designing policies for supporting high-growth

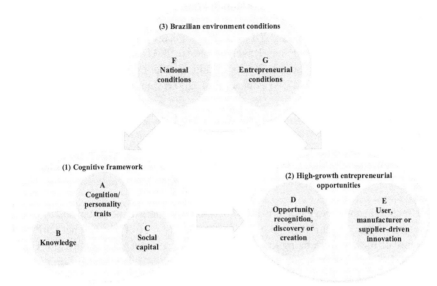

Fig. 1 Theoretical framework of the study

entrepreneurship that could eventually improve Brazil's economic growth (Singer et al. 2014; Drexler and Amorós 2015).

2   Theoretical Framework and Research Questions of the Study

The theoretical framework (Fig. 1) used to analyze the development patterns or formation over time of the cognitive frameworks of the high-growth entrepreneurs in Brazil, the high-growth entrepreneurial opportunities they exploited, and the influences of the countries environmental conditions was constructed from three clusters of factors. The first cluster characterizes the evolution of the cognitive framework of high-growth entrepreneurs, the second, the high-growth entrepreneurial opportunities they exploited, and the third, the influence of the Brazilian market conditions in fostering high-growth entrepreneurs and creating high-growth entrepreneurial opportunities (Degen 2017).

The cognitive framework cluster integrates three important factors—cognition/ personality traits, knowledge, and social capital. They have been identified in as significant in the process of opportunity recognition by entrepreneurs (George et al. 2016). More specifically these categories include the following factors:

- The cognitive/personality traits of entrepreneurs that lies in the realm of psychology include creativity (Ardichvili et al. 2003; Baron 2006; Nicolaou et al. 2009;

Ramos-Rodríguez et al. 2010; Heinonen et al. 2011), self-efficacy (Shane et al. 2003; Tominc and Rebernik 2007; Drnovšek et al. 2010; Cardon and Kirk 2015), risk-taking (Baron 2006; Foo 2011; Li 2011), need for achievement (McClelland 1976), need for independence (Rauch and Frese 2007; Nicolaou et al. 2009), and alertness or systematic search for opportunities (Fiet et al. 2005; McMullen and Shepherd 2006; Fiet 2007; Westhead et al. 2009; Zahra et al. 2009; Sarasvathy et al. 2010).

- The knowledge acquired by the entrepreneurs (Audretsch 1995; Venkataraman 1997; Shane 2000; Degen 2009; Haynie et al. 2009; Vaghely and Julien 2010) with the underlying factors—environmental information (Shane and Venkataraman 2000), knowledge of markets, ways to serve, and customer problems (Shane 2000), knowledge about how to innovate (Anderson et al. 2013, pp. 26–27).
- The social capital developed by the entrepreneurs refers to the actual and potential resources they obtain from knowing others, being part of a social network with them, or merely from being known to them and having a good reputation (Baron and Markman 2000; Shane and Venkataraman 2000; Alvarez and Busenitz 2001; Ardichvili et al. 2003; Baron 2006).

The high-growth entrepreneurial opportunities cluster includes two factors as suggested by the literature (Sarasvathy et al. 2010; von Hippel 1988) that contribute to the entrepreneurial opportunities identified by the high-growth entrepreneurs:

- Opportunity recognition: analyses how entrepreneurs find entrepreneurial opportunities (Sarasvathy et al. 2010).
- User, manufacturer, or supplier driven innovation: analyses the source of the innovation developed by entrepreneurs (von Hippel 1988).

The Brazilian environmental conditions include two factors as suggested by the literature (Kelley et al. 2016) that influence the cognitive framework of the high-growth entrepreneurs and the surge of the high-growth opportunities they developed:

- National conditions that include all the policy, social and economic factors that influence the entrepreneurs and the surge of entrepreneurial opportunities (Schwab 2015, 2016; WEF and GEM 2015).
- Entrepreneurial conditions that directly foster or hinder entrepreneurship like entrepreneurial finance, government entrepreneurship programs, entrepreneurship education, research and development transfer, and legal infrastructure (Macedo et al. 2013; Singer et al. 2014; WEF and GEM 2015; Ács et al. 2016; Kelley et al. 2016).

The connection between the three clusters of factors structured the research questions (RQs) as follows:

RQ1: How did potential entrepreneurs in Brazil develop their cognitive framework to exploit high-growth entrepreneurial opportunities?

RQ2: How did the Brazilian environmental conditions influence the development of the cognitive framework of the high-growth entrepreneurs?

RQ3: How did the Brazilian environmental conditions create the high-growth entrepreneurial opportunities?

The answers to these three research questions (RQs) leads by inductive logic to the answer of the central research question (CRQ):

CRQ: Why most of the early-stage entrepreneurs in Brazil did not have high-growth ambition and develop innovative activities?

3   Research Method

The explanatory multiple case study research method was chosen because the research questions driving the study demand an in-depth epistemological understanding of the factors that influence the behavior and cognition of entrepreneurs during the process of finding, starting, and building successful businesses (Grégoire et al. 2015). The study of these factors demands the qualitative epistemological examination of motivations, perceptions, and causal mechanisms as they unfold over time (Bluhm et al. 2011; Corbin and Strauss 2015, p. 5).

The theoretical framework and research questions were used to structure interview questions and determine the analytical direction of the study (Yin 2014, p. 136). The data on the cases were collected through face-to-face interviews with eight high-growth entrepreneurs recruited through the databank of high-impact entrepreneurs of Endeavor Brazil (Endeavor 2015), referrals by entrepreneurship professors, entrepreneurs, and angel-investors. The data collected was verified by secondary information about the entrepreneurs and the business ventures they started. The largest possible dispersion of demographic characteristics was sought to reduce gender, location, and industry bias (Table 1).

The transcripts of the interviews with the high-growth entrepreneurs were thematically analyzed and coded using NVivo software. The analysis was supplemented by frequency, matrix coding queries, and node metrics for the descriptive statistics. Pattern-matching logic for comparing empirical based patterns based on findings from the cases with theoretically predicted patterns found in the literature was used to build the explanations and conclusions of the study.

4   Results

The findings of the research organized according to their cluster categories have as follows:

Table 1 Demographic of high-growth entrepreneurs interviewed and their businesses

Entrepreneurs	E111	E121	E131	E141	E151	E161	E171	E181
Gender	Female	Male	Male	Male	Female	Male	Male	Male
Ethnicity	White	White	White	White	White	White	White	White
Age (years)	29	53	41	30	29	44	37	45
Formal education of parents	Father secondary and Mother graduated	Father graduated, and Mother graduated	Father graduated, and Mother secondary	Father secondary, and mother secondary	Father graduated, and Mother graduated	Father graduated, and Mother graduated	Father graduated, and Mother graduated	Father graduated, and Mother secondary
Profession of parents	Father entrepreneur, and Mother works with Father	Father entrepreneur, and Mother teacher	Father executive, and mother does not work	Father entrepreneur, and Mother does not work	Father entrepreneur, and Mother works with Father	Father entrepreneur, and Mother teacher	Father manager, and mother is a medical doctor	Father entrepreneur, and Mother does not work
Formal education	Graduated	Graduated	Graduated	Graduated	Graduated	Post Graduated	Graduated	Post Graduated
Previous professional experience (years)	10	24	14	7	3	14	2	17
Worked for a multinational company (years)	5	23	14	0	3	3	0	2
Last job title before starting the business	Manager	President	Director	Manager	Analyst	Director	Apprentice	Director
Previous entrepreneurial experience	0	0	1 unsuccessful	1 unsuccessful	1 successful	0	1 successful	2 successful

Age when started the business	40	23	30	25	25	32	49	27
Date business started (year)	2010	2002	2001	2012	2011	2007	2012	2014
Type of business	Manufacturing and sale of consumer products	Processing and distribution of food product	Digital Products	E-Service (rental)	Digital products	E-Commerce	Manufacturing	Service using technology
Start-up financing	Personal savings	Personal savings and family	Personal savings	Personal savings and family	Personal savings	Personal savings	Personal savings	Personal savings and family
Geographic location of the business	City of Rio de Janeiro	Interior of the state of Rio de Janeiro	City of Rio de Janeiro	City of São Paulo	Interior of the state of Minas Gerais	City of São Paulo	Interior of the state of São Paulo	City of São Paulo
Sales in 2015 (Reais)	15 million	9 million	32 million	5 million	10 million	60 million	11 million	0
Sales in 2016 (Reais)	19 million	11 million	52 million	8 million	37 million	120 million	3 million	70 thousand
Employees in 2015	72	75	200	70	99	180	60	6
Employees in 2016	80	93	404	67	210	250	25	8

Notes:
Some businesses were more resilient that others to Brazil's severe recession with a contraction of the GDP of −3.8% in 2015 and of −3.6% in 2016
E111 started developing the technology for its service in 2014 and started sales only in 2016
E121 was growing at almost 50% per year up to 2015 when it was hit by the Brazilian recession in 2016
E151 automated its systems and reduced its employees

4.1   Cognitive Framework of the High-Growth Entrepreneurs

4.1.1   Cognition and Personality Traits

- Self-efficacy was highlighted by all of the participants. Some of the reasons given were: "I always believed that we could innovate by making a better product or more intelligent product"; and "I have great confidence in my skills to develop any business".
- Determination, need for achievement and (or) high-growth ambition was highlighted by all of the participants, and some of the reasons they provided included: "My objective was not to create a business to improve my lifestyle or make money, it was to revolutionize recruitment in firms, and to have the greatest possible positive impact on the largest possible number of people"; and "I want to leave a legacy for my children and Brazilian society".
- Managing risk was identified by five participants, and some of the reasons given included: "Sharing of the risk with my partner helped me a lot in overcoming the natural risks of starting a new business"; and "When the opportunity appeared to buy the Brazilian subsidiary of the multinational, I was able to take on the risk because my wife had a very good salary in her job, and I knew that I would easily get a job if needed to".
- Alertness for Opportunities or systematic search for opportunities was highlighted by all participants (four mentioned alertness for opportunities and the remaining four mentioned the systematic search for opportunities). Some of the reasons given were: "I wanted to develop a business in the area I liked, and was looking for an opportunity for a high-growth business in this area"; and "I and my partner systematically searched for a business opportunity that was innovative, had the potential to grow, and that was good for all involved".

4.1.2   Knowledge

- Knowledge from working in multinationals was identified by six of the participants with statements like: "All the technical knowledge I acquired was working for multinational companies, living abroad, visiting factories, and having contact with people that use the products abroad"; and "I only worked for multinational companies in Brazil, and all my professional knowledge was acquired working for them".
- Knowledge of markets, knowledge of customer problems or knowledge of ways to serve customers was identified by all of the participants (four selected knowledge of markets, three knowledge of customer problems and one knowledge of ways to serve). Some of the justification they provided included: "I was 49 years old, had knowledge and experience in the business, and felt prepared when the multinational decided to close the factory of the Brazilian subsidiary I managed. I saw the opportunity to continue supplying products to the Brazilian clients, and I

decided to start my own business"; and "Because I had worked selling products to the C class in Brazil, I saw the opportunity of selling a similar product to this class with better performance and at a slightly higher cost than the those that were being offered to them in the market by the large companies".

- Environmental information about change was brought up by three of the participants. One of them noted: "We exploited the tendency of consumers towards conscious consumption by renting instead of buying that appeared at the time with Netflix, Spotify and Airbnb".

4.1.3 Social Capital

- Support from professional network was highlighted by six, participants and some of the reasons given included: "Because the multinational closed the factory that I managed in Brazil, I used all the relationships that I had developed with clients, suppliers and collaborators to develop my business"; and "My professional network developed at my former employers', always helped me in the development of our business".
- The same participant also referred to capitalizing on their personal reputation for their purposes. Some of the explanations given where: "What gave us some breathing space and tranquility to organize and develop our business was a service contract that I was able to get from my former employer"; and "My professional reputation, besides opening the doors of large clients, allows me to guarantee the credit of my supplier, who does not have credit to buy the raw material he needs to supply us".
- Support from family was highlighted .by five participants in statements like: "I followed the model recommended by my father: work for a multinational, learn the business, and when prepared start your own business"; and "I was born for the business, my father worked with direct sales of similar products, and I learned during my professional career the technical side of how to develop products, research and analyze the needs of consumers, develop new consumers, and sell in retail by orienting clients".
- Support from social network was highlighted by four participants. One of them said: "My social network, which I developed at the good school and universities I attended, always helped with contacts to do business".
- Support from entrepreneurial network was highlighted only by two (both female): "We (I and my partner) participated in many events on E-Commerce and entrepreneurship; in these events, we tried to contact people, especially entrepreneurs. We exposed our business ideas to these people in order to hear their criticism and get advice, and with these contacts we built a network of informal mentors that were a great help in the development of our business".

4.2 High-Growth Entrepreneurial Opportunities

4.2.1 Opportunity Recognition, Discovery, or Creation

- Opportunity discovery was mentioned by four of the participants and as one of them stated it was in the context of "curiosity of trying to understand the difficulties of the area in the firms made me recognize that there was on opportunity of offering a service to solve these problems".
- Opportunity recognition was identified by three of the participants. As one of them stated: "The opportunity appeared because the multinational decided to close the factory in Brazil, discontinue the supply of customized products from the factory, and concentrate on supplying standardized imported products with more technology".

4.2.2 User, Manufacturer, or Supplier Driven Innovation

- Manufacturer driven innovation was identified by four participants as a means of success for their business. One of them stated: "The innovation is in the quality of the product, how it is processed, and in the distribution logistics".
- User driven innovation was the means of growth by three of the participants. One of them stated: "Curiosity and knowledge of the area we were working made us aware of a problem in the area, and able to develop a digital product to solve this problem".
- Supplier drive innovation was only identified by one of the participants of its significance in the context of this research could be validated based on the remaining testimonials.

4.3 Brazilian Environmental Conditions

4.3.1 National Framework Conditions

- All of the participants indicated that their success was not the result of government policies or incentives.
- Favorable economic or social circumstances as a reason for success was highlighted by seven of the participants with statements such as: "There is a trend in the world towards people wanting to be happy in their work, searching not only for a salary, but also for a purpose that satisfies their expectations at that moment of their lives"; and "The tendency towards conscious consumption by renting instead of buying that appeared at the time with Netflix, Spotify and Airbnb".
- Complicated and costly labor and tax laws was highlighted as an inhibitor to growth by seven of the participants. Statements included: "I have to invest a lot of

my time to take all the necessary precautions, to follow all the labor and fiscal rules correctly so as not to have problems"; and "The Brazilian labor and tax laws are barriers to entrepreneurship, they are obsolete, complicated, and costly".

- Six of the participants identified social and cultural barriers that could also have inhibited growth. Some stated: "Firms, even Brazilian firms, have a prejudice against buying technology from Brazilian firms; they don't believe that Brazilian technology is equal to that of large global firms"; and "At the beginning of my business, I sold and delivered my product personally, and my middle-class acquaintances mocked me, because I was doing work that they considered humiliating".

4.3.2 Entrepreneurial Framework Conditions

- Favorable entrepreneurial environment was identified by four of the participants as a contributor to growth while the remaining did not consider it as significant to their success. One stated: "In the last years' entrepreneurship has become fashionable in Brazil, and today it is much easier to start a business than it was some years ago, when people did not know what entrepreneurship was".
- Support from other entrepreneurs was highlighted by three as a positive influence to their success. Aa one of them stated: "We had a lot of help from the entrepreneurs that became our mentors, they gave us ideas and advice that were an great help in finding the opportunity, and in starting and developing our business".

5 Findings on the Research Questions

The findings on the factors of each cluster validated by predicted factors found in the literature led to conclude the connections between the three clusters and so answer the three research questions (RQs) and the central research question (CRQ) as follows.

5.1 (RQ1): Why and How Did Potential Entrepreneurs in Brazil Develop Their Cognitive Framework to Exploit High-growth Entrepreneurial Opportunities?

The analysis of the findings on cognitive framework of the high-growth entrepreneurs and the high-growth entrepreneurial opportunities they exploited leads by inductive logic to the key factors in their cognition/personality traits, knowledge, and social capital responsible for their success and to understand how they acquired these factors.

The high-growth entrepreneurs in the interviews highlighted five cognition and personality traits they considered to be important to their success: self-efficacy, determination, need-to-achieve, high-growth ambition, and manage risk. Of these factors, as argued by Drnovšek et al. (2010), self-efficacy is important for understanding entrepreneurial success, and a substantial body of evidence supports its influence on start-up and business growth processes. Shane et al. (2003) posit that individual with high self-efficacy will exert more effort for a greater length of time on a given task, persist through setbacks, set, and accept higher goals, and develop better plans and strategies for the task. This explanation given suggests a direct relationship between self-efficacy and the other factors highlighted by the high-growth entrepreneurs—determination, need-to-achieve, high-growth ambition, and the ability to manage risk. The importance of self-efficacy for the success of the high-growth entrepreneurs can also be inferred by the significant hurdles they had to overcome do develop their businesses in Brazil—complicated and costly labor and tax laws, and social and cultural barriers—government support for entrepreneurs, and that all had to finance the start-up of their businesses with their own personal savings and only three had additional financing from their family.

From the statements of the high-growth entrepreneurs, the demographic data, and their experiences we can infer that their self-efficacy was acquired from the influence of university-educated parents, fathers that are or were entrepreneurs or managers, academic education, as well as professional, management and entrepreneurial experience (Bandura 1977, 1993; Boyd and Vozikis 1994; Bandura et al. 1996). This means they all belong to the very small minority of better educated and empowered elite in Brazil. Four belong to the 0.4% of the Brazilian population that had two parents that graduated in the early and mid-1990s, and three belong to the 4.7% for whom one parent graduated (Guedes 2008). All of them belong to the 11.3% that had the privilege of an academic education at the end of the 1990s or early twenty-first century (Censo 2012), and to the 45.5 of whites that earn on average twice as much as the 53.6% of mixed and blacks (Censo 2012; Ipea 2012; IBGE 2015a, 2015b; 2015c; Slavery's legacies 2016). They therefore belong to the country's empowered elite, consequence of the high inequality in Brazil with a GINI index of 52.7% (United Nations Development Program 2015) and a high-power distance, PDI (Power Distance Index), of 69 (Hofstede 2010; Hofstede et al. 2010). These influences in the formation of the high self-efficacy of the high-growth entrepreneurs that induced the believes they attribute being responsible for their success are resumed in Fig. 2.

The findings about the knowledge and demographics of the high-growth entrepreneurs imply that the differentiated initial human capital (acquired from graduate parents with entrepreneurial or management experience, and an academic education) complemented by professional and management experiences (knowledge of markets, customer problems or ways to serve, acquired in most cases working for multinationals, and having entrepreneurial experiences) was directly responsible for their success in discovering or recognizing entrepreneurial opportunities and successfully developing them into high-growth businesses. The statement: "Because I had worked selling products to the C class in Brazil, I saw the opportunity of selling

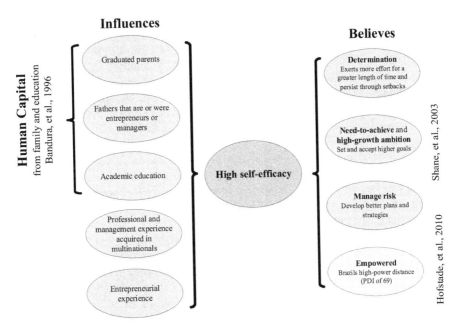

Fig 2 How the high-growth entrepreneurs acquired their high self-efficacy that induced the believes they attribute responsible for their success

a similar product to this class with better performance and at a slightly higher cost than the those that were being offered to them in the market by the large companies" support the importance of task-related knowledge to their success.

The finding that the knowledge (human capital) of entrepreneurs with task-related knowledge contributes to their success is corroborated by the findings of Cooper et al. (1994) and Unger et al. (2011). Cooper et al. (1994) found that the human capital of entrepreneurs with specific industry knowledge contributed to success in terms of both the survival and the growth of their businesses, and Unger et al. (2011) found that that the human capital-success relationship was higher for human capital that was directly related to entrepreneurial tasks compared to human capital with low task-relatedness.

The findings on the social capital and demographics of the high-growth entrepreneurs imply that their successful professional careers (most had been managers) secured support from their professional networks, which was decisive in the identification and development of their high-growth businesses, and that the support was based on their professional reputation. The statement "What gave us some breathing space and tranquility to organize and develop our business was a service contract that I was able to get from my former employer because they liked and trusted my work" supports the importance of their professional network based on their reputation for success.

An additional finding about the social capital of the high-growth entrepreneurs is that the support of families was important for their success. The statement "I followed the model recommended by my father: work for a multinational, learn the business, and when prepared start your own business" supports the importance of family in their success.

The finding that the social capital of the high-growth entrepreneurs—support from the professional network and support from family—are important factors is corroborated by the findings of Baron and Markman (2000), Hisrich and Peters (2002), Aldrich and Cliff (2003), Carr and Sequeira (2007), and Baron (2012). Baron and Markman (2000) posit that a high level of social capital, built on a favorable reputation, relevant previous experience, and direct personal contacts, often assists entrepreneurs to gain access to venture capitalists, potential customers, and others. Aldrich and Cliff (2003) and Carr and Sequeira (2007) explain that families influence entrepreneurs in opportunity recognition, start-up decisions and resource mobilization. Hisrich and Peters (2002, p. 69) highlight that having a father who is self-employed provides a strong inspiration for entrepreneurs. Baron (2012) points out that entrepreneurs obtain a wide range of benefits from their social capital, including support, advice, encouragement, acquisition of tangible financial resources, cooperation and trust from others, and enhanced access to information.

The finding that the high-growth entrepreneurs belong to the very small well-educated empowered Brazilian elite also has an influence on their social capital. This is because the empowered elite discriminates against those they consider to be below their social class. This discrimination was described by two high-growth entrepreneurs that started their businesses modestly, or by doing what is considered low paid work. The statements "My social network did not support me, on the contrary they mocked me because I was selling my product directly door to door. For them my work was humiliating and was below their social level" illustrate this discrimination".

5.2 (RQ2): Why and How Did the Brazilian Environmental Conditions Influence the Development of the Cognitive Framework of the High-growth Entrepreneurs?

The analysis of the findings on the Brazilian environmental conditions and the cognitive framework of the high-growth entrepreneurs leads by inductive logic to conclude that the country offers favorable economic or social circumstances to start a high-growth business, however it requires from the entrepreneur's alertness or systematic search for these opportunities and a high self-efficacy to overcome significant hurdles without support. The brighter side is that the environment is becoming more favorable for entrepreneurship and it is possible to get support from other entrepreneurs to start a business.

5.3 (RQ3): Why and How Did the Brazilian Environmental Conditions Create the High-growth Entrepreneurial Opportunities?

The analysis of the findings on the Brazilian environmental conditions the cognitive framework of the high-growth entrepreneurs, and the high-growth entrepreneurial opportunities leads by inductive logic to conclude that Brazil creates entrepreneurial opportunities due to favorable economic and social circumstances, however does not offer support and creates significant hurdles for entrepreneurs to explore them. Significant is that all the innovations were based on the professional experience of the high-growth entrepreneurs, which was mostly acquired in multinationals, and that the innovations were only innovations for the Brazilian market, filling a local need or market gap. None of the innovations came from private or government sponsored research, or were spinoffs of universities. Additionally, none of the innovations were disruptive innovations with the potential to shift the wealth creation curve at the industry and the individual level. Consequently, none of the eight high-growth entrepreneurs belonged to the sub-group defined by Ács et al. (2008) and Ács (2008) as high-impact entrepreneurs.

5.4 (CRQ): Why Most of the Early-stage Entrepreneurs in Brazil Did Not Have High-growth Ambition and Develop Innovative Activities?

The high self-efficacy of the high-growth entrepreneurs (Fig. 2) responsible for their success as entrepreneurs was acquired by the influence of parents who had graduated, fathers that are or were entrepreneurs or managers, academic education, as well as professional and management experience mostly in multinationals (Bandura 1977, 1993; Boyd and Vozikis 1994; Bandura et al. 1996). The demographic data of the high-growth entrepreneurs and the fact that all belong to the countries 45.5% white means that they all belong to the very small elite of better educated Brazilians (Censo 2012; Guedes 2008; Ipea 2012; IBGE 2015a, 2015b, 2015c) that is naturally empowered over the rest of the country's population, a consequence of the high inequality with a GINI index of 52.7% (United Nations Development Program 2015) and high-power distance index (PDI) of 69 (Hofstede 2010; Hofstede et al. 2010). This finding leads, by inductive reasoning, to the conclusion that high-growth entrepreneurs with high-growth ambition and innovation activity are rare in Brazil, and consequently, most of the countries early-stage entrepreneurs that don't belong to the very small well-educated and empowered elite have not acquire the factors, particularly high self-efficacy, in their cognitive framework that would have induced their high-growth ambition and innovation activity.

The corollaries from the finding on the central research question (CRQ) are: (1) There is no upward mobility from self-employed entrepreneurs to high-growth entrepreneurs; (2) Task-related knowledge, acquired mostly in multinationals, guided high-growth entrepreneurs to identify their entrepreneurial opportunities; (3) Due to the low quality of the Brazilian education system (Schwartzman 2012, 2014), high-growth entrepreneurs needed to acquire additional task-related knowledge through professional experience in order to identify entrepreneurial opportunities; and (4) Task-related knowledge, acquired through professional experience mostly in multinationals, can lead to innovations to fill needs and market gaps, but hardly to breakthrough innovations that can significantly move the wealth curve of the country and propel Brazil from the efficiency-driven stage to the innovation-driven stage of economic development.

6 Conclusions

The findings that the important factor in the cognitive framework of high-growth entrepreneurs in Brazil responsible for their success are high self-efficacy in the cognition/personality traits, knowledge (human capital) acquired from family and education complemented by task-related professional knowledge, and social capital that provided support from the professional network based on professional reputation and from family is corroborated by findings from other researchers, for example George et al. (2016). However, the finding that there is no social upward mobility from self-employed to high-growth early-stage entrepreneurs in Brazil is new and needs more research to confirm it. This lack of social upward mobility for early-stage entrepreneurs can be explained by the influence on the self-efficacy of early-stage entrepreneurs by the education of parents, as posited by Bandura et al. (1996), and by differences in social class or even in ethnic group because of the high inequality and the high-power distance in Brazil, as posited by Hofstede et al. (2010).

Also new is the finding that the task-related knowledge acquired mostly in multinationals by the high-growth entrepreneurs guided them to discover or recognize the entrepreneurial opportunities, that their average professional experience was 11 years, and that the average age was 31 when they started their successful ventures, leads us to infer that a fundamental factor for their success was their extensive professional experience and not knowledge acquired through education. A corollary of this finding is that, due to the low quality of the Brazilian education system (Schwartzman 2012, 2014), early-stage entrepreneurs needed to acquire additional task-related knowledge through extensive professional experience in order to go on to find entrepreneurial opportunities. In the case of Brazil, this finding puts into question the myth of the student entrepreneurs created by Steve Jobs, Michael Dell, Bill Gates, and Mark Zuckerberg. This finding implies that the best recommendation for aspiring entrepreneurs in Brazil is the recommendation followed by one of the high-growth entrepreneurs: "I followed the model recommended by my father: work for a multinational, learn the business, and when prepared start your own business".

Additionally, we can infer that task-related knowledge acquired through professional experience mostly in multinationals can lead to innovations to fill needs and market gaps, but hardly to breakthrough innovations that can significantly move the wealth curve of the country and propel Brazil from the efficiency-driven stage to the innovation-driven stage (the knowledge-driven stage) of economic development. A corollary of this inference is that, due to the low quality of the Brazilian education system, the country's early-stage entrepreneurs will hardly create breakthrough innovations. Both these inferences are new and need more research to validate them.

6.1 Implications for Brazil

Brazil is in what Drexler and Amorós (2015) have called an "entrepreneurial trap," with a high percentage of early-stage entrepreneurial activity, but with early-stage entrepreneurs that have almost no high-growth ambition, and generate almost no entrepreneurial innovation activity. Chile and Colombia that have similar inequality and power distance indexes (United Nations Development Program 2015; Hofstede 2010), have avoided the entrepreneurial trap with successful public-private policies that promoted high levels of new businesses to be launched by high-impact entrepreneurs (Drexler and Amorós 2015). These countries demonstrate that Brazilian policy makers could develop policies to support early-stage entrepreneurs in Brazil, and so promote the country's economic growth.

The need for policies authored by the Brazilian government to promote entrepreneurship is also demonstrated by the country's very low score of 26.1 and rank of 92 in the 2016 Global Entrepreneurship Index (GEI). In Latin America, this compares with Chile, which scored 62.1 and was ranked 16, and Colombia, which scored 44.8 and was ranked 43 (Ács et al. 2016). One of the Pillars of the GEI in which Brazil scored well below other Latin American countries is the Human Capital Pillar, which captures the level of education of entrepreneurs. The importance of human capital for generating a surge of high-impact entrepreneurs was highlighted by the findings of this study, and corroborated by Ács et al. (2016), who explain that a high score in human capital is important because entrepreneurs with higher education are more willing and capable of starting high-growth businesses.

6.2 Suggestions for Future Research

The World Economic Forum and Global Entrepreneurship Monitor (WEF and GEM 2015) used early-stage entrepreneurs' estimates of how many people they expected to employ in the medium term as a good proxy for their ambition. This is an oversimplification of the reasons why early-stage entrepreneurs in Brazil don't develop high-growth businesses and needs to be better understood through more research. Indicators like education, social class, and power distance are probably better at explaining why they are unable to develop high-growth businesses even when they have high ambition.

The report from the World Economic Forum and Global Entrepreneurship Monitor (WEF and GEM 2015) highlights that only two economies in their sample—Colombia and Chile—are all-round entrepreneurial economies that combine high early-stage entrepreneurial activity with a high proportion of ambitious and innovative entrepreneurs. All other economies fall within the average (or below the average) on at least one of these three dimensions. Drexler and Amorós (2015) explain that for countries to become all-round entrepreneurial economies like Chile and Colombia, their governments must pay attention to the balance of the three dimensions: the number of early-stage entrepreneurs, their innovativeness, and their growth ambitions. The authors point out that the pathways to thriving entrepreneurial economies are manifold, and the countries that try to copy the Chilean, Colombian, or well-known Silicon Valley model may well be disappointed. The reasons why Chile and Colombia, which have similar levels of inequality (United Nations Development Program 2015) and power distance (Hofstede 2010) as Brazil, were able to become entrepreneurial all-rounder economies needs more research, the findings of which may guide government policy makers in Brazil and other developing economies to help their countries become entrepreneurial all-rounder economies. One possible explanation is that these countries have a better education system (Schwab 2016).

The finding that there is no social upward mobility from self-employed individuals to high-growth early-stage entrepreneurs in Brazil is new and needs more research to confirm it, particularly if the lack of social upward mobility can be explained by the difference in the education of an entrepreneur's parents, which has an influence on their self-efficacy, as posited by Bandura et al. (1996), or by the difference in social class or even ethnic group because of the high inequality and the high-power distance in Brazil, as posited by Hofstede et al. (2010). Additionally, the inference that, due to the low quality of the Brazilian education system (Schwab 2015), early-stage entrepreneurs need to acquire additional task-related knowledge through extensive professional experience to find entrepreneurial opportunities, and that these innovations, which are found through professional experience, will rarely be breakthrough innovations needs to be confirmed through more research.

References

Ács, Z. J. (2008). *Foundations of high impact entrepreneurship*. Boston, MA: Now.

Ács, Z. J., Parsons, W., & Tracy, S. (2008, June). *Small business research summary: High-impact firms: Gazelles revisited* (Research Report No. 328). Washington, DC: SBA Office of Advocacy.

Ács, Z. J., Szerb, L, & Autio, E. (2016). *Global entrepreneurship index 2016*. Retrieved from http://thegedi.org/2016-global-entrepreneurship-index/

Aldrich, H. E., & Cliff, J. E. (2003). The pervasive effects of family on entrepreneurship: Toward a family embeddedness perspective. *Journal of Business Venturing, 18*(5), 573–596.

Alvarez, S. A., & Busenitz, L. W. (2001). The entrepreneurship of resource-based theory. *Journal of Management, 27*, 755–775.

Anderson, M., Grant, K., Halcro, K., Devis, J. M. R., & Genskowsky, L. G. (Eds.). (2013). *Innovation support in Latin America and Europe: Theory, practice and policy in innovation and innovation systems*. Burlington, NY: Gower.

Ardichvili, A., Cardozo, R., & Ray, S. (2003). A theory of entrepreneurial opportunity identification and development. *Journal of Business Venturing, 18*(1), 105–123.

Audretsch, D. B. (1995). *Innovation and industry evolution*. London, UK: Routledge.

Autio, E. (2011). High-aspiration entrepreneurship. In M. Minniti (Ed.), *The dynamics of entrepreneurship: Evidence from the global entrepreneurship monitor data* (pp. 251–276). Oxford, GB: Oxford University Press.

Bandura, A. (1977). Self-efficacy: Toward a unifying theory of behavioral change. *Psychological Review, 84*(2), 191–215.

Bandura, A. (1993). Perceived self-efficacy in cognitive development and functioning. *Educational Psychologist, 28*(2), 117–148.

Bandura, A., Barbaranelli, C., Caprara, G. V., & Pastorelli, C. (1996). Multifaceted impact of self-efficacy beliefs on academic functioning. *Child Development, 67*(3), 1206–1222.

Baron, R. A. (2006). Opportunity recognition as pattern recognition: How entrepreneurs "connect the dots" to identify new business opportunities. *Academy of Management Perspectives, 20*(1), 114–119. https://doi.org/10.5465/AMP.2006.19873412.

Baron, R. A. (2012). Entrepreneurship: A process perspective. In J. R. Baum, M. Frese, & R. A. Baron (Eds.), *The psychology of entrepreneurship* (pp. 71–102). New York, NY: Psychology Press.

Baron, R. A., & Markman, G. D. (2000). Beyond social capital: How social skills can enhance entrepreneurs' success. *Academy of Management Executive, 14*(1). https://doi.org/10.5465/AME.2000.2909843.

Bluhm, D. J., Harman, W., Lee, T. W., & Mitchell, T. R. (2011). Qualitative research in management: A decade of progress. *Journal of Management Studies, 48*(8), 1866–1891.

Boyd, N. G., & Vozikis, G. S. (1994). The influence of self-efficacy on the development of entrepreneurial intentions and actions. *Entrepreneurship Theory & Practice, 18*(4), 63–77.

Cardon, M. S., & Kirk, C. P. (2015). Entrepreneurial passion as mediator of the self-efficacy to persistence relationship. *Entrepreneurship Theory & Practice, 39*(5), 1027–1050. https://doi.org/10.1111/etap.12089.

Carr, J. C., & Sequeira, J. M. (2007). Prior family business exposure as intergenerational influence and entrepreneurial intent: A theory of planned behavior approach. *Journal of Business Research, 60*(10), 1090–1098.

Censo 2010. (2012). Retrieved September 29, 2016, from UOL educação website: http://educacao.uol.com.br/noticias/2012/12/19/ibge-quase-metade-da-populacao-com-25-anos-ou-mais-nao-tem-o-fundamental-completo.htm

Cooper, A. C., Gimeno-Gascon, F. J., & Woo, C. Y. (1994). Initial human and financial capital as predictors of new venture performance. *Journal of Business Venturing, 9*(5), 371–395.

Corbin, J., & Strauss, A. L. (2015). *Basics of qualitative research* (4th ed.). Thousand Oaks, CA: Sage.

Degen, R. J. (2009). *O empreendedor: Empreender como opção de carreira*. São Paulo, BR: Prentice-Hall do Brasil.

Degen, R. J. (2017). *Cognitive framework of high-growth entrepreneurs and reasons for the almost complete absence of high-growth ambition of early-stage entrepreneurs in Brazil*. Ann Arbor, MI: ProQuest.

Drexler, M., & Amorós, J. E. (2015). Guest post: How Chile and Colombia eluded the 'entrepreneur trap'. *Financial Times*, Blogs. Retrieved from http://blogs.ft.com/beyond-brics/2015/01/08/guest-post-how-chile-and-colombia-eluded-the-entrepreneur-trap/

Drnovšek, M., Wincent, J., & Cardon, M. S. (2010). Entrepreneurial self-efficacy and business start-up: Developing a multi-dimensional definition. *International Journal of Entrepreneurial Behaviour & Research, 16*(4), 329–348.

Endeavor. (2015). *Conheça os empreendedores endeavor do Brasil.* Retrieved from Empreendedores Endeavor website: https://endeavor.org.br/empreendedores-endeavor/

Fiet, J. O. (2007). A prescriptive analysis of search and discovery. *Journal of Management Studies, 44*(4), 592–611.

Fiet, J. O., Piskounov, A., & Patel, P. C. (2005). Still searching (systematically) for entrepreneurial discoveries. *Small Business Economics, 25*(5), 489–504.

Foo, M. D. (2011). Emotions and entrepreneurial opportunity evaluation. *Entrepreneurship Theory & Practice, 35*(2), 375–393.

George, N. M., Parida, V., Lahti, T., & Wincent, J. (2016). A systematic literature review of entrepreneurial opportunity recognition: Insights on influencing factors. *International Entrepreneurship and Management Journal, 12*(2), 309–350. https://doi.org/10.1007/s11365-014-0347-y.

Grégoire, D. A., Cornelissen, J., Dimov, D., & van Burg, E. (2015). The mind in the middle: Taking stock of affect and cognition research in entrepreneurship. *International Journal of Management Reviews, 17*(2), 125–142.

Guedes, M. C. (2008). A presença feminina nos cursos universitários e nas pós-graduações: Desconstruindo a idéia da universidade como espaço masculino [Women's presence in undergraduate and graduate courses: Deconstructing the idea of university as a male domain]. *História, Ciências, Saúde—Manguinhos, 15.* https://doi.org/10.1590/S0104-59702008000500006.

Haynie, J. M., Shepherd, D. A., & McMullen, J. S. (2009). An opportunity for me? The role of resources in opportunity evaluation decisions. *Journal of Management Studies, 46*(3), 337–361.

Heinonen, J., Hytti, U., & Stenholm, P. (2011). The role of creativity in opportunity search and business idea creation. *Education + Training, 53*(8/9), 659–672.

Hisrich, R. D., & Peters, M. P. (2002). *Entrepreneurship* (5th ed.). New York, NY: McGraw-Hill/Irwin.

Hofstede, G. H. (2010). *Country* [Fact sheet]. Retrieved from Geert Hofstede website: https://geert-hofstede.com/brazil.html

Hofstede, G. H., Hofstede, G. J., & Minkov, M. (2010). *Cultures and organizations: Software of the mind: Intercultural cooperation and its importance for survival* (3rd ed.). New York: McGraw-Hill.

IBGE. (2015a). *Brazil in figures.* Rio de Janeiro, BR: IBGE.

IBGE. (2015b). *Síntese de indicadores sociais: Uma análise das condições de vida da população brasileira.* Rio de Janeiro, BR: IBGE.

IBGE. (2015c). *Indicadores de desenvolvimento sustentável Brasil 2015.* Rio de Janeiro, BR: IBGE.

Ipea. (2012). *Políticas sociais: Acompanhamento e análise.* Rio de Janeiro, BR: Ipea.

Kelley, D., Singer, S., & Herrington, M. (2016). *Global reports: GEM 2015/2016 Global Report.* London, GB: Global Entrepreneurship Research Association.

Levie, J., & Autio, E. (2013). *ERC white paper: Growth and growth intentions* (Research Report No. 1). Retrieved from http://www.enterpriseresearch.ac.uk/wp-content/uploads/2013/12/ERC-White-Paper-No_1-Growth-final.pdf

Li, Y. (2011). Emotions and new venture judgment in China. *Asia Pacific Journal of Management, 28*(2), 277–298.

Macedo, M. D. M., Greco, S. M. D. S. S., Andreassi, T., Antunes, A. L., Borges, C., Pansarella, L., et al (2013). *National reports: Empreendedorismo no Brasil.* Retrieved from http://www.gemconsortium.org/report

McClelland, D. C. (1976). *The achieving society.* New York, NY: Free Press. (Original work published 1961).

McMullen, J. S., & Shepherd, D. A. (2006). Entrepreneurial action and the role of uncertainty in the theory of the entrepreneurs. *Academy of Management Review, 31*(1), 122–152. https://doi.org/10.5465/AMR.2006.19379628.

Nicolaou, N., Shane, S., Cherkas, L., & Spector, T. D. (2009). Opportunity recognition and the tendency to be an entrepreneur: A bivariate genetics perspective. *Organizational Behavior and Human Decision Processes, 110*(2), 108–117.

Ramos-Rodríguez, A. R., Medina-Garrido, J. A., Lorenzo-Gómez, J. D., & Ruiz-Navarro, J. (2010). What you know or who you know? The role of intellectual and social capital in opportunity recognition. *International Small Business Journal, 28*(6), 566–582.

Rauch, A., & Frese, M. (2007). Let's put the person back into entrepreneurship research: A meta-analysis on the relationship between business owners' personality traits, business creation, and success. *European Journal of Work and Organizational Psychology, 16*(4), 353–385.

Sarasvathy, S. D., Dew, N., Velamuri, S. R., & Venkataraman, S. (2010). Three views of entrepreneurial opportunity. In Z. J. Acs & D. B. Audretsch (Eds.), *International handbook series on entrepreneurs, Handbook on entrepreneurship research* (Vol. 5, 2nd ed., pp. 77–96). New York, NY: Springer.

Schwab, K. (Ed.). (2015). *Insight report: The global competitiveness report 2015–2016.* Retrieved from World Economic Forum website: http://www3.weforum.org/docs/gcr/2015-2016/Global_Competitiveness_Report_2015-2016.pdf

Schwab, K. (Ed.). (2016). *Insight report: The global competitiveness report 2016–2017.* World Economic Forum. Retrieved from http://www3.weforum.org/docs/GCR2016-2017/05FullReport/TheGlobalCompetitivenessReport2016-2017_FINAL.pdf

Schwartzman, S. (2012). Economic growth and higher education policies in Brazil: A link? *International Higher Education, 67*(Spring), 28–29.

Schwartzman, S. (2014). Academic drift in Brazilian education. In A. Maldonado-Maldonado & R. M. Bassett (Eds.), *Higher education dynamics series. The forefront of international higher education* (Vol. 42, pp. 61–72). New York: Springer.

Shane, S. (2000). Prior knowledge and the discovery of entrepreneurial opportunities. *Organization Science, 11*(4), 448–469.

Shane, S., Locke, E. A., & Collins, C. J. (2003). Entrepreneurial motivation. *Human Resource Management Review, 13*(2), 257–279.

Shane, S., & Venkataraman, S. (2000). The promise of entrepreneurship as a field of research. *Academy of Management Review, 25*(1), 217–226. https://doi.org/10.5465/AMR.2000.2791611.

Singer, S., Amorós, J. E., & Arreola, D. M. (2014). *Global report: GEM 2014 global report.* Retrieved from http://www.gemconsortium.org/report

Slavery's legacies. (2016). *The Economist, 420*(9006), 51–52.

Stam, E., Hartog, C., van Stel, A., & Thurik, R. (2011). Ambitious entrepreneurship, high-growth firms, and macro-economic growth. In M. Minniti (Ed.), *The dynamics of entrepreneurship: Evidence from the global entrepreneurship monitor data* (pp. 231–250). Oxford, GB: Oxford University Press.

Tominc, P., & Rebernik, M. (2007). Growth aspirations and cultural support for entrepreneurship: A comparison of post-socialist countries. *Small Business Economics, 28*(2/3), 239–255.

Unger, J. M., Rauch, A., Frese, M., & Rosenbusch, N. (2011). Human capital and entrepreneurial success: A meta-analytical review. *Journal of Business Venturing, 26*(3), 341–358.

United Nations Development Program. (2015). *Human development report.* New York, NY: United Nations.

Vaghely, I. P., & Julien, P. A. (2010). Are opportunities recognized or constructed?: An information perspective on entrepreneurial opportunity identification. *Journal of Business Venturing, 25*(1), 73–86.

Venkataraman, S. (1997). The distinctive domain of entrepreneurship research. In J. A. Katz (Ed.), *Advances in entrepreneurship, firm emergence and growth* (pp. 119–138). Greenwich, CT: Jai.

von Hippel, E. (1988). *The sources of innovation.* New York: Oxford University Press.

WEF, & GEM. (2015). *Leveraging entrepreneurial ambition and innovation: A global perspective on entrepreneurship, competitiveness and development.* Retrieved from http://www3.weforum. org/docs/WEFUSA_EntrepreneurialInnovation_Report.pdf

Westhead, P., Ucbasaran, D., & Wright, M. (2009). Information search and opportunity identification: The importance of prior business ownership experience. *International Small Business Journal, 27*(6), 659–680.

Yin, R. K. (2014). *Case study research: Design and methods* (5th ed.). Thousand Oaks, CA: Sage.

Zahra, S. A., Gedajlovic, E., Neubaum, D. O., & Shulman, J. M. (2009). A typology of social entrepreneurs: Motives, search processes and ethical challenges. *Journal of Business Venturing, 24*(5), 519–532.

Hindering Factors to Innovation: A Panel Data Analysis

Joana Costa, Anabela Botelho, and João Matias

Abstract The existence of companies developing innovative activities is a key factor for a competitive economy. Firms recognize the importance of performing innovative activities to raise their productivity and create an advantage towards their competitors, consolidate its position in the market and gain extra profits.

Innovation projects have a very uncertain outcome, thus exposing the firm to additional risks. When the economic environment is adverse, firms tend to reduce the amount spent in R&D and deleverage innovative activities. As many innovation projects succeed, others fail. Very often firms decide to abandon their innovative projects which were jeopardized for several obstacles.

The obstacles to innovation perceived by the firms will depend on their particular characteristics. The type of innovation being performed will naturally involve a different variety and extent of resources, moreover, the stage of the process will require the use of different resources with various intensities.

Using a panel of firms collected from the Portuguese CIS, we observe that the abandon of innovative activities fell during the crisis, contrarily to our first expectation. This finding reinforces the suspicions that firms continue their innovative actions in turbulent environments such as the crisis, going along with the Schumpeter Mark I hypothesis. A deep understanding about the effective the role of the different type of barriers firms face in their innovative process will allow the design of more accurate policy recommendations.

Keywords Innovation barriers · Innovation policy · Crisis · Panel data

J. Costa (✉) · A. Botelho · J. Matias
GOVCOPP and DEGEIT, University of Aveiro, Aveiro, Portugal
e-mail: joanacosta@ua.pt

© Springer International Publishing AG, part of Springer Nature 2018   269
S. Cubico et al. (eds.), *Entrepreneurship and the Industry Life Cycle*, Studies on
Entrepreneurship, Structural Change and Industrial Dynamics,
https://doi.org/10.1007/978-3-319-89336-5_12

1 Introduction

Successful innovation is determinant to the economic performance of firms. The engagement of innovative activities by developing new products or processes will raise the efficiency level, productivity, minimisation of the cost structure, thus generating an advantage towards their competitors. Firms' and industry specific characteristics may speed up the pace of achieving innovations (Acs and Audretsch 1987). Innovative firms grow more rapidly in terms of employment and profitability (Geroski et al. 1993).

The economic crisis that started in 2008 seriously affected innovation and R&D in Portugal likewise other countries. Furthermore, the existing weaknesses in the National System of Innovation (NSI) became wider. Further developments in the innovation policy are unclear, policy actions failed to address demand uncertainties, redeployment of both human and physical capital (OECD 2012).

Irreversible damage was generated due to the erosion of credibility of the financial system, exponential growth of firm insolvency, long term skilled unemployment, emigration, insufficient demand caused by negative expectations about the future as well as dramatic cuts in innovation policies as a result of budgetary constraints. Even though, Governments continue to allocate sums of money and resources in policy actions to promote R&D activities to heighten innovation. The European Commission has developed policy instruments to improve and intensify R&D activities through several instruments, whose effects are scarcely noticeable at present.

Innovation failure is an issue neglected by the literature, even though it is a natural condition of the process. Innovative activities are highly risky, due to the uncertainty regarding their outcomes: future earnings, scheduling, feasibility and market penetration are unpredictable; furthermore, and even with reliable forecasts unexpected drawbacks may happen.

When severe constraints, regardless of their nature, jeopardise the research projects, firms must abandon the innovative activities targeted to the development of new products or processes. Despite the eventual uniqueness or randomness of innovation failure we aim at finding some patterns concerning the determinants of abandon to anticipate failure or even to create theoretical and political contexts to reduce uncertainty, thus minimising losses. The study aims at systematizing the determinants of the abandon of innovative activities, understanding the eventual change it their structures caused by adverse economic environments and offering policy recommendations to hopefully put back innovation in the policy agenda.

Financing constraints are the most common obstacles to innovation discussed in the literature in works such as: Canepa and Stoneman (2002), Savignac (2008), and Tiwari et al. (2008) however they are not the single explanation for the weakening innovative activities. Currently, venture capital investments must reconsider participation in innovative activities; but policy-makers will play a determinant role in the design of accurate actions improving innovation and growth.

Modern markets face global competition standards, products and technologies are rapidly declining, consumer demand suffers constant variations; independent on their size, firms must be flexible enough to adapt to the new environment. Non-innovative markets will perish.

Understanding the full dimension of innovation and its hindering factors may help entrepreneurs, managers and financial investors to avoid several miscalculations. Approaching the framework proposed by the CIS, three major types of barriers will influence the abandon probability: lack of finance (internal or external), knowledge factors and market conditions.

Firms that perceive a favourable environment with reduced barriers to innovation will be more prone to perform innovative activities. Accordingly, policy makers must create the confidence conditions. As the firm is an open system, the exogenous economic and knowledge circumstance will determine the attitude of firms towards innovation; efforts should be made to nourish this milieu. Perception of obstacles from innovators varies across countries; consequently, policy makers should conceive a country specific innovation policy to overcome the limitations (Galia et al. 2012).

A particularly singular feature of this paper is that it compiles two CIS waves, to be exact the CIS 6 and the CIS 10 creating a panel of firms, gathering firms from all sectors, all technological intensities and all sizes, in sum, a broad sample of almost all SIC codes. The panel comprises 1496 firms, observed during the 2004–2006 and the 2008–2010 biennia. An analysis of the obstacles perceived by the Portuguese firms over the two CIS waves will be performed to shed some light into the hindering factors of innovation and produce some policy recommendations in order to incentive and finance the innovative activities of firms, moreover it is important to get a deep understanding of the possible changes caused by the evolution of the economic environment.

The econometric estimations prove that being an occasional innovator or a persistent innovator will influence the probability of abandoning the innovative activities. The perception of financial constraints strongly influences the probability of abandon, as well as the other sources such as the existence of trained workers or the uncertainty in terms of the demand.

The remainder of the paper is structured as follows. Section 2 presents the theoretical background, of barriers to innovation and their complementarity. It also discusses the role of barriers to innovation during the contractive phases of the business cycle. In Sect. 3 database, hypothesis, methodology and econometric modelling are defined. Hereinafter, Sect. 4 presents the econometric results, and the discussion. Lastly, Sect. 5 concludes and addresses some policy recommendations.

2 Critical Literature Review

Due to the uncertainties involved in innovative activities, many firms opt for not engaging innovation activities at all. The negative impact of the potential risk can be a significant obstacle to innovation within firms (Borgelt and Falk 2007).

Most of the literature is committed to explaining innovation success and its factors, very few has been done addressing what determines the failure of the innovation projects, if there is a possible systematisation, and what can policy makers do to minimise the negative consequences of this phenomenon.

Theoretical or empirical evidence about the determinants of innovation failures is scarce; and a recent point of interest among researchers. The most representative papers in this area are the works of Galia and Legros (2004), Landry et al. (2008), Mohnen et al. (2008), Savignac (2008), Tiwari et al. (2008), García-Vega and López (2010) and Madrid-Guijarro et al. (2009). In this section highlights concerning theoretical and empirical findings are presented. There are different strands of empirical literature addressing the issue of innovation failure and the barriers to innovation. As well as the analysis of the innovation activities over the business cycle.

This paper aims at addressing the influence of the barriers to innovation (economic factors, knowledge factors and market factors) in the probability of abandoning the innovative activities; additionally if these barriers affect differently the aspects of innovation (product, process, service, organizational and marketing innovation) and if the adverse economic environment changes the perception about the barriers and their importance.

The determinants of the innovation failure will be empirically tested by means of the construction of several models. In the first case, the probability of abandon will be tested in general, without any sectorial or innovative segmentation. The second model separates de firms according to their economic activity; the third, uses each of the innovation vectors illustrating the differences in their requirements and the fourth combines both.

2.1 Determinants of Innovation Failure

The existence of companies pursuing innovative activities is a key factor for a competitive economy; yet innovation exposes firms to additional risks. In the innovation process, failure can be inevitable; the outcome of innovation projects is uncertain, thus risky. Consequently, the prize to be paid to investors must be higher independent on relying on internal or external sources.

When firms launch new research projects they can make forecasts, but they do not know, for certain, if the project will succeed, its profitability and the difficulties they will find while pursuing these actions. Projects concerning innovative activities are unattractive to external investors as they cannot control the outcome of the firm's actions nor the evolution of the process; information asymmetries will disincentive venture capital due to the lack of warrantees, as the use of intangible assets as collateral is not commonly accepted.

Besides, firms fear delivering much information due to appropriability problems. Signalling the viability of innovative projects is costly Bhattacharya and Ritter (1985). Due to all these constraints, external sources of finance are often unavailable; firms prefer the use of internal rather than external funds, fostering their innovative activities based on internal liquidity (Myers and Majluf 1984).

The existence of financial constraints or restricted endowments forces firms to postpone their innovation activities; investments in innovation become even more unappealing due to risk aversion. There is an inverse correlation between innovation intensity and risk aversion of managers (Souitaris 2001). Taking more risks raises the financial exposure; this may disincentive internal and external financing.

Barriers affect in a different way the different types of innovations such as product innovation, service innovation, process innovation, organizational innovation, and marketing innovation. Better understanding of barriers to innovation can assist firms to foster development of an environment that supports innovation (Hadjimanolis 1999).

According to Asplund and Sandin (1999) and Cozijnsen et al. (2000) there is an obvious need to systematically assess factors decisive for success and failure of innovation. To van der Panne et al. (2003) innovation success is determined by positive impact of the firm culture; experience in innovation projects; availability of a variety of skills among the R&D team; coherent innovation strategy; managerial coherence with the innovative strategy; compatibility of the research with firm competences; matrix organization; competitive price and quantity compared to its substitutes; market opportunity. The viability of a certain product depends on Firm related factors; Project related factors; Product related factors; and Market related factors. Therefore, firms lacking these characteristics will be more prone to fail. The relation between R&D intensity and innovative output is moderated by such factors as regional knowledge spillovers, demand-pull effects or differences in technological opportunity.

Lack of financial resources is considered a predominant factor of failure. Mohnen et al. (2008) mainly analyzes the impact of financial constraints on firm decisions to abandon, prematurely stop, slow down or not start innovation projects.

A wide number of determinants affecting the failure of innovation projects, such as the creation of knowledge, firm strategies, external sources of knowledge, funding, obstacles to innovation, vulnerability and degree of novelty of innovation. Nevertheless financial obstacles and other obstacles related to innovation development are the most important ones (Canepa and Stoneman 2002; Landry et al. 2008).

Experience enables the firm to capitalize upon learning-by-doing and learning-by-failing effects. Whereas the first improves the firm's R&D efficiency, the latter exposes the firm's weaknesses (Maidique and Zirger 1985; Zirger 1997; García-Vega and López 2010). In sum, failure seems to be a natural component of the innovation process.

2.2 Innovation Barriers and Firm Characteristics

Successful firms are engaged in innovative activities to improve their performance in what concerns the cost structure and the advantage of their products. Sectoral and firm characteristics are established as determinants and advantages to produce innovation and patent licensing (Acs and Audretsch 1987, 1988).

The relationship between obstacles to innovation and firms' characteristics are studied in works such as Baldwin and Lin (2002), Galia and Legros (2004), Mohnen and Rosa (2002) and Tourigny and Le (2004). These studies consider two major vectors of characteristics, the first related to intrinsic features of the firm (such as size, sector, age, competitive environment, group membership, among others), and the second connected to the firm attitude towards innovation activity (such as technological intensity, financial support for innovation, of Sources of R&D for innovation activities, R&D intensity, introduction of technological innovations and novelty of innovation, among others). They reveal that firm heterogeneity has to be taken into account to evaluate the firms' perception of obstacles to innovation and their degree of importance.

There is a general belief that innovation barriers may differ according to firm size. Firm dimension seems to be a hampering factor as small firms tend to find more difficult to pursuit innovative activities than large firms. Small firms have lesser availability of finance being more constrained towards innovation, meaning a broader perception of barriers and their importance. Among SME's there is increased probability in finding difficult pursuing innovative actions (Hadjimanolis 1999). Despite their difficulty in finding finance, small firms also have absorptive capacity, and flexibility which can work as an innovative advantage compared to large firms. Large firms are threatened by innovation barriers in a different manner.

Increased productivity, growth potential and likelihood of survival will be enhanced in small firms that successfully pursue innovation as a core business strategy (Cefis and Marsili 2006; Heunks 1998; Geroski et al. 1993). Those who opt for not embracing these actions are highly prone to become uncompetitive because of the obsolescence of their products and processes. Companies operate under volatile environments facing global competition standards, shorted product and technology lifecycles; and unstable consumer demand. Regardless of their size, firms must achieve the benchmark otherwise being excluded from the market.

Young and small and medium sized firms pursuing these risky actions may fall in severe financial problems (Hadjimanolis 1999). Creating the accurate policy framework to incentive and finance the innovative activities of firms, mainly among SME's which tend to find more difficult to innovate is determinant for overcoming severe crisis and huge unemployment figures. Teece (1996) emphasized the need to understand and clarify how SMEs can overcome barriers to innovation. Public policies encouraging innovative attitudes, providing funds to SME's in their innovation will allow the start-up, the growth or even the survival of many entrepreneurial initiatives.

Innovating means doing something new, or doing the same in a different manner (Garcia and Calantone 2002). Being able to introduce innovations in the market depends on the small firm characteristics. Firms down weighting bureaucracy, with managerial expertise, and strong linkages in their productive chain will increase the probability if introducing successful innovations. Small firms achieve advantages in terms of flexibility and adaptability to compensate the disadvantage of resource constraints when attempting to become more innovative (Freel 2000). Understanding the full dimension of innovation and its hindering factors may help entrepreneurs, managers and financial investors to avoid several miscalculations.

2.3 Multiplicity of Innovation Barriers and Their Complementarity

Firms have a different perception to the barriers to innovation, according to their structural traits. Moreover, the perception of the weight of the innovation costs, the institutional constraints, the firm culture, the skills of the labour force are also of major importance (Mohnen and Röller 2005; Baldwin and Lin 2002).

A comprehensive knowledge about the barriers to innovation perceived interpreted by the entrepreneurs, the clients, the suppliers and other stakeholders may influence the innovative strategies as well as the positioning towards the market (Hadjimanolis 1999).

Complementarities between obstacles to innovation constitute a relevant branch of the literature, in this vein Mohnen and Rosa (2002) find cost factors and risk seem to go together; as well as problems of internal and external governance. On the other hand Galia and Legros (2004, 2012) find evidence pointing to the existence of important complementarities between obstacles to innovation in postponed projects, which decay of importance when analyzing abandoned projects. Mohnen and Röller (2005) propose a different approach to studying complementarities using a discrete test of supermodularity.

2.4 Effects of the Barriers to Innovation and the Innovative Activity

According to Schumpeter's process of *creative destruction*, recessive phases are a pool of opportunities for the agents improving the NSI. The innovation performance is jeopardized during downturns. Three major factors can be outlined to explain innovation performance during the crises: (a) uncertainty in demand; (b) availability of finance to develop R&D and innovative activities; (c) readjustments in terms of the Governmental innovation policy.

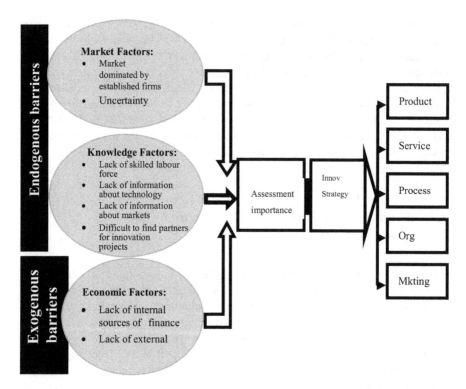

Fig. 1 Innovation barriers and innovation. Source: Author's organisation according to the CIS

Under uncertainty agents contract their willingness to develop risky projects such as innovation. Downturns make agents opt for the reduced exposition to activities generating uncertain pay-offs. Crises generally reduce the demand for products; reduces the liquidity, raises uncertainty, changes the innovation policy.

Mohnen et al. (2008) the variable obstacles has a positive or insignificant coefficient Savignac (2008) the same for financial constraints on innovation.

Innovation is approached by firms by means of two possible scenarios: (a) innovators, firms declaring to have introduced innovations independent on its vector which are new to the market; (b) Immitators are those introducing innovations new to themselves but not to the market (Sadowski and Sadowski-Rasters 2006).

In what concerns non innovative firms, we may find firms not engaging innovative projects as part of their managerial options (the non-innovative) and those firms that despite willing to innovate perceive barriers, therefore discouraged organisations are different from the unwilling. Firms not finding any obstacle and still not innovating are a synonym of unwillingness (Fig. 1).

Different strategies may coexist in the same sector, some have interest to innovate some to imitate (the innovators and the laggards). As a consequence absence of innovation and absence of obstacles directly connected. Non innovating firms are not outliers, they are a very common situation.

A large number of firms may survive or even grow with no innovation due to product characteristics. Innovation is not as fundamental in all sectors. Some firms opt not to innovate at all; other firms prefer to imitate innovators rather than performing their own innovative activities. In the Portuguese case, independent on the CIS session, in almost all economic sectors, nearly half of the firms refer not having performed innovative activities.

Market related factors are pointed as an important abandon due to competition of established firms and market uncertainty. Large firms tend to abandon due the lack of skills (qualified personnel) and availability of external finance. Public funding will help firms in supporting the costs and reducing the risk in fostering innovation projects.

Some articles analyze the impact of hampering factors on innovation, which is measured as R&D, innovation activities or innovation output. Several studies find the following counter intuitive result: obstacles to innovation have a positive effect on innovation (Mohnen and Röller 2005; Lööf and Heshmati 2006).

However, this result can be explained by a problem of endogeneity of hampering factors. There are common factors affecting both innovation and perception of obstacles. Savignac (2008), Hajivassiliou and Savingnac (2008) and Tiwari et al. (2008) analyse the role of endogeneity in innovation barriers. They underline the effect of financial constraints.

2.5 Importance of the Barriers to Innovation for the Panel of Firms

To produce a preliminary description about the barriers to innovation perceived by the firms in the panel, in both CIS waves, the following table was produced. For each type of barrier included in the CIS we have the importance attributed by the firm (in a 0–3 scale). The results are divided in two sections, being the first related to the CIS 6 and the second to the CIS 10.

In terms of the economic factors, the number of firms mentioning this barrier as being important rose; contrarily, the importance of the qualified personnel was to some extent less perceived. The perceptions of firms about the other knowledge factors were substantially steady in both periods.

Uncertainty about the demand has gained some momentum, reinforcing some negativity about the economic climate (Table 1).

2.6 Hypothesis of the Research

The analysis of the negative responses given to performing innovative activities is normally followed by questioning the reason. Normally, negative answers rely on

Table 1 Barriers to innovation—importance reported by firms

	Barriers		CIS 6				CIS 10			
			Not used	Low or very low	Medium	High and very high	Not used	Low or very low	Medium	High and very high
Economic factors	Insufficiency of equity (internal finance)	n	613	273	382	228	396	325	416	359
		%	41.0	18.2	25.5	15.2	26.5	21.7	27.8	24.0
	Lack of external sources of finance	n	683	297	313	203	445	300	400	351
		%	45.7	19.9	20.9	13.6	29.7	20.1	26.7	23.5
Knowledge factors	Lack of skilled labour force	n	506	389	429	172	419	472	476	129
		%	33.8	26.0	28.7	11.5	28.0	31.6	31.8	8.6
	Lack of information about technology	n	569	473	374	80	464	550	406	76
		%	38.0	31.6	25.0	5.3	31.0	36.8	27.1	5.1
	Lack of information about markets	n	615	469	329	83	472	546	401	77
		%	41.1	31.4	22.0	5.5	31.6	36.5	26.8	5.1
	Difficulty in finding innovation partners	n	680	319	336	161	504	408	420	164
		%	45.5	21.3	22.5	10.8	33.7	27.3	28.1	11.0
Market factors	Market dominated by established firms	n	599	317	393	187	417	399	485	195
		%	40.0	21.2	26.3	12.5	27.9	26.7	32.4	13.0
	Uncertainty about the demand	n	548	300	439	209	346	344	530	276
		%	36.6	20.1	29.3	14.0	23.1	23.0	35.4	18.4

Source: Author's computation based on the panel (CIS 6 and CIS 10)

some constraint. Hence, there is rationality in deciding not to innovate in the period, not to innovate at all, or to abandon the innovative activities (Blanchard et al. 2009).

The managerial strategy of the firm towards innovation is normally constrained; firms must be willing to innovate or not. Here, the focus is placed on those firms that do want to perform innovative activities despite not being capable to complete these actions due to due to the presence of obstacles (Blanchard et al. 2012). Former evidence refers that the negative effects of the obstacles are only effective for those firms willing to innovate. Whereas, the inference about innovative willingness is not possible in the CIS database, the data provides a binary classification of being innovative or not in the period.

Multiple innovative projects in different innovation vectors may coexist. Some of them will be completed others abandoned. Thus innovators will potentially abandon their innovative activities for several reasons: rationality or hampering factors.

Furthermore, among non-innovative firms two types of possible strategies emerge: firms that spontaneously opted for not innovating at all, therefore not being influenced by the barrier; firms that did not perform innovation in the period for strategic reasons, such as huge barriers to such an extent that these actions not even started and those that were not fortunate to conclude innovation due to the complete abandon of the projects in course. So, we have opted to consider the nil responses to the innovation question as it is important seizing the heterogeneity in this category. Exploratory analysis of the correlation allows decision to be made.

Hypothesis 1 Larger firms will have a lower probability of abandoning their innovative activities.

Very often the underlying reason to abandon the innovative activities is connected to the existence of financial constraints. Larger firms are expected to have an easier access to different financing sources either internal or external.

The access to public grants, bank overdrafts, venture capital or other credit and event to internal equity is easier in larger firms. With lower constraints in financing these actions large organizations are expected to have a simplified journey in pursuing innovative activities. Consequently is expectable that size negatively influences the abandon of innovative activities.

Hypothesis 2 Firms performing, at least, one innovation vector during the biennium will have a lower probability of abandoning their innovative activities.

If firms perform successful innovation, accumulation and feedback will be generated; the literature uses the expression "virtuous cycles". In consequence, firms perceive the advantages of introducing these novelties to the market and develop innovation in a continuous base, discouraging these organisations will be tougher as they understand the advantages and abandon only those projects which are economically unfeasible. Thus, innovative firms tend to be embedded in the innovation cycle and present a lower probability of abandon.

Hypothesis 3 The availability of top educated workers will reduce the probability of abandoning innovative activities.

In this point, the analysis will be twofold: in one side, by means of the analysis of the education intensity; on the other hand, the perception about the lack of qualified personnel (which operates as a barrier to the innovative projects).

Top educated workers will enhance the development of innovations and boosting the absorptive capacity. The human resources by using their skills with allow the firm to behave as an innovator or as an adopter. These human means will solve the problems in a daily basis, so the innovative processes have no reason to be delayed or postponed.

To our knowledge, more educated workers will rise the probability of success, therefore, the probability of abandon will follow; moreover, when the firms do not possess these employees they will probably perceive the lack of qualified personnel; the effects of these vectors on the probability to abandon will go in an opposite direction.

Hypothesis 4 Financial constraints will act as hampering factors in the development of innovative activities.

Innovation activities are by nature highly risky. When successful, these actions will produce high pay offs, although, the probability of failure is high. In adverse economic contexts managers tend to increase risk aversion, postponing risky actions. Lacking financing options will force in concentrating in routinely actions rather than in activities with uncertain results. As a consequence financial constraints are expected to positively influence the abandon of innovative activities.

Hypothesis 5 Public financing to develop innovative activities will reduce the probability of abandoning the innovative activities.

Due to information asymmetry and other failures, seizing external financing is a complex task. Hence, firms normally have insufficient internal finance to develop these actions; public financing will fulfill the gap of private investors, boosting innovative actions. Public funds will act as substitutes to private investors, thus reducing the probability of abandon the innovative activities.

Hypothesis 6 Uncertainty about the demand will raise the probability of abandoning the innovative activities.

The development of innovative activities face two major hurdles, the first being the feasibility of the project and the second its performance in the market (success towards the demand). Fearing a poor reception in the market may disincentive pursuing innovative actions. As a consequence, the uncertainty about the demand behavior is expected to raise the probability of abandoning the innovative activities.

3 Database and Panel Structural Traits

The panel of firms used for this analysis is extracted from the CIS. Firms were asked about their structural characteristics, their perception of the innovation barriers and about abandoning their innovative activities; this data will be used to highlight the systematization of abandoning firms, their individual heterogeneity, their perception about barriers and the effect of the crisis in these decisions observed by time variability.

3.1 Database

The analysis will comprise a panel of Portuguese firms constructed using data from the CIS 2006 and the CIS 2010 as firms are asked about innovation barriers each four years The two CIS waves include a total number of observations 10,881 firms (4721 firms in the CIS 6 and 6160 firms in the CIS 10), however, when building the panel we get 1496 firms observed in both periods.

A general overview about the panel of firms was run to identify biasedness or eventual insignificance of certain groups; the balanced results allowing segmentation through size, economic activity and technological intensity among others. Following a similar procedure of the CIS, barriers to innovation will be grouped, when needed, into funding factors, knowledge factors and market factors.

The database provides direct information about the abandon of innovative activities; perception about the different barriers to innovation and a set of firm structural characteristics such as size, SIC code, economic sector, technological intensity, sources of innovation, education intensity, R&D intensity which will be used to run the econometric estimations.

3.1.1 Size

The questions about innovation barriers are posed each 4 years, the periods of analysis are the CIS 6 and the CIS 10. The structural traits of the constructed panel, in what concerns the size, remain almost unchanged.

Small and medium sized firms comprise nearly four fifths of the panel, achieving similar proportions, and around one fifth includes large firms. The literature mentions the fact the small firms face increased barriers to innovation as they need to tackle financial constraints and risk aversion, whereas large firms will overcome eventual constraints based on internal equity or credibility towards creditors (Fig. 2).

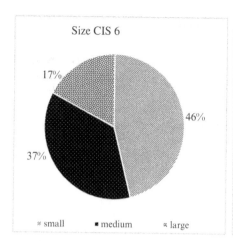
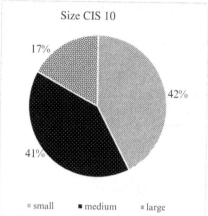

Fig. 2 Proportion of firms in the panel per size. Source: Author's computation based on the panel (CIS 6 and 10)

3.1.2 Economic Sector

No changes are found in the two time periods respectively to the economic sector, the proportion of firms is exactly the same. This result was absolutely predictable as the firm economic sector is a time invariant individual characteristic, considering that we are observing exactly the same firms no changes were expected to happen. The panel includes 60% of firms operating in the secondary sector, 38% in the tertiary and 2% in the primary. This portrait is illustrative of the aggregate Portuguese reality. The intense representation of industrial activities will allow for the conventional analysis in terms of innovation activities, even though this study is comprehensive (Fig. 3).

3.1.3 Economic Group

The majority of the firms in the panel belongs to an economic group. The fact of integrating a group will enhance the endowments of financial and human resources, therefore the perception in terms of the barriers is expected to decrease. In the firm waves of the panel 60% of the firms belong to a group, and societal changes were operated in such a way that in the CIS 10 this percentage went to 55% (Fig. 4).

3.1.4 Technological Intensity

Nearly a half of the firms belongs to a high tech sector, the expectable dynamism in terms of innovative activities is high, forcing the firms to overcome the difficulties in terms of innovation (Fig. 5).

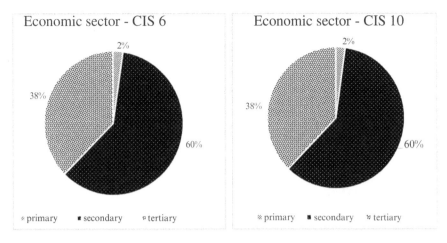

Fig. 3 Proportion of firms in the panel per economic sector. Source: Author's computation based on the panel (CIS 6 and 10)

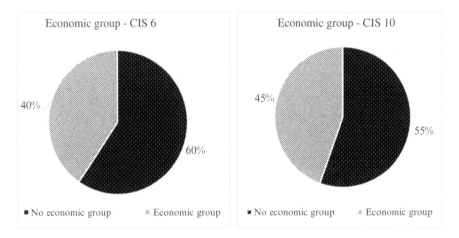

Fig. 4 Proportion of firms in the panel per economic group. Source: Author's computation based on the panel (CIS 6 and 10)

In the first wave the proportion of high tech firms was 51% moving to 47% in the second wave; in the mid tech 31% in the first and 34% in the second. Low tech firms represented 18% in the first wave, 19% in the second. The explanation for this result relies on the fact that Portuguese firms have two alternative SIC codes and the one that absorbs the higher percentage of the turnover is reported to the questionnaire.

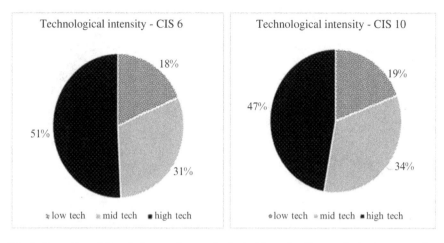

Fig. 5 Proportion of firms in the panel per technological intensity. Source: Author's computation based on the panel (CIS 6 and 10)

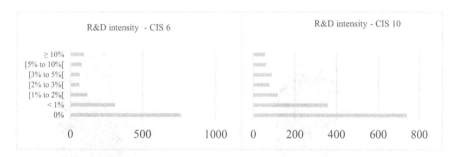

Fig. 6 Proportion of firms in the panel per R&D intensity. Source: Author's computation based on the panel (CIS 6 and 10)

3.1.5 R&D Intensity

Most of the firms in the panel reported not devoting any financial resources to R&D activities. The total number of firms was 763 for the CIS 6 and 739 in the CIS 10. The pattern remained almost unchanged in both periods, a remarkable proportion of firms mentioned R&D intensities above the European target of 3% in both cases. The economic effects of the crisis were expected to decrease the firms' propensity to pursuit these actions, the changes are not noticeable. Indeed, the top intensities grasp a smaller proportion of firms but on average the results are similar (Fig. 6).

3.1.6 Education Intensity

An important evolution in terms of the education intensity is noticed among the respondent firms. The proportion of firms with no top educated workers felt

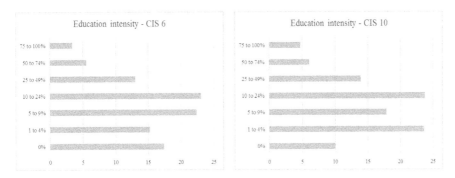

Fig. 7 Proportion of firms in the panel per Education intensity. Source: Author's computation based on the panel (CIS 6 and 10)

significantly from 17.4 to 10%. Contrarily, the proportion of firms mentioning having 1–4% of the labour force highly educated rose from 15.2 to 23.7%. In the extreme scales the proportion remained almost unchanged. This evidence unveils the policy efforts developed to provide the working population with higher schooling degrees. This effort aims to furnish the entrepreneurs the human capital required to develop innovative actions thus raising productivity levels (Fig. 7).

3.1.7 Openness

Firms are expected to rely on the sources to overcome eventual barriers in their individual endowments of resources. The development of networks will enhance the construction of innovative projects in cooperation with other institutions while overcoming the eventual barriers. Still any internal constraints may act as barriers themselves, such as the poor absorptive capacity. Not using any of the possible sources was 39.4% in the CIS 6 and 37.8% in the CIS 10, no remarkable changes were presented. The highest score reaches 14.1% in the CIS 6 and 21.1% in this CIS 10. This suggests economic environment influenced the second (Fig. 8).

3.1.8 Funds

A frequent handicap towards innovative activities is the lack of finance. Policy makers actively seek to provide the firms the possibility to use public finance to support their innovative activities. Public funding is a strong policy recommendation in the present economic environment, whereas its full extent has not yet been quantified. In the panel we observed that in the first wave 88% of the firms did not rely on public funning to develop their innovative activities, and this proportion decreased in the second wave, being 79%,. Desirably, public funding will allow overcoming the internal scarcity on finance, illustrated by means of the financial barriers (Fig. 9).

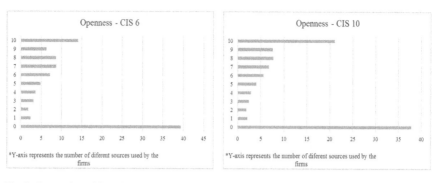

Fig. 8 Proportion of firms in the panel per openness intensity. Source: Author's computation based on the panel (CIS 6 and 10)

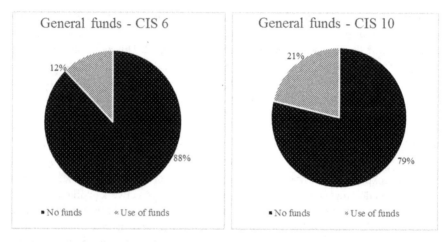

Fig. 9 Proportion of firms in the panel using funds. Source: Author's computation based on the panel (CIS 6 and 10)

4 Econometric Estimations

In this part, underlying methodological issues will be discussed along with the estimations and the results. To summarise the previous theoretical debate, the following table describes the hypothesis in test and the empirical findings. The details will be found in the rest of this section (Table 2).

4.1 Model Specification

The analysis of the probability of abandoning the innovative activities will be modeled by means of a panel comprising two time periods. The objective is to get

Table 2 Summary of the hypothesis in analysis

Hypothesis	Description	Results
[H1]	Larger firms will have a lower probability of abandoning their innovative activities	Unsupported
[H2]	Firms performing at least on innovation vector in the period are less prone to abandon their innovative	Supported
[H3]	Availability of too educated workers will reduce the innovation abandon (education intensity and lack of qualified personnel)	Supported
[H4]	Financial constraints will force the firms to abandon their innovative activities: internal and external	Supported
[H5]	Relying on public funds to develop the innovative activities will reduce the probability of abandoning the innovative activities	Unsupported
[H6]	Uncertainty about the demand will increase the probability of abandoning the innovative activities	Supported (opposite direction of the effects)

Source: Author's composition according to the literature and the econometric results

a full understanding about the role of the obstacles to innovation in the abandon of the innovative activities. Due to self-selection, firms which start an innovation activity are very prone to succeed. If firms perceive important obstacles they will naturally tend to postpone or even to abandon their innovative activities.

4.2 Operationalisation (Proxies)

To examine the determinants of abandoning the innovative activities at the firm level the endogenous variable (abandon), will be binary. It will take the value 1 if the firms did mention having abandoned innovative activities in the period, zero otherwise.

As explanatory variables, the models include firms's structural traits, innovative performance in the different innovation vectors, the use of some sources of innovation and the different barriers.

It is worth mentioning that the CIS collects information about barriers to innovation in a multinomial scale: the barrier can be considered as not being experienced (0), experienced but with a low impact (1), medium (2) or high (3). Consequently, dummy variables are generated to capture the marginal impact of the different intensities perceived. In Appendices 1 and 2 variable description and estimation results can be found.

4.3 Econometric Estimations

The random effects probit model to explain the determinants of the abandon of the innovative activities are run the different models. It is of worth mentioning that correlation tables were run and the different barriers to innovation are positively correlated with a high degree of significance. The abandon of the innovative activities will be determined by the firm structural traits, some innovation determinants and the innovation barriers. Firms are asked about innovation barriers each four years; this means that to construct the panel we have taken into account the CIS 6 and the CIS 10.

Despite the awareness of the aggregation made in the CIS, the models include each innovation barrier in separate as well as a dummy variable to capture the marginal effect of the intensity to capture the detailed effect of each hampering factor in the different degrees.

The panel is strongly balanced as only firms responding to the two CIS waves were taken into account. Thus the structure comprises 1496 firms observed in the two biennia. A random effects probit model is run having the abandon of the innovative activities as endogenous variable and different combinations of explanatory variables in the different models. Model 1 illustrates the general model of innovation abandon considering structural traits and innovative variables; Model 2 controls per economic sector, being the benchmark the primary sector.

The random effects probit regression constructed to capture the general effects of the structural traits, the innovation strategies and the barriers to innovation produced the following general results: structural traits, with the exception of being an innovator fail to be statistically significant, the perception of the barriers increases the probability of abandoning the innovative activities as expected.

Being an innovator, independent on the vector, during the period decreases the probability of abandoning the innovative activities in 22.4 percentage points compared to the non-innovative firms. Figure is a natural part of the innovative process, still firms performing innovative actions perceive the gains obtained from these actions; therefore, they will continue the innovative path facing its positive and the negative achievements. This result goes along with our understanding that analysing only innovative firms in the period may be insufficient.

Innovation is a strategic option and part of a general behaviour; firms following this strategy will be less prone to abandon the innovative activities.

Being an occasional innovator will raise the probability of abandoning the innovative activities in 12 percentage points compared to the non-occasional innovators. In the case of persistent innovators, the probability of abandoning increases for 21.4 percentage points compared to the not persistent. These results and its significance allow us to understand that firms with a very active approach towards innovative activities are also those who abandon them more often.

Performing innovative activities by means of drawing upon external knowledge raises the probability of abandoning the innovative activities.

The perception of financial barriers with low intensity raises the probability of abandoning the innovative activities by 8.3 percentage points compared to the firms that found the availability of internal finance as being irrelevant.

Finding the availability of internal finance as a very important barrier rises the probability of abandoning innovative activities by 10.6 percentage points, compared to the firms that found it irrelevant.

Therefore, the lack of internal finance is a determinant to the increased probability of abandoning innovative activities. The perception of external finance as a barrier to innovative activities is significant, although, increasing the perception of the difficulty decrease the probability of abandon; the expected effect is opposite from this result (Table 3).

Finding the cost of innovation as being high, therefore a barrier to innovation, at a low level, raises the probability of abandoning the innovative activities in 6.6 percentage points compared to those firms that found this barrier as not experienced.

The difficulty in finding innovation partners is also significant. Firms that did find this component as a very important barrier to the innovative activities have an increased probability of abandoning the innovative activities of 10.7 percentage points compared to those that find it irrelevant.

The fact of perceiving the operation in a dominated market will also raise the probability of abandoning innovative activities by 9 percentage points (Table 4).

When controlling for the economic sector, similar results hold. Innovative firms, independent on the vector have a lower probability to abandon the innovative activities.

The lack of internal finance will increase the probabilities of abandoning the innovative activities. External finance is another significant barrier, although the estimated signal is opposite from what was expectable.

The consideration of innovation to be too expensive is also statistically significant. Firms that did find innovative activities as being too expensive at a low or moderate degree have an increased probability to abandon the innovative activities of 6.7 and 6.8 percentage points compared to those who found it irrelevant.

The lack of trained personnel is a significant barrier to innovative activities. Firms that perceive the lack of qualified personnel with a high degree of importance raise the probability of abandoning the innovative activities.

5 Conclusion

According to either Schumpeter mark I or II, firm size should affect the propensity to abandon the innovative activities, still, the econometric results point to the irrelevance of size in terms of abandoning the innovative processes. These findings shed some light to the preconceived idea that small firms have weaker innovative structures which become more volatile under unstable environments thus raising the abandon.

Table 3 Model 1—Average marginal effects Random effects probit estimation without sectoral control

Probit	Variable Pr (Use)	Probit (cont.)	Variable Pr (Use)	Probit (cont.)	Variable Pr (Use)	Probit (cont.)	Variable Pr(Use)	Probit (cont.)	Variable Pr(Use)
Size_medium	0.010 (0.025)	Intern_sourc_med	0.003 (0.049)	Education_intensity	−0.003 (0.008)	_Ibarr_inov_1	0.066* (0.038)	Barr_mkt_info_med	−0.055 (0.043)
Size_large	0.037 (0.030)	Intern_sourc_high	0.008 (0.048)	Occasional_Innov	0.120*** (0.027)	_Ibarr_inov_2	0.067* (0.037)	Barr_mkt_info_high	−0.103 (0.064)
Group	−0.027 (0.025)	Univ_source_low	−0.049 (0.035)	Persistent_innov	0.214*** (0.027)	_Ibarr_inov_3	0.050 (0.042)	Barr_partner_low	0.046 (0.033)
Tech_intens_medium	−0.024 (0.029)	Univ_sou_medium	−0.024 (0.036)	Innov_ext_know	0.057*** (0.022)	Barr_person_low	0.008 (0.039)	Barr_partner_med	0.031 (0.035)
Tech_inte_high	−0.012 (0.028)	Univ_sou_high	−0.012 (0.028)	Barr_capin_low	0.083** (0.036)	Barr_person_med	0.039 (0.041)	Barr_partner_high	0.107** (0.043)
Innov_geral	−0.224** (0.095)	Public_sou_low	0.061 (0.044)	Barr_capin_med	0.002 (0.037)	Barr_person_high	0.100** (0.048)	Barr_mkt_low	−0.036 (0.035)
Expenditures_RD	1.95×10^{-9} (1.8×10^{-9})	Publ_sou_medium	0.017 (0.033)	Barr_capin_high	0.106** (0.042)	Barr_tech_info_low	0.019 (0.041)	Barr_mkt_med	0.004 (0.035)
Funds	0.017 (0.023)	Public_sou_high	0.061 (0.038)	Barr_capex_low	−0.128*** (0.035)	Barr_tech_info_med	−0.007 (0.048)	Barr_mkt_high	0.090** (0.039)
Openness	0.005 (0.007)	RD_intensity	0.012 (0.053)	Barr_capex_med	−0.106*** (0.036)	Barr_tech_info_high	−0.021 (0.068)	Barr_uncert_low	−0.086** (0.034)
Intern_sourc_low	−0.001 (0.065)	Turnover_growth_rate	0.00 (0.001)	Barr_capex_high	−0.129*** (0.041)	Barr_mkt_info_low	−0.040 (0.035)	Barr_uncert_med	−0.051 (0.034)
			1.547×10^{-4} (1.145×10^{-4})					Barr_uncert_high	−0.048 (0.041)

Source: Author's computation based on the panel constructed considering the CIS 6 and CIS 10. Standard errors (in brackets) are showed. ***, ** and * indicate the significance on a 1%, 5% and 10% level, respectively

Note: Details about innovation barriers likewise Table 1

Table 4 Model 2—Average marginal effects Random effects probit estimation with sectoral control (industry and services—benchmark, agriculture)

Probit — Variable	Pr (Use)	Probit (cont.) — Variable	Pr (Use)	Probit (cont.) — Variable	Pr (Use)	Probit (cont.) — Variable	Pr(Use)	Probit (cont.) — Variable	Pr(Use)
Size_medium	0.009 (0.025)	Intern_sourc_high	0.007 (0.048)	Persistent_innov	0.212*** (0.027)	Barr_person_low	0.008 (0.039)	Barr_partner_med	0.031 (0.035)
Size_large	0.035 (0.030)	Univ_source_low	−0.051 (0.035)	Innov_ext_know	0.058*** (0.022)	Barr_person_med	0.039 (0.041)	Barr_partner_high	0.107** (0.043)
Group	−0.025 (0.024)	Univ_sou_medium	−0.026 (0.036)	Barr_capin_low	0.085** (0.036)	Barr_person_high	0.097*** (0.048)	Barr_mkt_low	−0.036 (0.035)
Tech_intens_medium	−0.016 (0.030)	Univ_sou_high	−0.026 (0.036)	Barr_capin_med	0.003 (0.037)	Barr_tech_info_low	0.017 (0.041)	Barr_mkt_med	0.004 (0.035)
Tech_inte_high	−0.007 (00.029)	Public_sou_low	0.059 (0.044)	Barr_capin_high	0.106** (0.042)	Barr_tech_info_med	−0.008 (0.048)	Barr_mkt_high	0.089** (0.039)
Innov_geral	−0.225** (0.095)	Publ_sou_med	0.061 (0.039)	Barr_capex_low	−0.129*** (0.035)	Barr_tech_info_high	−0.022 (0.068)	Barr_uncert_low	−0.086** (0.034)
Expenditures_RD	2×10^{-9} (1.81×10^{-9})	Pub_sou_high	0.011 (0.053)	Barr_capex_med	−0.107*** (0.036)	Barr_mkt_info_low	−0.040 (0.035)	Barr_uncert_med	−0.051 (0.034)
Funds	0.016 (0.023)	RD_intensity	0.001 (0.001)	Barr_capex_high	−0.131*** (0.041)	Barr_mkt_info_med	−0.055 (0.043)	Barr_uncert_high	−0.048 (0.041)
Openess	0.005 (0.006)	Turnover_growth_rate	1.554×10^{-4} (1.151×10^{-4})	Barr_too_exp_low	0.067* (0.038)	Barr_mkt_info_high	−0.102 (0.064)	Industry	0.114 (0.087)
Intern_sourc_low	1.54×10^{-5} (0.065)	Education_intensity	−0.002 (0.008)	Barr_too_exp_med	0.068* (0.037)	Barr_partner_low	0.046 (0.033)	Services	0.101 (0.089)
Intern_sourc_med	3.822×10^{-4} (0.049)	Occasional_Innov	0.121*** (0.027)	Barr_too_exp_high	0.050 (0.042)				

Source: Author's computation based on the panel constructed considering the CIS 6 and CIS 10. Standard errors (in brackets) are showed. ***, ** and * indicate the significance on a 1%, 5% and 10% level, respectively

Note: Details about innovation barriers likewise Table 1

Another common belief is that firms belonging to economic groups have smoother innovative behaviours, meaning that the abandon was expectably lower in these cases. The results contradict this idea, being part of a group is statistically insignificant to the probability of abandoning the innovative actions; this finding is of particular interest as policy makers frequently argue in favour of fiscal benefits to be granted to these firms as they are seen as innovation anchors.

As expected, being an innovator decreases the probability to abandon, independent on the model in consideration; this result should reinforce the design policy innovation actions to benefit innovative firms, independent of the type of innovation in progress.

To prove the strategical bases of abandon, expenditures in R&D or even R&D intensity fail to be significant in affecting the propensity to abandon; this reinforces the idea that interrupting innovative processes is a natural managerial option with underlying economic rationale. Most of the theoretical contributions justify the abandon with scant economic resources; still it is not so linear.

Reinforcing the logic of strategic abandon, variables like openness, and the dummies proxying sources such as Universities or Public institutes fail to be relevant to determine the propensity to abandon. Overall, using these external sources of relevant knowledge to innovation could perhaps minimise some scarcity of funds, particularly under a period of economic turbulence, which does not happen.

The availability of skilled labour force among the staff members should rise the effectiveness of the innovative activities and as well as the abandon on innovation; again, no significance is found, which to some extent reinforces the thesis that interrupting these projects proves tactical view rather than incapability. Policy makers should be careful in analysing these results and consider that artificially maintaining some innovative project may constitute a waste of public resources.

Notwithstanding, the innovative strategy of the firm should not be neglected by the authorities when designing the policy instruments, as being an occasional or a persistent innovator raises the probability to abandon compared to the non-innovative firms. Occasional innovators are, for certain, problem solvers, firms that show smart strategic innovative tactics and they are ready to abandon innovative projects when they feel to. At a first glance the expected result of these controls was believed to be negative, but, once more, abandon appears as being intentional.

Our findings highlight in one hand the fact that firms performing innovation are less prone to abandon the innovation this will reinforce the theoretical, framework of innovation persistence; on the other hand, persistent innovators have a higher propensity to abandon. Combined, these results show that firms will pursue the projects they believe as being profitable and naturally releasing the burden of the non-profitable ones. So, there is a deliberate strategy of (non)continuity which should be carefully taken into account by the authorities when financing innovation.

Most of the literature points the lack of finance as being the major hampering factor towards the innovative activities (e.g. Galia et al. 2012; Galia and Legros 2004; García-Vega and López 2010; Savignac 2008). Due to the ability of seizing finance from external sources, large firms will be less prone to find innovative barriers, therefore less prone to abandon the innovative activities. To us, this hypothesis is not supported.

As expected, financial constraints raise the probability of abandoning the innovative activities as discussed by Galia and Legros (2004), and García-Vega and López (2010).

In our models, finance should be meticulously analysed given that multiple effects are included in the regression: relying on public funds, using internal and external finance. The first does not affect the probability to abandon, which to some extent is interesting as it seems that the abandon will happen, independent of the availability of funds, as firms find useless continuing these actions even benefitting from public finance. It was expectable that firms relying on public funding would be less prone to abandon the innovative activities as their financial constraints are reduced.

Internal financial constraints play a major role in the abandon of the innovative activities, reinforcing the idea that the availability of external funds to pursue innovation is scarce due to moral hazard. Low finance seems to be determinant in innovation abandon.

The perception of external financial constraints exerts an opposite effect, which is eventually preoccupying, as it may suggest that fearing the misjudgments of the external investors may force firms to continue projects otherwise abandoned. Perhaps managers prefer some waste of resources in less effective innovation rather than eroding the confidence of their investors.

Those organisations with difficulties in hiring qualified personnel are also more vulnerable to innovation abandon, which from a tactical point of view is logic. Fearing some weaknesses in terms of development, adoption or diffusion of the novelties, they prefer to abandon the projects rather than wasting the endowments of resources.

Diffusing the risk of the innovative activities by means of implementing these actions together with some partners is something firms often adopt; therefore, those firms that are incapable of finding partners to innovate in their productive chain are more prone to abandon innovation. Yet again, authorities should promote the establishment of solid linkages among firms and draw policy schemes to positively discriminate cooperant firms. In the Portuguese context where an important part of firms is young and small this action is even more useful. Moreover, the results highlight the higher probability of abandon when firms perceive that the market is dominated by already established companies.

It seems that innovation abandon far more deliberate than one should think; and, this is happening for strategical reasons more often than for the lack of finance. In one hand it seems that the available funds are insufficient to convince the corporations to continue some projects, but, on the other hand it seems a wise use of the public funds. The irrelevance of size should convince policy makers that large corporations should not absorb the public funds. The same should happen concerning sectors of activity as they are shown as irrelevant, so, efficient firms should be granted rather than specific activities.

Considering the present implementation of the RIS3 (Regional innovation strategy for smart specialization) that has been taken the public debate in Europe, special attention should be paid the insignificant coefficients of the University and the increased abandon caused by the inexistence of partners. To some extent these results point to an inoperative triple helix whose consolidation should be made under the leadership of the authorities conglomerating a cohesive policy strategy at all Governance levels. The future brings serious challenges as resources must be efficiently used and sustainable outcome are required.

Appendix 1

Model 1: Determinants of the Abandon of the Innovative Activities Random Effects Probit Regression—General Model

Variable	Description	Estimate	SE	p-value	[95% Conf. Interval]	
_Isize_3	Firm Size—Medium	0.038	0.098	0.697	−0.154	0.230
_Isize_4	Firm Size—Large	0.143	0.116	0.217	−0.084	0.370
group	Economic Group	−0.103	0.095	0.276	−0.289	0.083
_Itech_inte_2	Tech Intensity—Mid Tech	−0.092	0.114	0.417	−0.315	0.130
_Itech_inte_3	Tech Intensity—High Tech	−0.045	0.107	0.674	−0.254	0.164
innov_general	In in one vector (at least)	−0.870	0.373	0.02	−1.601	−0.139
Exp/RD_TOTAL	Exp RD T (RDTOTAL) €	7.54×10^{-9}	7.01×10^{-9}	0.282	-6.2×10^{-9}	2.13×10^{-8}
FUNDS_GEN	Use of funds to innovate	0.064	0.087	0.461	−0.107	0.235
OPENNESS	Openness to sou innov	0.018	0.025	0.477	−0.031	0.067
Internal_S_Low		−0.006	0.250	0.982	−0.496	0.485
Internal_S_Mid		0.010	0.190	0.959	−0.362	0.382
Internal_S_High		0.030	0.187	0.873	−0.336	0.396
University_Low		−0.188	0.137	0.171	−0.457	0.081
University_Mid		−0.093	0.139	0.505	−0.366	0.180
University_High		0.235	0.172	0.172	−0.103	0.573
Public_Low		0.066	0.127	0.605	−0.183	0.314
Public_Mid		0.236	0.150	0.115	−0.058	0.530
Public_High		0.048	0.205	0.816	−0.355	0.450

(continued)

Variable	Description	Estimate	SE	p-value	[95% Conf. Interval]	
RD_intensity	R&D exp to Turnover Ratio	0.002	0.002	0.39	−0.003	0.007
Turnover_GR	Turn Growth Rate—(%)	0.001	4.456×10^{-3}	0.179	-2.74×10^{-4}	0.001
Education_intensity	% LF undergr training or more	−0.012	0.031	0.695	−0.073	0.049
_IOcasio_act_i_1	Performing Innov Act Ocas	0.465	0.108	0.000	0.253	0.677
_IPersis_act_i_2	Performing Innov Act Pers	0.829	0.116	0.000	0.602	1.056
act_in_extl_know	R&D Act Ext Knowledge	0.221	0.084	0.008	0.056	0.385
_Ibarr_capi_1		0.323	0.140	0.021	0.049	0.597
_Ibarr_capi_2		0.007	0.143	0.962	−0.274	0.287
_Ibarr_capi_3		0.409	0.164	0.013	0.088	0.730
_Ibarr_capia1		−0.495	0.139	0.000	−0.767	−0.222
_Ibarr_capia2		−0.410	0.140	0.003	−0.685	−0.136
_Ibarr_capia3		−0.502	0.161	0.002	−0.816	−0.187
_Ibarr_inov_1		0.255	0.149	0.087	−0.037	0.547
_Ibarr_inov_2		0.261	0.146	0.074	−0.025	0.547
_Ibarr_inov_3		0.192	0.162	0.238	−0.126	0.510
_Ibarr_pess_1		0.030	0.151	0.845	−0.266	0.325
_Ibarr_pess_2		0.152	0.158	0.334	−0.157	0.462
_Ibarr_pess_3		0.387	0.186	0.038	0.021	0.752
_Ibarr_info_1		0.073	0.160	0.649	−0.241	0.386
_Ibarr_info_2		−0.027	0.184	0.883	−0.388	0.334
_Ibarr_info_3		−0.083	0.264	0.754	−0.601	0.435
_Ibarr_infoa1		−0.156	0.138	0.257	−0.426	0.114
_Ibarr_infoa2		−0.214	0.167	0.201	−0.543	0.114
_Ibarr_infoa3		−0.399	0.250	0.11	−0.888	0.091
_Ibarr_parc_1		0.179	0.127	0.158	−0.069	0.428
_Ibarr_parc_2		0.118	0.135	0.382	−0.147	0.383
_Ibarr_parc_3		0.414	0.169	0.014	0.083	0.744
_Ibarr_merc_1		−0.138	0.136	0.31	−0.404	0.128
_Ibarr_merc_2		0.017	0.135	0.90	−0.247	0.281
_Ibarr_merc_3		0.348	0.154	0.024	0.047	0.650
_Ibarr_ince_1		−0.335	0.134	0.013	−0.597	−0.072
_Ibarr_ince_2		−0.198	0.134	0.141	−0.461	0.065
_Ibarr_ince_3		−0.185	0.161	0.252	−0.501	0.132
_cons		−0.610	0.405	0.132	−1.404	0.184

Source: Author's computation based on the panel constructed considering the CIS 6 and CIS 10
Note: Random effects probit regression N = 1839 responses from 1167 subjects; Wald test of H0: $\alpha = \beta = 0$ has $\chi^2_{51} = 160.63$ (p-value < 0.001)

Appendix 2

Model 2: Determinants of the Abandon of the Innovative Activities Random Effects Probit Regression—Controlling by Sector

Variable	Estimate	SE	p-value	[95% Conf. Interval]	
_Isize_3	0.034	0.098	0.727	−0.157	0.226
_Isize_4	0.135	0.116	0.246	−0.093	0.362
group	−0.098	0.095	0.300	−0.283	0.087
_Itech_inte_2	−0.060	0.118	0.610	−0.292	0.171
_Itech_inte_3	−0.027	0.114	0.815	−0.250	0.196
innov_general	−0.871	0.373	0.019	−1.602	−0.141
gastos_rd_total	7.76×10^{-9}	7.05×10^{-9}	0.271	-6.05×10^{-9}	2.16×10^{-8}
FUNDS_GEN.	0.061	0.088	0.488	−0.112	0.234
OPENNESS	0.019	0.025	0.453	−0.030	0.068
Internal_S_Low	5.95×10^{-4}	0.251	1.000	−0.491	0.491
Internal_S_Mid	0.001	0.191	0.994	−0.372	0.375
Internal_S_High	0.028	0.187	0.883	−0.340	0.395
University_Low	−0.196	0.138	0.154	−0.466	0.074
University_Mid	−0.101	0.139	0.471	−0.374	0.173
University_High	0.227	0.173	0.189	−0.112	0.566
Public_Low	0.068	0.127	0.595	−0.181	0.316
Public_Mid	0.237	0.151	0.116	−0.058	0.532
Public_High	0.042	0.205	0.836	−0.360	0.445
RD_intensity	0.002	0.002	0.376	−0.003	0.007
Turnover_growth_rate	0.001	4.483×10^{-4}	0.179	-2.763×10^{-4}	0.001
Education_intensity	−0.009	0.032	0.782	−0.073	0.055
_IOcasional_act_i_1	0.468	0.108	0.000	0.255	0.680
_IPersistent_act_i_2	0.823	0.117	0.000	0.594	1.052
act_innov_external_know	0.223	0.084	0.008	0.059	0.388
_Ibarr_capi_1	0.331	0.140	0.018	0.057	0.605
_Ibarr_capi_2	0.013	0.143	0.928	−0.268	0.293
_Ibarr_capi_3	0.412	0.164	0.012	0.091	0.734
_Ibarr_capia1	−0.500	0.139	0.000	−0.771	−0.228
_Ibarr_capia2	−0.417	0.140	0.003	−0.691	−0.143
_Ibarr_capia3	−0.507	0.160	0.002	−0.821	−0.193
_Ibarr_inov_1	0.259	0.149	0.081	−0.032	0.551
_Ibarr_inov_2	0.262	0.146	0.073	−0.024	0.547
_Ibarr_inov_3	0.195	0.162	0.228	−0.122	0.513
_Ibarr_pess_1	0.031	0.151	0.835	−0.264	0.327
_Ibarr_pess_2	0.153	0.158	0.333	−0.156	0.462
_Ibarr_pess_3	0.378	0.186	0.043	0.012	0.743
_Ibarr_info_1	0.067	0.160	0.674	−0.247	0.382
_Ibarr_info_2	−0.029	0.184	0.874	−0.390	0.332
_Ibarr_info_3	−0.086	0.264	0.745	−0.603	0.432
_Ibarr_infoa1	−0.153	0.138	0.267	−0.424	0.118
_Ibarr_infoa2	−0.214	0.168	0.201	−0.543	0.114
_Ibarr_infoa3	−0.396	0.250	0.113	−0.885	0.094

(continued)

Variable	Estimate	SE	p-value	[95% Conf. Interval]	
_Ibarr_parc_1	0.178	0.127	0.16	−0.071	0.427
_Ibarr_parc_2	0.119	0.136	0.38	−0.147	0.385
_Ibarr_parc_3	0.415	0.169	0.014	0.084	0.747
_Ibarr_merc_1	−0.140	0.136	0.302	−0.406	0.126
_Ibarr_merc_2	0.015	0.135	0.909	−0.249	0.280
_Ibarr_merc_3	0.344	0.154	0.026	0.042	0.647
_Ibarr_ince_1	−0.333	0.134	0.013	−0.595	−0.070
_Ibarr_ince_2	−0.199	0.134	0.138	−0.463	0.064
_Ibarr_ince_3	−0.185	0.161	0.251	−0.501	0.131
_Isector_2	0.440	0.338	0.193	−0.222	1.103
_Isector_3	0.392	0.344	0.254	−0.281	1.066
_cons	−1.051	0.526	0.046	−2.081	−0.020

Source: Author's computation based on the panel constructed considering the CIS 6 and CIS 10
Note: Random effects probit regression N = 1839 responses from 1167 subjects; Wald test of H0: $\alpha = \beta = 0$ has $\chi^2_{53} = 160.85$ (p-value < 0.001)

References

Acs, Z., & Audretsch, D. (1987). Innovation, market structure, and firm size. *The Review of Economics and Statistics, 69*(4), 567–575.

Acs, Z., & Audretsch, D. (1988). Innovation in large and small firms: An empirical analysis. *American Economic Review, 78*, 680–681.

Asplund, M., & Sandin, R. (1999). The survival of new products. *Review of Industrial Organization, 15*, 219–237.

Baldwin, J., & Lin, Z. (2002). Impediments to advanced technology adoption for Canadian manufacturers. *Research Policy, 31*, 1–18.

Bhattacharya, S., & Ritter, J. (1985). Innovation and communication: Signalling with partial disclosure. *Review of Economic Studies, 50*, 331–346.

Blanchard, P., Huiban, J.-P., Musolesi, A., & Sevestre, P. (2009). Where there is a will, there is a way? Assessing the impact of obstacles to innovation. In *Paper presented at 3rd ICEE*, Ancona, Italy.

Blanchard, P., Huiban, J.-P., Musolesi, A., & Sevestre, P. (2012). Where there is a will, there is a way? Assessing the impact of obstacles to innovation. *Industrial and Corporate Change, 22*(3), 679–710.

Borgelt, K., & Falk, I. (2007). The leadership/management conundrum: Innovation or risk management? *Leadership & Organization Development Journal, 28*(2), 122–136.

Canepa, A., & Stoneman, P. (2002). *Financial constraints on innovations: A European cross-country study* (Working Paper no. 02–11, Kiel Institute of World Economics).

Cefis, E., & Marsili, O. (2006). Survivor: The role of innovation in firms' survival. *Research Policy, 35*, 626–641.

Cozijnsen, A., Vrakking, W., & IJzerloo, M. (2000). Success and failure of 50 innovation projects in Dutch companies. *European Journal of Innovation Management, 3*(3), 150–159.

Freel, M. (2000). Do small innovating firms outperform non-innovators? *Small Business Economics, 14*(3), 195–210.

Galia, F., & Legros, D. (2004). Complementarities between obstacles to innovation: Evidence from France. *Research Policy, 33*, 1185–1199.

Galia, F., & Legros, D. (2012). Complementarities between obstacles to innovation: Empirical study on a French Data Set. *Paper presented at the DRUID Summer Conference 2003 on industrial dynamics of the new and old economy – Who is embracing whom?* June 2003.

Galia, F., Mancini, S., & Morandi, V. (2012). Obstacles to innovation: What hampers innovation in France and Italy? *Paper presented to DRUID Society 2012*.

Garcia, R., & Calantone, R. (2002). A critical look at technological innovation typology and innovativeness terminology: A literature review. *The Journal of Product Innovation Management, 19*, 110–132.

García-Vega, M., & López, A. (2010). Determinants of abandoning innovative activities: Evidence from Spanish firms. *Cuadernos de Economía y Dirección de la Empresa, 13*, 69–91.

Geroski, P., Machin, S., & van Reenen, J. (1993). The profitability of innovating firms. *The RAND Journal of Economics, 24*(2), 198–211.

Hadjimanolis, A. (1999). Barriers to innovation for SMEs in a small less developed country (Cyprus). *Technovation, 19*, 561–570.

Hajivassiliou, V., & Savingnac, F. (2008). Financing constraints and a firm's decision and ability to innovate: Establishing direct and reverse effects. Notes d'Études et de Recherche 202, Banque de France.

Heunks, F. (1998). Innovation, creativity and success. *Small Business Economics, 10*, 263–272.

Landry, R., Amara, N., & Becheikh, N. (2008). Exploring innovation failures in manufacturing industries. *Paper presented at the 25th DRUID Conference*. Available at http://www2.druid.dk/conferences/viewpaper.php?id=3378&cf=29

Lööf, H., & Heshmati, A. (2006). On the relationship between innovation and performance: A sensitivity analysis. *Economics of Innovation and New Technology, 15*(4/5), 317–344.

Madrid-Guijarro, A., Garcia, D., & Auken, H. (2009). Barriers to innovation among Spanish manufacturing SMEs. *Journal of Small Business Management, 47*(4), 465–488.

Maidique, M. A., & Zirger, B. J. (1985). The new product learning cycle. *Research Policy, 14*(6), 299–313.

Mohnen, P., & Röller, L.-H. (2005). Complementarities in innovation policy. *European Economic Review, 49*, 1431–1450.

Mohnen, P., & Rosa, J. (2002). Barriers to innovation in service industries in Canada. In M. Feldman & N. Massard (Eds.), *Institutions and systems in the geography of innovation* (Vol. 25, pp. 231–250). Boston: Kluwer Academic Publishers.

Mohnen, P., Palm, F. C., Loeff, S., & Tiwari, A. (2008). Financial constraints and other obstacles: Are they a threat to innovation activity? *De Economist, 156*(2), 201–214.

Myers, S., & Majluf, N. (1984). Corporate financing and investment decisions when firms have information that investors do not have. *Journal of Financial Economics, 13*, 187–221.

OECD. (2012). *Innovation in the crisis and beyond*. OECD Science, Technology and Industry Outlook 2012.

Sadowski, B., & Sadowski-Rasters, G. (2006). On the innovativeness of foreign affiliates: Evidence from companies in The Netherlands. *Research Policy, 35*(3), 447–462.

Savignac, F. (2008). Impact of financial constraints on innovation: What can be learned from a direct measure? *Economics of Innovation and New Technology, 17*(6), 553–569.

Souitaris, V. (2001). External communication determinants of innovation in the context of newly industrialised country: A comparison of objective and perceptual results from Greece. *Technovation, 21*, 25–34.

Teece, D. (1996). Firm organization, industrial structure, and technological innovation. *Journal of Economic Behavior & Organization, 31*, 193–224.

Tiwari, A., Mohnen, P., Palm, F., & van der Loeff, S. (2008). *Financial constraint and R&D investment: Evidence from CIS* (Working Paper Series 2007-011). United Nations University.

Tourigny, D., & Le, C. (2004). Impediments to innovation faced by Canadian manufacturing firms. *Economics of Innovation and New Technology, 13*(3), 217–250.

van der Panne, G., van Beers, C., & Kleinknecht, A. (2003). Success and failure of innovation: A literature review. *International Journal of Innovation Management, 7*(3), 1–30.

Zirger, B. (1997). The influence of development experience and product innovativeness on product outcome. *Technology Analysis & Strategic Management, 9*(3), 287–297.

Part III
Entrepreneurship for Change

Women Entrepreneurship in India: A Work-Life Balance Perspective

Ajay K. Jain, Shalini Srivastava, and Serena Cubico

Abstract The purpose of this empirical study is to study women entrepreneurs' psychological well being as supported by their family members in terms of support network so that effect of role overload and dependent care could be minimized. In any society, women receive relatively less support in order to fulfill their career aspirations. In a study on south Indian women entrepreneurs, researchers have examined the factors of work life balance for women entrepreneurs. These factors are termed as, *role overload, dependent care, quality of health, time management and support network*.

Due to some limitations of past studies, we felt a strong need to conduct another study on women entrepreneurs with an improved research design. Hence, this study is aimed at exploring the moderating impact of support network on the relationship of role overload and dependent care on quality of health and time management on a sample of north Indian women entrepreneurs. The data were collected from a sample of 130 women entrepreneurs located in Northern India. Results of moderating regression analysis showed the significant impact of support network on the relationship between predictor and criterion variables. Implications are discussed for women in Indian society.

Keywords Women entrepreneurship · Work life balance · Role overload · Social support · India

A. K. Jain (✉)
Institute of Management Studies, Ghaziabad, India
e-mail: ajay.jain@imsgzb.com

S. Srivastava
Jaipuria Institute of Management, Noida, India

S. Cubico
University of Verona, Verona, Italy
e-mail: serena.cubico@univr.it

© Springer International Publishing AG, part of Springer Nature 2018
S. Cubico et al. (eds.), *Entrepreneurship and the Industry Life Cycle*, Studies on Entrepreneurship, Structural Change and Industrial Dynamics,
https://doi.org/10.1007/978-3-319-89336-5_13

1 Introduction

Women Entrepreneurship in India

Before the beginning of twentieth century, women were operating a business as a way to supplementing family's income in order to meet with a sudden financial crisis or personal crisis e.g., loss (death or divorce) of the spouse. However, during 1900s, the society has developed a more progressive thinking due to the rise of feminism, so female entrepreneurship began to be a widely accepted term in the process of gaining a flexibility and autonomy in their life. So women started developing their own ventures in order to create jobs, strengthening innovation and economic development of the nation through entrepreneurial activities.

In India, women comprise about 30% of corporate senior management positions, which is notably higher than the global average (24%). But in the overall workforce, India is ranked 113th out of 135 when it comes to the gender gap and women entrepreneurs constitute only 10% of the total number of entrepreneurs in the country (Source: Forbes India). Being a family driven society, the success of women entrepreneurs in India depends on the social support from their family members (https://thegedi.org/research/womens-entrepreneurship-index/). So we are aimed at studying the moderating effect of support network on women entrepreneurs.

Literature indicates that women entrepreneurs in India face technical problems that are hindering their business efforts (Nayyar et al. 2007) or motivation and stress related issues (Das 2001; Lilian 2009). Meanwhile, the work life balance issues of women entrepreneurs in India have not been addressed by the researchers. Women constitute half of the total population so their participation in entrepreneurial activities needs to be encouraged for social and economic development of such societies. Women entrepreneurs will facilitate in creating more jobs, however female entrepreneurship is growing with a slow pace. Women entrepreneurs have confided themselves to a very small cottage industries. In patriarchal-Indian society, a woman entrepreneur is in a search of her independent identity away from their father's or husband's identity. Since business gives them more freedom to look after their family and to do something meaningful. However, there are several challenges women entrepreneurs face e.g., financial support, scarcity of raw materials, limited mobility, stiff competition, lack of education, male dominance, low-risk bearing ability, social biases. So keeping all these aspects in mind, the present paper attempts to understand the challenges as perceived by women entrepreneurs from life balance perspective. How does support-network facilitate in managing the time and health of women entrepreneurs?

2 Changing Status of Women Entrepreneurs in India

With increased awareness of their potential through educational opportunities, females an India have gained confidence in establishing their own identities by becoming an entrepreneur. The support they are getting with the government, NGO's and the increased industrialization and urbanization have boosted their morale to come out as budding entrepreneurs. Female entrepreneurs, apart from getting the financial support, are also getting opportunities to train themselves in their respective entrepreneurial domains and thereby establishing themselves in their entrepreneurial journey.

2.1 Women Entrepreneurs and Work-Life Balance (WLB)

It is very difficult for a fairer sex to maintain work life balance. When they try to enter in this domain, they either get a cold response by doubting their credibility (Nayyar et al. 2007) or they perceive lack of support and motivation to achieve their dreams (Das 2001; Lilian 2009). The irony is that this issue has not been taken seriously and nothing has been done to address this cause. The issue that is prevailing in Indian context is far different from those perceived in western world (Godwyn 2009). This issue of balancing work life for women entrepreneurs in such nations thus needs to be recognized of vital importance to the society and needs intensive research in order to encourage entrepreneurship among women.

2.2 Support-Network as a Moderator Variable

Previous studies have identified the "buffering" effect of different types of social support on the stressor/stress relationship (Parasuraman et al. 1992). Other studies have established the importance of social support as a coping resource in dealing with stressors in different life domains (House 1981). In a study by LaRocco et al. (1980), it was found that if the employees get social support, they are able to cope up with stress in a positive way which in turn leads to more committed to the organization and thereby, increased job satisfaction. This suggests that support acts in two ways—it acts as a moderator in the relationship between different organizational stressors and indicators of wellbeing as well as buffering the magnitude of the organizational stress experienced. A significant impact of perceived organizational support as a moderator for organizational stressor and organizational citizenship behavior was also found by Jain, Giga and Cooper (2012) who conducted their study on BPO sector employees. They have identified that perceived organizational support reduces employees' involvement in some of the OCB activities which may be a source of strain for employees. For example, a negative link between the Individual Initiative dimensions of OCB with role overload and work-family conflict (Bolino and Turnley 2005) suggests that individuals who take initiative and perceive higher demands reduce the level of pressure by withdrawing their involvement in some OCB activities.

Based on social exchange theory, it can be argued that employees who are treated well by their organizations may reciprocate by engaging in OCBs. However, as argued by Jain et al. (2012) that high stressful jobs, e.g., operators in BPOs, does not show the positive moderating impact of POS on stressors-OCB relationship. Sometimes, employees may prefer to withdraw their efforts from extra-role behavior in order to save energy. Likewise, entrepreneurship can take a heavy toll on the well being and health of women while managing household activities and establishing a business venture.

Thus it can be argued that support network may produce differentiating impact on the relationship of role overload and dependent care with quality of health and time management. As women entrepreneurs may differ in their perception of role overload and dependent care, therefore support network may act differently with both of the predictor variables. It might be possible that role overload may interact negatively while dependent care may interact positively with support network. As it can be argued that women entrepreneurs might feel more responsible for taking care of their dependents and support network may generate positive emotions of affection and attachment with the family. However, support network may not produce such emotions for role-overload. Role-overload may inhibit in creating such perception of high stress. Hence support network can interact with role overload negatively. Thus it means "support-network" might act as a moderator variable, so the following hypothesis is proposed:

Hypothesis Support-network moderates the effect of role overload and dependent care on quality of health and time management".

3 Hypothesis Development

It has been found and felt that there is a significant difference between female entrepreneurs who are married than ones who are unmarried. Moreover, one who stay in nuclear family perceive more stress than staying in joint one. Factors like lack of opportunities, support from family, hesitation in taking initiative, preference for secure and traditional jobs were perceived as inhibiting forces behind for females staring their own venture Harinarayana (1991).

Nayyar et al. (2007) in their study found that women entrepreneurs face several constraints in the areas related to financial, marketing production, work place facility and health problems. Because of preconceived notion, it was a challenge for women in terms of getting loans from banks as well as in marketing their products. An important issue that also added as a challenge was lack of support from the family

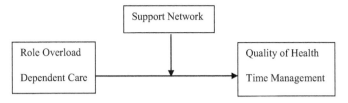

Fig. 1 The proposed conceptual scheme for examining the moderating impact of support-network

which led to stress. A study done by Caputo and Dolinsky (1998) indicated that business knowledge and spouse support are strong contributors of entrepreneurial success for women. The study also suggested that it is a high time for the governments to realize the importance and contribution of female entrepreneurs and provide theme the facility to undergo the desired training. Thus it might be argued that family support might act as a moderator variable.

4 Research Design

This study is aimed at exploring the moderating impact of social network on the relationship of role overload and dependent care with quality of health and time management. Grounded in the social support literature, we assume that women need a strong family support if they want to be a successful entrepreneur in the Indian society. The conceptual scheme of the study is presented in Fig. 1.

5 Method

5.1 Participants and Procedure

The present study consisted of 130 female entrepreneurs. Although 154 entrepreneurs were contacted for the purpose of data collection, however 130 responses were found to be appropriate for the final analysis. These females had their set up in remote as well as urban areas of Delhi region of India. The female entrepreneurs belonged to diversified background and occupations. There were females who were forced to start their business whereas there were some who took the initiative of fulfilling their dreams of becoming an entrepreneur. Some of them owned their beauty salons, boutiques, handicrafts business, and few were involved in their family business or were having their tuition centres. Out of the total sample, ten females were medical practitioners and had their own nursing homes or pathology centres. It was easy to approach the medical professionals and those running their family business but approaching entrepreneurs involved in beauty salon or boutique was a difficult task as they were hesitant of revealing their views as fearing the intentions

Table 1 Demographic details

Qualification	Marital status	Tenure (years)	Age (years)
Graduation (40)	Married (92)	1–5 (42)	21–30 (26)
Post-graduation (45)	Unmarried (38)	6–10 (64)	31–40 (28)
Others (45)		11–15 (19)	41–50 (42)
		16–20 (3)	51–60 (23)
		Above 20 (2)	Above 60 (11)

Source: Author's Survey

behind. But once they were assured of the purpose and were applauded for their work, they came out free and relaxed when they were asked about the opinions. Due to a significant variation in the nature of work they were involved, the income varied to a significant amount. The entrepreneurs were contacted in person and were briefed about the purpose of the study. They were assured about the confidentiality of their responses. The demographic profile of the respondents is presented in Table 1.

5.2 Measures

The questionnaire was adapted from Mathew and Panchanatham (2011). The study involved non-probability convenient sampling as the study is related to examining the WLB issues of women entrepreneurs in northern India. In order to ensure the reliability and appropriateness of the items, pilot testing was conducted on a sample of 25 women entrepreneurs. Examples of the items are as follows; (1) Role Overload—"I have to perform many roles in a given time", (2) Quality of Health—"Due to the work/family issues and lack of time, I find it difficult to take care of my health", (3) Dependent Care—"I feel free and enjoy my profession as I have no dependent care issues" (R). (4) Time Management—"I often came from the office very late in the evening", (5) Support Network—"My social support network is very helpful in dealing with the dependent care issues".

5.3 Results

We have used factor analysis and moderated regression analysis for data analysis through SPSS 21. The results have showed the validity and reliability of questionnaire. The results of descriptive statistics are presented in Table 2. After conducting the reliability test, 39 items out of 44 items were used for the final analysis categorized into five factors. Results of factor analysis are not presented here. These five factors have explained a total of 67.58% of variance with **Role Overload** (component 1) contributing 24.42%, **Quality of health** (component 2) contributing14.44%, **Dependent care**, (component 3) contributing 11.24%, **Time**

Table 2 Means, standard deviations, correlations and reliabilities among the variables (N = 130)

No	Variables	Mean	SD	1	2	3	4	5
1	Role Overload	26.84	5.63	*0.88*				
2	Dependent Care	33.82	5.31	0.85**	*0.75*			
3	Support Network	19.01	2.08	−0.71**	−0.67**	*0.66*		
4	Quality of Health	24.70	2.22	−0.59**	−0.30**	0.61**	*0.71*	
5	Time Management	34.36	4.21	−0.54**	−0.27**	0.63**	0.79**	*0.65*

Note: ** $p < 0.01$, *Reliabilities are represented diagonally in italics and bold*

Table 3 Results of moderated regression analysis: independent variable-role overload; moderator variable-support network

Predictor and moderator	Main effect of role overload		Main effect of support network		Interaction effect of role overload × support network	
Criterion Variables	Beta	Adj R^2	Beta	Adj R^2	Beta	Adj R^2
Quality of health	−0.59**	0.32	0.61**	0.36	−0.36**	0.12
Time management	−0.54**	0.29	0.63**	0.40	−0.27**	0.07

Note: ** $p < 0.01$, Source: Authors' Survey

Table 4 Results of moderated regression analysis: independent variable-dependent care; moderator variable-support network (N = 130)

Predictor and moderator	Main effect of dependent care		Main effect of support network		Interaction effect of dependent care * Support network	
Criterion variables	Beta	Adj R^2	Beta	Adj R^2	Beta	Adj R^2
Quality of health	−0.26**	0.08	0.61**	0.36	0.16**	0.02
Time management	−0.27**	0.07	0.63**	0.40	0.23**	0.04

Note: ** $p < 0.01$, Source: Authors' Survey

management (component 4) contributing 9.28% and **Support network** (component 5) contributing 8.18% respectively.

Moderator regression analysis was used as the principal method for analyzing data (Aiken and West 1991). On step 1, Role overload was entered; on step 2, support network was entered; and on step 3, role overload along with support network and the interaction term (product of role overload and social network) was added to the regression equation. The procedure was repeated for dependent care. The results of moderated regression are presented in Tables 3 and 4.

Table 3 reflects the results of Moderated Regression Analysis. Results show that Role overload had a negative impact on Quality of Health as well as on Time management ($\beta = -.59** * \beta = -.54**$) respectively and Support network had a positive and significant impact on Quality of Health and Time Management ($\beta = 0.61**$, $\beta = 0.63**$) respectively. The interaction effect between role overload and support network have reduced the impact of role overload on Quality of health and time management ($\beta = -.36**$, $-.27**$) respectively.

Results from Table 4 show that Dependent Care had a negative impact on Quality of Health as well as on Time management. ($\beta=-.26$** * $\beta=-.27$**) respectively and Support network had a positive and significant impact on Quality of Health and Time Management ($\beta = 0.61$**, $\beta = 0.63$**) respectively. The interaction impact between Dependent Care and support network have converted the negative impact of Dependent Care on Quality of health and time management into the positive effect ($\beta = 0.16$**,-0.27**). Thus support network plays a significant role in moderating the relationship between Role overload and dependent care on quality of health and time management.

6 Discussion

The main objective of this study was to see the moderating impact of social network on the relationship of role overload and dependent care with quality of health and time management of women entrepreneurs in northern India. It is evident from the analysis that women entrepreneurs in northern Indian region are facing the issues of role overload and dependent care and that had a negative relationship with quality of health and time management. Grounded in social support and OCB literature, we argued that it should reduce the negative impact of role overload and dependent care on quality of health and time management. However, we found that support network had a significant and positive moderating effect on the relationship of dependent care and quality of health and time management; however it had a significant and negative effect on the relationship of role overload and quality of health and time management. As discussed before, Indian women take moral and social responsibility of dependents and support network plays a positive role. So dependent care is part of their essence and creates positive emotions of attachment and affection for the family. Support network help in enhancing these emotions. The findings are consistent to social support and POS literature (e.g., House 1981; Jain et al. 2012).

Dependent care issue is an important factor which affects the quality of health and time management of women entrepreneurs in north India. Most of the women entrepreneurs are overloaded by their demanding household duties and responsibilities (Dileepkumar 2006; Vikas 2007; Rizvi and Gupta 2009). Women entrepreneurs, moreover, have to spend long hours on planning and managing their business to achieve progress. Regularly they cannot take care of their dependents leading to nervousness and work-life conflict. However, support network can play a significant role in reducing this perception. The women entrepreneurs in this study have reported that childcare and elder care management are their major responsibilities. But they enjoy it and such care makes them happy with the support from their family members. The presence of elderly people facilitate in taking care of their younger family members. So support network and dependent care play an instrumental role in creating positive emotions of satisfaction, affection and attachment with the family.

However, role overload may create stress and strain among women, so the perception of support network does not produce a positive impact on the relationship of role overload and criterion variables. Jain et al., (2012) observed that stressors and POS does not produce a positive interaction on operators in BPO industry due to a very stressful working conditions of these employees e.g., working in late night hours. Similarly, the perception of high stress due to the role-overload does not help in seeing the positive impact of support network and women may consider it in a negative manner. Our results are consistent to the findings that conflict between work and family occurs when individuals have to perform multiple roles (Greenhaus et al. 2003), such as spouse, parent, housekeeper, employee and entrepreneur. Each of these roles needs time and energy, which is if once spent on one role, will not be used for another. It may reduce the quality of health and ability to manage their time. According to Nayyar et al. (2007), role overload may occur in a society where women have to play a multiple role within a limited amount of time. Role overload was an attribute of most of the women's lives in the present study, leading to poor quality of health and time management. So role overload is obviously produces negative effect on quality of health and time management, support network is failed to reduce the effect as women are compelled to perform their social roles.

This study indicates that social support from family members leads to a better health and time management. Women entrepreneurs in this study have reported satisfaction when they received the support from their spouse and children in their entrepreneurial activities. However, sometimes, it becomes very tough to get support from family for dependent care and/or other household activities, as it is considered it as part of their responsibilities. However, role overload still remains a factor of concern as support network does not help in it. Women entrepreneurs believe that they do not want to be a successful entrepreneur at the cost of their family members. So support structure around them needs to be strengthened if India wants to produce more number of women entrepreneurs.

Quality of health and time management both are found to be relevant criterion variables for women entrepreneurs. As health and time management does not only worsen a work-family imbalance but also affect the success of women entrepreneurs. According to the respondents in this study, work-life balance of many women entrepreneurs suffers when they have to work during unusual hours and weekends and which a problem of overload and dependent care is not a burden on them.

7   Conclusion

The study assesses the impact of support network on the relationship of role overload and dependent care with quality of health and time management of women entrepreneurs in north India. The questionnaire has been borrowed from Mathew and Panchanatham (2011), however we have developed a moderating impact model of the factors of work-life balance questionnaire. These factors do not act upon women entrepreneurs independently rather they interact with each other. Women entrepreneurs are confronted with problems related to role overload and dependent care; however the perception of social and family support helps in reducing the negative impact of these stressors on their health and well being. Support network is found to be positively related with health and time management of women entrepreneurs.

The women entrepreneurs struggle to maintain a balance between work and family life because workloads and their personal and family roles rather often overlap with one another. Therefore, work life imbalances and conflicts have become a common facet of many inspiring women entrepreneurs. This study is important especially in the context of India because more and more women are entering into the arena of entrepreneurial activities as a result socio economic changes. In this highly competitive environment survival and proper management of business have become extremely complex and difficult.

Women entrepreneurs may use these dimensions to realize the plausible work-life balance issue and plan to take preventive measures. Moreover, professional organizations may accommodate these dimensions in their corporate culture. At social level, the society needs to understand the gender stereotype and needs to overcome with this issue in order to support the emergence of women entrepreneurship in India. So, social awareness may play a key role in helping the women entrepreneurs to overcome with the problems related to role overload and dependent care.

The study has some limitations. The study has not considered the psychological and social aspects that might have an influence on the quality of health e.g., personality type, social and economic status etc. The study has been conducted in Delhi region taking relatively a small size, which is only a very small portion of the north India. So, the results of the study may not represent the whole country. Therefore, in a country like India, where there are multicultural and multi-religious . people and societies include various economic groups, further research across all the major cities may produce more representative output. As the present study has been conducted on women entrepreneurs of Delhi region, it is enviable to conduct further studies on a broader extent taking all the major cities into account. The studies may also be conducted to assess the adverse impact of role overload and dependent care on women empowerment, economic development and employment, economic and social development. It is desirable to pursue further studies on a larger scale by taking all of the Indian states into account, particularly given the multifaceted nature of Indian society. As the prevailing roles of Indian women in the family and society are comparable to those of many other developing and underdeveloped countries, research in this direction could help international policymakers and organizations to design more coherent and internationally applicable policies towards women in the entrepreneurial sector. As entrepreneurship among women is considered to be an avenue of female empowerment, rapid economic development and employment, studies related to the adverse impact of work-life balance issues in these areas, as well as the issues' manifestations in national and international economic and social development, are also worth pursuing.

Notwithstanding, Indian women entrepreneurs' delicate act of balancing personal life and business needs to be studied more thoroughly and should be compared with women from individualistic culture. As women in India may feel more dissonance then western women while not able to fulfill their family roles and responsibilities. Indian women experience emotions of guilt and shame more than western women if unable to deliver their family responsibilities. Indian man should show their willingness to extend a helping hand in order to promote entrepreneurship in their mothers and wife. After 70 years of India's independence, women are still looking for their true freedom in order to establish their independent identity through more entrepreneurial opportunities.

References

Aiken, L. S., & West, S. G. (1991). *Multiple regressions: Testing and interpreting interactions.* Newbury Park, CA: Sage.

Bolino, M. C., & Turnley, W. H. (2005). The personal costs of citizenship behavior: The relationship between individual initiative and role overload, job stress and work-family conflict. *Journal of Applied Psychology, 90*, 740–748.

Caputo, R., & Dolinsky, A. (1998). Women's choice to pursue self-employment: The role of financial and human capital of household members. *Journal of Small Business Management, 36*(3), 8–17.

Das, M. (2001). Women entrepreneurs from India: Problems, motivations and success factors. *Journal of Small Business and Entrepreneurship, 15*(4), 67.

Dileepkumar, M. (2006). *Problems of women entrepreneurs in India.* Retrieved December 3, 2010, from http://www.indianmba.com/Faculty_column/FC293/fc293.html

Godwyn, M. (2009). This place makes me proud to be a women: Theoretical explanation for success in entrepreneurship education for low-income women. *Research in Social Stratification and Mobility, 27*(1), 50–64.

Greenhaus, J. H., Collins, K. M., & Shaw, J. D. (2003). The relation between work, family balance and quality of life. *Journal of Vocational Behaviour, 63*, 510–531.

Harinarayan, R. C. (1991). Promotion of women entrepreneurship: A brief comment. *SEDME, 18* (2), 21–28.

House, J. S. (1981). *Work stress and social support.* Reading, MA: Addison-Wesley.

Jain, A. K., Giga, S. I., & Cooper, C. L. (2012). Perceived organizational support as a moderator in the relationship between organizational stressors and organizational citizenship behaviors. *International Journal of Organizational Analysis, 21*(3), 313–334.

LaRocco, J. M., House, J. S., & French, J. R. P. (1980). Social support, occupational stress, and health. *Journal of Health and Social Behavior, 21*, 202–218.

Lilian, D. (2009). A cross-cultural study of entrepreneurial role stress among Eritrean and Indian women entrepreneurs. *International Journal of Management Sciences, 5*(2), 9–19.

Mathew, R.V. & Panchanatham N. (2011, July). An exploratory study on the work-life balance of women entrepreneurs in South India. *Asian Academy of Management Journal, 16*(2), 77–105. © Asian Academy of Management and Penerbit Universiti Sains Malaysia.

Nayyar, P., Sharma, A., Kishtawaria, J., Rana, A., & Vyas, N. (2007). Causes and constraints by women entrepreneurs in entrepreneurial process. *Journal of Social Science, 14*(2), 99–102.

Parasuraman, S., Greenhaus, J. H., & Granrose, C. S. (1992). Role stressors, social support, and well being among two career couples. *Journal of Organizational Behavior, 13*, 339–356.

Rizvi, A. F., & Gupta, K. L. (2009). Women entrepreneurship in India – Problems and prospects. *OORJA Journal of Management and IT, 7*(2), 35–41.

Vikas, K. (2007). *Problems of women entrepreneurs in India.* Retrieved 3 December 2010, from http://www.123eng.com/form/viewtopic.php? P = 18304

The Pentagonal Problem and the Offshore Energy Sector in Portugal: Why Does It Matter?

Ana Pego

Abstract The relationship between circular economy and offshore energy is a big step for "eco-innovation industries." The use of renewables has become one of the main issues in the European economy. Therefore, the latest European agenda for 2020 set up policies in order to implement new business models based on sustainability, cooperation, and collaboration between industries, towards more environment efficiency. This article shows the importance of offshore energy in Portugal and its linkages to a circular economy based on technology and innovation where natural recourses comprise a business model based on natural innovation system which performs a new method of analyzing the economy. The methodology will be based on the pentagonal problem (resources gap, technical challenges, public challenges, climate change challenges, problem statement) focusing on the Portuguese organizations which use renewable energy. In order to analyze the offshore energy sector, a quantitative analysis (IO matrix) and a qualitative analysis (Porter's model) are used. The use of renewable in the circular economy is expected to have an impact on three main areas: economic, environmental, and communal. The sharing of economic savings and collaborative consumption between organizations will contribute to redistribution markets and collaborative lifestyle platforms. The new challenge is to move towards a new business model based on eco-products, service providers, and energy recovery.

Keywords Circular economy · Offshore energy cluster · Pentagram problem · Innovation ecosystem

A. Pego (✉)
Centre for Interdisciplinary Social Sciences and Humanities, Nova University of Lisbon, Lisbon, Portugal
e-mail: anapego@campus.fcsh.unl.pt

© Springer International Publishing AG, part of Springer Nature 2018
S. Cubico et al. (eds.), *Entrepreneurship and the Industry Life Cycle*, Studies on Entrepreneurship, Structural Change and Industrial Dynamics,
https://doi.org/10.1007/978-3-319-89336-5_14

1 Introduction

The world is changing towards a better use of renewable and environment resources.

Changing attitudes and valuing natural resources is the biggest step for economies. Circular economy provides a framework to face challenges and a guide for rethinking and redesigning the future. Therefore, in the global economy, the challenge is to prove the benefits of belonging to a circular economy and natural innovation system.

Circular economy underlines a few points which organizations face: the value added from circular products, reusing materials to reduce waste, the use of raw materials, forward and reverse logistics, supply chain efficiency, and innovative materials for innovative products (e.g. bio-based materials) (MacArthur and MackKinsey & Company 2014) from innovative ecosystems (Oh et al. 2016).

The linkage between circular economies and renewable energy will decrease the direct costs for production. Renewable energy offers effective technologies to tackle global energy challenges: climate change, the rising demand for energy, and the security of energy supplies (Zhang and Cooke 2009).

The challenge is to describe the linkages between offshore energy and circular economy and to set up a business model where market strategies can be put into practice towards more economy efficiency based on product performance, value added, and potential savings by sharing materials. The key is to create positive externalities in the economy to obtain more efficiency and competitiveness based on a business model where innovation and technology allows better natural resources uses.

The business model created by these vectors will promote innovation and networking in labor, products, and capital, having the pentagonal problem in consideration.

Another challenge for entrepreneurs, related with renewable energy and externalities in the circular economy value chain, is the capacity of the organizations to go forward and introduce new methodologies for the production of raw materials. This means changing the production process, making new investments, and finding market value for eco products.

This paper tries to analyze the potential of the Portuguese circular economy market when using offshore renewable energy, based on solving the pentagonal problem. The solution is still very incipient since the supply of offshore energy to the demand market is only an emerging cluster, (Pego et al. 2016) and also because few organizations are adopting the circular economy model for their businesses.

2 The Business Model and The Circular Economy

Innovation constitutes a problem in a modern economy related with new products, such as eco innovation, eco technologies, and a new process for production. The innovation problem derives from the concept of more sustainability and new challenges for production.

The natural innovation systems concept is the linkage between the innovation, technology, and multi-stakeholders collaboration (Oh et al. 2016). The circular economy is the concept where these relationships happen.

The circular economy (CE) refers to the industrial character of the economy, which becomes self-sustainable through the use of renewable energy, and there duction of toxic substances and waste (Costea-Dunarintu 2016: 150).

The concept of CE (Su et al. 2013; Lieder and Rashid 2016) presented in fig 1 is well known for the transition, which allows materials to safely re-enter the biosphere or continue to circulate as high-quality production resources; the opposite of a linear model where the 'take, make and dispose' is applied. The CE model is consistent with three aspects: environmental impact, economics benefits and resource scarcity. The question is solve the amount of waste substances and give them utility.

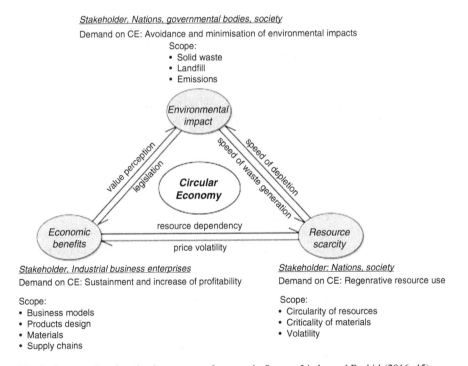

Fig. 1 A comprehensive circular economy framework. Source: Lieder and Rashid (2016: 45)

2.1 The Business Model

The concept of business model is based on industrial innovation of the future productivity and competitiveness between organizations. Di Fonzo and Hime (2017: 15) point out some features of the business models based on CE, such as decision-making support for business, measure and value decision-making, regulators, and research funders.

The CE business model solution can be improved if the companies transfer knowledge from their previous experience based on the relationship with costumers and stakeholders (Oh et al. 2016), monetizing capacity, having better control of the product life cycle, and creating stable revenue streams and premiums (MacArthur and MackKinsey & Company 2014: 47).

CE provides four types of resource benefits: improving resource security and decreasing import dependency; Environmental benefits: less environmental impact; Economic benefits: opportunities for economic growth and innovation; and Social benefits: sustainable consumer behavior and job opportunities (EEA 2016: 13).

The potential gaps to address include: the development of more accurate metrics i.e. regional rather than global and country level data; improved biodiversity and soil metrics (through consideration of relevant definitions and ways to report changes in context); strengthening the linkage between any suggested metrics and core business processes (Di Fonzo and Hime 2017: 23).

On the other hand, the network system and the potential for collaborative markets constitute the goal of CE system (MacArthur and MackKinsey & Company 2014: 39).

Further researches in this field can be based on top-down (legislation and policy, support infrastructure, social awareness) or bottom-up (collaborative business models, product design, and supply chain, information and communication technology) approaches (Lieder and Rashid 2016: 47).

Another perspective put forward by Genovese et al. (2017: 355), reveals that there are four types of regions with competitiveness and sustainability in CE. The transition to CE includes a new challenge involving political, cultural, human, and economic structures, as well as technological limitations. In the authors' perspective, there are four types of sustainability systems: Type IV (products) is a subset of System Type III (Businesses) which in turn is a sub-set of System Type II (Regions/Cities). An aggregation of regions and cities then forms System Type I (The Earth).

Therefore, the business model based on this methodology is consistent with sustainable solutions at the product level, and it can be aggregated across businesses in order to improve their sustainability, as well as economic systems. This means a new challenge to improve business based on ecosystems and human well-being. The business models can be reliable with natural ecosystems projects, "systems thinking", shape ideias of technopolis and innovation, high-tech regional economic development, geographic activities location, and knowledge from biological systems (Oh et al. 2016: 5).

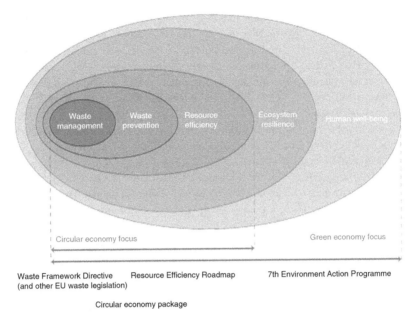

Fig. 2 Circular economy and green economy. Source: EEA (2016: 31)

Moreover, a business strategy based on CE needs to optimize materials and energy flows inside the regions or industrial ecosystems. This raises a new challenge for resource recovery and tax exemption policy for companies involved in reverse supply chain activities. Additionally, the expectation stakeholder's expectations regarding the CE business based on production, value chain and competiveness constitute an important vector for social, environment and resources efficiency in economy (Fig. 2).

Action plans and strategic directions are the vectors for the future of CE in Europe. Nevertheless, some technical, social, political and economic barriers are pointed out: companies are often not aware or do not have the ability or the knowledge to choose circular economy solutions; systems, infrastructures, business models and technology of today can lock the economy into a linear model; investments in efficiency measures or innovative business models remain insufficient and are considered risky and complicated; the demand for sustainable products and services can remain low, especially if they involve changes in behavior; often, the prices reflect actual costs incurred by the company for the consumption of resources and energy; the signals of political transition to a circular economy are not strong enough and consistent (Costea-Dunarintu 2016: 158).

The business model presented in this paper is completed if considering the Portuguese strategy for the sea and the emergent topic on innovation systems. Therefore, the Portuguese pentagonal problem of offshore energy relays on the strategy for the maritime economy (OECD 2016: 21) and the potentiality of innovation ecosystems. SEA has the capacity to understand the decisional and development context and to drive development opportunities into pathways that are inclusive of environmental and sustainability priorities (Partidário and Gomes 2013: 36). This means a relationship between a few vectors which comprise the environmental system and its linkage to a circular economy. Those vectors are the ecosystem services, governance, drivers of change and human well-being (Partidário and Gomes 2013: 39).

The Portuguese strategy to achieve an environmental performance is National Strategy for Integrated Coastal Zone Management (SICZM) (December 2008) and Maritime spatial Plan (MSP) (June 2009). In terms of ecosystems performance and its relation to the SEA activities, both apply for a better use of natural resources, where on SICZM the ecosystem approach is related with sustainable management of human activities that ensure the integrity of ecological systems and the valorization of ecosystem services; the MSP applies for Ecosystem Services related to evaluation of the ability to provide ecosystem services, taking into account thresholds of acceptable change with coordination and multi-purpose logic (Partidário and Gomes 2013: 40).

To sum up, despite the problems which arise from the pentagonal problem, the innovation ecosystem supports the ability to supply services and technology based on innovation towards more competitiveness between the multi-stakeholders.

2.2 The CE Benefits on Economy

EASAB (2015: 4) point out some benefits of CE: fostering competitiveness by creating savings and reducing raw materials and energy dependency; security of supply and control of rising costs; contributing to EU climate change policy by reducing greenhouse gas emissions; employment opportunities; reducing environmental impact of resource extraction and waste disposal; opportunities for new businesses by selling goods or offering services.

The following table shows the indicators for the study of CE.

Table 1 Indicators of circularity in an economy

Scope	Indicator
Resource productivity	GDP per kilogram of domestic material consumption
Circular activities	Recycling rate Eco-innovation index (index of green investment, employment, patents, etc.)
Waste generation	Amount of waste per GDP output Amount of municipal waste per capita
Energy and greenhouse emission	Share of renewable energy Greenhouse gas emission per GDP output

Source: EASAB (2015: 10)

Fig. 3 The simplified circular economy. *r* Recycling, *W* waste, *P* production, *C* consumption, *K* capital goods, *U* utility, *R* natural resources. Source: Andersen (2007: 134)

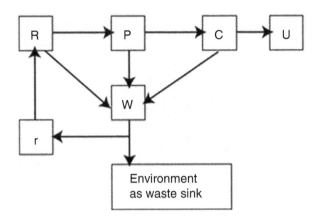

One of the vectors to analyze circularity and its benefits on economy is the share of renewable energy and greenhouse gas emission per GDP output; additionally, to complete the analysis other factors need to be considered (Table 1).

Consequently, studying offshore energy and its linkages to CE value chain and direct or indirect impact is one of the advantages to study the relationship between production and value added on the economy. A better comparison can be achieved if the values for CE and linear economy or efficiency, competiveness, value added and environment impacts are compared.

Energy savings represent an essential component of meeting climate goals, and energy management is an unparalleled opportunity to enable organizations across all sectors to achieve on-going energy consumption reductions. This shift from a focus on the merits of individual projects to a more systematic, comprehensive, and strategic focus can enable organizations to develop their full potential to achieve improved energy performance overtime. Accomplishing this goal would enhance economic development at the organizational, national, and global levels, and would contribute greatly to address urgent global concerns regarding emissions from the use of non-renewable energy sources and associated climate change impact (EMES 2017: 7).

The importance of CE in the economic system is consistent with the relationship between economic agents, as shown in fig 3. The relationship between economic agents performs the direct inputs and outputs where the impacts on the economic system can be explored.

The analogy with renewables is quite easy to understand if we consider the overall benefits on the economic system. The system with renewable energy will promote the recycling of goods that will not be wasted because resources, economic agents and resources use are maximized with the minimum of waste. From this perspective, the environment can be acknowledged as fulfilling four basic welfare economic functions: (1) amenity values; (2) a resource base for the economy; (3) a sink for residual flows; (4) a life-support system (Andersen 2007: 135) (Fig. 4).

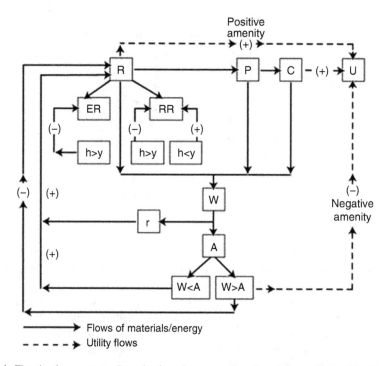

Fig. 4 The circular economy. *P* production, *C* consumption, *K* capital goods, *U* utility, *R* natural resources, *r* recycling, *W* waste, *ER* exhaustible resources, *RR* recyclable resources, *A* assimilative capacity, *h* harvest, *y* yield. Source: Andersen (2007: 136)

In other words, CE is a concept which involves a set of competences, useful for the welfare. This means a network with the ability to foster system thinking, goals, strategy and their adoption, with external and internal effects, and which promotes positive externalities in the economy.

Renewable energy is considered in this system as a factor which allows for the minimization of wastes and external costs.

The previous model is applicable to interaction between all sectors in the economy and CE. The model gives the idea of interaction and externalities which come from all sectors.

This means that CE, in a cumulative way, can be a positive externality when there are flows of material/energy between sectors. For this reason, the CE components are the positive vectors which allow linear economy for resource savings.

To sum up, the importance of CE in the business model is related with the capacity of the organization to provide externalities to the economy. The value-added generated by the symbioses of different sectors in CE promotes different levels of waste.

3 The Cleantech Model

The word Cleantech (green) is the new concept of clean energy, and it is related to transport; recycling &waste; materials; building & energy efficiency; renewable energy; air, water environment; agriculture & food sectors (Henriksen et al. 2012: 18). Cleantech is defined as (clean technology) products and services that use technology to compete for favourable price and performance while reducing pollution, waste, and use of natural resources (Burtis et al. 2004: 11). The table 2 shows the industries and the materials which apply for cleantech model.

The main areas involving cleantech are : *renewable energy* (Onshore, Offshore Wind, Solar, Geothermal and Bioenergy); *clean cities* (Green Buildings, Clean Water, Smart Grid, Solid Waste, Clean Road Transport) and *perspectives* (Maritime Cleantech, Carbon Storage, Energy Storage) (Cluster 2012: 10).

The Cleantech capacity involves regions, markets, consumers and renewable energy, as the niche activities, which are directly related to regional development,

Table 2 Cleantech industries category

Industry	Examples
• Advanced Materials and Nanotechnology	• Non-platinum catalysts for catalytic converters • Nano-materials for more efficient and fungible solar photovoltaic panels;
• Agriculture and Nutrition	• Innovative plant technologies and modified crops • Designed to reduce reliance on pesticides or fungicides
• Air Quality	• Stationary and mobile emission scrubbers • Testing and compliance services
• Consumer Products	• Biodegradable plastic ware • Nontoxic household cleaners
• Enabling Technologies and Services	• Advanced materials research services • High throughput screening research equipment;
• *Energy Generation, Storage, and Infrastructure*	• *Solar photovoltaic technology* • *Wind power* • *Hydrogen generation* • *Batteries and power management technology*
• Environmental Information Technology	• Regulatory and policy compliance software • Geographic Information Services (GIS)
• Manufacturing/Industrial Technologies	• Hardware and software to increase manufacturing productivity and efficiency
• Materials Recovering and Recycling	• Chemical recovery and reprocessing in industrial Manufacturing • Remanufacturing
• Transportation and Logistics	• Fuel cells for cars • Diesel retrofits equipment • Hybrid electric systems for cars, buses, and trucks
• Waste and Water Purification and Management	• Biological and chemical processes for water and waste purification • Fluid flow metering technology

socio-technical transitions in organizations, coordinated activities, and institutional involvement (McCauley and Stephens 2012).

Few institutions developed Cleantech studies [e.g. Finland (2014) and Henriksen et al. 2012)] in order to classify methodologies about renewable energy. Cleantech clusters comprise benefits, such as: the specialization of regions in activities, higher employment and greater expansion rates, reducing the cost of production and the cost of exchanging by strengthening trading relationships, local knowledge spill-over, local R&D institutions, business collaboration and research activities, and strong clusters in the same geographical region (Davies 2013: 1289).

In this paper, we point out three main models which show the linkages within the cleantech cluster based on offshore energy and the possibility of a relationship with CE model.

The *Helix Model* (Finland 2014: 6) combines five points: costumers needs, enterprise/private sector, coordination of cooperation, education and research and public sector. The goal is to develop strategies in order to maximize the cooperation between all sectors of the economy, through an innovative business where the needs of the market, Government, research, and networking are combined.

The *Convas Model* is usedto understand green business models and green business innovation. This model is based on eleven factors: growth strategy, key partners, key activities, key resources, value proposition, costumer's relationships, costumers segments, channels, cost structure, revenue streams, and comparative strategy (Henriksen et al. 2012: 33).

The *Diamond Model* comprising the analysis of collaboration and competitive-ness between organizations towards a cluster was presented by Porter (1990). Maxoulis et al. (2007), Zhao et al. (2011), Dögl et al. (2012), and Monteiro et al. (2013). A diamond model is used to explain the competitiveness of economies for renewables through demand conditions, factors conditions, firm strategy structure and rivalry, and related and supported industries.

To summarize, the use of each model in green clusters where CE acts constitute an important issue in the green market, since it will promote organization compet-itiveness, maximized consumers utility, and innovation and collaboration.

4   The Impact of Offshore Energy in Portugal

The first study made on the impact of offshore energy in Portugal presented by Pego et al. (2016) concludes that there is an emerging sector. The study reflects also the direct, indirect, and induced effect on economy.

Most of the authors (Benito et al. 2003; Wijnolst 2006), agree that a good indicator of a cluster's relevance can be assessed by analyzing the strength of the connections (agglomeration economies) between its members, namely by the trade transaction figures that are at stake. In general terms, sectors in a successful cluster have a strong dependence on one another and on the way buyers and suppliers are related. In fact, there is a debate on whether it is more important to have these

Table 3 Suppliers with higher technical coefficients

NACE	Industry	Technical coefficients
351	Electr. Prod.	0.45
352	Gas Distr.	0.06
69 + 70 + 71	Services (Law, Manag, Archit.)	0.03
64	Financial Serv.	0.02
27	Electric Equip.	0.01
33	Mach &Eq Services	0.01
42	Civil Engin.	0.01
82	Other Serv.	0.01

Table 4 Energy production (351) Keynesian multipliers

Multiplier type 1 (output)	Multiplier type 2 (output)	Employment multiplier
2.53	3.18	2.11

connections between the same or different sectors (Titze et al. 2011; Boschma et al. 2012; Van der Panne 2004), with the majority of the later studies arguing that the development of clusters benefits more from a larger range of activities.

On the other hand, Nooteboom et al. (2007) argue that spillovers are more fruitful between sectors that are neither too cognitive close or distant.

The study presented by Pego et al. (2016) shown that there is a few linkages between the electric sectors which revels a potential clusters.

Results show that sector 351 (Electric power generation, transmission, and distribution) has a strong relationship with itself (6400 million euros of intra-commercial relations) (Table 3).

This is probably due to the large size of the main company and the concentration of activities (energy production, distribution and commercialisation). Taking into account all the 97 sectors' technical coefficients of the Leontief matrix $[a_{ij}]$, we may conclude that there are just a small number of "average linkages" (technical coefficient >0.02) between "Energy Production" and the rest of the economy .

The direct and indirect impact from the offshore energy sector was estimated with a Keynesian multiplier (Pego et al. 2016).

Taking into account the e Windfloat investment (2011), in an amount of about 23 million euros had 58.2 million euros of direct and indirect effects and 73.1 million euros of total (direct + indirect + induced) effects. In what concerns the effects on employment, we cannot add a number, as the number of workers at Windfloat is not available. The table 4 shows the keynesian multiplier for energy production in Portugal for investments. Therefore, the investment and employment will increase substancially in the renewable offshore energy sector.

5   The Pentagonal Model

The pentagonal problem on sustainable economies became very popular for facilitators. This means that a new vision of CE and its future started to be discussed by stakeholders which are part of the CE. For this reason, the CE problem starts with a question *who are we?*(Matti et al. 2016).

The study presented by Moser and Ekstrom (2010) about climate changes and its impact on the economy, shows that there are a few points that society is dealing with. This means a new concept of planning and explores new challenges for *climate problem and economy*, related to understanding, planning and managing barriers. Consequently, the main concept is the transition, where the plan for excellence within a collective, an organization or a sector is broadly defined.

The pentagonal problem is also related to natural resources sustainability and consumer's needs. The optimization of renewable resources and its linkages to an organization is the "perfect marriage" if there is an adequate exploitation of natural resources and market needs by Cleantech organizations.

Therefore, smart grid technologies, low impact on the transportation system, stimulating local and regional economic development by creating the conditions that attract and promote innovative firms can be seen as the vectors of Cleantech performance in regions (McCauley and Stephens 2012; Lam et al. 2011).

In this paper, the relationship between the pentagonal problem and offshore energy towards a sustainable business model is discussed.

The IWA (2016: 13) report shows that there is a tight linkage between renewables and the environment. This means that energy and carbon strategies should be centered around reducing costs for customers and minimizing the impact on the environment. The energy portfolio should aim at reducing carbon-based energy consumption, increasing renewable energy consumption, increasing renewable energy production, and making a positive contribution to zero-carbon cities.

For this reason, studying the renewable energy path towards more sustainability in economy is one of the main achievements to solve the pentagonal problem.

Therefore, the innovative business model is globally accepted when there are important linkages between the vectors which are part of the CE.

6   Why Does the Pentagonal Solution Matter in the Portuguese Offshore Energy?

The emerging offshore energy sector in Portugal (2017) is the first pre-commercial phase for this type of energy.

Porter's diamond model makes possible for some conclusions on the potential of the supply sector. The study presented by Pego et al. (2016) points out the existence of virtually all the conditions for a swift development an offshore energy cluster.

According to Pego et al. (2016), we may conclude that the first study made on the offshore energy cluster with Porter's methodology will lead to a competitive sector with a collaborative performance. Although, it did not study the linkages between the capacities of stakeholders to change their business model to a better performance based on environment and CE model.

For this reason, a new vision about the stakeholders and their ability to develop instruments based on climate change, business strategy, collaboration with others sectors is presented, with the following vectors: (1) *problem statement*; (2) *climate change challenges*; (3) *societal challenges*; (4) *technical challenges and* (5) *resources gap* (Matti et al. 2016).

The business strategy relies on a very simple way to solve a pentagonal problem regarding offshore energy. Firstly, the awareness of the stakeholders which are part of the energy sector and its linkages with one another; secondly, the very problem of the interaction on the cluster, which means better support to help business and prevent offshore business to flooding in the future; climate change can lead to lower profit of offshore investments; commercial insurance of offshore energy supply, and government help to the cluster towards more competitiveness and collaboration with other aggregated sectors, with financial and employment benefits; renewable energy is not mainstream, it needs technology, development, and research; lack of technical human resources and private financial support.

The importance of the pentagonal problem is based on a set of skills gathered to develop the offshore cluster project, and therefore circular economy projects (Fig. 5). Those are implemented taking in account more innovation and technology towards human well-being

The figure shows the capacity of offshore energy projects to become important in CE. The big challenge for the current business model is the capacity of offshore energy projects to be linked to CE in Portugal.

Solving the pentagonal problem is the basis for the change of the Portuguese business model towards a market strategy. This involves the implementation of environmental solutions, contributing positively to CE, cooperation with other environment-friendly organizations, innovation, expertise network, public interest, and intensive R&D activities.

Additionally, the importance of an agreement on a business model for offshore energy related with CE and the potential economic impact constitute an important point for organizations.

Therefore, solving the pentagonal problem for offshore energy in Portugal will allow for the identification of benefits and catalyzing enabling mechanisms focusing on five key areas of economic and environmental impact: material inputs, labor inputs, energy inputs, carbon emissions, and the balance of trade. Additionally, using a "circularity calculator" it is possible to compare the inputs needed to make a new product in today's linear system with those required to make the same product using pure materials flow (MacArthur and MackKinsey & Company 2014: 53).

For this reason, the Portuguese business model based on offshore energy development can be applied to public-private partnerships on innovative solutions, simultaneously developing a networking platform to foster the global agenda on science,

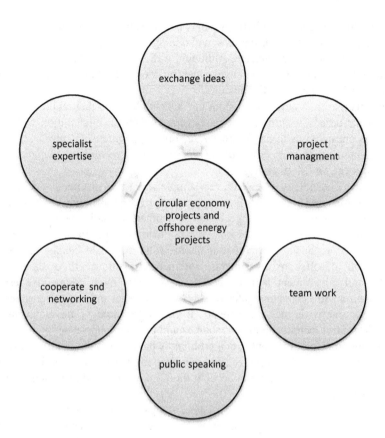

Fig. 5 Offshore energy projects and circular economy

technology, and innovation (innovation ecosystems). The goal is to find a solution for the pentagonal problem and address new challenges on business with synergies between the partners. Another point of view stressed the importance of information technologies (IT) in CE. Its trace the materials and products, organizing reverse logistics and accelerating innovation and technology (ecosystems). CE is one of the challenges for Portuguese business networking and for the emerging offshore cluster. Others like smart cities, sustainability buildings, and eco production will also bring up new challenges.

7   Conclusions

The interest of considering CE together with offshore energy is becoming more attractive bearing in mind the benefits of potential economic externalities. Thus, the analysis made along this paper showed that there is a positive economic impact from using renewables in green economy. Therefore, resources productivity, circular activities, waste generation and greenhouse emissions constitute important vectors for studying this relationship.

Considering the positive impact of offshore energy sector in Portugal (Pego et al. 2016), Porters' cleantech model, and the pentagonal problem related with CE and offshore energy projects in Portugal, this paper concluded that organizations face an important change towards a market strategy based on materials, labor, energy inputs, and natural innovation ecosystems. This means changing attitudes towards innovation and technology through new business from CE.

References

Andersen, M. S. (2007). An introductory note on the environmental economics of the circular economy. *Sustainability Science, 2*(1), 133–140.

Benito, G. R., Berger, E., De la Forest, M., & Shum, J. (2003). A cluster analysis of the maritime sector in Norway. *International Journal of Transport Management, 1*(4), 203–215.

Boschma, R., Frenken, K., Bathelt, H., Feldman, M., & Kogler, D. (2012). Technological relatedness and regional branching. *Beyondterritory. Dynamicgeographies of knowledge creation, diffusion and innovation* (pp. 64–81). London: Routledge.

Burtis, P., Epstein, R., & Hwang, R. (2004). *Creating the California cleantechcluster*. Environmental Entrepreneurs and Natural Resources Defense Council. Accessed June 10, 2017, from https://www.nrdc.org/sites/default/files/cleantech.pdf

Cluster, C. C. (2012). *The global cleantech report 2012*. Copenhagen: Copenhagen Cleantech Cluster.

Costea-Dunarintu, A. (2016). The circular economy in the European Union. *Knowledge Horizons. Economics*, *8*(1): 148–150.

Davies, A. R. (2013). Cleantech clusters: Transformational assemblages for a just, green economy or just business as usual? *Global Environmental Change, 23*(5), 1285–1295.

Di Fonzo, M. & Hime, S. (2017). *How businesses measure their impacts on nature: A gap analysis* (Working Paper 01/2017). University of Cambridge Institute for Sustainability Leadership (CISL).

Dögl, C., Holtbrügge, D., & Schuster, T. (2012). Competitive advantage of German renewable energy firms in India and China: An empirical study based on Porter's diamond. *International Journal of Emerging Markets, 7*(2), 191–214.

Energy Management and Energy Savings (EMES). (2017). *Draft Business Plan ISO TC 301*. Accessed June 6, 2017, from http://isotc.iso.org/livelink/livelink/open/tc301

European Academic Science Advisory Board (EASAB). (2015). *Circular economy: A commentary from the perspectives of the natural and social sciences*. Accessed May 31, 2017, from http://vatt.fi/documents/2956369/3244616/European+Academies+Science+Advisory+Council+Circular+economy+a+commentary+from+the+perspectives+of+the+natural+and+social+sciences/82982e56-56f6-466d-8fe6-dc2b8079cb7b

European Environment Agency. (2016). *Circular economy in Europe. Developing the knowledge base* (EEA Report No. 2/2016).

Finland, C. (2014). *About Cleantech Finland*. Accessed June 10, 2017, from http://www.rohevik.ee/2012/wp-content/uploads/2012/08/Lauri_Hietaniemi_191012.pdf

Genovese, A., Acquaye, A. A., Figueroa, A., & Koh, S. L. (2017). Sustainable supply chain management and the transition towards a circular economy: Evidence and some applications. *Omega, 66*, 344–357.

Henriksen, K., Bjerre, M., Øster, J., & Henriksen, T. (2012). *Green business model innovation-policy report*. Nordic Council of Ministers.

IWA. (2016). *Water utility pathways in a circular economy*. London: International Water Association.

Lam, H. L., Varbanov, P. S., & Klemeš, J. J. (2011). Regional renewable energy and resource planning. *Applied Energy, 88*(2), 545–550.

Lieder, M., & Rashid, A. (2016). Towards circular economy implementation: A comprehensive review in the context of manufacturing industry. *Journal of Cleaner Production, 115*, 36–51.

MacArthur, E. & MackKinsey & Company. (2014). *World economic forum*. Accessed May 28, 2017, from http://www3.weforum.org/docs/WEF_ENV_TowardsCircularEconomy_Report_2014.pdf

Matti, C., de Vicente López, J., Sargeantson, E., Burn, C., & Dahl, P. L. S. (2016, June). *Practice-based knowledge on system innovation and climate change. A learning approach for practitioners through active-blended format*. https://www.ris.uu.nl/ws/files/22582552/WEB040716_POSTER_EDUCATION_A1.pdfv

Maxoulis, C. N., Charalampous, H. P., & Kalogirou, S. A. (2007). Cyprus solar water heating cluster: A missed opportunity? *Energy Policy, 35*(6), 3302–3315.

McCauley, S. M., & Stephens, J. C. (2012). Green energy clusters and socio-technical transitions: Analysis of a sustainable energy cluster for regional economic development in Central Massachusetts, USA. *Sustainability Science, 7*(2), 213–225.

Monteiro, P., de Noronha, T., & Neto, P. (2013). A differentiation framework for maritime clusters: Comparisons across Europe. *Sustainability, 5*(9), 4076–4105.

Moser, S. C., & Ekstrom, J. A. (2010). A framework to diagnose barriers to climate change adaptation. *Proceedings of the National Academy of Sciences, 107*(51): 22026–22031.

Nooteboom, B., Van Haverbeke, W., Duysters, G., Gilsing, V., & Van den Oord, A. (2007). Optimal cognitive distance and absorptive capacity. *Research Policy, 36*(7), 1016–1034.

OECD. (2016). *OECD factbooks 2015-2016: Economic, environmental and social statistics*. Paris: OECD Publishing.

Oh, D. S., Phillips, F., Park, S., & Lee, E. (2016). Innovation ecosystems: A critical examination. *Technovation, 54*, 1–6.

Partidario, M. R., & Gomes, R. C. (2013). Ecosystem services inclusive strategic environmental assessment. *Environmental Impact Assessment Review, 40*, 36–46.

Pego, A., Marques, M., Salvador, R., Soares, G., Monteiro, A. (2016). The potential offshore energy cluster in Portugal. In C. Guedes Soares (Eds.), *Progress in renewable energy offshore* (pp. 867–873). London: Taylor & Francis.

Porter, M. E. (1990). New global strategies for competitive advantage. *Planning Review, 18*(3), 4–14.

Su, B., Heshmati, A., Geng, Y., & Yu, X. (2013). A review of the circular economy in China: Moving from rhetoric to implementation. *Journal of Cleaner Production, 42*, 215–227.

Titze, M., Brachert, M., & Kubis, A. (2011). The identification of regional industrial clusters using qualitative input–output analysis (QIOA). *Regional Studies, 4*(1), 89–102.

Van der Panne, G. (2004). Agglomeration externalities: Marshall versus Jacobs. *Journal of Evolutionary Economics, 14*, 593–604.

Wijnolst, N. (2006). *Dynamic European maritime clusters* (Vol. 30). Amsterdam: IOS Press.

Zhang, F., & Cooke, P. (2009). *Global and regional development of renewable energy*. Project "Green innovation and entrepreneurship in Europe" funded EU FP6

Zhao, Z. Y., Zhang, S. Y., & Zuo, J. (2011). A critical analysis of the photovoltaic power industry in China—From diamond model to gear model. *Renewable and Sustainable Energy Reviews, 15*(9): 4963–4971.

Entrepreneurial Urban Revitalization

Carlos José Lopes Balsas

Abstract Business Improvement Districts (BIDs) in north-America were used during the last two decades as instruments capable of making communities more attractive for residents and visitors. The purpose of this chapter is to discuss the application of this revitalization mechanism in downtown Stockton (California). The argument is that BIDs can provide an answer to many of the livability problems faced by city centers (Balsas, Planning Practice and Research 19(1):101–110, 2004). The key finding is that the proactive implementation of this urban revitalization mechanism can increase the livability of communities and their economic development opportunities in part because of its entrepreneurial perspective. The chapter closes with a series of recommendations for the successful implementation of an entrepreneurial urban revitalization strategy.

Keywords Entrepreneurial management · Urban revitalization · Business improvement district—BID · Stockton—California · North-America

1 Introduction

Business Improvement Districts (BIDs) in north-America were used during the last two decades as instruments capable of making communities more attractive for residents and visitors. The purpose of this chapter is to discuss the application of this revitalization mechanism in downtown Stockton (California). The argument is that BIDs can provide an answer to many of the livability problems faced by city centers (Balsas 2004). The key finding is that the proactive implementation of this urban revitalization mechanism can increase the livability of communities and their economic development opportunities in part because of its entrepreneurial perspective.

C. J. L. Balsas (✉)
Geography and Planning AS210, University at Albany, Albany, NY, USA
e-mail: cbalsas@albany.edu

© Springer International Publishing AG, part of Springer Nature 2018   329
S. Cubico et al. (eds.), *Entrepreneurship and the Industry Life Cycle*, Studies on Entrepreneurship, Structural Change and Industrial Dynamics,
https://doi.org/10.1007/978-3-319-89336-5_15

Table 1 Importance of city center revitalization

Improves image	The center is the area that usually gives visitors their first impressions of a community
Makes use of existing buildings	Assists communities in managing growth through reuse of property
Develops a sense of community	Provides central location for community-wide projects
Provides variety of retail options	The more stores there are in an area, the more people will gather and shop
Prevents blight and abandonment	Reduces health and safety costs and concerns; discourages vagrancy and vandalism
Perpetuates community character and history	Visible signs of the past can be retained and stories can be passed on to the next generation
Encourages new and complementary businesses	Businesses want to be where people are and money is being spent, so it strengthens an existing building cluster
Expands the tax base	Generates local revenues to pay for community services
Increases employment opportunities	Replaces jobs lost through natural attrition and encourages entrepreneurs
Regains status as central shopping district	Pulls in shoppers from a radius beyond the city limits

Source: Adapted from Community Assistance Center (1999)

In the United States, the first activities of city center revitalization started shortly after the end of World War II. They started probably more intensely during the 1960s when cities started to be affected by the growing processes of suburbanization and when retail activities relocated to out-of-town locations. If initially those revitalization activities only involved signs and billboards to attract customer's attention that retail was still located downtown, in the 1970s and 1980s they evolved to better organized and better financed revitalization interventions (Gratz and Mintz 1998; Gibbs 2012; Balsas 2017a).

These interventions have been aggregated into four main areas (Robertson 1997). First, the pedestrianization of main streets. Second, the conversion of historical buildings in specialty retail, restaurants and entertainment centers. Third, the construction of downtown shopping centers. And fourth, the construction of mixed-use complexes ranging from hotels to convention centers and transportation hubs. Besides these four main types, there is still a set of more eclectic interventions. Among these there is the designation of the downtown area as a historic district, the establishment of a Main Street Program, tax increment financing, and strategies aimed at centralized retail management (Frieden and Sagalyn 1991; Francaviglia 1996; Grodach and Ehrenfeucht 2016).

The most recent trend in commercial development in the United States is that city centers are regaining their traditional role as centers of commerce and shopping (Ford 2003; Gibbs 2012). Even though this development includes a great variety of commercial formats and solutions, the main goal is to take advantage of the urban context and of its sense of place. Table 1 shows the importance of city center revitalization.

2   Business Improvement Districts (BIDs)

The Business Improvement Districts are important instruments in the commercial revitalization of city centers in the United States and Canada (Houstoun 2003). BIDs can have different names depending on the state and cities where they are developed. They can be called Special Improvement Districts, Business Improvement Zones and Special Services Districts. Even though there is no consensus about their exact number, projections indicate that the number of BIDs in existence throughout the United States has surpassed more than 1500.

A BID is a financial instrument that allows property owners in a certain geographical area to have several supplemental services through the payment of a property fee. BIDs are formed and controlled by the property owners in a specific area. After being legally approved, all property owners in that pre-defined area have to pay an additional fee to have additional services in their area. These services include maintenance, safety and marketing among others. Even though there are residential and industrial BIDs, the great majority targets commercial properties.

The need for these services resulted from the increased competition from the new shopping malls in out-of-town locations and the decrease in the volume of sales by the merchants in traditional downtowns. On the other, hand BIDs can be an alternative way to pay for new infrastructures and new common services such as maintenance and safety.

In general, BIDs are created in areas that suffered or are in risk of urban decline. Even though they can be criticized by some who do not want to pay any more fees, BIDs are efficient ways to increase safety, cleanliness, attract customers back and to increase the value of commercial properties.

The establishment of a BID is preceded by state legislation. Past experience has demonstrated that many merchants are skeptical at first before knowing the fee structure and the program of additional services to be proposed. But the legislation that authorizes the creation of BIDs also contains rules about its dissolution and frequent revision and monitorization after an initial period of about 5 years. As long as property owners give their support the BID can be in place. Once established, BIDs can charge an agreed fee to all property owners in the intervention area. This possibility to charge a compulsory fee in an area previously defined makes sure that there is no "free rider" since all property owners who benefit from the services of the organization have to contribute to its costs. The city normally collects the fees and gives the money to the organization in charge of managing the BID.

BIDs have several key elements in common: (1) the initiative comes from business leaders who seek common services beyond those that the city can provide; (2) the city determines the boundaries, approves the annual budget and the financing strategy, and determines what services may be provided; (3) business leaders shape the annual budget, hire staff, led contracts, and generally oversee operations (Table 2).

This financing mechanism is being used and is even proposed as a useful structure that allows property owners, merchants and local authorities to achieve common

Table 2 Benefits provided by BIDs in north-America

Supplementary government services	• Hiring uniformed security personnel • Cleaning and maintaining parks and other public spaces
Non-governmental services	• Sidewalk cleaning • Snow removal • Marketing, promotions, and advertising • Business retention and recruitment
Advocacy	• Speak collectively • Develop and promote unified positions • Help government services through performance and monitoring
Cooperative enterprises	• Joint advertising • Purchase of services • Special needs common to many but not all businesses
Capital improvement financing	• Allow BIDs to borrow to pay for streetscaping programs under applicable state laws
Research and planning services	• Collect and analyze economic and demographic data • Monitor progress • Set and revise goals • Develop multi-year redevelopment programs

Source: Houstoun (2003)

goals. This unifying characteristic allows them to solve common problems but above all makes sure that entities that otherwise would not work together do have a shared forum to solve common problems. The main lesson one can learn from the BID implementation seems to be that merchants are using these organizations to make city centers more competitive. The key to their success seems to be the entrepreneurial perspective that is being applying to the creation and maintenance of livable urban areas (Eisinger 1988).

3   Case Study: Stockton

Stockton is a regional city and county seat located on Interstate Highway I-5 in California's San Joaquin Central Valley, almost halfway between San Francisco and the state's capital of Sacramento. This area is one of the most fertile agricultural areas in the country but it is suffering tremendous urbanization pressures due to its proximity to San Francisco bay area and the Silicon Valley. With a population of 291,000 people in 2010, the city grew and developed as a result of its privileged location in the middle of a very fertile agricultural hinterland irrigated by the San Joaquin River and its intricate canal system. In recent decades, a considerable amount of land has been converted to new subdivisions to the north and northwest, in many cases according to unscrupulous land use development practices, which look, feel, and function more like car-dependent suburban sprawl than sustainable urbanism neighborhoods.

The city's growth and dispersal have impacted the downtown area negatively reducing it mostly to institutional uses, limited retail, some entertainment offerings, and almost no residential structures (Balsas 2017b). Stockton also has an inland port and a high quantity of derelict available land from light industry uses in the southern and eastern districts, just a few blocks from downtown. Fortunately, urban revitalization programs implemented since the 1990s have led to the rehabilitation of historic buildings with architectonic significance, the construction of a new multimodal transit station in the mid-2000s according to federal Transit Oriented Development (TOD) station area guidelines, and the improvement of the waterfront Weber Point Park, which now constitutes a central lively public space for many cultural and sports events (Lyndon 2005).

The designation of Stockton as an "All America City" by the National Civic League in July of 1999 was the result of years of joint work by the city's different institutions and local residents. This designation shows that civic and pro-active participation, together with a governmental action that incorporates volunteerism and shares information to generate a strong vision, can bring many benefits to all citizens. The strategy for the city center included the creation of a new private organization to promote, develop and maintain the city center area. Besides the funds coming from the compulsory fee to all property owners, in a range of 65 blocks, the establishment of many partnerships and other collaborations with private and public organizations have been critical to the success of the city center revitalization activities.

4 Discussion

Table 3 presents a synthesis of the entrepreneurial urban revitalization BID in Stockton. Downtown Stockton Alliance is a new private non-profit organization with an autonomous staff and an intervention area well delimitated, with a specific budget and with a relatively high number of representatives on the board of directors. These members are representatives from the local community. Usually, there are several working groups that have to meet frequently to analyze, coordinate or simply to assess the progress obtained in the implementation of a certain project.

The great majority of these revitalization organizations are created for a period of 3–5 years. In the case of the business improvement districts there is a need to re-authorize their existence every 5 years. The intervention area in Stockton comprises approximately 65 blocks. The main objective of this organization is not only the revitalization of the commercial component of the city center but also the encouragement of residential living downtown, the preservation of historical buildings, the implementation of streetscape improvements, the coordination of parking and the promotion of the area through cultural events and city marketing campaigns (Speck 2012). Many of these organizations initially start by improving the cleaning and safety of the intervention area. Only after improving these basic services, they broaden their scope to also include economic development activities and the attraction of new economic activities and technical support to the existing ones.

Table 3 Synthesis of the entrepreneurial urban revitalization BID in Stockton

	Stockton (CA)
Type of organization	Downtown Stockton Alliance—private nonprofit organization
Partnership objectives	Promotion, development, and maintenance of the Stockton city center
Juridical structure	Board of directors; executive team
Geographical area	65 blocks in the city center; population: 18000 residents and about 2000 economic activities
Type of management	One executive director; one secretary (part-time); three marketing and economic development technicians; one coordinator of events; one coordinator of hospitality; seven local guides; eight cleaning and maintenance employees
Main activities	Maintenance; hospitality and safety; economic development; marketing, promotions and special events
Budget structure	Maintenance (25%); hospitality and security (23%); marketing and economic development (27%); organization (20%); others (5%)
Funding nature	Variable compulsory levy on property depending on the property's location within the BID precinct
Website	https://www.downtownstockton.org/

The revitalization activities in Stockton included maintenance, hospitality and safety, economic development, marketing, promotions and special events. These activities were very similar to the revitalization activities in other downtowns. It is important to mention that property owners in different areas of the BID pay different amounts depending on their location. The funds to finance the activities of these organizations have two different sources. The revitalization funds come directly from the application of the compulsory fee to the properties within the district. But these organizations can also ask for loans and establish funding collaborations. Even though what these organizations can do is always limited by their budgets (Gelinas 2013) and by their technical capacity, it is important to mention the important role of volunteering activities.

5 Conclusion and Recommendations

In conclusion, the objective of the city center intervention mechanism reviewed above is to create better ways to manage a city center. Due to the specific nature of city centers, these models give priority to partnerships between the private and the public sectors. This mixed nature includes traditional aspects from both sectors (Nawratek 2011; Barber 2013). The representatives from the public authorities were democratically elected and should aim at preserving the common interest derived from a revitalized downtown. The representatives from the private interest are unconditional partners in the sense that they can influence the role of the local elected officials. Beyond the characteristics of the revitalization programs identified in Table 1, the existence of a full time professional management team and the existence of local sustainable funds seem to be the two most critical aspects to the good functioning of the city center.

It is important to emphasize that these models are not static. Similar to city centers, they go through evolutive phases. What is important is that the proactive implementation of this urban revitalization instrument can increase the livability of communities and their economic development opportunities. The recommendations at the local level include working principles for a city center management office, for the municipality, for the chamber of commerce, and for economic activities [see Balsas (2006)]. These recommendations were derived from the author's almost two decades of investigations on urban transformations and the responses crafted and implemented to facilitate transitions through cyclical changes in the economy. Like Savitch and Kantor (2002), it is also important to recognize that these recommendations are not suggested here to create more homogenized urban areas. They have been distilled from the analysis of multiple cities and towns across the Atlantic Ocean in both Anglo-Saxon (Balsas 2014) and southern European contexts (Balsas 2007). At least from a U.S. perspective and according to Wachs (2013, p. 1159), they seem to have contributed to creating "the most vibrant residential and commercial centers throughout a largely suburban continent".

5.1 City Center Management Office

Create effective public-private partnerships The foreign experiences show that public-private partnerships are a critical element in the success of the city center revitalization operations. In this partnership the main characteristics include joint decision-making and sharing responsibilities among the different partners in order to benefit the entire community. More recently, the private sector is taking the leadership in many revitalization partnerships. Even beyond the public and the private sector, many foreign partnerships include the participation of civic and voluntary associations.

Create the position of city center manager The existence of a city center manager is critical to the implementation of a revitalization partnership and to the future management of a city center. Its main function is to help the board of directors to develop a strategy for the city center, including the implementation of the action plan and the program of activities and, the creation and coordination of the working groups. The manager is also the coordinator of the existing interests in the city center and the person responsible for gathering more funds to the city center management office. It is important that the city center manager is on board from the start of the partnership or is nominated very soon thereafter.

Create a long-term strategic vision The most successful revitalizations include a clear strategic, pro-active and consensual vision for the city center in the future, for instance in the next 5–10 years. It is important that all partners contribute to the definition of this strategic vision and that all are responsible for it, and believe that it is realistic and capable of being achieved.

Holistically analyze the city center Before defining the intervention strategy, it is necessary to holistically analyze the city center in its different dimensions. For instance, the commercial position in the regional hierarchy, strengths (e.g. diversified offer), weaknesses (e.g. accessibility), opportunities (e.g. collaborative environment) and threats (e.g. peripheral retail areas). Many of these analyses can already be done in studies of the municipality or of the chamber of commerce; however, it is important that the partnership can produce a concise and clear document with the main diagnosis of the city center.

Have a coherent intervention strategy The intervention strategies in the city center must contain action plans that allow the management office to successfully achieve the previously defined vision and capture the opportunities identified in the market study. This action plan results directly from the diagnosis, it must be detailed to the point of identifying all the activities that need to be done, their beginning and end, who is responsible for them, how much money is allocated to each action, and where the money comes from. This action plan must be revised and updated annually.

Be selective and define priorities With the exception of small cities, regular city centers can have considerable dimensions, which can make it difficult to solve multiple problems through only one program. On the other hand, there are always more skeptical partners who like to see immediate results. Due to these two limitations, the most successful city center programs are those, which direct their (necessarily limited) resources to the target areas identified by the different partners. The concentration of resources in a certain geographical area makes it easy for the revitalization efforts to become more visible. It is important to take incremental action with realistic activities.

Have a city marketing plan A city center partnership must have a city marketing plan that allows the management office to communicate effectively with the targeted consumers. This plan must give a positive image of the city center and of its activities. It must include promotional campaigns, tourist guides, maps, brochures, as well as the realization of events and public festivals. These festive events should portray the city center as an interesting and safe place to shop, reside, work and be entertained. It is important to communicate the results of these activities to the elected officials and to the people at large, so that they can keep their interest in the activities being done by the management office.

Encourage and promote local leadership In order to create successful partnerships, it is important that the leaders are from the local community and that they find resources within their own community. Sustainability should be one of the main goals of the partnership. Local leadership involves establishing links with the most influential people in the community and between them and the merchants, and not only the ones located in the city center but those representing the entire community.

Promote sustainable funding The management unit must have a mechanism that allows it to gather funds in adequate amounts so that the action plan can be implemented. The most successful partnerships abroad are the ones where the public government subsidies are minimal. Normally, public funding is used to create the management office and to keep it functioning for a certain period of time, during which the manager is supposed to gather funds from other sources as well, in order to achieve a sustainable funding level.

Recognize and value voluntary contributions Voluntary contributions are very important to the functioning of the partnership. They can be monetary amounts, goods, services or even time to participate in the working groups. Public funds are normally given to partnerships with the condition that they have to be matched with local funds. In these cases, it is important that the city center manager can be very persuasive in showing potential contributors what they can gain by contributing to the partnership.

Monitor and evaluate management activities regularly The manager must conduct inspections to the city center as regularly as possible. In these inspections the manager should pay attention to cleanliness, safety, attractiveness services available in the center, parking, and conflicts between users, etc. The manager must also regularly monitor a set of statistical indicators that can give the elements of the board of directors an idea of how the revitalization activity is evolving. These indicators include, vacant properties, number of pedestrians, crime, and the number of new jobs created, etc.

5.2 Municipality

Promote the revitalization of the center The revitalization of the city center must be an economic development and political priority for the municipality. It is the municipality's responsibility to promote the identity and the diversity of the city center through its active participation in the partnership. To have competitive economic activities in the city centers, municipalities have to review local ordinances and licensing processes in order to expedite investments in the center. These processes must be fast, but without the loss of quality or rigor in the revitalization interventions.

Create Commercial Development Plans These instruments are being developed in many municipalities in order to coordinate commercial interventions. It is believed that the operationalization of such plans with traditional planning documents (e.g. master plans, ordinances and regulations) and processes (e.g. licensing, permitting, and GIS analyses) can expedite intervention processes and help the work of the city center manager.

Integrate retail activities in the municipal plans It is a responsibility of the planning technicians working for the municipality to include commercial activities in the municipal plans (e.g. strategic, master, urbanization and site plans). It is important that retail is taken into consideration as any other activity with profound implications in the organization of the territory, but also in terms of the socio-economic dynamics of the localities.

Promote high standards of cleanliness, maintenance and safety The cleaning and maintenance of public spaces must have very high standards of quality and hygiene. These standards must apply to the mechanical and manual cleaning of streets and sidewalks, the emptying of litter and wastebaskets, and to the cleaning and removal of graffiti and other unwanted publicity. The maintenance of trees, flower pots and bushes, as well as the maintenance of street furniture, signal and lights is very critical to the appearance and safety in the city center.

Promote a compact and sustainable development To promote mixed-use develop-ments and to control suburbanization, reducing the need to use private cars in urban areas must be a critical objective of municipal planning. The implementation of this objective not only reinforces the livability of the center but it also increases the quality of life of all city users.

5.3   Chamber of Commerce

Promote the creation of city center management offices The chambers of commerce have a critical role in the revitalization programs and in the creation of city center management offices, since their direct activity involves the promotion of commercial activity in the community. In many foreign cities, the chamber of commerce temporarily houses the city center management office and allows the manager to share its resources (e.g. installation, equipment, administrative support, etc.); this may help the city center revitalization initiative. However, it is important to mention that the chamber of commerce normally has a territorial area broader than the city center, which can lead to long-term conflicts.

Mobilize retailers to become involved in the direction of the center The chamber of commerce can have a critical role in making its members involved in the activities of the city center management office. This involves the organization of events, the coordination of promotions, festivals and the production of marketing materials.

Cooperate in the organization of events The chamber of commerce can cooperate in the organization of events that aim to promote the activities in the center. The gathering of sponsorship, the naming of a coordinator, and the promotion of the event well ahead of time can make a real difference in terms of the number of participants.

Promote best practices of commercial management The chamber of commerce must be ready to promote best practices of commercial management. It can also organize and promote professional training sessions capable of increasing the competitiveness of the small businesses.

Develop alternative ways of doing business In cooperation with the city center management office and the municipality, the chamber of commerce can develop and promote alternative ways of doing business. It can, for instance, promote business over the Internet such as e-commerce. It can even identify niche markets of traditional local products and sell them in cooperation with the tourism services of the municipality.

5.4 Economic Activities

Follow market principles The realization of a diagnosis market study is critical to know who the customers are, which other customers can be attracted, what kind of goods do customers want, what their future preferences will be and finally, how to create loyal customers.

Target differences In order to compete, the city center retail must be able to create and be known for a certain type(s) of product(s). This calls forth the notion of niche market. The retail located in the city center cannot sell the exact same merchandise as the stores in the peripheral shopping malls. They can instead target certain themes, and certain age groups. The idea is to coexist with the big shopping malls and not compete directly with them. So, the difference should not be on price but on the type of product.

Be unique Even though now there are many new ways to buy the same product, city center retail can prosper by providing a friendly and quality service to their customers. For instance, this might involve personalized service and an after sale assistance program.

Participate in the resolution of common problems The mission to create a livable center capable of attracting customers is not a responsibility of the municipality alone. It is up to the individual merchants to keep their establishments attractive, as well as to participate in the resolution of the problems of the city center as a whole. The support of the city center management office can go beyond money contributions, support can be offered with goods and services, time, equipment and installations.

Acknowledgement This chapter revises and references more generously material from two previously published pieces: Balsas, C. (2004). BIDs as Instruments of City Center Revitalization. *APA Economic Development Newsletter,* vol. Winter, pp. 7–12, and Balsas, C. (2006). Commercial urbanism in Portugal, evolution and future perspectives (pp. 357–369), In D. Feehan & M. Feit (Eds.), *Making Business Districts Work.* New York: The Haworth Press. The author is very grateful to the original publishers.

References

Balsas, C. J. L. (2004). Measuring the livability of an urban center: An exploratory study of key performance indicators. *Planning Practice and Research, 19*(1), 101–110.

Balsas, C. J. L. (2006). Commercial urbanism in Portugal, evolution and future perspectives. In D. Feehan & M. Feit (Eds.), *Making business districts work*. New York: The Haworth Press.

Balsas, C. J. L. (2007). City center revitalization in Portugal: A study of Lisbon and Porto. *Journal of Urban Design, 12*(2), 231–259.

Balsas, C. J. L. (2014). Downtown resilience: A review of recent (re)developments in Tempe, Arizona. *Cities—The International Journal of Urban Policy and Planning, 36*, 158–169.

Balsas, C. J. L. (2017a). Lemons into Lemonade: Materializing utopian planning in Providence, Rhode Island (RI). In M. Monteiro, M. Kong, & M. Neto (Eds.), *PHI Utopia(s)—Worlds and frontiers of the imaginary*. London: CRC Press.

Balsas, C. J. L. (2017b). Sustainable urbanism in temperate-arid climates: Models, challenges and opportunities for the Anthropocene. *Journal of Public Affairs.*. https://doi.org/10.1002/pa.1663

Barber, B. (2013). *If mayors ruled the world—Dysfunctional nations, rising cities*. London: Yale University Press.

Community Assistance Center. (1999). *Learning to lead: A primer on economic development strategies*. Seattle: Washington State Department of Commerce.

Eisinger, P. (1988). *The rise of the entrepreneurial state*. Madison: The University of Wisconsin Press.

Ford, L. (2003). *Revitalization or reinvention? America's new downtowns*. Baltimore: The Johns Hopkins University Press.

Francaviglia, R. (1996). *Main street revisited—Time, space, and building in small-town America*. Iowa City: University of Iowa Press.

Frieden, B., & Sagalyn, L. (1991). *Downtown Inc. How America rebuilds cities*. Cambridge: The MIT Press.

Gelinas, N. (2013). What to do when you're broke—New York's insolvent municipalities could learn from California's bankrupt ones. *City Journal, Summer*: 36–43.

Gibbs, R. (2012). *Principles of urban retail planning and development*. Hoboken: Wiley.

Gratz, R., & Mintz, N. (1998). *CITIES back from the edge—New life for downtown*. New York: Preservation Press.

Grodach, C., & Ehrenfeucht, R. (2016). *Urban revitalization—Remaking cities in a changing world*. London: Routledge.

Houstoun, L. (2003). *BIDs: Business improvement districts* (2nd ed.). Washington, DC: ULI—The Urban Land Institute.

Lyndon, D. (2005). Editorial—Cover image: Weber point. *Places, 17*(3), 2.

Nawratek, K. (2011). *City as a political idea*. Plymouth: University of Plymouth Press.

Robertson, K. A. (1997). Downtown retail revitalization: A review of American development strategies. *Planning Perspectives, 12*(4), 383–401.

Savitch, H. V., & Kantor, P. (2002). *Cities in the international marketplace*. Princeton: Princeton University Press.

Speck, J. (2012). *Walkable city—How downtown can save America, one step at a time*. New York: North Point Press.

Wachs, M. (2013). Turning cities inside out: Transportation and the resurgence of downtowns in North America. *Transportation, 40*, 1159–1172.

Unconventional Entrepreneurship and the Municipality: The Role of Passion and Competences

Francesca Simeoni and Federico Testa

Abstract The purpose of this research is to investigate unconventional entrepreneurship and its relationship with the municipality. In particular, the research seeks to deepen the understanding of passion and competences in this special context. A case study method was utilised, focusing on the recreational–vehicle–equipped parking area in Monzambano (Italy), which is one of the best of its kind in Italy and Europe. Two critical findings emerge from the case study. First, the relationship between the entrepreneur and the municipality. Since the beginning (of the recreational–vehicle–equipped parking area), this relationship has provided business opportunities and threats at the same time; at a later stage of development, this relationship might lead to better results in terms of sustainability (economic, environmental and social) for the firm *in primis* and for the whole territory. The second critical finding relates to the role of passion and competences of the entrepreneur in a similar context.

Keywords Unconventional entrepreneurship · User entrepreneurs · Passion and competences · Municipality · Tourist destination · Recreational vehicles

1 Introduction

Unconventional entrepreneurship is a relatively new concept in the literature and not well defined. Since the eighties, some authors have talked about the possibility that a form of entrepreneurship could be considered a form of consumption rather than production, particularly in the case of tourism entrepreneurship (Williams et al. 1989); they have also demonstrated some important dimensions of noneconomic decision-making. For tourism entrepreneurship, it was revealed that the new entrepreneurs were attracted to the possibility of consuming (enjoying) the landscape and

F. Simeoni (✉) · F. Testa
Department of Business Administration, University of Verona, Verona, Italy
e-mail: francesca.simeoni@univr.it; federico.testa@univr.it

© Springer International Publishing AG, part of Springer Nature 2018   341
S. Cubico et al. (eds.), *Entrepreneurship and the Industry Life Cycle*, Studies on Entrepreneurship, Structural Change and Industrial Dynamics,
https://doi.org/10.1007/978-3-319-89336-5_16

acquiring a lifestyle mode of self-employment. Sometimes this phenomenon was related to the life cycle and so with the post-retirement period or as a half-way stage to retirement. Some of these entrepreneurs 'had relatively little relevant job experience or training and there were few opportunities to acquire the latter anyway' (Williams et al. 1989, p. 1650). Moreover, some of these entrepreneurs were classified as 'without capital entrepreneurs' (p. 1640); the research showed that the capital required was modest because of the domestication of the labour force and the self-service economy (Gershuny and Miles 1983) that could reduce the operating costs.

The role of entrepreneurs in a destination's development has been too often considered only in the early stages of the Tourism Area Life Cycle (Butler 1980) without consideration of the human as an active entity in the others stages of Butler's model. Differently, some authors now declare that it is important 'to understand the dynamic and historical role of entrepreneurs' to study tourism development (Ryan et al. 2012, p. 2; Ritchie and Crouch 2003; Li 2008). The role of entrepreneurs can be considered to help and stimulate the transformation of an area to a tourism destination (Koh and Hatten 2002) and promote the involvement of other businesses in the tourism destination (Ryan et al. 2012; Pearce 1995).

Further, it is interesting to understand the role of the municipality in this type of transformation and development of a tourism area. The complexity but also the discretion and leeway of the public administration and public servants 'clearly require nonroutine or creative behavior (...) what makes public administration innovative, proactive, and sometimes even risk taking' (Meynhardt and Diefenbach 2012, p. 761; Currie et al. 2008; Morris and Jones 1999).

Regarding these concepts, this chapter discusses the unconventional entrepreneur figure's role in the development of an area into a tourist destination, with active participation of the municipality. We find that the principal strengths and weaknesses lie in the passion and competences of the involved actors. From this analysis, it will also be possible to underline future opportunities and threats for the destination and entrepreneurship in the area. To do so, we will analyse a case study: the birth and development of the RV-equipped parking area in Monzambano (Italy).

The purpose of this research is to investigate unconventional entrepreneurship and the relationship with the municipality. The research seeks to deepen the understanding of the role of passion and competences in this special context. The case study method was chosen because our aim is to increase our understanding on this matter, rather than only suppose from the literature the possible characteristics of these special entrepreneurs.

First, a literature review of the user and unconventional entrepreneurs is presented in a tourism context. Second, we examine the industry context and then the territorial context. Following the methodology of this research was shown. Finally, the findings are presented, with discussion and conclusions.

2   The Literature Review

Shah and Tripsas (2007, p. 124) define user entrepreneurship as 'the commercialization of a new product and/or service by an individual or group of individuals who are also users of that product and/or service'. This type of entrepreneurship remains under-recognised and under-studied.

Of the two categories of user entrepreneurs indicated by Shah and Tripsas (2007, p. 124), we refer to the case of end-user entrepreneurs who are the first individuals to use a product in their day-to-day lives. Therefore, we exclude reference to 'professional users' who could become entrepreneurs.

The benefits that derive from the activity followed by user entrepreneurs (Haefliger et al. 2010) are, in general, identified in the use of the created product or service and in the financial benefit from the commercialisation.

This paper contributes to the entrepreneurship literature by extending the knowledge of user entrepreneurship, naming it in this case 'unconventional entrepreneurship'. The case study we present demonstrates and confirms what Shah and Tripsas (2007) theorise about regarding 'the conditions that make user entrepreneurship more prevalent in some industries than others' (p. 126). That is, user entrepreneurship is more likely in industries where:

- Use provides enjoyment as opposed to purely economic benefits
- Users have relatively low opportunity costs
- There is high variety in demand and, hence, many small-scale niche market segments
- Markets are nascent, amid high turbulence and characterised by uncertain, ambiguous and evolving demand conditions.

Starting from this point, with reference to Cardon et al. (2009, p. 511), it is important to understand the role and influence of entrepreneurial passion in the entrepreneur process (Presenza et al. 2016). In this research, we focus on the object of entrepreneurial passion to develop new ventures, one's work or other opportunities in general. The premise is that 'passion is aroused not because some entrepreneurs are inherently disposed to such feelings but, rather, because they are engaged in something that relates to a meaningful and salient self-identity for them' (Cardon et al. 2009, p. 516).

The focus of our research is in the middle of two different entrepreneur identities. The first is the inventor identity, 'when the entrepreneur's passion is for activities involved in identifying, inventing, and exploring new opportunities' (Cardon et al. 2009, p. 516). The second is the developer identity, 'where the entrepreneur's passion is for activities related to nurturing, growing, and expanding the venture once it has been created' (Cardon et al. 2009, p. 516).

We ask if an unconventional entrepreneur is good in any ways, both inventor and developer, above all in the case that the property of the venture is of others.

Wiggings (1995, pp. 54–68) demonstrates that it is necessary for the property to be of the entrepreneur (in the case of small firms) because of the possibility, only in this case, to incentivise the entrepreneur in the case of success.

According to Kotha and George Thesy (2012, p. 525), in the case of entrepreneurs without capital, 'entrepreneurs with specific industry experience and start-up experience are able to provide ownership more selectively and raise more resources from their helpers'. Nevertheless, if the passion experienced seems to facilitate an entrepreneur's efforts to adapt and cope with environmental challenges, it is also true that 'this does not presume that the resulting adaptation and coping are necessarily functional. Instead, we acknowledge that the experience of entrepreneurial passion may produce response patterns that are obsessive, blind, or misdirected' (Cardon et al. 2009, p. 518; Vallerand et al. 2003).

As it was well explained by Cardon et al. (2005) with a parenthood metaphor, there are various features of entrepreneurship to develop depending on the different stage of the progression of ventures. From a "childhood and adolescence" stage to a "maturity" stage, it is necessary to search for a less involvement in daily decision making and a more consideration of professional managers. The role of the passion changes. Similarly, another research supported, with an analysis on a sample of 380 nascent entrepreneurs, "human capital in predicting entry into nascent entrepreneurship, but only weakly for carrying the start-up process towards successful completion" (Davidsson and Honig 2003, p. 301).

In the specific industry context, we analysed—entrepreneurs as contributors to tourism destination development—the role of individual entrepreneurs has been highlighted only recently (Enright and Newton 2004; Legohérel et al. 2004). In addition, Komppula (2014, p. 369) has declared that 'the role of individual enterprises and entrepreneurs is largely underestimated in the literature and models of destination competitiveness. The role of DMOs in the models has been over-emphasized'.

Ryan et al. (2012, p. 2) have shown instead 'how entrepreneurs are implicated in stimulating specific developments, advancing vital infrastructure, promoting particular approaches to development and cultivating particular entrepreneurial cultures in local tourism context'.

As the findings of Komppula (2014) challenged the prevailing DMO (Destination Management Organization)-dominated approach to destination competitiveness development, with this research we will confirm the role of individual entrepreneurs in the development of destination competitiveness. Komppula (2014), for the specific case of rural tourism destination, focused on the potentiality of a collaboration between small businesses and the municipality. 'Municipalities have a crucial role as facilitators of the entrepreneurial environment, but without innovative, committed, and risk-taking entrepreneurs no destination will flourish' (Komppula 2014, p. 361).

Some authors have also argued that 'the existence of so many small businesses in tourism means that many owner–managers lack the skills, expertise or resources to function efficiently and effectively' (Ritchie and Crouch 2003, p. 141).

Finally, it seems that the influence of entrepreneurs could be considered in the creation of an entrepreneurial environment (Letaifa and Goglio-Primard 2016) in particular when 'where the focus for development is on the area in general and not just individual businesses' (Komppula 2014, p. 369).

3 The Specific Context

3.1 The Industry Context

Our study is particularly interesting because it examines a case inside the tourism industry that is traditionally presented as an industry with a high level of dual relationships between the business and humanities perspectives (Tribe 2010; Prideaux and Carson 2011). We focus on the recreational vehicle (RV) equipped parking area industry that offers equipped areas for motorhomes. In the literature, there are few academic researchers focused on the campgrounds industry (Brooker and Joppe 2014) and for the RV-equipped parking area the situation is worse.

Something similar to this matter is described by Caldicott and Scherrer (2013) for the caravan park. The caravan park in this context is defined 'as one that is actively engaged in the tourism industry through the provision of short-term and/or long-term accommodation to the general public and provides powered or unpowered sites and toilet, shower and laundry facilities to guests' (p. 118). What is considered an RV-equipped parking area in Italy is similar to the caravan park definition, even if in Italy it is not possible to park the caravans in these areas, but only the motorhomes. Nevertheless, if we consider the services offered to the tourists, the concept is quite similar, especially if we consider the four principal types of equipped areas provided in Italy:

- Rest area ('punto sosta'): the simpler area with the most essential services for a break.
- Specific service area for motorhomes ('camper service'): an area only for the provision of the vehicles (loading and unloading of water, loading of the batteries and similar); it is not possible to stop for a long period.
- RV-equipped parking area ('area attrezzata'): an area with the same services as the above two, but also with the possibility to camp for more days. It could be similar to the campgrounds, but the access is only for motorhomes.
- Integrated area ('area integrata'): a rest area inside other accommodation structures, such as agritourism or thermal centres.

Of these different cases, we focus on the third one: the RV-equipped parking area. The total number of these entities is difficult to evaluate. Different sources in Italy give each one a different total number, because it is in continuous evolution. For instance, for the three first types of area, the major specialist magazine *PleinAir* gives a total number of 2734. However, we arrive at the number of 5,830 if we consider an important web site, Camper On Line.

There are different ways to open these areas and register a business. In some cases, we find public owners in other private ones. The principal role as managers has been given to the club of motorhomers who often work to open a similar area in the proper territory to promote itinerant tourism. This recognises the club's capacity to promote a direct, motivated and constant relationship with the tourists (APC 2013, p. 10). These clubs can demonstrate the possibility to develop itinerant tourism in a destination with few resources and with a low impact on environment and community, and an important uptick for the economy of the territory (Fjelstul and Fyall 2015).

Research by the Italian Association of Camper and Caravan Producers found that for a small rest area of 15 laybys without personnel, it is necessary to invest around 160,000€, with a payback period of 9 years and a difference between annual incomes and costs of 17,000€. For a similar but bigger rest area (40 laybys), it is necessary to invest around 302,000€, with a payback period of 5/6 years and a difference between annual incomes and costs of 55,000€ (APC 2014). This research also shows that a small rest area can generate an economic effect on the territory of around 175,000€, whereas the bigger ones generate around 470,000€.

The specific tourist industry linked to the RV-equipped parking area is interesting for the study on entrepreneurship because of the relationship between the business and humanities perspectives, and because this business could have an important effect on sustainable tourism destinations (Aronsson 2000; Modica 2015).

Further, it is important to study the relationship between the entrepreneurs and the municipality because the law gives the municipality jurisdiction over equipped parking areas (art. 7, comma 1, lettera h, Nuovo Codice della Strada). The research will also demonstrate that this 'must' (due to the law) offers an important opportunity for the municipality.

3.2   The Territorial Context

It is important to analyse the territorial context because the structure of the local tourism economy influences the different ways of entrepreneurship development (Williams et al. 1989, p. 1641). It is also worth while to examine the reasons why an entrepreneur chooses a particular location for his or her business. From the research of Williams et al. (1989, p. 1649), these reasons appear to be related to economic reasons, to environmental preference for a particular tourism destination and to the chance of 'being there anyway'.

The considered territorial context is the Municipality of Monzambano, not a particularly touristic province by itself, but it is located near Verona and Mantova (Italy) and Garda Lake. The tourist development of this territory began in the twenty-first century and has been constantly growing, as shown in Figs. 1 and 2.

In 2002, in this locale, the RV-equipped parking area was established, at a time when other tourism was absent. Therefore, it is possible to assert that the RV-equipped parking area began the development of Monzambano as a tourism

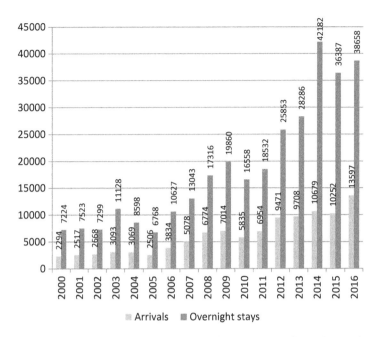

Fig. 1 Arrivals and overnight stays in Monzambano, 2000–2016 (excluding arrivals and overnight stays in the RV-equipped parking area). Source: our elaboration on Éupolis Lombardia, 2017

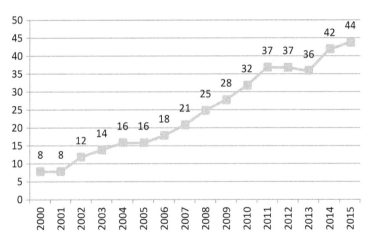

Fig. 2 Number of accommodation structures in Monzambano, 2000–2015. Source: our elaboration on Éupolis Lombardia, 2017

destination. In more recent years, the overnight stays trend in other Monzambano accommodation structures are better than for the RV-equipped parking area (see Fig. 3).

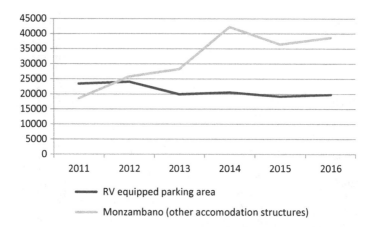

Fig. 3 Trend of overnight stays in Monzambano, 2011–2016. Source: our elaboration on Éupolis Lombardia and RV-equipped parking area documents, 2017

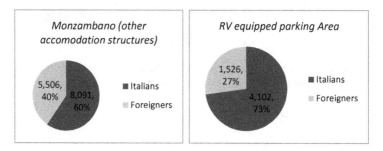

Fig. 4 Arrivals by visitor's country of origin, 2016. Source: our elaboration on Éupolis Lombardia and RV-equipped parking area documents, 2017

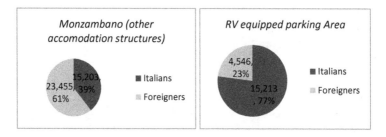

Fig. 5 Overnights stays by visitor's country of origin, 2016. Source: our elaboration on Éupolis Lombardia and RV-equipped parking area documents, 2017

As demonstrated in Figs. 4 and 5, the tourists in Monzambano now mainly comprise Italians. This remains the case in terms of guests of the RV-equipped parking area even if the situation is changing; for instance, in the last year there has been an increase of the foreigner overnight stays of +38% against a decrease of the

Fig. 6 The area before the reclamation. Source: RV-equipped parking area documents

Fig. 7 The area after development. Source: RV-equipped parking area documents

Italian overnight stays of −4%. The most important foreign tourists in the RV-equipped parking area are Germans, comprising 67.8% of the total foreign tourist overnight stays in 2016.

Given these quantitative results, the entrepreneurial activity has also made possible the qualitative redevelopment of an area that had been swamp and abandoned land. The people (named 'unconventional entrepreneurs') began the reclamation of the swampland in 2002 (Figs. 6 and 7).

This image of the land—now decisively improved—has given to the territory a new way to live the Monzambano (the area is in the Monzambano centre) even for the tourists that for the citizens who should look to the RV-equipped parking area managers with gratitude.

4 Methodology

Several authors encourage qualitative methodologies for tourism research (e.g., Pernecky and Jamal 2010; Riley and Love 2000; Ryan 2010). As the purpose of this study is to increase our understanding of unconventional entrepreneurship in the tourism development context, a qualitative approach was chosen as a research methodology.

The chosen research strategy is a single case study (Yin 2003): the RV-equipped parking area in Monzambano (Italy). It was chosen because it is one of the best RV-equipped parking areas in Italy and Europe; hence, it may represent an important benchmark case.

In addition, Simon (1979) emphasised the crucial role of the case study in research, particularly on research into the decision-making processes. According to Bonoma (1985), the case study 'is a description, directly obtained, of a management situation based on interview, archival, naturalistic observation, and other data, conducted to be sensitive to the context in which management behavior takes place and to its temporal restraints'. Hence, in this chapter we present the case study from the beginning of the activity to the present, in the special industry context of tourist services and in a territorial context originally not well-known as a tourist area. This case study could be considered an intrinsic case study: 'In an intrinsic case study the researcher seeks for an in-depth understanding of the particular case, meaning that the case is interesting itself, not only as a representative of similar cases' (Stake 2005).

In this research strategy utilising a single case study in which we seek an in-depth understanding, through November 2016 to June 2017 we collected data via in-depth interviews with the four most important actors of the investigated field: the two entrepreneurs/managers of the RV-equipped parking area, the Mayor of Monzambano and the City Council Member in charge of tourism matters.

Based on and inspired by the literature, interview themes were chosen (Komppula 2014, p. 366) and then presented in a linear–analytic structure (Yin 2003). Interviews were conducted with a semi-structured questionnaire containing open questions. The interviews were manually transcribed and analysed. The empirical materials collected during the interviews were integrated with other data, documents and information originating from other cited sources (Guercini 2014). This made it possible to check the accuracy and honesty of the data and information provided by the interviewees, as required by the triangulation principle (Eisenhardt 1989; Woodside and Wilson 2003). In addition, this objective was achieved because one of the authors has considerable experience as a motorhomer.

The structure of the presented findings from the interviews utilises a linear–analytic structure, with use of sub-headings to isolate specific themes with the perspectives from the interviewees.

As Siggelkow (2007) recommended, in this section we provided a description of the theories on unconventional entrepreneurs and their relationship with the municipality; we will now present the specific case study through a narrative of the case and testing of these theories. In this way, the case study will able to inspire new ideas and suggestions and motivate new research questions.

5 Findings

5.1 The Description of the Case Study: The Origin

The origin of the RV-equipped parking area of Monzambano dates to the autumn of 2002 when, on the occasion of the twenty-ninth anniversary of an important event for this territory, motorhomers began to arrive in large numbers.

Some motorhomers of Monzambano understood the demands that would arise, and so a few days later they went to see the Mayor where they discussed their idea—then still vague—to create a special RV-equipped parking area. Realising the tourist potential for Monzambano, the City Council put its support behind the project. After a few months, on 1 June 2003, the area was inaugurated. For the occasion, the official group, Motorhomers of Monzambano (the 'Gruppo Amici Camperisti Monzambano'), was born.

From that day, the Motorhomers of Monzambano together decided to manage this area with dedicated professionalism and were, above all, driven by a great passion. After another year and a half, the Motorhomers of Monzambano became the Motorhomers Association of Monzambano ('Associazione Camperisti di Monzambano'), a non-profit association consisting entirely of volunteers. Today, the principal members of this association are Luigi and Mirca, the two volunteers who manage the RV-equipped parking area and take care of the tourists who arrive.

The findings presented are the results of interviews with these two people. In addition, we present the responses of two other interviewed actors: the Mayor of Monzambano and the Council Member in charge of tourism.

5.2 Who Are the People Involved in the Management of the Area?

The land is owned by the municipality, but management of the area is entirely in the hands of the Motorhomers Association of Monzambano, particularly the two volunteers, Luigi and Mirca.

They work in the area 365 days a year, during the daytime, against a minimal reimbursement of their expenses. During night-time, there is no one from the association present, but the Italian Police make frequent passes (thanks to an ad hoc agreement with the Italian Police).

These two persons have no other experience in the tourism sector. Luigi is a retired technician of an electrical station, with some special competence in construction. Mirca is a retired post office director, with some special competence in administration. Each has a great passion for en plein air tourism with motorhomes; Mirca also knows three foreign languages.

Due to the characteristics of these two persons, it is possible to talk about a specific case of unconventional entrepreneurs. Passion is the principal motivation that made possible the development of the area by these two unconventional entrepreneurs. They find pleasure in being occupied by work that they like and enjoy and the feeling of taking part in the plein air system; for Mirca, there is also pleasure in practicing foreign languages. The major benefit they have with this work is personal satisfaction.

5.3 What Are the Relations Between the Owners of the Land and the Management of the Area?

The municipality has no competences in the tourism sector and no knowledge of motorhome tourists; hence, the Mayor and the Council Member in charge of tourism gave the area managers autonomy. Further, in some cases the municipality asks for advice from the area managers on tourism matters in Monzambano.

In terms of the economic relationship, at the beginning the municipality paid for the utilities against a minimal annual contribution by the area (500€). Then since the second convention (past 5 years from birth), the area alone paid for all utilities, except those to be paid to the municipality. From 2017, the area has paid a fee for each motorhome that enters the area (1€/motorhome). This latest agreement expires in 2020.

Luigi and Mirca publish and comment on the annual balance with all the members of the Motorhomers Association of Monzambano and with the Mayor to demonstrate the work done and provision for the future. It is important to note that the area has a bank overdraft with Luigi (the president of the association) as guarantor. It means that there is for this 'volunteer' the typical economic risk of the entrepreneur. Further, this unconventional entrepreneur has put into the enterprise personal money to the sum of 30,000€.

5.4   What Are the Principal Problems with Governance of the Area?

The principal problem with governance of the area is the availability of other volunteers. It is very difficult for two people to manage all the questions asked of them and work every day in the area. However, the small management group means each person knows the entire structure and the management organisation can be simplified, which accelerates the decision-making process, with a problem-solving approach.

However, there is a different problem that makes difficulties in the relationships and stresses the company climate. In some moments and with respect to some persons, there are many questions to discuss, particularly with a political perspective.

Finally, there is a problem with lack of specific competences that are required for the improvement of the area. The two managers have great passion and willpower, but they feel they do not have sufficient competences and resources to further improve the area.

Despite this, there are numerous potential entrepreneurs who want to open similar areas in other regions who come to Monzambano to ask them (the two unconventional entrepreneurs) how to do it. They are becoming special representatives of entrepreneurs in this sector.

5.5   What About the Future of the Area?

The municipality understands that the role of these two persons is fundamental for the development of the area, but in the same way they need to be transparent and open to the different possibilities that could come from potential competition. The municipality has to guarantee the best use of public resources (in this case, the estate).

Conversely, the entrepreneurs have to show the complexity of the work in maintaining the area beyond its initial foundation (too many similar areas opened by municipalities have failed because of the lack of competent management). If this area is considered one of the best in Italy and Europe—as stated by international supervisors and tourists. Some tourists also write on the area's website (see Fig. 8)—it means that the continuing presence and quality of the offered services by Luigi and Mirca are very important.

Both the municipality and the entrepreneurs have clear that this business has an important economic effect on the territory. According to recent research of the area management, every motorhomer spends 10€/day in the territory; if we consider that the area has around 20,000 overnight stays a year, it means that the area contributes 200,000€ a year to Monzambano businesses. According to the member of the City Council in charge of tourism, many economic organisations survive in Monzambano thanks to the area guests; for instance, the open-air market held every Sunday would

11 June 2015
'(...) I want to congratulate you on the management and maintenance of the RV-equipped parking area (...).'

17 April 2015
'(...) I didn't know that would exist, in Italy, a place so beautiful and for motorhomers (...). I congratulate your Association on the creation of this so beautiful RV-equipped parking area, that it preserved with much care and attention and that finally call a lots of tourists. I have quite travelled in Europe with our motorhome and in this case I feel proud to be Italian!
I will certainly return'.

23 December 2014
'(...) To you, who are always at disposal and ready to help.
To you, who patiently hear our problems and don't speak of yours.
To you, who, with diligence and effort, have created and now maintain this small Eden of beauty and peace. (...)'

29 April 2013
'We will point out this RV-equipped parking area as an example to follow in many other Italian municipalities, excellent hospitality from the people who manage with passion and competences, the organisation is really motorhomers oriented and surely the municipality will benefit from the area to the tourism that could help the entire local economy. (...)'

28 April 2012
'I seize the opportunity to congratulate you for the excellent and kind management from all the personnel always present. (...)'

Fig. 8 A selection of messages from the Guest Diary ('Diario Ospiti'). Source: Our free translation from Guest Diary ('Diario Ospiti'), www.camperisidimonzambano.it

be dead if only attended by Monzambano citizens. Further, the flows of tourists encouraged from this area are very important to develop and to promote, at the international level, important special events of this territory.

In contrast to when the area first opened, there are now a number of other tourist structures in the municipality that host tourists. For the development of tourism in Monzambano, the municipality has to work with the motorhomer area and promote itself around the tourism fairs and other different contexts as one of the best such areas in Italy and Europe. So, all the involved parties have an interest to go on with this business and further invest to improve the area.

6 Discussion

The role of unconventional entrepreneur figures for the development of an area into a tourist destination is strictly connected with the active participation of the municipality. We found that the principal strengths and weaknesses lie in the passion and competences of the involved actors.

In particular, it emerged that the role of passion is important because it is linked to a service organisation where human contact is essential. We also found that the inventor identity for the unconventional entrepreneur leads to better results than the developer identity. Indeed, the role of inventor, as a person who identifies, invents and explores new opportunities, was of success and it gave a great opportunity to the business and to the territory. Conversely, the role of developer, as a person who nurtures, grows and expands the venture once it has been created, yields minor results.

From this case study, it seems that passion has had a great role in the first phase of the Butler's model, but it is not sufficient in the developing phase. In this stage, the role and importance of competences seems to be greater (Cardon et al. 2005, 2009). In this context, the unconventional entrepreneurs, who have some important competences but not all the necessary ones (e.g., marketing competences), show their limits (Cova et al. 2007).

As in the early stages, the municipality's role is to cover the existing lack (e.g. the no capital disposal), even now it would be necessary an intervention of the public institution. Indeed, if we consider the future opportunities and threats for the tourist destination and all the entrepreneurship of the area, we have a lot of points to cover.

First, the fact that the law ascribes jurisdiction for the RV-equipped parking area institution to the municipality is in favour of the Monzambano case, because the municipality knows to have some experts who have already demonstrated their value if supported. This business development then yields results in terms of contribution to the promotion of the tourist destination area.

In addition, the fact that the agreement from 2017 predicts the payment of a fee from the area to the municipality offers a good opportunity to review the governance of the area and the human resources involved. The statute of the association responsible of the area predicts the hypothesis to employ a new person (also different from the association members). Until now, this hypothesis has been rejected by the entrepreneurs because of the economic question. The positive tourist development of Monzambano shows that the flows of tourists in this area can increase and a contribution from the municipality could not only cover the cost of this new person, but perhaps give greater results for all the involved parts: the Association of Motorhomers, the so-named unconventional entrepreneurs and the entire territory (citizens, other entrepreneurs and political entities).

Finally, the case shows the importance of the age of the entrepreneurs. In a positive lecture, we see the major knowledge of the context and the many human relationships with other stakeholders who can give support and advice; conversely, we see the opposition to make important investments for the long term. Further, in this case, the collaboration with the municipality and the institutional objective to develop the territory with a long-term perspective could provide a great opportunity for the development of the area.

7 Conclusions

Entrepreneurs have the responsibility to develop a tourist destination (Ryan et al. 2012; Koh and Hatten 2002; Komppula 2014). In addition, the municipality has a crucial role in the entrepreneurial climate formation and in the support of entrepreneurs, especially if the entrepreneurs are 'unconventional' (Koh and Hatten 2002; Golembski and Olszewski 2010; Rusko et al. 2009).

Unconventional entrepreneurship is necessary in the case of development of an unfavoured and atypical industry, in this case a tourist destination considered neither important or well-known. The unconventional entrepreneurship has to count on, above all, passion and competences. Passion is necessary in the first stages of the birth and development; meanwhile, the competences are decisive for the later stages of development and improvement of the organisation.

Finally, we agree with Gillingan (1987) and Williams et al. (1989, p. 1651), who argue that 'there are two important consequences for the regional economy of this process of firm formation. First (. . .) such businesses may be unresponsive to policy initiatives (. . .), second, many of these businesses survive by operating at suboptimal levels and by accepting suboptimal profits. Their lower prices may, however, act to undercut the prices charged by and even to undermine the profits achieved by the "full-time professionals" in some areas'.

To avoid these risks, it is necessary to continue research in this field; for instance, to research the economic effect on the territory from this business reality and different possibilities to cover the lack of governance and improve the performance of the area. It might also be interesting to examine if, in this case, it is possible to talk about social entrepreneurship (Muñoz and Kibler 2016) and, if so, review the role of the municipality. Lastly, from a managerial point of view, this case study could be considered an interesting in-depth research benchmark for other entrepreneurs and municipalities.

References

APC. (2013). *Linee guida. Aree di sosta a servizio del turismo itinerante*. Italy: Zaffina.
APC. (2014). *Rapporto nazionale sul turismo in libertà in camper e in caravan*. Italy: APC Rapporto.
Aronsson, L. (2000). *The development of sustainable tourism*. London: Continuum.
Bonoma, T. V. (1985). Case research in marketing: Opportunities, problems and a process. *Journal of Marketing Research, 22*(2), 199–208.

Brooker, E., & Joppe, M. (2014). A critical review of camping research and direction for future studies. *Journal of Vacation Marketing, 20*(4), 335–351.

Butler, R. W. (1980). The concept of a tourist area cycle of evolution: Implications for management of resources. *Canadian Geographer, XXIV*(1), 5–12.

Caldicott, R. W., & Scherrer, P. (2013). Facing divergent supply and demand trajectories in Australian caravanning: Learnings from the evolution of caravan park site-mix options in Tweed Shire. *Journal of Vacation Marketing, 19*(2), 117–131.

Cardon, M. S., Wincent, J., Singh, J., & Drnovsek, M. (2009). The nature and experience of entreprenrial passion. *Academy of Management Review, 34*(3), 511–532.

Cardon, M. S., Zietsma, C., Saparito, P., Matherne, B. P., & Davis, C. (2005). A tale of passion: New insights into entrepreneurship from a parenthood metaphor. *Journal of Business Venturing, 20*, 23–45.

Cova, B., Kozinets, R. V., & Shankar, A. (2007). *Consumer tribes*. Oxford: Butterworth-Heinemann.

Currie, G., Humphreys, M., Ucbasaran, D., & McManus, S. (2008). Entrepreneurial leadership in the English public sector: Paradox or possibility? *Public Administration, 86*, 987–1008.

Davidsson, P., & Honig, B. (2003). The role of social and human capital among nascent entrepreneurs. *Journal of Business Venturing, 18*, 301–331.

Eisenhardt, K. M. (1989). Building theories from case study research. *The Academy of Management Review, 14*(4), 532–550.

Enright, M. J., & Newton, J. (2004). Tourism destination competitiveness: A quantitative approach. *Tourism Management, 25*(6), 777–788.

Fjelstul, J., & Fyall, A. (2015). Sustainable drive tourism: A catalyst for change. *International Journal of Tourism Research, 17*, 460–470.

Gershuny, J. I., & Miles, I. D. (1983). *The new service economy: The transformation of employment in industrial societies*. London: Frances Pinter.

Gillingan, H. (1987). Visitors, tourists and outsiders in a Cornwall town. In M. Winter (Ed.), *Who from their labours rest? Conflict and practice in rural tourism*. Aldershot, Hants: Avebury Press.

Golembski, G., & Olszewski, M. (2010). The spas of Salt Mine Bochnia – a Polish case. In P. Weiermair, H. Keller, H. Pechlaner, & F. Go (Eds.), *Innovation and entrepreneurship. Strategies and processes for success in tourism* (pp. 135–149). Berlin: Erich Schmidt Verlag GmbH.

Guercini, S. (2014). New qualitative research methodologies in management. *Management Decision, 52*(4), 662–674.

Haefliger, S., Jäger, P., & von Krogh, G. (2010). Under the radar: Industry entry by user entrepreneurs. *Research Policy, 39*, 1198–1213.

Koh, K. Y., & Hatten, T. S. (2002). The tourism entrepreneur: The overlooked player in tourism developmente studies. *International Journal of Hospitality & Tourism Administration, 13*(1), 21–48.

Komppula, R. (2014). The role of individual entrepreneurs in the development of competitiveness for a rural tourism destination – A case study. *Tourism Management, 40*, 361–371.

Kotha, R., & George, G. (2012). Friends, family, or fools: Entrepreneur experience and its implications for equity distribution and resource mobilization. *Journal of Business Venturing, 27*, 525–543.

Legohérel, P., Callot, P., Gallopel, K., & Peters, M. (2004). Personality characteristics, attitude toward risk, and decisional orientation of the small business entrepreneur: A study of hospitality managers. *Journal of Hospitality & Tourism Research, 28*(1), 109–120.

Letaifa, S. B., & Goglio-Primard, K. (2016). How does institutional context shape entrepreneurship conceptualizations? *Journal of Business Research, 69*, 5128–5134.

Li, L. (2008). A review of entrepreneurship research published in the hospitality and tourism management journals. *Tourism Management, 29*, 1013–1022.

Meynhardt, T., & Diefenbach, F. E. (2012). What drives entrepreneurial orientation in the public sector? Evidence from Germany's Federal Labor Agency. *Journal of Public Administration Research and Theory, 22*, 761–792.

Modica, P. (2015). *Sustainable tourism management and monitoring*. Milan: FrancoAngeli.

Morris, M. H., & Jones, F. F. (1999). Entrepreneurship in established organizations: The case of the public sector. *Entrepreneurship Theory and Practice, 24*, 71–91.

Muñoz, P., & Kibler, E. (2016). Institutional complexity and social entrepreneurship: A fuzzy-set approach. *Journal of Business Research, 69*, 1314–1318.

Pearce, D. (1995). *Tourism today. A geographical analysis*. Longman Group Limited: UK.

Pernecky, T., & Jamal, T. (2010). (Hermeneutic) Phenomenology in tourism studies. *Annals of Tourism Studies, 37*(4), 1055–1075.

Presenza, A., Yucelen, M., & Camillo, A. (2016). Passion before profit in hospitality ventures. Some thoughts on Lifestyle Entrepreneur and the case of *Albergo Diffuso*. *Sinergie Italian Journal of Management, 99*, 221–239.

Prideaux, B., & Carson, D. (Eds.). (2011). *Drive tourism: Trends and emerging markets*. New York: Routledge.

Riley, R. W., & Love, L. I. (2000). The state of qualitative tourism research. *Annals of Tourism Research, 27*(1), 164–187.

Ritchie, J. R. B., & Crouch, G. I. (2003). *The competitive destination. A sustainable tourism perspective*. UK: CABI Publishing.

Rusko, R., Kylänen, M., & Saari, R. (2009). Supply chain in tourism destination. The case of Levi resort in Finnish Lapland. *International Journal of Tourism Research, 11*(1), 71–87.

Ryan, C. (2010). Ways of conceptualizing the tourist experience. A review of literature. *Tourism Recreation Research, 35*(11), 37–46.

Ryan, T., Mottiar, Z., & Quinn, B. (2012). The dynamic role of entrepreneurs in destination development. *The Journal of Ttourism Planning & Development, 2*, 1–19.

Shah, S. K., & Tripsas, M. (2007). The accidental entrepreneur: The emergent and collective process of user entreprenership. *Strategic Entrepreneurship Journal, 1*, 123–140.

Siggelkow, N. (2007). Persuasion with case studies. *Academy of Management Journal, 50*(1), 20–24.

Simon, H. A. (1979). Rational decision making in business organizations. *American Economic Review, 69*(4), 493–513.

Stake, R. E. (2005). Qualitative case studies. In N. K. Denzin & Y. S. Lincoln (Eds.), *Handbook of qualitative research* (2nd ed., pp. 443–466). Thousand Oaks, CA: Sage.

Tribe, J. (2010). Tribes, territories and networks in the tourism academy. *Annals of Tourism Research, 37*(1), 7–33.

Vallerand, R. J., Mageau, G. A., Ratelle, C., Leonard, M., Blanchard, C., Koesner, R., & Gagne, M. (2003). Les passions de l'ame: On obsessive and harmonious passion. *Journal of Personality and Social Psychology, 85*, 756–767.

Wiggins, S. N. (1995). Entrepreneurial enterprises, endogenous ownership, and the limits to firm size. *Economic Inquiry, 33*(1), 54–69.

Williams, A. M., Shaw, G., & Greenwood, J. (1989). From tourist to tourism entrepreneur, from consumption to production: Evidence from Cornwall, England. *Environment and Planning A, 21*, 1639–1653.

Woodside, A. G., & Wilson, E. J. (2003). Case study research methods for theory building. *Journal of Business & Industrial Marketing, 18*(6/7), 493–508.

Yin, R. K. (2003). *Case study research. Design and methods*. Thousand Oaks, CA: Sage.

Assessing Entrepreneurial Profiles: A Study of Transversal Competence Gaps in Four European Countries

Marlene Amorim, Marta Ferreira Dias, Helena Silva, Diego Galego, Maria Sarmento, and Carina Pimentel

Abstract The need to develop entrepreneurial competences in young professionals has been a key priority in the agendas of policy makers and industry leaders for some time. This chapter offers several contributions to address this issue, drawing on the results of an in-depth study addressing the meaning, and the requirements, for entrepreneurial competences across four European contexts (Cyprus, Lithuania, Poland and Portugal). Building on the literature as well as on exploratory data from interviews with employers and young graduates, the chapter starts by identifying and characterizing ten transversal entrepreneurial competences that were identified at the forefront of requirements for economic and social development, as determinants for job creation, employability, social emancipation and personal fulfilment in labour contexts. Using this competence framework, a scale for the assessment of entrepreneurial competences has been developed and empirically validated. The chapter then presents the results of the application of the scale in the four countries addressed in the study. This investigation addressed a sample of 449 young professionals and 88 employers, and offers insights on two perspectives: (1) the competence profile of young professionals, from different educational backgrounds, and across distinct European contexts; (2) the entrepreneurial competence requirements reported by the employers of leading industries. These two perspectives are matched in order to infer the importance of the gap between the requirements of employers and the offer from the graduates. The chapter therefore offers a timely contribution for the understanding of the span of psychological and behavioural characteristics, along with management and technical knowledge and skills that need to be at the forefront of education and training, and aligned with societal development goals.

M. Amorim (✉) · M. F. Dias · H. Silva · C. Pimentel
GOVCOPP, Department of Economics, Management and Industrial Engineering, University of Aveiro, Aveiro, Portugal
e-mail: mamorim@ua.pt

D. Galego · M. Sarmento
Department of Economics, Management, Industrial Engineering and Tourism, University of Aveiro, Aveiro, Portugal

© Springer International Publishing AG, part of Springer Nature 2018
S. Cubico et al. (eds.), *Entrepreneurship and the Industry Life Cycle*, Studies on Entrepreneurship, Structural Change and Industrial Dynamics,
https://doi.org/10.1007/978-3-319-89336-5_17

Keywords Entrepreneurial competences · Industry needs analysis · Competences gaps

1 Introduction

At present, the European Union (EU) context faces several challenges, such as poverty, social exclusion, an aging population, environmental changes, unemployment and in particular, youth unemployment. With the emergence of new technologies and innovations, old jobs and the skills associated call for renewal, giving way to new jobs which require new skill sets across the board. Simultaneously universities produce an increasing number of graduates, who, after leaving the education system cannot find straight away a place in the labour market, notably cannot find jobs in their field of study or a job which they desire. On the other hand, many employers report that graduates are not well prepared to enter into the labour market.

Entrepreneurship has been considered as a key element to promote growth and competitiveness through employment, skills, innovation and technology. These are the key issues which will enable the EU to meet the targets set out in the Europe 2020 Strategy for Smart, Sustainable, and Inclusive Growth (European Commission 2010a). Education, namely Higher Education Institutions (HEI), have an important role to help students developing their entrepreneurial competences, fostering youth employability and, enhancing self-employment.

Considering these factors, it is necessary to gain knowledge about the existing gaps in what concerns the development of entrepreneurial skills among young people as a preliminary step for devising strategies to promote the development of entrepreneurial capabilities in a generalized manner, as well as to implement adequate assessment methods.

This chapter aims to share some insights that result from research work conducted under the project EU Youth: From theory to action—ActYouth EU that are relevant to this discussion. The research work conducted in this context was driven by the aim of contributing to foster the employability and innovative potential of young people, notably of young graduates by upgrading and developing their competences for entrepreneurship, entrepreneurial attitudes and other transversal competences necessary for them to enter the labour market successfully. ActYouth's aim is, thus, to respond to the educational challenges of the higher education system in Europe and all members of the EU through the development of a system to diagnose, measure and develop such competences.

The project's goals are aligned with the European vision of building smart, sustainable and inclusive growth, especially on the priority themes of Youth on the Move, A digital agenda for Europe and An Agenda for new skills and jobs, and also Entrepreneurship 2020 Action Plan (Xavier and Lannoo 2013).

The present chapter is organized into three sections that offer a contextualized description of the essential concepts that framed the work, after which some key results are presented. Therefore, a preliminary literature review is offered as an overview of the key elements that characterize the most important competences for youth employability used to frame and support the subsequent data collection with industry representatives and young graduates. At the end, this chapter provides a conclusion that lists the main key points arising from the literature review and data analysis that should be a framework for the definition of the competence profile, evidencing dimensions and indicators to fill gaps on this field of study.

1.1   On the Relevance of Entrepreneurial Competences in Contemporary Economies

The pace of technological innovation coupled with the increasingly strong demands from employers vis-a-vis students qualifications for entering the active life have been pushing universities to reframe their educational strategies and methods. In particular, there has been a growing demand for the development and implementation of strategies to foster entrepreneurial capabilities in young people. Moreover, in order to meet to the dynamics of the current changing economy, employers expect workers to acquire and continuously update much diversified skills. There is a demand for competency at the technical level, but also regarding transversal skills, such as ICT competences, problem-solving, planning, organization and communication (World Bank Development and Private and Financial Sector Development Departments 2011; Lapiņa and Ščeulovs 2014).

Education, in particular the tertiary education sector is a key societal resort for the development of competences, and can play a key role in reducing the gaps between market demands and the profile of job seekers, therefore contributing to reduce unemployment rates (World Bank Development and Private and Financial Sector Development Departments 2011; Górniak 2013; Lapiņa and Ščeulovs 2014). Universities show a high degree of concern about the level of employability of their students (Ortiz-Medina et al. 2016), and in empowering students with the competences most valued by employers. Although some employers screen future employees according to their degree classification, for others, the grades are not the most important aspect as they pay attention to a whole range of competences not necessarily covered directly in the academic curricula (Saunders and Zuzel 2010). Entrepreneurship education appears as an important vehicle to stimulate the development of transversal skills in young people, both as an attribute for enabling them to create their own jobs, and for qualifying them to make the difference in the competitive labour market (Premand et al. 2016; Lapiņa and Ščeulovs 2014). Several studies have examined this topic and demonstrate that the employability of young people is boosted by entrepreneurship skills (Premand et al. 2016; Bustamam et al. 2015). In this new social and economic landscape several authors have also been highlighting the relevance of the models of entrepreneurial universities (Guerrero et al. 2016).

While education programs for entrepreneurship focus on skills and development of competences, they also aim to stimulate the capacity of students to act and think differently, and in making them more effective people, not only at work but also at a personal level (Bagheri and Pihie 2013). This first part of the chapter clarifies key concepts on the field of young graduates' transition into the labour market.

1.2   Challenges of the Contemporary Economy

The World economy has faced significant changes throughout the last decades. Globalization has brought new dynamics, such as businesses trading via the internet and connections between countries with very different cultures and features. These new global contexts asks for unprecedented levels of flexibility and adaptability from individuals, and consequently from organizations. Employers expect their employees to be increasingly more prepared for the competitive national and international markets (Lapiņa and Ščeulovs 2014; Nowacka 2015). Such requirements are demanded even from young graduates, and across all kinds of job categories (Lapiņa and Ščeulovs 2014).

Simultaneously, with the increasing number of graduates, the job market becomes more competitive. Moreover, the recent economic and financial crisis requires great adaptive capabilities from companies, for which they need strong collaborators (OECD/European Commission 2015). Overall, countries are facing serious employability problems (OECD/ILO 2014), with young and inexperienced graduates having difficulties in the their search for a job (Górniak 2013). Demographic trends also contribute to this scenario. In Europe, data shows that in a near future the older segment of the workforce will be a major proportion of the population. Forecasts advanced suggest that the proportion of people aged over 65 in relation to those aged 15–64 will increase from 26% in 2008 to 38% by 2030, and that this will have important impacts in the skills that will be available in the job market. This scenario will lead to increasing pressures for expanding labor market participation, notably for women as well as for the requalification of unemployed and immigrant populations (European Commission 2010b).

1.3   Youth Unemployment

Unemployment is one of the greater challenges faced by EU, with youth unemployment being of particular concern (European Policy Centre 2014). Youth unemployment is defined as the unemployment among citizens under 25 years old (between the ages of 15 and 24) compared to the total labour force (employed and unemployed) in that age group (Eurostat 2015c). A large proportion of people in this age group is actually out of the labour market, because many young people are still full-time students. In 2012, the youth unemployment rate in EU-28 achieved the worrying number of 23% (Eurostat 2015c), registering only a slight decrease in 2014, to 21.8%, and to 20.1% in 2015 (Eurostat 2015a).

Although one of the functions attributed to the education system is to prepare students to enter the labour market, and considering that the number of people in tertiary education continues to increase (with 2012 registering an approximate number of 4.8 million students graduating in the EU-28), it is likely that the labour market will be unable to absorb these people (Eurostat 2015b). It is commonly accepted that competences are an essential part of an individuals' development, for businesses and for society, in general. They assume a great importance, not only in the face of the economic crisis, but also in the face of a world that is increasingly globalized (Klosters 2014). Nevertheless, although there is a common concern on Education, many employers consider there is a gap between the competences required for jobs and the ones that young graduates actually have (World Economic Forum 2014; OECD and ILO 2014).

Job candidates go into the labour market with specific knowledge in several areas, with competences and other individual characteristics, such as work experience, choices of education, training, innate abilities and preferences (Klosters 2014), that may constitute factors that will allow a successful transition from school to work. However, it is not uncommon for candidates to show a low level of development of some competences that are required to respond to the expectations placed on them (Gillinson and O'Leary 2006). Demos (2006) refers, for instance, that since they come from the university used to working in the peer-to-peer environment, it leads them to find difficulties when a shift occurs to organizational hierarchies, and they tend to have some problems in their relationship with their bosses (Gillinson and O'Leary 2006).

Entrepreneurship is regarded as one possible solution to youth unemployment (OECD/European Commission 2015), since it could re-activate economies and create jobs. At the same time, studies recognize the importance of entrepreneurial competences to foster employability and reduce the risk of unemployment (World Bank Development and Private and Financial Sector Development Departments 2011).

2 Key Competences for Youth Employability

Over time, various definitions of competences have been proposed by different authors. There is often even a lack of agreement about what is the correct term to use, and for this reason the speech can be sometimes confusing, since "skills", "expertise", "acumen" and "competency" are used in the literature as synonyms (Mitchelmore and Rowley 2010). Boyatzis (1982) was the first to popularize the term "competency", defining a competency as "a capacity that exists in a person that leads to behaviour that meets the job demands within the parameters of organizational environment, and that, in turn brings about desired results".

Overall, competences are defined as an integration or combination of components of knowledge, attitudes, skills, values and behaviours that a person needs to successfully accomplish a task or an activity (Kyndt and Baert 2015; Morris et al. 2013). Considering that competences are changeable, they could be acquired, learned, developed and reached by experience, training or coaching and practice (Kyndt and Baert 2015). Yet, it is important to highlight that while competences could be enhanced with practice, if they are not practiced, they may be lost (Morris et al. 2013).

Regarding the area of entrepreneurship, the literature establishes a number of competences that determine the performance and the success of an entrepreneur. There is still some ambiguity in the studies concerning the entrepreneurial skills, and in an entrepreneurial context there is no consensus regarding the relative importance of each competence specifically (Morris et al. 2013).

The list of entrepreneurial skills is endless and there is no general agreement about the classification of those competences. Nevertheless, many authors refer entrepreneurial competences as covering personal characteristics, attitudes and skills such as problem solving, leadership, communication, self-awareness and assessment skills like business and managerial competences (Frank, 2007; Morris et al., 2013)

Attempting to answer the question about what transversal competences the young professionals need to present on their profile, the first phase of this research aims to develop a system which may recognize, evaluate and develop horizontal skills of people, students and graduates (particularly entrepreneurial skills). The following topic provides an analysis of key literature in the field of entrepreneurship competences that contributed to identify the essential dimensions to this study. With the aim of investigating the alignment between the contributions of literature and the skills required by employers in the real context of the workplace, the research involved also the analysis of 40 job offers, for graduates, from the different European countries addresses in the study (Cyprus, Lithuania, Poland and Portugal). This helped to identify the competences needed for a successful entrance into the labour market.

2.1 Key Competences to Find a Job: Insights from the Literature

Notwithstanding the huge number of studies in the field of entrepreneurship competences, there is few literature concerning the competences that graduates need to have when they leave university and make the transition to the labour market, regardless of creating their own job or working for others.

Considering that there is no set of characteristics that every entrepreneur and young graduate must have, a core list of entrepreneurial skills has been defined. Fig. 1 identifies a group of relevant competences for young students/graduates to successfully enter the labour market, deriving from the literature (Frank, 2007;

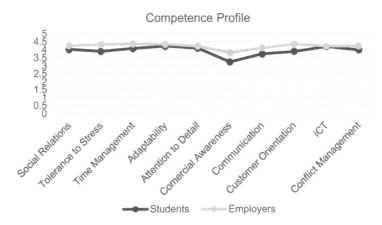

Fig. 1 Comparison of competence profile between students and employers: average for the sample

García-Aracil and Van der Velden 2008; Mitchelmore and Rowley 2010; World Bank Development and Private and Financial Sector Development Departments 2011; Morris et al. 2013; Saunders and Zuzel 2010).

Firstly, contributions of notably literature on the topics of the entrepreneurship area and competences needed to young people in the labour market were required from all project partners for the identification of key competences addressed in the current literature. In addition, in order to assure that all relevant literature would be considered, after an in-depth literature analysis, the most identified key competences were chosen and assumed as essential for development. These were grouped in two main categories: (1) transversal competences and (2) technical competences, which complement each other (Lima et al. 2013).

Entrepreneurial competences presented in Table 1 represent a summary of the most referred characteristics found in the literature.

2.2   Most Desirable Competences: Preliminary Insights from Employers

Many students invest in their university education in order to have specific knowledge and skills with the intent to obtain better employment prospects and to be successful in the labour market. Simultaneously employers expect that young people to be endowed with well-developed skills in order to become efficient right from the moment of recruitment (Saunders and Zuzel 2010). However, many employers consider that there is a gap between the competences required for jobs and the ones that candidates have (World Economic Forum 2014; OECD and ILO 2014).

Sometimes the level of skills acquired at school and those required in the labour context do not match (García-Aracil and Van der Velden 2008). Saunders and Zuzel (2010) analyses the employability skills in the vision of employers and the students

Table 1 Preliminary identification of relevant competences: insight from the literature

Transversal competences		Technical competences
Personal competences	Generic competences	
• Adaptability	• Commercial awareness	• Theoretical knowledge
• Attention to detail	• Communication	• Understanding concepts
• Commitment	• Ethical issues	• Knowledge of methods
• Cooperation	• Foreign languages	• Application of knowledge
• Creativity	• Management skills	
• Decisiveness	• Negotiation	
• Dependability	• Networking	
• Enthusiasm	• Numeracy	
• Initiative	• Planning & organisation	
• Integrity	• Problem solving	
• Self-awareness	• Questioning/listening	
• Timekeeping	• Self-management	
• Tolerance to stress	• Team work	
• Work ethic	• Use of ICT	
• Interpersonal relationships		
• Leadership		
• Willingness to learn		

perceptions, and obtained a good agreement between them. However, the priority assigned to each of the competences was different according to the group (students vs. employers). More than technical and subject-specific skills, even in highly technical jobs, employers value a range of personal characteristics and generic skills (Saunders and Zuzel 2010).

Employers who complain about difficulties in recruiting usually report a lack of soft/transversal skills (Gillinson and O'Leary 2006), namely in: occupational skills (related to the specific qualities of activities performed in the given occupation); self-organizational (self-organization and motivation to work, showing initiative, timeliness, entrepreneurship, and resilience to stress) and interpersonal (contacts with people, both colleagues and clients, and cooperation in the group) (Gillinson and O'Leary 2006; Kocór and Strzebońska 2011, Górniak 2013). Also communication skills and creative thinking are seen as competences which are lacking in new employees who have recently left education (Gillinson and O'Leary 2006).

In order to identify the competences required by employers in the real workplace, the study looked at the content of job offers, from a selected sample of ten examples per each country addressed in the study. The sources considered included offers from government or public institutions (e.g. Ministries), such as Employment and Vocational Training Institutes, Universities or their careers services and public employment pools. A time limit was established and set for job offers advertised in the period between 2014 and 2016. This phase of the research was complemented with the conduction of semi structured interviews with stakeholders such as training organizations and employers.

Interviewees were asked to score on a scale from 1 to 5 a list of transversal competences, namely personal and generic competences, regarding their importance for employability. It was also a semi-open question in order to give the opportunity for respondents to state the most important competences to find a job. In this question, respondents were invited to list up to a maximum of three other competences not mentioned in the previous question, and also scoring them in a scale from 1 to 5.

The results from this analysis are summarized in Table 2.

From the descriptive analyses it can be concluded that in all countries, job offers are focused mainly on the desired transversal skills, namely generic competences, rather than focused on technical competences. Only for functions of a more technical level, the technical skills are called and described in more detail.

The most frequently mentioned skills in job offers are fluency in foreign languages mainly in English idiom, ICT competences (e.g. "Fluent in Microsoft Excel/ Google Sheets"; "Good PC skills") and management skills (e.g. "management of the materials and financial means available"; "Project management skills"). The following competences appeared to be the most referred to: attention/focus on details, communication skills, creativity, customer-orientation, flexibility, initiative, motivation, multi-tasking, organizational skills, problem solving, self-reliance, stress resistance, team work, time management, willingness to learn, the ability to work independently and to work under pressure. All the above and most cited competences in the job offers, fit in the transversal competences category. Less often mentioned but not less important, the following skills were highlighted: autonomous learning; availability to travel; driving license; motivation; networking; numeracy; organizational skills; persuasiveness; previous experience; results orientation; stress resistance; and time-management.

Several job offers referred to the need for future employees to have a university degree, but only in one case was asked a "very good grade". This fact is in line with the authors view that less importance is attributed to grades by employers (Saunders and Zuzel 2010). Universities have an important role in the development of skills and the entrepreneurial culture of their students, that can produce a range of desirable outcomes, providing them several differentiator factors for their working and personal life. This issue is of high relevance to society and the current economy, and it is already a target of attention by policymakers.

3 A Deeper Enquiry About Competence Demands: Building on Data from Young People and Employers

The following stage in the research involved the development of questionnaires to address young people and employers about the existing and the needed competences for employability. The questionnaires were developed with the purpose of collecting data about the entrepreneurial competences that young people would need in order to make a successful transition from their studies to the labour market. The questionnaire was composed of 144 statements, associated with 38 competences, which had been previously identified in the research stage before, and the interviews with

Table 2 Most competences requested in job offers by country

Country	Transversal competences	Technical competences
Cyprus	• Communication skills • ICT skills • Initiative • Language skills • Self motivation • Team work • Work under pressure	• Promote new campaigns and sell the company's product • Process data and apply in accurate manner to the database using technical and financial knowledge • Ability to carry out financial and management research reports
Lithuania	• Attention to details • Communication skills • Flexibility • ICT skills • Independence • Initiative • Language skills • Management skills • Problem solving skills • Customer-oriented	• Experience with standard template library • Manage the reconciliation of supplier invoices to the various invoice systems (which includes eProcurement (R2P) and SAP AIP direct invoicing. • Process payments and security transactions related to new issues for Swedbank clients
Poland	• Attention to detail • Communication skills • Creativity • ICT skills • Language skills • Management • Multi-tasking • Team work • Work independently	• Knowledge on SAP system • Basic knowledge on Java • Working knowledge of flash, rich media • Analyse data using VLOOKUP, COUNTIF, SUMIF, and IF functions
Portugal	• Communication skills • Dynamic • ICT skills • Interpersonal relationship skills • Language skills • Management • Responsibility • Problem solving	• Modeling and design MySQL databases, SQL server, SQL server compact edition and Oracle application data to support • Projection and estimated sales • Experience in the management and implementation of quality management systems ISO 9001 • Prospecting for new customers

employers and stakeholders described in previous section. This preliminary analysis led to the identification of 20 personal competences and 18 generic skills. In the questionnaire for students, they were asked to make a self-assessment about their own skills, using a scale from 1 to 5 ("strongly disagree" [1] and "strongly agree" [5]). The

Table 3 Number of students and employers surveyed per country

	Questionnaire for students	Questionnaire for employers	Total
Cyprus	103	20	123 (22.9%)
Lithuania	108	27	135 (25.1%)
Poland	100	21	121 (22.5%)
Portugal	138	20	158 (29.4%)
Total	**449**	**88**	**537 (100%)**

Table 4 Final transversal competences

Final transversal competences	
Personal competences	Generic competences
Adaptability	Commercial awareness
Attention to detail	Communication
Social relations	Customer orientation
Time management	Conflict management
Tolerance to stress	ICT

questionnaire addressed students with diverse academic profiles. Employers, on their turn, were invited to score the statements listed, in the same scale ("not desirable at all" [1] and "strongly desirable" [5]), considering their opinion about how desirable each competence was for young graduate to hold.

The questionnaire was answered by a total of 537 people, divided in 449 graduates and 88 employers. Table 3 shows the sample by each country.

Data collection was followed by a statistical and psychometrical analysis in order to define the final version of the competence assessment scale. The psychometric analysis includes the assessment of the quality of a measuring instrument, based on the validity and reliability. The reliability refers to the repeatability of findings, which means, the reliability evaluates the extent to which a measurement procedure yields the same results on repeated trials. The validity is the extent to which the construct measures what it says it is measuring. To this aim, a sequence of steps and criteria were followed in order to clarify and identify the most important competences for transition to the labour market.

The assumptions needed to assure the adequacy of the analysis were tested, resulting in a two final factor structures, one for personal competences and another one for generic competences, which are presented below in Table 4.

Data analysis led to the development of a final scale including ten different competences.

Afterwards, a deep analysis of the students and employer's questionnaires was performed, considering the ten final transversal competences. The findings of this study are presented on the next paragraphs. The global relationship between the employer's perceptions, about the transversal competences importance for a smooth

Fig. 2 Representative competence gaps per country

transition of young graduates to the labour market, and the students own perception is presented in Fig. 2.

Aiming to analyse the needs of students, concerning the development of competences for entrepreneurship and other transversal ones, a gap analysis was developed across the questionnaire's results from the perspective of employers versus students, by country.

Gaps were calculated considering the difference between the importance of a given competence for employers and young students/graduates preparation, with positive values (above 0) meaning that the competence requires some training.

Values below 0 mean that such skills do not require training, revealing that the self-assessment value of students is higher than the expectation stated by employers.

The results obtained in all the countries under consideration show that in general the employers consider that all the ten competences are important. In all of them the average score achieved is higher or equal to 4, except for the commercial awareness competence in which the average is equal to 3.8, both in Portugal and in Lithuania. In addition to this, the results presented in Fig. 2 also show that employers seem to expect young graduates to be more prepared than they fell they are, since for all the competences the gaps reached represent positive values in the four countries considered in this study.

The data also show that the competences with higher gaps are tolerance to stress and commercial awareness, in which the gaps are higher or equal to 0.44 and 0.58, respectively, in every country. This is observed in all the countries under consideration, although in Cyprus and Poland the differences are more expressive. It is also interesting to note that both in Cyprus and Poland the communication competence emerges as the third most critical one, considering again the gap between the importance attributed by employers and young graduates preparation. Finally, we would also like to emphasize the customer orientation competence results, in which in all the countries the gap falls between 0.42 and 0.46.

On the other side, ICT and adaptability competences are the ones in which the above mentioned gap is smaller in all the countries. The adaptability competence gap values ranged between 0.08 and 0.16, and from 0.03 to 0.2 for the ICT competence.

From this analysis we are able to conclude that there is a need to improve students/graduates skills, particularly the tolerance to stress and commercial awareness competences, as they are the personal and generic competences with greater gaps.

Figures 3 and 4 exhibit the averages reported score by employers and students, per country.

As stated in Fig. 3 the results of employer's perceptions, considering the four countries, show that tolerance to stress, time management, adaptability and customer orientation are the most valued competences. On the other side, commercial awareness is the less valued one. In addition to this, Fig. 4 demonstrates for the ten competences that there are not relevant differences per country among the students' answers.

To summarize, we emphasize that the most worrying gap between the employers' expectations on personal competences and students' assessment, were found in tolerance to stress. Also, commercial awareness is the generic competence that most concerns, regarding the highest gap results.

This analysis allowed us to conclude that there are competences that need training, across all countries, particularly the ones with higher gaps. Therefore there is a demand for the offer of tools and training mechanisms to develop both personal and generic competences, towards which ActYouth Project can provide a relevant answer.

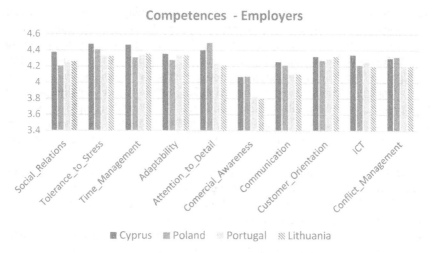

Fig. 3 Total representation of the average reported answers by employers per country

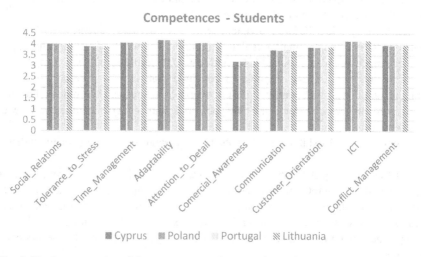

Fig. 4 Total representation of the average reported answers by students per country

4 Conclusion

As a result of several factors as well as the current economic crisis, the increase in the number of graduates, the reduction in the number of jobs and the increase in the retirement age, challenges such as youth unemployment have emerged. Young people leaving the education system find it increasingly difficult to enter the labour market. This is a concern for many policymakers, who believe that one way to combat this problem is to give more attention to the development of entrepreneurial skills in HEI.

This chapter has proposed a theoretical and practical framework from the work-place context to entrepreneurial profiles for young graduates. In order to realize the progressive potential and transformative capacity of young graduates in finding a job, carrying the required abilities to enter in the labour market. Skills can be acquired and developed throughout life which represent a key and differentiating factor for individual success. Many of the entrepreneurial skills could be acquired and developed in the school/university context (Frank 2007). Although there are other factors that influence the availability and characteristics of entrepreneurship, such as the existence of familiar business, innate factors and individual differences (Frank 2007; Morris et al. 2013). These factors lead to a change in how a student is influenced by entrepreneurship education.

The literature lists a number of entrepreneurial skills which are important for new entrepreneurs or people who want to enter the labour market better prepared. A list of key entrepreneurship competences were defined which are the most referred in the literature, divided in two main categories: transversal competences and technical competences. The most cited transversal competences are: adaptability, creativity, initiative, self-awareness, tolerance to stress, communication, foreign languages, leadership, management and use of ICT.

Furthermore, 40 job offers from the four countries were analysed. In the real labour market, a good knowledge in ICT, foreign languages, management skills, communications skills, problem solving and team work seem to be the skills most required by employers and, therefore, good indicators of high performance. It seems that there exists a strong degree of agreement between the skills that the literature consider as important for young people to have when entering the labour market and the skills requested (in job advertisements) by employers.

The emphasis, both in the literature and in the job offers analyzed, is given to transversal competences. With respect to technical skills the job offers refer to them less often, with the exception of work with a very specific technical component (e.g. software developer). This is consistent with what is reported in the literature and may be linked with the fact that in jobs that require more technical skills these can be provided through on-the-job-training (Frank 2007; World Bank Development and Private and Financial Sector Development Departments 2011).

It is clear that competences such as communication skills, team work (working with others), initiative, networking (contacts with people) are requested, and according to the literature they are the ones most often lacking in future employees (Gillinson and O'Leary 2006; Kocór and Strzebońska 2011; Górniak 2013). Possibly due to this fact, they are specifically requested in job advertisements. Knowledge of foreign languages is also referred to both in the literature and in job offers as a differentiating factor in the employability of young graduate (Araújo et al. 2015).

According to the literature review and data analysis resulting from this research, it is important to ask young people/students/graduates and employers their opinion about the competences needed to enter into the labour market with success. This kind of methodology to acquire Data Collection Tools, targeting students/graduates, employers, training organizations and stakeholders aims to verify if the information extracted in preliminary phases, as in the literature review, match with the reality. So, in this chapter we also present the results of a survey conducted with the aim to identify a set of most important transversal competences for youth employability. The following set of competences emerged: adaptability, attention to detail, social relations, time management, tolerance to stress, commercial awareness, communication, customer orientation, conflict management and ICT. According to our analysis tolerance to stress and commercial awareness are the competences that need more attention, since they are the ones in which the gaps are higher.

Such an initiative, which encourages dialogue between employers and employees can be a first step in approaching the mission of universities in terms of their relationship with the business sector, taking the realities of the workplace and the practical requirements of employers into account. This could allow universities to reframe their teaching methods and the focus of their research in order to provide students with the skills and abilities that they need in the field of entrepreneurship.

References

Araújo, L., Costa, P. D., Flisi, S., & Calvo, E. S. (2015). *Languages and employability*. Luxembourg: Publications Office.

Bagheri, A., & Pihie, Z. A. L. (2013). Role of University Entrepreneurship Programs in developing students' entrepreneurial leadership competencies: Perspectives From Malaysian undergraduate students. *Journal of Education for Business, 88*, 51–61. Retrieved http://search.proquest.com/docview/1197624209?accountid=14116%5Cn, http://ensor.lib.strath.ac.uk/sfxlcl41?url_ver=Z39.88-2004&rft_val_fmt=info:ofi/fmt:kev:mtx:journal&genre=article&sid=ProQ:ProQ:abiglobal&atitle=Role+of+University+Entrepreneurship+Programs+

Boyatzis, R. E. (1982). *The competent manager: A model for effective performance*. New York: Willey.

Bustamam, U. S. A., Mutalib, M. A., & Yusof, S. N. M. (2015). Graduate employability through entrepreneurship: A case study at USIM. *Procedia – Social and Behavioral Sciences, 211*, 1117–1121. Retrieved http://linkinghub.elsevier.com/retrieve/pii/S1877042815054890

European Commission. (2010a). *Communication from the commission, Europe 2020 – A strategy for smart, sustainable and inclusive growth*. Retrieved http://hdl.voced.edu.au/10707/89925

European Commission. (2010b). *New Skills for new jobs: Action now – A report by the expert group on new skills for new jobs*. Luxembourg. Retrieved http://ec.europa.eu/social/main.jsp?catId=568&langId=en%5Cn, http://ec.europa.eu/education/focus/focus2043_en.htm

European Policy Centre. (2014). *Challenges and new beginnings: Priorities for the EU's new leadership*. Brussels: European Policy Centre.

Eurostat. (2015a). *Euro area unemployment rate at 10.8%*. pp. 1–6.

Eurostat. (2015b). Tertiary education statistics. *Eurostat Statistics Explained*.

Eurostat. (2015c). Youth unemployment. *Eurostat Statistics Explained*.

Frank, A. I. (2007). Entrepreneurship and enterprise skills: A missing element of planning education? *Planning Practice and Research, 22*(4), 635–648. Retrieved http://www.tandfonline.com/doi/abs/10.1080/02697450701770142

García-Aracil, A., & Van der Velden, R. (2008). Competencies for young European higher education graduates: Labor market mismatches and their payoffs. *Higher Education, 55*(2), 219–239.

Gillinson, S., & O'Leary, D. (2006). *Working progress: How to reconnect young people and organisations*. London: Demos. Retrieved http://www.demos.co.uk/press_releases/workingprogress

Górniak, J. (Ed.). (2013). *Youth or experience? Human capital in Poland*. Warszawa, Poland: Polish Agency for Enterprise Development. Retrieved https://en.parp.gov.pl/images/PARP_publications/pdf/2013_bkl_youth_or_experience_en.pdf

Guerrero, M., Urbano, D., Fayolle, A., Klofsten, M., & Mian, S. (2016). Entrepreneurial universities: emerging models in the new social and economic landscape. *Small Business Economics, 47*(3), 551–563.

Klosters, D. (2014). Matching skills and labour market needs: Building social partnerships for better skills and better jobs. *World Economic Forum, 28*. Retrieved http://www3.weforum.org/docs/GAC/2014/WEF_GAC_Employment_MatchingSkillsLabourMarket_Report_2014.pdf

Kocór, M., & Strzebońska, A. (2011). *Who's wanted in Poland's labour market?* Warszawa, Poland. Retrieved https://en.parp.gov.pl/images/PARP_publications/pdf/2011_pl_labor_en.pdf

Kyndt, E., & Baert, H. (2015). Entrepreneurial competencies: assessment and predictive value for entrepreneurship. *Journal of Vocational Behavior, 90*, 13–25. Retrieved http://linkinghub.elsevier.com/retrieve/pii/S0001879115000767

Lapiņa, I., & Ščeulovs, D. (2014). Employability and skills anticipation: Competences and market demands. *Procedia – Social and Behavioral Sciences, 156*(April), 404–408. Retrieved http://linkinghub.elsevier.com/retrieve/pii/S1877042814060315

Lima, R., Mesquita, D., & Rocha, C. (2013). Professinals' demands for production engineering: Analysing areas of professional practice and transversal competences. (pp. 352a1–352a7). *22nd International Conference on Production Research* (*ICPR*). Foz do Iguassu.

Mitchelmore, S., & Rowley, J. (2010). Entrepreneurial competencies: A literature review and development agenda. *International Journal of Entrepreneurial Behavior & Research, 16*(2), 92–111. Retrieved http://www.emeraldinsight.com/doi/10.1108/13552551011026995

Morris, M. H., Webb, J. W., Jun, F., & Singhal, S. (2013). A competency-based perspective on entrepreneurship education: Conceptual and empirical insights. *Journal of Small Business Management, 51*(3), 352–369. Retrieved http://doi.wiley.com/10.1111/jsbm.12023

Nowacka, U. (2015). Entrepreneurship as a key competence – Implications for the education process in Poland. *Society, Integration, Education. Proceedings of the International Scientific Conference, 1*, 293–302. Retrieved http://journals.ru.lv/index.php/SIE/article/view/324

OECD/European Commission. (2015). *Youth entrepreneurship support in Poland*. OECD. Retrieved http://www.oecd.org/industry/Rapid-policy-assessment-Poland-Final.pdf

OECD/ILO. (2014). *Promoting better labour market outcomes for youth*. Melbourne. Retrieved https://www.oecd.org/g20/topics/employment-and-social-policy/OECD-ILO-Youth-Apprenticeships-G20.pdf

Ortiz-Medina, L., Fernández-Ahumada, E., Lara-Vélez, P., Taguas, E., Gallardo-Cobos, R., del Campillo, M., & Guerrero-Ginel, J. (2016). Designing an accompanying ecosystem to foster entrepreneurship among agronomic and forestry engineering students. Opinion and commitment of university lecturers. *European Journal of Engineering Education, 41*(4), 393–410. https://doi.org/10.1080/03043797.2015.1079815

Premand, P., Brodmann, S., Almeida, R., Grun, R., & Barouni, M. (2016). Entrepreneurship education and entry into self-employment among university graduates. *World Development, 77*, 311–327. Retrieved http://linkinghub.elsevier.com/retrieve/pii/S0305750X15002090

Saunders, V., & Zuzel, K. (2010). Evaluating employability skills: Employer and student perceptions. *Bioscience Education, 15*(1), 1–15. Retrieved http://www.tandfonline.com/doi/full/10.3108/beej.15.2

World Bank Development and Private and Financial Sector Development Departments. (2011). *Europe 2020 Poland – Fueling growth and competitiveness in Poland through employment, skills, and innovation overview*. Warsow: Protea-Taff Studio DTP. Retrieved papers3://publication/uuid/8A10CF72-E4F5-45A2-AF9F-EAE892BCBEDC

Xavier, G. L., & Lannoo, R. (2013). Communication from the commission to the European Parliament, the council, the European Economic and Social Committee and the Committee of the Regions – Entrepreneurship 2020 Action Plan – Reigniting the Entrepreneurial Spirit in Europe (pp. 1–11). Retrieved http://www.eesc.europa.eu/?i=portal.en.int-opinions.25759